Exploring Disability Identi
Disability Rights through N..........

Building on David M. Engel's and Frank W. Munger's work analyzing the narratives of people with physical and learning disabilities, this book examines the life stories of 12 physically disabled Canadian adults through the prism of the social model of disablement. Using a grounded theory approach and with extensive reporting of the thoughts of the participants in their own words, the book uses narratives to explore whether an advocacy identity helps or hinders dealings with systemic barriers for disabled people in education, employment and transportation.

The book underscores how both physical and attitudinal barriers by educators, employers and service providers complicate the lives of disabled people. The book places a particular focus on the importance of political economy and the changes to the labour market for understanding the marginalization and oppression of people with disabilities. By melding socio-legal approaches with insights from feminist, critical race and queer legal theory, Ravi Malhotra and Morgan Rowe ask if we need to reconsider the social model of disablement, and propose avenues for inclusive legal reform.

Dr Ravi Malhotra is Associate Professor at the Faculty of Law, Common Law Section at the University of Ottawa and a graduate of Harvard Law School and the University of Toronto. Disabled since birth, he has published widely on disability rights.

Morgan Rowe is a graduate of the University of Ottawa's Common Law program and Carleton University's Journalism program. Throughout her education, she has volunteered with community and advocacy groups working on behalf of individuals with disabilities. She anticipates continuing this work through her legal career.

"This book provides a thoughtful analysis of how qualitative research can contribute to social change and transformation. Using narratives and life stories of disabled people, the authors contribute to law reform proposals for improving equality rights of disabled people." Ruby Dhand, Faculty of Law, Thompson Rivers University

Exploring Disability Identity and Disability Rights through Narratives
Finding a Voice of Their Own

Ravi Malhotra and Morgan Rowe

Routledge
Taylor & Francis Group

LONDON AND NEW YORK

First published 2014
by Routledge
2 Park Square, Milton Park, Abingdon, Oxfordshire OX14 4RN

Simultaneously published in the USA and Canada
by Routledge
711 Third Avenue, New York, NY 10017

First issued in paperback 2014

Routledge is an imprint of the Taylor and Francis Group, an informa business

British Library Cataloguing in Publication Data
A catalogue record for this book is available from the British Library

Library of Congress Cataloging-in-Publication Data
A catalog record has been requested for this book

ISBN 978-0-415-53235-8 (hbk)
ISBN 978-1-138-91882-5 (pbk)
ISBN 978-0-203-72134-6 (ebk)

Typeset in 11/12 Garamond 3 by
Servis Filmsetting Ltd, Stockport, Cheshire

Dedicated to the memory of "Andrea" who died far too young
And to our families, Lalitha and Mohan Malhotra, and
Geoff Rowe, Judi Reid and Laurel Rowe

Contents

Preface

Writing a book such as this—based on in-depth interviews with disabled participants—is a rewarding but time consuming task. Writing it as a collaboration is all the more rewarding but that much more complicated as different visions are considered, explored and revised. Originally, this project started out far less ambitiously and with a very small research budget in 2006. One of us (Malhotra) has been disabled since birth and has devoted his career to disability rights. The other (Rowe) came to the field of disability studies through her work as a journalist and her own experiences with chronic illnesses. Over time, this project grew in scope until it became the full length volume you are holding in your hands today. We owe an enormous debt to David Engel and Frank Munger, whose erudite book, *Rights of Inclusion: Law and Identity in the Life Stories of Americans with Disabilities*, remains a touchstone and essential reading for all who care about the relationship between disability rights and identity. The collegiality and warmth of Engel and Munger made this endeavour that much more satisfying even as we, at times, asked different questions and made different choices in our approach and scope. We hope that academics and disability rights advocates on the ground will find our commentary useful. The 12 participants who gave generously of their time to share their life stories and personal analysis are also owed a debt which we can never fully repay. We only hope that we have done justice to their voices, dreams and aspirations. That all of them did not live to see the publication of this book is a matter of deep sorrow.

A brief word on terminology. Throughout, we embrace those scholars in Britain and elsewhere who use the phrase "disabled people" rather than people-first language to signify our political commitment to a vibrant disability rights movement in which people embrace their disabilities. Hence, our usage follows our politics and we use both terms as appropriate.

Foreword

This book by Professor Ravi Malhotra and Ms Morgan Rowe examines the relationship between civil rights in Canada and the identity of persons with a disability. Path-breaking in its own right, their study builds on work that we began two decades ago, shortly after the passage of the Americans with Disabilities Act of 1990 in the United States. We welcome the opportunity to draw attention to the continuing development of this field of research through important studies like this one, which incorporates some of our insights but also thoughtfully critiques some of our assumptions and extends others.

When we began our work in 1992, we thought too few studies took account of the subtle interplay between the conditions that can turn an impairment into a disability—and the capacity of individuals to manage the challenges that follow. We were by no means the first to perceive or examine this interplay, but our study was undertaken in the immediate aftermath of a major new development in American civil rights law. We took advantage of the early years of this moment of legal change to explore law's capacity to transform peoples' lives, change social attitudes, and make institutions more inclusive and accepting of those who are too often labeled "different." Our research gradually led us to understand that whether law becomes active depends in the first instance on the construction of identities, a subtle and complex process that is only partially dependent on judicial decisions, legislative enactments, or constitutional innovations.

Our research drew on the work of others who pioneered the use of narratives in socio-legal research, and we were able to adapt that approach by making life story narratives the centerpiece of our research methodology. Identities are shaped over a lifetime, in part through circumstances and relationships encountered by an individual, but also by creation of a narrative of the Self. Our starting point, therefore, was the life story of the individual, though we did not intend this to be the exclusive vantage point on rights, identity, or social change. As Malhotra and Rowe note, some of our critics have seen our emphasis on the formation of a narrative of identity, and relative lack of attention to social formations, as a weakness. But we believed, and continue to believe, that our emphasis on the individual in his or her immediate surroundings, while by no means offering a comprehensive description of society, provides one exceptionally powerful tool for understanding the meaning of disability in particular social contexts and, more broadly, the relevance of law in everyday life.

Malhotra and Rowe generously credit us with suggesting a starting point and a methodology, but they have moved beyond our study, building on it but not confining themselves to replication. Their data differ from ours because they chose interviewees at moments they were engaged in advocacy, opening the way to new and complex insights about the circumstances that can influence the narratives individuals create about themselves. The authors have adapted, modified, and disagreed with some of our assumptions and approaches, thus, in our view, renewing and extending the value of the research we began two decades ago, but moving forward beyond our work. We welcome such contributions, and, in turn, will incorporate their insights as we continue our own research.

Even more important, we applaud and endorse this new addition to a growing cross-cultural literature on law and disability that expands the inquiry beyond the unique and in many ways atypical experience of the United States. This exploration of legal and social issues related to disability rights in Canada is highly instructive. The work of Malhotra and Rowe should be read alongside that of other comparative scholars, such as Katharina Heyer,[1] Arlene Kanter[2] and Peter Blanck.[3]

Malhotra's and Rowe's study displays extraordinary sensitivity to the lives and thoughts of the individuals who participated in their research. They clearly feel, as we did, that the interviewees and informants provided much more than "data" about themselves. By generously sharing portions of their lives with the researchers, the interviewees enriched the understandings of the authors as well as the readers. We owed a profound debt of gratitude to those we interviewed, since they not only changed our understanding of disability and law but even steered us toward the decision to use life story narratives as a research methodology. We were impressed that Malhotra and Rowe chose to express their gratitude, as we did, by inviting their interviewees to join in the interpretation of the narratives they had provided.

Malhotra and Rowe conclude with a plea for a reconsideration of the social model of disability that is more attentive to "the complexity of the lived experience of disabled people." Their book eloquently demonstrates the power and persuasiveness of such an approach. They listen carefully and respectfully to their interviewees, they present the narratives with sensitivity, and they then involve the interviewees in the search for meaning and significance. Such work requires enormous time and effort, but it provides the most convincing insights possible into the workings of civil rights law—for better or for worse—in the lives of those who are its intended beneficiaries. Documenting law's successes and failures through this presentation of life story narratives represents law and society research at its very best. The authors are to be commended for their important and selfless contribution to the literature on disability rights.

Professor David M. Engel and Frank W. Munger

Notes

1 K. Heyer, 'The ADA on the Road: Disability Rights in Germany' *Law & Social Inquiry*, 2006, vol. 27, pp. 723–62; K. Heyer, 'From Special Needs to Equal Rights: Japanese Disability Law' *Asian-Pacific Law & Policy Journal*, 2000, vol. 1, pp. 7:1–7:21 at p. 7:6.
2 A. Kanter, 'The Globalization of Disability Rights Law' *Syracuse Journal of International Law & Commerce*, 2003, vol. 30, pp. 241–70.
3 J. Nakagawa and P. Blanck, 'Future of Disability Law in Japan: Employment and Accommodation' *Loyola of Los Angeles International and Comparative Law Review*, 2010, vol. 33, pp. 173–221; M. Soffer, A. Rimmerman, P. Blanck and E. Hill, 'Media and the Israeli Disability Rights Legislation: Progress or Mixed and Contradictory Images?' *Disability & Society*, 2010, vol. 25, pp. 687–99.

Acknowledgements

In writing a book such as this, authors accumulate many debts. It is simply not possible to thank each and every one of you who has helped us along the way. First and foremost, we thank our 12 participants for their support and patience. In addition to our respective families, Lynda Collins, Frank Smith, Richard Jochelson and Alex Lubet provided encouragement and support. Katie Carpenter, Stephen Gutierrez and Mark Sapwell at Routledge have been patient and responsive to our every need. We thank Ann Andrzejewska for her thorough assistance with indexing. Interviews and focus groups with participants were conducted by the many patient and hard working research assistants, including Suzie Kotzer and Jordana Laporte. Many others who cannot be identified to preserve the confidentiality of participants we can thank only anonymously. Readers who took the time to provide valuable feedback on drafts include Jihan Abbas, Pamela Block, Amy Derickx, Ruby Dhand, Dustin Galer, Rachel Garaghty, Rachel Gorman, Christine Kelly, Suzie Kotzer, Emily Perkins, Daniel Tucker-Simmons, Mark Walters, audience members of the Chicago and Honolulu sessions of the Law and Society Association and, last but not least, Mark Weber. Professor Weber exemplifies the true meaning of mentorship in a world gone awry with commodification and commercialism. While we did not follow the advice in every case, we carefully considered all of it. All remaining errors are our responsibility.

We also wish to thank Dean Bruce Feldthusen of the Faculty of Law, Common Law Section, University of Ottawa for his commitment to equality rights in general and critical scholarship in particular. We gratefully acknowledge the financial support of the University Research Scholarship of the University of Ottawa and the Law Foundation of Ontario, without which this research would not have been possible.

1 Disability rights, narratives and identities: an overview

Disabled people have long experienced economic and political marginalization. Throughout the West, disabled people are significantly disadvantaged and ostracized whether one evaluates well-being by labour market participation rates, education levels or rates of poverty.[1] Our study aims to make a small contribution toward correcting this oppressive state of affairs through the reporting and analysis of in-depth narrative interviews. Our participants were mostly young physically disabled adults in a large Canadian city. Inspired by David Engel's and Frank Munger's recounting of the life stories of disabled Americans,[2] we provide these life stories in the voices of disabled people themselves. We then consider how law may be effectively used to address the policy issues we identify.

In this chapter, we begin by explaining the importance of the social model of disablement. It is the operating paradigm and core of our work. Simply put, the social model stresses an emphasis on structural barriers as the fundamental cause for the marginalization and oppression of disabled people. Second, we consider why narratives are important generally and for legal scholars in particular. We examine the work of Francesca Polletta and the writing team of Patricia Ewick and Susan Silbey, and critically assess the attack on narrative scholarship by Daniel Farber and Suzanna Sherry. Third, we explore insights gleaned from the use of feminist, critical race, and queer narratives in legal scholarship. We consider the scholarship of feminist theorists such as Kathryn Abrams, Susan Estrich, Martha Mahoney and the writing team of Lisa Webley and Liz Duff on a variety of topics, including sexual violence, spousal abuse and the attrition of women barristers and solicitors in the profession. We also evaluate the insights of critical race theorists, such as Anthony Farley and Nitya Duclos, as well as the contributions of William Eskridge Jr on queer legal theory. All of these scholars emphasize the importance of hearing the voices of marginalized people: listening to stories from the bottom is essential for social change. Fourth, we suggest ways in which qualitative research in general, and the analysis of narrative specifically, may contribute to social transformation and equality for disabled people, a profoundly marginalized group. We survey a range of disability narratives and qualitative scholarship, paying particular attention to the work of David Connor and Dustin Galer, as well as reflections on the writing of narratives by Robert Dinerstein and G. Thomas Couser. Lastly, we provide a brief overview of the chapters that follow.

The social model of disablement

The social-political or social model of disablement constitutes the core of the critique that the disability rights movement makes of society and its animating political concept.[3] We embrace the social model and use it throughout our analysis; its tenets have also guided the methodological choices we have made in designing our survey. It stands for the proposition that structural barriers lie at the root of the marginalization of disabled people. In other words, akin to earlier work done by feminists on patriarchy and anti-racism scholars on race, it maintains disability is socially constructed and shifts the focus away from physiological impairment.[4] It encompasses both physical barriers, such as a staircase that prevents a wheelchair user from accessing a school or office, and attitudinal barriers, such as an assumption that a wheelchair user would not be able to satisfactorily perform a task. To illustrate the distinction between disability and impairment, the fact that a woman has broken her spine and can no longer move nor feel her legs is an *impairment*. The fact that she cannot work as a bank teller because the bank has no wheelchair ramp at the entrance nor accessible washrooms which she can use is the creation of a *disability*. These barriers can be removed given the appropriate legal and policy framework. In other words, the problem is not the spinal cord injury but the fact that the bank and the laws that regulate public space and the architectural environment have not established an inclusive service model that would provide accessibility to all.

This sharply contrasts with a medical or individual model that emphasizes individual medical impairments as the cause for social and economic marginalization of disabled people. The problem of disablement in this model is regarded as one of personal troubles and personal tragedy caused by individual deficits.[5] On this view, the desired policy outcomes are medical intervention by qualified professionals, rehabilitation and preferably cure.[6] An array of professionals such as physicians, physiotherapists, occupational therapists, social workers and psychologists are deemed to be objective experts on the lives of disabled people and the optimal policies suited for them.[7] Both the power and numbers of rehabilitation professionals grew tremendously in the years following the end of the Second World War. These years were marked in most Western countries by economic growth and full employment.[8] When a cure does not transpire, the disabled person's life is regarded as a failure and she is expected to adopt what the sociologist Talcott Parsons famously identified as the sick role: permanent dependence and care in exchange for highly stigmatized passivity and a lack of responsibility.[9] The medical model posits a series of stages of grief that disabled people who acquire impairments are expected to pass through akin to the response of someone who is in bereavement as they attempt to adapt to society.[10]

Just as feminists had to transform public discourse by creating a new language to identify and analyze the concepts, both legal and sociological, they were developing in order to educate the media and the public at large about their importance, disability rights have had to do the same to challenge the legacy of dependency. This has been a long and ongoing battle with considerable backlash by rehabilitation professionals who have often remained skeptical and felt threatened by the argument.[11] Where feminists transformed a discourse that blamed women and girls who dressed as what was seen as inappropriately in the workplace as inviting sexual attention to one of sexual harassment focused on male conduct and responsibility, disability rights scholars have transformed the assumption of automatic institutionalization of those who require physical assistance with activities of daily living such as bathing, dressing and toileting to one of providing appropriate attendant services. Consequently, disabled people can live independently in the community.[12]

There is no single version of the social model just as there is no single disability rights movement. The disability rights movement is best regarded as a coalition of disparate groups run by and for disabled people including advocates for physically disabled people, proponents of equality for those with sensory impairments such as blindness and hearing impairments, and disability rights activists who struggle for equality for people with intellectual disabilities. Cross-disability organizing is often, but not necessarily always, a feature of the disability rights movement.[13] With respect to the social model, a vast literature in disability studies has swallowed entire forests dissecting the numerous competing schools, and we cannot possibly deal with every contributor to this debate.[14] In what follows, we are influenced primarily but not exclusively by the British version of the social model articulated and pioneered by scholars such as Michael Oliver, Colin Barnes, Vic Finkelstein and Paul Abberley.[15] This has been further developed by American scholars such as Marta Russell, Nirmala Erevelles and Sunny Taylor.[16] Sometimes known as the "strong social model,"[17] it articulates a materialist understanding of disability. In other words, it focuses on identifying structural relationships inherent in the capitalist mode of production that create disabilities which marginalize some people.[18] This means what constitutes a disability will change over time depending on the state of the economy and the state of technology in a given society. Numeracy and literacy may be so unimportant in a predominantly agricultural society that dyslexia may not constitute a disability.[19] A striking example is the documented cases when the United States in the 1970s began to make eligibility criteria for disability pensions more generous, effectively altering what was supposedly a medically objective definition of disability by creating a legal presumption of disability for certain types of impairments, at a time when unemployment rates were rapidly increasing. This had the effect of lowering official unemployment rates.[20] On other occasions, the definition of disability has been narrowed in countries such as Britain to reduce expenditures by refusing to deem certain disabled people as incapable of working.[21]

One of the most important developments in the propagation of the social model was the pioneering work of the Union of the Physically Impaired Against Segregation (UPIAS) in Britain. Founded by activists such as Vic Finkelstein and others in 1974, it condemned the control of disability organizations by professionals and highlighted the important distinction between impairment and disability that is foundational to the social model.[22] It challenges the notion that disability inevitably *follows* from impairment.[23] To return to the illustration of Jessica, her spinal cord injury has no impact on her functioning as a bank teller where the bank is fully accessible to wheelchair users. Instead of purely rehabilitation, the social model suggests collective political action as a remedy for oppression and exclusion to fight the marginalization of disabled people.[24] In our view, this struggle against the barriers that produce disability and for full citizenship can take any number of forms including political lobbying for legislation such as the Americans with Disabilities Act of 1990 (ADA) in the United States and the inclusion of disability in section 15 of the Canadian Charter of Rights and Freedoms, civil disobedience, street demonstrations, boycotts or strategic litigation.[25] Disability rights struggles from below are as valid a potential strategy as litigation: the two need not be counterposed but can work effectively in tandem.[26] Radical mobilization by rank and file disability rights advocates has played a crucial role at times in shaping public policy. Perhaps the most notable example is the 1977 demonstrations and sit-ins, lasting weeks in some cities, by American disability rights advocates across the United States to demand that the Carter Administration release regulations relating to accessibility pursuant to the Rehabilitation Act of 1973. In San Francisco, demonstrators were endorsed by the Black Panthers Party, which supplied food and publicity.[27]

The social model thereby encourages disabled people to think of themselves as an oppressed identity group and social movement, just as women, people of colour and gays, lesbians, bisexual, transsexual and asexual people have done.[28] Eventually, it encouraged a reconceptualization by the World Health Organization of how it classified disabilities, leading to the 2001 release of the International Classification of Functioning, Disability, and Health (ICF) that incorporated elements of the social model in its understanding of disablement.[29]

At the same time, we agree with those scholars who argue that it is important to acknowledge that physical impairments have very real and occasionally subtle implications on the quality of life of disabled people and need to be fully analyzed. Effectively arguing that the social model needs to "bring the body back in,"[30] they worry that a strong version of the social model ignores the important need to theorize impairment sociologically. In so doing, they rightly reject a Cartesian mind/body dualism that ignores the politics of the body and a conception of the impaired body as intersubjective and capable of action.[31] It is simply untenable, if we may return to the example at the outset of this chapter, to regard Jessica's life purely in terms of how social organizations create disability through physical barriers such as a lack of wheelchair accessible entrances. Rather, Jessica is likely to experience a range of what has been characterized as impairment effects.[32] These might include fatigue, incontinence, painful shoulders from constant use of a wheelchair and emotional exhaustion as a result of constantly having to advocate for wheelchair accessibility in a world designed for walking. Feminist scholars in particular have challenged the traditional version of the social model for marginalizing what are particularly crucial experiences of the lived experiences of disabled women, many of whom often have invisible impairments that nevertheless cause chronic pain.[33] In acknowledging this critique of the social model, we nevertheless maintain that a materialist understanding of disablement is crucial to advance the interests of disabled people, a distinct minority group with its own common needs and interests.

We do not, however, adopt the Universalist or human variation view articulated by some scholars that holds disability is merely a spectrum encompassing all human beings on which different people simply sit on a different point.[34] This approach has become influential particularly but not exclusively among those who advocate Universal Design (UD) in fields such as architecture and urban planning to eliminate barriers in products and environments so that they may be used by all without adaptation or modification.[35] By attempting to transform the environment rather than provide accommodations to particular individuals, UD could be regarded as an attempt to operationalize the Universalist paradigm of disablement. UD seeks to eliminate the notion that the provision of accessibility for disabled people reinforces segregation, that it is focused primarily on wheelchair access to the exclusion of accommodating other impairments and the concern by some architects and designers that accessibility modifications tended to be completed so poorly as to undermine the aesthetic quality of buildings.[36] However, we agree with those scholars who suggest that UD ignores the fact that technological progress is always mediated by a given social context. It does not flow automatically to create a utopia for disabled people, but critically depends on human agency to ensure accessibility. An illustration that grows in salience later in this book (see Chapter 5 on transportation) is the fact that accessible design to allow wheelchair users on public buses is completely useless if bus drivers harass disabled people.[37] We also believe the critics are correct to worry about the market orientation of UD product designers which may marginalize the needs of those who are not deemed to be profitable to UD innovators yet ought to have a right to accessible services and technology.[38] There is also an unmistakeable technocratic thread running through the UD paradigm which suggests that the scientific experts are in charge of the creation of products passively used by disabled people. This is worrying as products will not be effective without active input from disabled people.[39] Lastly, UD seems to inherit from the Enlightenment a rational paradigm of universalism that may not be sufficiently sensitive to the need to accommodate individual differences. The cultural claims of Deaf people are an example of a constituency that might actually be marginalized by UD principles that did not take into account their unique claims to be a linguistic minority.[40] For all these reasons, we endorse a modified version of the social model rather than a Universalist approach.

What might be the best approach for applying the social model to understanding the life stories of disabled adults? One particularly fruitful approach for analyzing the body is phenomenology or the study of the "essences that constituted the original basis of the meaning of the possibilities of consciousness, correlatively with its object."[41] It emphasizes subjective immediate experience and the central role of the body in understanding the human experience because it is through the body's interaction with the world that we perceive such phenomena as tactile sensation and colour.[42] Rooted in the theories of Edmund Husserl and modified by Maurice Merleau-Ponty in his landmark book, *Phenomenology of Perception*,[43] a phenomenological paradigm of impairment would be able to effectively acknowledge critiques of the social model raised by, among others, feminists by stressing the capacity for perception and action inherent in each individual and by giving new critical focus to the fact of embodiment and the possibility of human agency to transform the world to better suit disabled people.[44] As Turner correctly argues, the phenomenology of the body "recognizes the complex interplay between the objectified body of medical discourse, the phenomenal body of everyday experience, and the body image that, as it were, negotiates the social spaces between identity, experience and social relationships."[45] It would allow disability rights theorists to acknowledge the reality of embodied pain, which is always embedded in a cultural context that provides meaning,[46] while blazing social-political paths to create the conditions that minimize and resist it. Its inherently intersubjective character, rooted in the idea that the meaning of bodies is dependent on the relationships with other bodies, opens up the potential to challenge discriminatory attitudes toward disabled people.[47] We return to the question of methodology in more detail in Chapter 2, but now focus on the importance of narratives as an open window into the phenomenological world of disabled people and their reality.

Narratives and their uses

"It is not the consciousness of men [sic] that determines their being, but, on the contrary, their social being that determines their consciousness."[48] Karl Marx famously expressed this idea that is foundational to appreciating the importance of narratives or storytelling in situating the perspective and lived experiences of marginalized people as central to their understandings of the world. As Engel and Munger have argued, narrative relies on "remembered experiences, perceptions and feelings."[49] The resonance with phenomenological approaches is unmistakable. They are social practices that not only reflect their context but actively shape it.[50] By using life stories to ground proposals for law reform, one is able to vividly communicate knowledge about an otherwise alien experience and make it real for one's audience. Narrative accounts of particular life events such as, for instance, childbirth convey an experience with an emotive richness and authenticity that is not otherwise readily understandable to men or women who have not shared the experience.[51] One should readily recognize the impact of narratives for understanding the phenomenological experience of disablement is equally true. To the extent that this notion is challenging, it is largely because one is unaccustomed to thinking about disability issues in a political way. Without narrative to provide the phenomenological understanding, it is likely as difficult for an able-bodied woman to appreciate what it is truly like to require assistance with toileting and bathing on a daily basis as it is for a man to appreciate the experience of childbirth.[52] Narratives serve a purpose that cannot be easily filled by dry quantitative analysis, especially when attempting to challenge engrained stereotypes, by making the vivid immediacy of the situation crystal clear and facilitating empathy for oppressed people.[53] It brings a human face to the problem, thereby facilitating appreciation of the legal barriers and discrimination experienced by marginalized groups including disabled people. Narratives can take many forms including prose text, poetry or even fiction.[54] And they are a fundamentally different mode of cognitive thought than argument: narrative stresses the verisimilitude of a story to convey the specificity of experience.[55]

Francesca Polletta demonstrates how narratives of political events relating to the American civil rights movement for racial equality, the wave of sit-ins to protest racial segregation in the American South in 1960, played a fundamental role in shaping the consciousness of, and helped to mobilize, the participating students despite the perceived spontaneous character of the sit-ins.[56] In doing so, she identifies a number of purposes for narrative. First, she argues that by analyzing and structuring events over time, narratives transform individual insights of identity into fully-formed wholes. She notes that by locating events in a life story, one can make sense of the past, present and the potential future, identifying a basis for identity and action.[57] Narratives also help to form a collective identity or epistemic community. They act to strengthen them where they already exist.[58] By requiring the interpretive participation of readers, Polletta argues that narratives keep the public engaged by soliciting them in determining gaps and evaluating ambiguities in the narrative.[59] Lastly, narrative must always contend and grapple with the dominant cultural understanding of a particular problem. Since there are a "limited number of culturally resonant plots,"[60] activists trying to change the world have to construct a counter-plot that is convincing to the public or a segment thereof.[61] A counter-plot reframes an issue from the dominant understanding to a new appreciation for another perspective. A feminist counter-plot would reframe sexual harassment away from a focus on the alleged improprieties of the woman's attire to the sexist conduct engaged by men with power in the workplace.

The use of narrative in legal scholarship is still relatively marginal but has grown over the years. Writing on the relationship between narrative and legal scholarship, Patricia Ewick and Susan Silbey identify two grounds on which narrative is celebrated. First, narratives have the capacity to teach us truths that are flattened by conventional methods of legal scholarship and the social sciences. In other words, narrative analysis is an epistemological approach that allows us access to consciousness and meaning in its full context, without the distortions that inevitably accompany interpretation by legal scholars.[62] Second, narratives have a counter-hegemonic potential to subvert or transform society by allowing voices traditionally ignored to speak out and by recognizing the fact that the production of knowledge is profoundly political.[63] Ewick and Silbey also suggest a trichotomy of ways in which scholarly research in law may use narratives. First, narratives may be the object of inquiry: the researcher explores how narratives are produced in a given community to articulate a specific understanding of the world. They describe a study that compares how two communities evaluated the verisimilitude of stories by a variety of criteria.[64] Second, narratives may be the means to study a question in social life such as jury decision-making.[65] As we discuss in more detail in Chapter 2, we analyze the narratives of mostly young, Canadian adults in this book precisely in this way to study the policy implications for disabled people in a number of areas. Lastly, legal scholars may create narratives themselves that are either accounts from their own lives that reflect upon legal issues or entirely fictional stories.[66] This has been particularly popular, as we discuss below, amongst feminist and critical race legal scholars seeking to challenge racism and patriarchy, and increasingly by disability rights advocates.

Ewick and Silbey usefully distinguish between hegemonic tales and subversive stories. Hegemonic tales function to reproduce existing power structures by acting as mechanisms of social control. Whether it is the importance of family values or the importance of hard work and the dangers of rebelliousness, narratives may be used to reinforce conformity.[67] They also "colonize consciousness" by collectively constituting through accretion a world view that becomes difficult for others to challenge. The recovery of American dignity and the rehabilitation of traumatized war veterans in the aftermath of the loss in Vietnam is an example of such a narrative, which precludes more radical consideration of the purposes of American foreign policy objectives.[68] Hegemonic tales also mask the relationships between the particular and general that reflect unspoken general understandings and assumptions of how the world works. For instance, narratives of domestic violence in family law mediation have been shown to marginalize women's experience of violence because the norms of mediation have in some cases mandated that all stories are relative, thereby trivializing acts of male violence that in fact constitute criminal conduct.[69]

In contrast, subversive or counter-hegemonic stories locate the particular within the organization of society and disclose the relationships between them that are not typically scrutinized. Interestingly, Ewick and Silbey cite the counter-hegemonic narrative that parents of disabled children must construct to fight the medicalized stigma that accompanies giving birth and raising a disabled child who does not conform to the conventional expectations of society.[70] Moreover, subversive stories understand how hegemony is constructed. By knowing the rules of the established order, subversive stories are able to effectively challenge it. A comprehensive understanding of the regulations governing the eligibility of purchases by welfare recipients, for instance, is required in order to challenge restrictions such as the type of shoes which are covered.[71] Lastly, subversive narratives are facilitated where there is both a common opportunity to narrate stories and a common content to them. From racial segregation in the United States and elsewhere to experiences specific to women such as childbirth, oppressed groups have often had both the opportunity and content to articulate stories that speak to their oppression. In this sense, the very oppressive structures manifest in society contains the seeds of its own transformation through the telling of stories by outsider groups.[72]

The use of legal narratives is not without controversy. Daniel Farber and Suzanna Sherry have published a critique of the use of legal narratives, particularly concerned that narratives describing the experiences of oppressed groups ought to comply with universal conceptions of truth in order for scholars to be able to evaluate their validity. They worry that third party claims about discrimination may be one-sided and unreasonably rely on intuition to determine the validity of the truth-claim.[73] Without agreeing with their full argument which strikes us as rooted in an ideological skepticism of embodied knowledge, we agree with their critique that narratives of multiple participants should never be collated to create a fictional montage that may mislead the reader.[74] We have not altered the participants' stories that follow in this book in any way, except to preserve anonymity in accordance with standard research protocols, and we do not claim that their stories are the absolute truth. They are, however, an important perspective from individuals whose voices have been badly neglected in public discourse. Moreover, we attempt in Chapter 7 to link the narratives to practical law reform projects. We now turn to consider how subversive stories have empowered and enriched our understanding of outsider groups through feminist, critical race and queer legal theory.

Feminism, critical race theory, queer theory and narratives

Feminist legal narratives have been enormously influential in raising consciousness about the experiences of women in legal discourse challenging a patriarchal world. The same is true for critical race and queer legal narratives and their impact for people of colour and queers. Stories from the bottom provide a glimpse into a world the majority ignores and which lawyers need to hear. Our purpose here is not to provide a comprehensive account of this vast literature but to provide the reader with some of the overall insights to bear in mind when evaluating the focus of our inquiry on disability narratives. Kathryn Abrams has eloquently outlined a defense of the narrative method in feminist legal scholarship through a review of various examples.[75] She analyzes how American legal scholar Susan Estrich famously introduced a law review article of sexual assault law in the United States with a detailed description of her own rape, illustrating how Estrich's legal perspective has been shaped by both the violence she experienced and the hostile police reaction to the violence.[76] As an emotionally traumatic experience that men do not share and is often not discussed in public, Estrich's introduction provided a vivid—and, at the time, controversial—documentation of the brutality of the crime and a foundation for her proposals in the remainder of her article for the revision of problematic and sexist legal doctrines to ensure consent to sexual activity is consistent with the perspective of female victims of violence.[77]

Abrams also shows how Martha Mahoney uses narratives to help readers understand legal and policy issues relating to domestic violence and battered women to challenge the stereotype that only certain kinds of women are prone to domestic violence.[78] Mahoney's analysis creatively develops a new concept, which she calls "separation assault," to better understand the context in which women are battered by spouses when they try to terminate a relationship.[79] Unlike Estrich, Mahoney uses narratives throughout her piece.[80] She also uses multiple narratives of various lengths from many different women, apart from her own story, to illustrate the complexity of battering and how battered women make effective parents. She does so in order to influence legal debates about custody battles.[81] In weaving narrative through the legal analysis, Abrams notes how Mahoney's work aesthetically resembles at times performance art and sociology, as well as legal analysis, providing the audience with a richer insight into the problem.[82] While Estrich and Mahoney use narratives in different ways, the richness of the experience conveyed through narrative provides a grounding that would simply be impossible through a statistical account of the impact of sexual violence or battering on women and allows male decision-makers a window into a world that they normally ignore.

A methodology closer to the traditional social sciences is illustrated by the study undertaken by Lisa Webley and Liz Duff to determine why British women solicitors have left the profession in large numbers and are not promoted at rates similar to their male colleagues. They use focus groups of women solicitors who had taken a break from the practice of law in the last five years to probe their experiences of the legal profession.[83] They use the narratives of the women solicitors to show how the practice of law was increasingly becoming commodified with a focus on maximizing billable hours. The pressure of firms for profitability and expectations that lawyers participate in time consuming networking activities during evening hours were making life burdensome for women who faced responsibilities in both the workplace and at home.[84] The short narratives together make the marginalization of British female solicitors real.

Critical race narratives in American and Canadian legal scholarship have also played an important part in articulating the perspective of racialized people.

Scholars such as Derrick Bell,[85] Patricia Williams,[86] Richard Delgado,[87] Anthony Farley[88] and Nitya Duclos[89] have all creatively used narratives— sometimes fictional, sometimes autobiographical—to illustrate how racism and white supremacy have shaped and distorted legal discourse and relied on experiential knowledge to do so.[90] It is thus an outgrowth of critical legal studies which interrogates the ambiguity of the legal positivist and legal realist traditions, but with an explicit focus on challenging racism and white supremacy which they regard as a normal part of North American society.[91] Delgado identifies the importance of oppressed groups using what he calls 'counterstorytelling' to challenge the presuppositions and received wisdoms of mainstream society.[92] Women of colour have importantly used narrative to raise the issue of intersectionality, namely how those who experience personal identity on more than one categorical form of oppression and subordination have both a unique history and forms of resistance that cannot simply be reduced to a single ground.[93] Narratives have thus played a pivotal role in the development of Critical Race Theory (CRT). Given space constraints, we will focus our commentary on the work of Farley and Duclos.

Anthony Farley's highly theoretical reflection on racism centres on his thesis that race is a form of sadomasochistic pleasure in one's own body and achieved through the humiliation of people of colour. However, denial of the humiliation is an integral part of the process that creates this racial hierarchy.[94] Applying the work of, among others, Frantz Fanon, Michel Foucault, James Baldwin and Elaine Scarry to better explore the dynamics of race as a form of pleasure, Farley's intervention is an intimidatingly sophisticated response to debates in CRT.[95] Yet for all its complexity, Farley captivates his audience by commencing his piece by recounting an episode from his childhood when he watched a Tarzan film with his younger brother. In the film, the white hero and his love interest traverse the jungle along a treacherous mountain path, followed by an army of Black men who carry the provisions on their head. When a Black man falls off the path to his death, the hero exclaims his horror at the loss of the supplies. The death of the Black man goes unnoticed.[96] A second story is equally evocative. Farley is on a school trip in junior high school to Washington DC and a classmate combed her long hair at great length, before inquiring to whom the comb belonged. Another classmate falsely claimed that the comb belonged to Farley, the only African American student on the trip. The class laughed at the racial transgression that was alleged while the comber burst into tears and turned crimson. The notion of interracial intimacy was so improper as to be a violation.[97] Farley writes:

> I was the collective soul of my white classmates. They transformed me with their jests, tears, and laughter. I could feel myself extruded as vomit, as sweat, as spit, as abjection itself. Their souls flowed out through their tongues and I, silent and excrementalized, was filled with the nobodyness they desired of me.[98]

Together, these narratives of racial humiliation from the author's childhood provide the depth that makes Farley's otherwise highly abstract argument about racial pleasure come alive.

Nitya Duclos also uses narrative effectively to make her argument about how the discrimination experienced by Canadian women of colour is not properly addressed by the human rights tribunals charged with addressing the problem. Duclos suggests that human rights tribunals fail to capture the intersectionality raised by complainants who are women of colour and whose experience cannot be captured completely either by the concepts of racism or sexism. Indeed, she notes how the indexing of reported tribunal decisions makes it difficult to even determine the race of human rights complainants.[99] Duclos begins her landmark piece with a haunting story about how she, a woman of colour, is unable to have her coffee cup re-filled as she finishes breakfast in a restaurant in which all the other customers and servers are white. She comments:

> I lift my empty cup and stare pointedly at a waitress pouring another unrequested refill for the man at the next table. She does not see me. I call out. She does not hear. I have fantasies of leaping up and seizing the pot from her hands, of stalking over to the next table and drinking the refilled cup, of making a SCENE. Everyone in the restaurant, everyone in the city, has coffee except for me. I seethe with frustration. Still nothing happens. I despair. It is late. Even if I could get more coffee, I would not have time to drink it now. I feel small and miserable. Invisible still, I rise from my table, gathering my notes. At the cash register I become visible, briefly, as I pay my bill. I wonder whether I will disappear again before I can hail a cab.
>
> Hours later, alone and safe in my room, I still wonder. Was it because I was a woman alone? Because I wasn't white? Because I looked too young? Too short? Was it discrimination? Was it them or was it just me?
>
> I still wonder.[100]

She is repeatedly ignored and yet, in a way that symbolizes her legal argument, she is unable to ascertain whether she is being ignored because she is a woman, she is a person of colour or both.[101]

With respect to qualitative research, Malagon, Huber and Velez have argued that CRT is compatible with qualitative approaches, particularly grounded theory which we discuss in detail in Chapter 2.[102] They suggest, however, that an anti-racist focus must be foundational, in the same way that the social model of disablement guides our own work, for research that seeks to liberate people of colour and challenge white supremacy.[103] They identify four sources of cultural intuition that can facilitate the research process for CRT scholars. They are the researcher's personal background and life experiences, the researcher's academic experiences, the researcher's professional experiences and the research process itself.[104] Together, they constitute an approach that attempts to involve participants in a meaningful and respectful manner that enhances social justice.[105]

Queer legal theorists have also turned to narrative to give voice to their experiences in a world of homophobia. William Eskridge Jr identifies three benefits of gay narratives. First, he argues, writing in the context of homophobic policies that historically prohibited queer people from serving in the American military, that such narratives make the public aware of the patriotic and effective contributions of queer soldiers. By putting a human face on the issue, administrators are less able to defend ignorant and homophobic policies.[106] Given the profound lack of public knowledge about disability issues, the same principle likely applies to many disability issues of which the general public is simply unaware. Second, he argues that narrative allows one to test abstract principles through specific cases. The weaknesses of the exclusion of queer people from the military and the dysfunctional periodic witch hunts which accompanied the policy are revealed by considering the narratives of queer soldiers.[107] Third, he maintains that narratives effectively demonstrate the relationship of disparate policies. While he does not use the term intersectionality, he highlights the case of an African American gay soldier, Watkins, who was allowed to re-enlist in Vietnam. Eskridge speculates that it may well have been racist assumptions that Watkins would die in service as an African American that allowed him to join in the first place despite being queer. Eskridge also shows how women soldiers who refused to agree to improper sexual demands by male superiors were then falsely accused of lesbian conduct and subjected to investigations under the military's homophobic policies.[108] Narratives thus work to combat homophobic stereotypes and bring the lived experience of queer people—a world invisible to many—to the surface.

Narratives and critical disability theory: the ultimate outsiders

As critical disability theory in the field of law is in its infancy compared to older social movements, we cast our net slightly wider, explore disability narratives more broadly and defer our account of Engel's and Munger's pathbreaking work for Chapter 2.[109] Why are narratives of disability in particular an excellent methodological choice? Four characteristics of when qualitative research has been said to be warranted are: (a) the research program emphasizes individual results; (b) the in-depth information about the phenomena is required; (c) the study's focus covers the diversity of individuals; and (d) there is no standardized instrument.[110] As so little is known about the life experiences of disabled people and their relationship to law, we submit that in-depth disability narratives are fully warranted to analyze the constellation of questions that surround the lives of disabled people.

Feminists were among the first to include narratives of disablement. Numerous anthologies of disabled women's personal experiences have given voice to their insights into the barriers they face as a result of both ableist barriers and patriarchy. Susan Browne, Debra Connors and Nanci Sterne followed by Marsha Saxton and Florence Howe edited two of the earliest such anthologies in the United States in 1985 and 1987, respectively.[111] The first collection is striking in its open discussion of how the various impairments of the editors greatly impacted the production of the book. They experienced hospitalizations or temporary blindness as a result of their impairments, deaths in their families and amongst treasured pets, and the news that friends had become terminally ill.[112] The stories convey the emotional and physical reality of growing up with impairments. One particularly haunting narrative recounts the helplessness of childhood orthopedic surgery at age nine. The child is simply subjected to what turns out to be a highly experimental and detrimental surgery to lengthen her leg without adequate explanation. The sense of violation is palpable and the impact is far-reaching: she is placed in a segregated crippled children's class, a highly stigmatized environment whose pupils are marginalized and regarded as Other by the able-bodied students attending regular classes. As an adult, she has significant body image issues, and the fear of anesthesia used for surgery makes it difficult for her to enjoy orgasm during sexual intercourse.[113] The various contributors to Saxton and Howe's anthology, consisting of a heady mix of personal accounts, poetry and fictional stories, passionately describe coping with the effects of their impairments, the impact of sexual violence and trying to survive on minimal incomes.[114] They also poignantly describe the difficulties in finding appropriate orthopedic shoes and the stigma that carries, particularly for disabled teenagers.[115] These narratives give voice to the stories that have largely been ignored. A more recent collection featuring the writings of Canadian disabled women, edited by Diane Driedger, appeared in 2010. It included various contributions on themes such as assisted suicide, violence against women, intersectionality and poverty.[116] However, it should be said that relatively little scholarship has been produced that simultaneously addresses gender, disability *and* race.[117]

A more specialized book is Mary Mason's insightful ethnographic study of the work lives of disabled women in the United States. She conducts interviews with 30 women with a range of physical and sensory impairments about their work experiences, education, family upbringing, sexual relationships and their sense of disability identity.[118] She documents how the attitude of parents, socioeconomic status, and having a social support system were key factors in determining success beyond simply physical accessibility in the workplace.[119] Although the study is restricted to disabled women and largely eschews academic references and even commentary by the author, it thus bears some striking resemblances to our own project in certain respects. Other specialized books, such as the recounting of the experience of mothering as a disabled woman, have also appeared.[120]

Anne Finger, a radical disability and feminist theorist, novelist and academic, has authored at least two different works that combine reflections from her life as a woman who acquired polio as a young girl with sharp political insights.[121] In *Past Due*, Finger eloquently describes her pregnancy as a disabled woman.[122] In a subsequent book, *Elegy for a Disease*, Finger mixes autobiographical elements from her childhood with an account of the cultural effects of polio in the United States.[123] She provides gleaming and often contradictory insights that force the reader to rethink one's assumptions about disablement. For instance, while noting that in the 1950s, many parents worried that their disabled children, especially boys, would grow up to be queer, at a time when queer identity was severely persecuted and feared as part of the anti-Communist McCarthyism discourse dominant at the time, Finger also points out that as a disabled child who had polio, she was liberated in the scope of her employment horizons beyond the confines of the patriarchal world view which held sway. She could imagine any career path without stigma and constantly had the late President Franklin Roosevelt held up as an example of a successful role model who had polio, whereas virtually all of her able-bodied female acquaintances aspired to be either teachers or nurses, in conformity with the acceptable gender roles for women of the time.[124]

Historians have also used disability narratives to illuminate the conditions experienced by disabled people. Canadian historian Geoffrey Reaume employs narratives of former patients and hospital workers to deepen his analysis of life at Lyndhurst, Canada's first rehabilitation centre for people with spinal cord injuries.[125] He documents how patients, often military veterans in the early days, worked to subvert the strict regulations of the facility, such as the prohibition of beer in the rehabilitation facility, so that they could enjoy life while recuperating, at times with the acquiescence of sympathetic nurses.[126] Reaume provides a deeper understanding of the intricacies of institutional life that are alien to the vast majority of people and demonstrate the agency that even hospitalized patients possess. In an earlier book, Reaume uses extant medical files of institutionalized patients, including correspondence to families, at a psychiatric facility in Toronto to paint an in-depth portrait of patient life at the facility. He documents how patients at times resisted oppressive treatment and forces the reader to rethink one's conception of madness.[127]

A compelling example of cutting edge qualitative research with respect to disabled people is David Connor's innovative study of eight African American and Latino/a working class youths between the ages of 18 and 23 living in New York City who had all been labeled as having learning disabilities at various points in their lives.[128] Connor used a variety of techniques over many sessions to garner the participation of the disabled people in the production of the research and to emphasize the importance of their intersectional oppression on the basis of disability, race and gender. He began by having participants compose prose narratives about how urban learning-disabled youth understand their status within the discursive universe of learning disability through their lived experience.[129] He then operated individual meetings or focus groups to discuss the work, which he called self-portraits, which his participants produced.[130] Connor then utilized an approach known as collective memory work whereby participants shared their stories, in prose or poetry form, so that each one could envision the commonalities and overlap with the experiences of others. The idea, influenced by poststructuralist theory, is to break down the divisions between researcher and participants by recognizing the embodied moments that lead to knowledge.[131] Connor then conducted group analysis of the portraits composed by the participants for accuracy.[132]

Lastly, Connor and the participants constructed monologues based on the data that formed the substance of his book, using Delgado's insights on counterstorytelling as a basis to construct narratives that were both authentic and challenged the conventional portrayal of learning disabled youth in mainstream special education paradigms.[133] One participant remarks on her experience living with learning disabilities:

> It is hard for me sometimes because I always wanted to see myself above everyone and being able to do a lot of things that General Ed. can do. They seem so popular to me and I wanted to be the same way as them. I would feel intimidated by boys because of their intelligence, if they liked me, or if they were my friends. I always rubbed my hands together as if I was nervous because their speech was so perfect. I know when I was with the General Ed. girls I felt more comfortable and more open with them. My strengths are: explaining how I feel, dance, behavior, and good hygiene. I can work.[134]

Connor recommends a number of reforms to transform public education including the introduction of disability into the public school curriculum, using a menu of testing methods to accommodate different learning styles, and collaborative team teaching in a single classroom to better include students with all levels of intellectual ability.[135] He also recommends that the process by which parents of learning disabled children are consulted about educational accommodations be restructured because of the way racialized, working class parents are marginalized in the current system.[136]

A second intriguing and more methodologically traditional qualitative research project on disability and narratives is Canadian scholar Dustin Galer's study of the work history narratives of 29 disabled people in Toronto and the surrounding area, and its relationship to identity formation.[137] As we note in Chapter 4, employment often lies at the core of how one establishes identity and the acquisition of a disability can disrupt one's identity. Galer examines people with a wide range of impairments including intellectual, physical, sensory and mental health impairments from across the age spectrum.[138] Participants were asked about the importance of work in their lives and how it affected their identity using a grounded theory approach.[139] NVivo 9.0 qualitative data analysis software was used and four themes were identified: material drivers, performative sociocultural roles, image management and emotional aspects.[140]

Galer found that material drivers of work include a desire for autonomy, avoiding dependency and self-respect.[141] On the question of performative sociocultural roles, Galer observes how both men and women found psychological and emotional benefits from work. However, consistent with an intersectional understanding of the world, some women also faced considerable sexism in the workplace, especially if they worked in mostly male environments.[142] On the other hand, many men in his sample accepted conventional gender norms about working and found unemployment to be humiliating and degrading.[143] A participant comments:

> It was humiliating. I'm a guy who likes to work. I just found myself stuck. Like a tire stuck in snow, just can't get out, no matter spinning my wheels trying to get out. I did everything they wanted, I was willing to do anything. I was young, had a family. Even when my kids were [age] seven to nine, it's like "Daddy why don't you work? Mommy goes to work." It's kind of embarrassing, humiliating, like why can't I be more productive.[144]

With respect to image management, Galer noted how some participants felt a need to make the public more comfortable with their impairments. In other cases, participants were concerned about the stigma they felt that volunteer work and gaps in labour market participation carried. Some participants spoke passionately about how gaps relating to mental illness were frowned upon, even though gaps relating to pregnancy were seen as acceptable.[145] Lastly, work was closely related to self-esteem. Participants emphasized how paid work provided a sense of fulfillment and achievement. Connor and Galer present two strikingly different ways of performing qualitative research with disabled people. Connor uses the most radical of data collection methods to aggressively challenge traditional approaches of understanding learning disability. While Galer is clearly committed to social justice and allows for participant input in his work, his approach is relatively conventional and backs up his theoretical understanding of disablement with a rigorous methodology including even the use of software. As we see in Chapter 2, our own approach may be situated somewhere between the two poles.

Turning to specifically legal narratives, Ruth O'Brien's anthology, *Voices from the Edge: Narratives about the Americans with Disabilities Act*,[146] consciously sets out to do for disability rights what Derrick Bell, Patricia Williams and Richard Delgado had done for critical race theory: employing a mix of fictional and non-fictional narratives to tell the stories of disabled Americans.[147] She structures her book so that the narrative and the legal commentary appear separately and the reader is left to gather the chapters into a cohesive whole. For instance, one chapter recounts the happy childhood of an affluent Baltimore woman, Aleshire, with malformations in her hands who goes on to be the first woman in her family to attend college. She becomes a poet and teaches creative writing. Her family encouraged her to succeed despite the fact that she was born during the Great Depression, decades before a social model approach took hold in American public policy.[148] There are no direct references to law in Aleshire's narrative. A subsequent chapter then analyzes the complex American law relating to who qualifies as having a disability under the ADA through the prism of Aleshire's life.[149] The weaving of narrative and law allows the reader to have a vivid picture of the application of the abstract principles being discussed.

A qualitative approach that combines autobiographical narrative may be found in Carrie Griffin Basas' study of 38 disabled women lawyers in the United States.[150] She begins her tale with a compelling description of how she was subjected to patronizing behaviour by a faculty member while a physically disabled student at Harvard Law School.[151] The professor, clearly uncomfortable with her impairments, would inappropriately refer to her impairments in class, go out of his way to open doors for her and shower her with lavish praise.[152] On the final day of class, he kept the class over time and directly targeted Basas for unwanted attention. She comments:

> As he provided the customary adieus, he deviated from norms of any kind when he began to talk about a "special person" in class who would go far, "serve on the Supreme Court," and "has helped so many unfortunate handicapped people."[153]

With respect to the work experiences of disabled women lawyers, Basas identifies three ways in which disabled women engage in what she calls self-accommodation to enable them to work. They are: the acquisition of adaptive equipment or making physical space alterations, choosing jobs that are flexible and disability-friendly and the adoption of an entrepreneurial path that eliminates bosses.[154] Yet as she rightly points out, self-accommodation is a pragmatic and wise choice for many, especially given the poor success rate of the ADA in employment discrimination cases. Nevertheless, it also means few novel disability discrimination cases involving legal counsel are heard.[155] She also conveys how disabled women lawyers face unique barriers as a result of their intersectional position. Although able-bodied women often face stigma because of concerns relating to child care and competing demands on their time that place them on a mommy track, the accommodations that disabled women typically require are more fundamental as they must literally ensure that the workplace is accessible to gain entry before they can consider issues relating to career advancement.[156]

The very practice of law also involves narratives. In an insightful work, Robert Dinerstein has shown how lawyers of disabled clients shape the narratives of their cases in ways that may conform to stereotypes or contest them depending on the strategy undertaken by legal counsel.[157] Referring to what he calls the "prism of tactical calculation,"[158] Dinerstein argues that lawyers shape narratives in ways that are likely to win them favour with judges and juries.[159] However, this can lead to ethical challenges if there is a conflict between the lawyer's goals and the client's objectives because the strategy most likely to win might very well be at the cost of the client's dignity.

Dinerstein cites the complex and emotionally laden case of a horrific sexual assault of an intellectually disabled young teenage female by a group of young men in New Jersey where the prosecutor wanted to emphasize the woman's inability to consent due to her impairments, while disability advocates were uncomfortable with a legal narrative that called into question the ability of intellectually disabled people to *ever* consent to sexual intercourse.[160]

How might one assess legal narratives? G. Thomas Couser thoughtfully develops a typology of the relationships between personal narratives and law for the American context.[161] He maintains that narratives may anticipate legal developments, seek confirmation in the law or risk disconfirmation, have a hypothetical relationship to the law or be tacitly informed by the law.[162] An example of anticipatory narrative would be how Representative Coehlo, who was a sponsor of the ADA, was denied admission to the priesthood because of his epilepsy. This shaped his commitment to accessibility for disabled people. Similarly, Couser recounts how a blind woman, Adrienne Asch, lobbied for legislation that enabled her to be accepted in the workplace. She did so by altering the cultural narrative of disability.[163] Second, he notes how narratives of disability discrimination may be either confirmed or disconfirmed. He cites the well-known problem of the narrow definition of disability under the ADA. Couser observes how successful ADA discrimination confirms the narratives of disability, while the many cases that result in a finding that the plaintiff does not meet the definition of disability disconfirms the narrative, forcing advocates to transform the political culture if they want to succeed in litigation.[164]

The third category in Couser's typology is one where there is a hypothetical relationship between the narrative and the law. Perhaps most salient for our own work, he cites the example of Aleshire described by Ruth O'Brien and discussed above. Aleshire may well qualify as having a disability under the ADA, but O'Brien presents separately her narrative of growing up wealthy in Baltimore and O'Brien's own legal analysis. In fact, it is far from clear that Aleshire would be entitled to accommodations under the ADA and the hypothetical approach that O'Brien uses illuminates the issues far more clearly than a purely doctrinal analysis.[165] Lastly, a text may be tacitly informed by disability rights law, even when the text never discusses disability rights law directly. Couser illustrates how narratives of younger disabled people may simply assume the existence of accessibility is so commonplace that they fail to mention access features. It is so obvious that it simply does not merit consideration, while the narratives focus on the everyday life of the disabled narrator. Yet they are beneficiaries of accessibility rather than litigants and their entire lives and identities were constituted through a relationship with disability rights law.[166] The wheelchair user who attends a public school that was retrofitted with an elevator may be blissfully unaware of battles previous generations of disability rights advocates took to make it accessible. In the same way a feminist memoir might take the ready availability of birth control to be so obvious as not worth commentary. We would caution, however, that this type of widespread availability of wheelchair accessibility is largely restricted to the United States, suggesting that the tacitly informed paradigm may have less salience where systemic barriers are more widespread.

Overview of chapters

This first chapter has provided insight into the social model of disablement and why narratives are an appropriate and insightful way of understanding the experience of disability. Second, we then explored the merits of narrative generally and its application in feminist, critical race theory and queer legal theory. Third, we considered how narratives have been used in critical disability theory. In Chapter 2, we discuss in detail the methodological approach taken in this qualitative study, the merits of grounded theory and the profound influence of Engel and Munger on our work. We show how we decided that grounded theory is the most suitable research method for the type of open-ended inquiry we were making and to highlight the narratives of our participants. In Chapter 3, we examine and analyze the experience of our participants in facing physical and attitudinal barriers in education. This encompasses public school education and post-secondary education, as well as some of the unique issues relating to summer camps exclusively for disabled children. In Chapter 4, we explore how barriers impact on the ability of our participants to enter and maintain employment in a world where all too often disabled people are regarded as inefficient burdens. We pay particular attention to the changes that have affected many workplaces with the shift from permanent full time employment to the expansion of poorly paid part time employment. As we note, this has ominous implications for the provision of accommodations that would make workplaces truly inclusive. In Chapter 5, we evaluate the experience of our participants in using transportation in its myriad forms when the built environment systematically ignores the accessibility needs of disabled Canadians. We consider how barriers in both door-to-door paratransit services and public transportation marginalize disabled people and limit their access to community life. And we explore how other forms of transportation such as taxis, airplanes and automobiles impose barriers that marginalize the lives of disabled people. In Chapter 6, we examine how gender affects the lives of our male and female participants. We explore how the expected performance of gender differs for men and women, leading to difficulties for both disabled men and women, as they attempt to conform to gendered expectations. We specifically consider issues such as body image, harassment, and caregiving and their relationship to gender. Lastly, in Chapter 7, we examine how law reform can be implemented to address some of the barriers that we identify earlier in the book and suggest avenues for further inquiry. Collectively, we hope this text makes a small contribution to better understanding the relationship between disability rights, law and narratives and does justice to the voices of the participants who so graciously gave their time.

Notes

1 For American statistics, see A.M. Smith, 'Persons with Disabilities as a Social and Economic Underclass' *Kansas Journal of Law and Public Policy*, 2002–2003, vol. 12, p. 21. For Canadian statistics, see G. Brodsky, S. Day and Y. Peters, *Accommodation in the 21st Century*, Ottawa: Canadian Human Rights Commission, 2012, p. 2, available online at http://www.chrc-ccdp.ca/pdf/accommodation_eng.pdf (last accessed January 4, 2013) (noting disabled people are twice as likely to be poor and significantly less likely to have graduated from high school than their able-bodied counterparts).

2 D.M. Engel and F.W. Munger, *Rights of Inclusion: Law and Identity in the Life Stories of Americans with Disabilities*, Chicago, IL: University of Chicago Press, 2003. Work based on their study also appeared in D.M. Engel and F.W. Munger, 'Rights, Remembrance, and the Reconciliation of Difference' *Law and Society Review*, 1996, vol. 30, pp. 7–54; D.M. Engel and F.W. Munger, 'Civil Rights and Self-Concept: Life Stories of Law, Disability, and Employment' *Droit et Cultures*, 1998, vol. 35, pp. 43–73; D.M. Engel and F.W. Munger, 'Re-Interpreting the Effect of Rights: Career Narratives and the Americans with Disabilities Act' *Ohio State Law Journal*, 2001, vol. 62, pp. 285–333; D.M. Engel and F.W. Munger, 'Narrative, Disability and Identity' *Narrative*, 2007, vol. 15, pp. 85–94. To the best of our knowledge, this is the first study to replicate Engel's and Munger's methodology.

3 M. Oliver and C. Barnes, *The New Politics of Disablement*, Basingstoke: Palgrave Macmillan, 2012, p. 21. This is an update to the iconic work, M. Oliver, *The Politics of Disablement*, London: Macmillan, 1990.

4 Oliver and Barnes, ibid; Oliver, ibid. Comprehensive citations regarding gender and race as social constructs would take us too far afield. However, see C. MacKinnon, 'Feminism, Marxism, Method and the State: An Agenda for Theory' *Signs*, 1982, vol. 7, pp. 516–17 (analyzing patriarchy and sexuality as social constructs); T.W. Allen, *The Invention of the White Race: Volume 1: Racial Oppression and Social Control*, 2nd edn, London: Verso, 2012, p. 23 (analyzing white supremacy as a social construct).

5 M. Rioux and F. Valentine, 'Does Theory Matter? Exploring the Nexus between Disability, Human Rights and Public Policy' in D. Pothier and R. Devlin (eds) *Critical Disability Theory: Essays in Philosophy, Politics, Policy and Law*, Vancouver: University of British Columbia Press, 2006, pp. 48–51.

6 Rioux and Valentine, ibid. To save space, we have skipped over Jerome Bickenbach's insightful analysis of what he calls an economic model of disablement which focuses on how barriers create work disabilities and how disability serves as a boundary between those deemed capable of paid work and entitled to accommodations and vocational rehabilitation and those who are not and consigned to a life on social assistance. See J.E Bickenbach, *Physical Disability and Social Policy*, Toronto: University of Toronto Press, 1993, pp. 93–134. For Bickenbach, disablement has three dimensions: medical, economic and social. Law and economics scholars in the United States and elsewhere, however, are increasingly applying principles of neoclassical economics to understand disability accommodation. See M.A. Stein, 'The Law and Economics of Disability Accommodations' *Duke Law Journal*, 2003, vol. 53, pp. 79–191; M.A. Stein, 'Labor Markets, Rationality and Workers with Disabilities' *Berkeley Journal of Employment and Labor Law*, 2000, vol. 21, pp. 314–34.

7 See V. Finkelstein, *Attitudes and Disabled People*, New York, NY: World Rehabilitation Fund, 1980, p. 10, available online at http://www.leeds.ac.uk/disability-studies/archiveuk/finkelstein/attitudes.pdf (last accessed December 18, 2012).

8 Oliver and Barnes, op. cit., n. 3, p. 15. Oliver and Barnes date the start of the post-war boom at a slightly later time period but the overall point is the same. On the implications of the Keynesian post-war boom, see L. Boltanski and E. Chiapello, *The New Spirit of Capitalism*, trans. G. Elliott, London: Verso, 2005.

9 Oliver and Barnes, op. cit., n. 3, p. 11; W. Hanna and B. Rogovsky, 'Women with Disabilities: Two Handicaps Plus' in L. Barton (ed.) *Overcoming Disabled Barriers: 18 Years of Disability and Society*, Abingdon: Routledge, 2006, p. 47.

10 A. Borsay, 'Personal Trouble or Public Issue? Towards a Model of Policy for People with Physical and Mental Disabilities' in L. Barton (ed.) *Overcoming Disabled Barriers: 18 Years of Disability and Society*, Abingdon: Routledge, 2006, p. 152.

11 See the astonishingly defensive reactions by rehabilitation professionals who were invited to respond to Vic Finkelstein's landmark 1980 critique of rehabilitation: J. Siller, 'Commentary on Finkelstein's "Changing Attitudes and Disabled People": Issues for Discussion' in V. Finkelstein, *Attitudes and Disabled People*, New York, NY: World Rehabilitation Fund, 1980, pp. 30–32. He concludes (at p. 32) his scathing commentary with the remark: "I once was told by a fine psychoanalysist had severe residuals from polio about his own first session in psychoanalysis. At the end of the interview he was told, 'And don't forget. After all of this you are still going to be a cripple.'"

12 See I. Young, *Inclusion and Democracy*, Oxford: Oxford University Press, 2000, pp. 72–73.

13 In Canada, an example would be the Council of Canadians with Disabilities. One of us (Malhotra) serves on its Human Rights Committee. See Council of Canadians with Disabilities, available online at http://www.ccdonline.ca/ (last accessed January 16, 2013). That is not to suggest that organizations representing, for instance, parents do not at times do valuable work. For an overview of the Canadian disability rights movement, see W. Boyce *et al.*, *A Seat at the Table: Persons with Disabilities and Policy Making*, Montreal and Kingston: McGill-Queen's University Press, 2002. See also C. Kelly, 'Toward Renewed Descriptions of Canadian Disability Movements: Disability Activism outside of the Non-profit Sector' *Canadian Journal of Disability Studies*, 2013, vol. 2, pp. 1–27, available online at http://cjds.uwaterloo.ca/index.php/cjds/article/view/68/119 (last accessed January 18, 2013).

14 In addition to the works already cited, good overviews include G.L. Albrecht, K.D. Seelman and M. Bury (eds) *Handbook of Disability Studies*, Thousand Oaks, CA: Sage, 2001; L.J. Davis (ed.) *The Disability Studies Reader*, 3rd edn, New York, NY: Routledge, 2010; S. Linton, *Claiming Disability: Knowledge and Identity*, New York, NY: New York University Press, 1998.

15 Oliver and Barnes, op. cit., n. 3; Finkelstein, op. cit., n. 7; P. Abberley, 'The Concept of Oppression and the Development of a Social Theory of Disability' *Disability, Handicap & Society*, 1987, vol. 2, pp. 5–19. In 1993, the journal changed its name to *Disability & Society*.

16 See M. Russell, 'What Disability Civil Rights Cannot Do: Employment and Political Economy' *Disability and Society*, 2002, vol. 17, pp. 117–35; M. Russell, *Beyond Ramps: Disability at the End of the Social Contract*, Monroe, ME: Common Courage Press, 1998; M. Russell, 'Backlash, the Political Economy and Structural Exclusion' *Berkeley Journal of Employment and Labor Law*, 2000, vol. 21, pp. 335–66; M. Russell, 'Inequality, Neo-Liberalism and Disability' *Disability Studies Quarterly*, 1999, vol. 19, p. 372; M. Russell and R. Malhotra, 'Capitalism and Disability' *Socialist Register*, 2002, pp. 211–28; N. Erevelles, *Disability and Difference in Global Contexts: Enabling a Transformative Body Politic*, Basingstoke: Palgrave Macmillan, 2011; S. Taylor, 'The Right Not to Work: Power and Disability' *Monthly Review*, 2004, vol. 55, pp. 30–44.

17 See T. Shakespeare, *Disability Rights and Wrongs*, Abingdon: Routledge, 2006, p. 52.

18 M. Priestley, *Disability: A Life Course Approach*, Cambridge: Polity Press, 2003, p. 14.

19 R. Lang, *The Development and Critique of the Social Model of Disability*, London: Leonard Cheshire Disability and Inclusive Development Centre, 2007, p. 22, available online at http://www.ucl.ac.uk/lc-ccr/centrepublications/workingpapers/WP03_Development_Critique.pdf (last accessed December 27, 2012).

20 D. Stone, *The Disabled State*, Philadelphia, PA: Temple University Press, 1984, pp. 165–67. Note, however, that Stone is very careful to indicate that this correlation does not prove intent on the part of policymakers.

21 Oliver and Barnes, op. cit., n. 3, p. 15.

22 Oliver and Barnes, op. cit., n. 3, p. 21.

23 Priestley, op. cit., n. 18, p. 14.

24 Oliver and Barnes, op. cit., n. 3, p. 22.

25 Hence, we think those academics who rightly are skeptical about the limits of law as a tool for social transformation are too quick to adopt the universalist model of disability as a result, which we critique later in this chapter, instead of recognizing the potential for disability rights struggles from below. But see R.K. Scotch and K. Shriner, 'Disability as Human Variation: Implications for Policy' *Annals of the American Academy of Political and Social Science*, 1997, vol. 549, pp. 148–59 at p. 148 (arguing for the human variation model). An excellent overview of the grassroots disability rights movement in the United States is D.Z. Fleischer and F. Zames, *The Disability Rights Movement: From Charity to Confrontation*, updated edn, Philadelphia, PA: Temple University Press, 2011. For an overview of the Canadian disability rights movement, see D. Stienstra and A. Wight-Felske (eds) *Making Equality: History of Advocacy and Persons with Disabilities in Canada*, Toronto: Captus Press, 2003.

26 We discuss this further in Chapter 5 on transportation.

27 S.N. Barnartt and R.K. Scotch, *Disability Protests: Contentious Politics 1970–1999*, Washington, DC: Gallaudet University Press, 2001, p. 24.

28 Priestley, op. cit., n. 18, p. 14. For brevity, we use the term 'queer'.

29 Oliver and Barnes, op. cit., n. 3, p. 24. But see M. Barile, 'Globalization and ICF Eugenics: Historical Coincidence or Connection? The More Things Change the More They Stay the Same' *Disability Studies Quarterly*, 2003, vol. 23, pp. 208–23 (arguing that the ICF model is still too reliant on the medical model approach).

30 The reference is of course to the famous anthology: P.B. Evans, D. Rueschemeyer and T. Skocpol (eds) *Bringing the State Back In*, Cambridge: Cambridge University Press, 1985. However, the noted disability studies sociologist, Irving Zola, later also used the expression. See I.K. Zola, 'Bringing Our Bodies and Ourselves Back in: Reflections on a Past, Present and Future "Medical Sociology"' *Journal of Health and Social Behavior*, 1991, vol. 32, pp. 1–16.

31 See e.g. B. Hughes and K. Paterson, 'The Social Model of Disability and the Disappearing Body: Towards a Sociology of Impairment' *Disability and Society*, 1997, vol. 12, pp. 325–40; B.S. Turner, 'Disability and the Sociology of the Body' in G. Albrecht, K. Seelman and M. Bury (eds) *Handbook of Disability Studies*, Thousand Oaks, CA: Sage, 2001, pp. 252–66; K. Paterson and B. Hughes, 'Disability Studies and Phenomenology: The Carnal Politics of Everyday Life' *Disability and Society*, 1999, vol. 14, pp. 597–610 at p. 600.

32 C. Thomas, *Female Forms: Experiencing and Understanding Disability*, Buckingham: Open University Press, 1999, pp. 42–44.

33 The literature on this is massive. See e.g. J. Morris, *Pride against Prejudice: Transforming Attitudes to Disability*, London, The Women's Press, 1991; S. Wendell, *The Rejected Body: Feminist Philosophical Reflections on Disability*, New York, NY: Routledge, 1996. A recent anthology of the experiences of disabled women whose impairments are invisible is D. Driedger and M. Owen (eds) *Dissonant Disabilities: Women with Chronic Illnesses Explore Their Lives*, Toronto: Canadian Scholar's Press/Women's Press, 2008.

34 For advocates of the Universalist approach in the American and Canadian legal contexts, respectively, see K. Barry, 'Toward Universalism: What the *ADA Amendments Act of 2008* Can and Can't Do for Disability Rights' *Berkeley Journal of Employment and Labor Law*, 2010, vol. 31, pp. 217–21; and J. Penney, 'A Constitution for

the Disabled or a Disabled Constitution? Toward a New Approach to Disability for the Purposes of Section 15 (1)' *Journal of Law and Equality*, 2002, vol. 1, pp. 83–94. While we do not engage their specific arguments here, we would suggest Barry's principled concerns about the definition of disability under the ADA can in fact be fully addressed by the social model and the judicial failure in the United States on this matter rather reflects a deficiency in American courts' reasoning for equality-seeking groups (including religious minorities) that is not replicated in other countries with broader conceptions of equality. One of us has written about this. See R. Malhotra, 'The Legal Genealogy of the Duty to Accommodate American and Canadian Workers with Disabilities: A Comparative Perspective' *Washington University Journal of Law and Policy*, 2007, vol. 23, pp. 1–32.

35 R. Imrie, 'Universalism, Universal Design and Equitable Access to the Built Environment' *Disability & Rehabilitation*, 2012, vol. 34, pp. 873–82 at p. 873.

36 Imrie, ibid, p. 873.

37 Imrie, op. cit., n. 35, p. 877.

38 Imrie, op. cit., n. 35, p. 878.

39 Imrie, op. cit., n. 35, p. 878. Screen readers for blind people are an illustration of a product that has evolved over time due to input from blind users.

40 Imrie, op. cit., n. 35, pp. 879–80.

41 F. Dosse, *History of Structuralism, Volume 1: The Rising Sign, 1945–1966*, trans. D. Glassman, Minneapolis, MN: University of Minnesota Press, 1997, p. 37.

42 G. Gutting, 'What Have We Been Missing? Science and Philosophy in Twentieth Century French Thought' in B. Leiter and M. Rosen (eds) *The Oxford Handbook of Continental Philosophy*, Oxford: Oxford University Press, 2007, pp. 201–3.

43 M. Merleau-Ponty, *Phenomenology of Perception*, trans. C. Smith, London: Routledge and Kegan Paul, 1962, pp. 84–102 (discussing phenomenology of people with phantom limbs). See also M. Iwakuma, 'The Body as Embodiment: An Investigation of the Body by Merleau-Ponty' in M. Corker and T. Shakespeare (eds) *Disability/ Postmodernity: Embodying Disability Theory*, London: Continuum, 2002, pp. 76–87. Merleau-Ponty's critique of Sartrean phenomenology is beyond the scope of our work. Similarly, while poststructuralist approaches have been very influential in disability studies, we largely but not entirely ignore them. But see D. Mitchell and S. Snyder (eds) *The Body and Physical Difference: Discourses of Disability*, Ann Arbor, MI: University of Michigan Press, 1997; T. Siebers, *Disability Aesthetics*, Ann Arbor, MI: University of Michigan Press, 2010.

44 See T. Baldwin, 'The Humanism Debate' in B. Leiter and M. Rosen (eds) *The Oxford Handbook of Continental Philosophy*, Oxford: Oxford University Press, 2007, p. 683; Turner, op. cit., n. 31, p. 255.

45 Turner, op. cit., n. 31, p. 254.

46 Paterson and Hughes, op. cit., n. 31, p. 602.

47 On the question of intersubjective bodies, see Erevelles, op. cit., n. 16, p. 8.

48 K. Marx, *A Contribution to the Critique of Political Economy*, trans. N.I. Stone, Chicago, IL: Charles H. Kerr & Co., 1904, pp. 11–12. See also G.A. Cohen, *History, Labour and Freedom: Themes from Marx*, New York, NY: Oxford University Press, 1988, pp. 37–42 (discussing concept of consciousness in Marxist theory).

49 Engel and Munger, 'Narrative', op. cit., n. 2, p. 85.

50 P. Ewick and S.S. Silbey, 'Subversive Stories and Hegemonic Tales: Toward a Sociology of Narrative' *Law and Society Review*, 1995, vol. 29, pp. 197–226 at p. 211.

51 See, e.g. M. Ashe, 'Zig-Zag Stitching and the Seamless Web: Thoughts on "Reproduction" and the Law' *Nova Law Review*, 1989, vol. 13, pp. 355–84.

52 Even toileting is profoundly political. For an interview with a rehabilitation professional who argues for the need to regulate disabled children to encourage independent toileting so as to lessen the burden on school boards, see E. Ignagni, 'Disabled

Young People, Support and the Dialogical Work of Accomplishing Citizenship', PhD Dissertation, Ryerson University, 2011, p. 105. She also reports (at p. 140) how every young female she interviewed had been encouraged to go on birth control pills so as to eliminate her menstrual periods and eliminate the need for assistance with menstruation, a shockingly invasive suggestion. None complied. Disabled activist and scholar Anne Finger also reports the irritation of a nurse who was tasked to assist Finger with menstrual care when Finger was nine. See A. Finger, *Elegy for a Disease: A Personal and Cultural History of Polio*, New York, NY: St. Martin's Press, 2006, p. 138.

53 D.W. Carbado and M. Gulati, 'The Law and Economics of Critical Race Theory' *Yale Law Journal*, 2003, vol. 112, pp. 1784–85.

54 A notable example is a series of interrelated fictional stories written by the legal scholar, Richard Delgado, concerning a fictional graduate law student and later professor, Rodrigo Crenshaw. See R. Delgado, *The Rodrigo Chronicles: Conversations about America and Race*, New York, NY: New York University Press, 1995.

55 J. Bruner, *Actual Minds, Possible Worlds*, Cambridge, MA: Harvard University Press, 1986, pp. 11–14. See also J. Bruner, 'The Narrative Construction of Reality' *Critical Inquiry*, 1991, vol. 18, pp. 1–21.

56 F. Polletta, '"It Was Like A Fever . . ." Narrative and Identity in Social Protest' *Social Problems*, 1998, vol. 45, pp. 137–59. See also F. Polletta, *It Was Like A Fever: Storytelling in Protest and Politics*, Chicago, IL: University of Chicago Press, 2006.

57 Polletta, '"It Was Like A Fever . . ." Narrative and Identity in Social Protest', ibid, p. 140.

58 Polletta, '"It Was Like A Fever . . ." Narrative and Identity in Social Protest', op. cit., n. 56, pp. 140–41.

59 Polletta, '"It Was Like A Fever . . ." Narrative and Identity in Social Protest', op. cit., n. 56, p. 141.

60 Polletta, '"It Was Like A Fever . . ." Narrative and Identity in Social Protest', op. cit., n. 56, p. 142.

61 Polletta, '"It Was Like A Fever . . ." Narrative and Identity in Social Protest', op. cit., n. 56, p. 142.

62 Ewick and Silbey, op. cit., n. 50, p. 199. See also P. Ewick and S.S. Silbey, *The Common Place of Law: Stories from Everyday Life*, Chicago, IL: University of Chicago Press, 1998. For a famous account of the relationship between narrative and law in the constitutional law context, see R.M. Cover, 'The Supreme Court, 1982 Term – Foreword: Nomos and Narrative' *Harvard Law Review*, 1983–84, vol. 97, pp. 4–68.

63 Ewick and Silbey, op. cit., n. 50, p. 199.

64 Ewick and Silbey, op. cit., n. 50, p. 202.

65 Ewick and Silbey, op. cit., n. 50, pp. 202–3.

66 Ewick and Silbey, op. cit., n. 50, p. 203.

67 Ewick and Silbey, op. cit., n. 50, p. 213.

68 Ewick and Silbey, op. cit., n. 50, pp. 213–14. The quoted phrase is Ewick's and Silbey's.

69 Ewick and Silbey, op. cit., n. 50, pp. 214–15.

70 Ewick and Silbey, op. cit., n. 50, pp. 220–21. Melanie Panitch has written about parents' role as disability advocates in the Canadian context. See M. Panitch, *Disability, Mothers and Organization: Accidental Activists*, New York, NY: Routledge, 2008.

71 Ewick and Silbey, op. cit., n. 50, p. 221. A Canadian example would include the challenges by welfare rights activists for a special diet allowance. See K. Kraus, 'McGuinty's Axing of the Special Diet Program is a Catastrophe to Poor and Sick Ontarians', Rabble.ca, May 7, 2010, available online at http://rabble.ca/news/2010/05/mcguintys (last accessed January 26, 2013).

72 Ewick and Silbey, op. cit., n. 50, pp. 221–22.

73 D.A. Farber and S. Sherry, 'Telling Stories Out of School: An Essay on Legal Narratives' *Stanford Law Review*, 1992, vol. 45, pp. 835–38. Harsher and more ideological critiques are D.A. Farber and S. Sherry, *Beyond All Reason: The Radical Assault on Truth in American Law*, Oxford: Oxford University Press, 1997, and R. Posner, 'Skin Trade' *New Republic*, 1997, vol. 217, pp. 40–43 (favourably reviewing Farber and Sherry's *Beyond All Reason*).

74 Farber and Sherry, 'Telling Stories Out of School', ibid, p. 834.

75 K. Abrams, 'Hearing the Call of Stories' *California Law Review*, 1991, vol. 79, pp. 971–1052. But see C. Weisbrod, 'Divorce Stories: Readings, Comments and Questions on Law and Narrative' *Brigham Young University Law Review*, 1991, pp. 143–96 (illustrating difficulties in using narratives as a tool for legal transformation in the context of divorce law).

76 Abrams, ibid, pp. 983–87. For Estrich's piece, see S. Estrich, 'Rape' *Yale Law Journal*, 1986, vol. 95, pp. 1087–184. Estrich begins her piece with the sentence, "Eleven years ago, a man held an ice pick to my throat and said: 'Push over, shut up, or I'll kill you.'" (at p. 1087).

77 Abrams, op. cit., n. 75, p. 985.

78 Abrams, op. cit., n. 75, pp. 987–95. For Mahoney's piece, see M.R. Mahoney, 'Legal Images of Battered Women: Redefining the Issue of Separation' *Michigan Law Review*, 1991, vol. 90, pp. 1–94. An example of Mahoney's powerful narrative (at p. 17) includes the following: "When I finally called the Battered Women's Center for help, I was just looking for advice—my husband had threatened to move back in without my consent while I was recovering from a Cesarian section . . . He said you can't stop me . . . I told the counselor I was just looking for a referral, as I didn't qualify for their help as my marriage had not been violent, although I had left after he attacked me with a loaded shotgun. There was a tiny pause, and then she said gently: 'We classify that as extreme violence.'"

79 Mahoney, ibid, p. 6.

80 Abrams, op. cit., n. 75, p. 990.

81 Abrams, op. cit., n. 75, pp. 988–91.

82 Abrams, op. cit., n. 75, p. 991.

83 L. Webley and L. Duff, 'Women Solicitors as a Barometer for Problems within the Legal Profession—Time to Put Values before Profits?' *Journal of Law and Society*, 2007, vol. 34, pp. 382–83.

84 Webley and Duff, ibid, pp. 387–97.

85 D. Bell, *And We Are Not Saved: The Elusive Quest for Racial Justice*, New York, NY: Basic Books, 1987. Professor Bell, who died in 2011, is often regarded as one of the founding scholars of critical race theory and was a sponsor of the socialist journal, *New Politics*, along with many others including one of the authors of this volume.

86 P.J. Williams, *The Rooster's Egg: The Persistence of Prejudice*, Cambridge, MA: Harvard University Press, 1995.

87 Delgado, op. cit., n. 54.

88 A.P. Farley, 'The Black Body as Fetish Object' *Oregon Law Review*, 1997, vol. 76, pp. 457–535.

89 N. Duclos, 'Disappearing Women: Racial Minority Women in Human Rights Cases' *Canadian Journal of Women and the Law*, 1993, vol. 6, pp. 25–51. She now writes as Nitya Iyer.

90 On the importance of experiential knowledge, see M.C. Malagon, L.P. Huber and V.N. Velez, 'Our Experiences, Our Methods: Using Grounded Theory to Inform a Critical Race Methodology' *Seattle Journal of Social Justice*, 2009–2010, vol. 8, pp. 252–72 at p. 259.

91 G. Ladson-Billings, 'Racialized Discourses and Ethnic Epistemologies' in N.K. Denzin and Y.S. Lincoln (eds) *Handbook of Qualitative Research*, 2nd edn, Thousand

Oaks, CA: Sage, 2000, p. 264. A full discussion of critical legal studies is well beyond the scope of our book. But see M. Kelman, *A Guide to Critical Legal Studies*, Cambridge, MA: Harvard University Press, 1987; R.W. Bauman, *Ideology and Community in the First Wave of Critical Legal Studies*, Toronto: University of Toronto Press, 2002 (critiquing critical legal studies).

92 R. Delgado, 'Storytelling for Oppositionists and Others: A Plea for Narrative' in R. Delgado and J. Stefancic (eds) *Critical Race Theory: The Cutting Edge*, Philadelphia, PA: Temple University Press, 2000, p. 61.

93 Intersectionality theory challenged the tendency of courts, policymakers, and researchers to consider instances of discrimination from only one ground at a time so that sex discrimination was evaluated in terms of white women only and race discrimination was considered in terms of black men only, further marginalizing black women who experienced both. The concept has since been broadened to become a multi-disciplinary theory and to encompass other elements of personal, categorical identity. See e.g. K. Crenshaw, 'Demarginalizing the Intersection of Race and Sex: A Black Feminist Critique of Antidiscrimination Doctrine, Feminist Theory and Antiracist Policy' *University of Chicago Legal Forum*, 1989, pp. 139–67 (showing how courts fail to effectively address discrimination alleged by African American women under Title VII); K. Crenshaw, 'Mapping the Margins: Intersectionality, Identity Politics, and Violence against Women of Color' *Stanford Law Review*, 1991, vol. 43, pp. 1241–99.

94 Farley, op. cit., n. 88, p. 464.

95 Farley, op. cit., n. 88, pp. 457–535.

96 Farley, op. cit., n. 88, pp. 461–63.

97 Farley, op. cit., n. 88, pp. 480–82.

98 Farley, op. cit., n. 88, p. 481.

99 Duclos, op. cit., n. 89, pp. 30–32.

100 Duclos, op. cit., n. 89, p. 26.

101 Duclos, op. cit., n. 89, p. 26.

102 Malagon, Huber and Velez, op. cit., n. 90.

103 Malagon, Huber and Velez, op. cit., n. 90, p. 254.

104 Malagon, Huber and Velez, op. cit., n. 90, p. 265. They rely on the work of Delgado Bernal for this typology.

105 Malagon, Huber and Velez, op. cit., n. 90, p. 266.

106 W.N. Eskridge Jr, 'Gaylegal Narratives' *Stanford Law Review*, 1994, vol. 46, pp. 614–16. Eskridge was specifically writing about gay, bisexual and lesbian soldiers.

107 Eskridge, ibid, pp. 616–17.

108 Eskridge, op. cit., n. 106, pp. 617–20.

109 Our own autobiographies are not the focus of our study. However, one of us (Malhotra) was disabled at birth. In commenting on his own upbringing, he writes: "When I was a physically disabled youth, accessibility was not a concept and integration of disabled children in regular schools was not the norm and not a part of public discourse. Although I was always integrated, all the work of integration was placed on my family and I. I had to crawl up stairs to attend class every day as I did not yet have the ability to climb. Not one of the three publicly funded schools I attended before university in the late 1970s and 1980s had an elevator or any kind of accessibility feature. My high school, which I attended for its gifted program, had three stories plus a basement. My high school guidance counselor told me since I use crutches, I should become an accountant and you had to read a book a week to be a lawyer. At my graduation, the principal applauded the fact that I had climbed every day without complaint but nothing was done about the access barriers for years."

110 S.C. Brown, 'Methodological Paradigms That Shape Disability Research' in

G. Albrecht, K. Seelman and M. Bury (eds) *Handbook of Disability Studies*, Thousand Oaks, CA: Sage, 2001, p. 148.

111 S.E. Browne, D. Connors and N. Sterne (eds) *With the Power of Each Breath: A Disabled Women's Anthology*, Pittsburgh, PA: Cleis Press, 1985; M. Saxton and F. Howe (eds) *With Wings: An Anthology of Literature by and about Women with Disabilities*, New York, NY: The Feminist Press, 1987. See also P. Dossa, *Racialized Bodies, Disabling Worlds: Storied Lives of Immigrant Muslim Women*, Toronto: University of Toronto Press, 2009; Driedger and Owen, op. cit., n. 33; C. Krause (ed.), *Between Myself and Them: Stories of Disability and Difference*, Toronto: Second Story Press, 2005 (anthology of young disabled adults, both men and women featuring stories on identity, sexuality, education, the workplace and family); D. Driedger and S. Gray (eds), *Imprinting Our Image: An International Anthology by Women with Disabilities*, Charlottetown: Gyenrgy Books, 1992.

112 S.E. Browne, D. Connors and N. Sterne, 'Introduction' in S.E. Browne, D. Connors and N. Sterne (eds) *With the Power of Each Breath: A Disabled Women's Anthology*, Pittsburgh, PA: Cleis Press, 1985, p. 10.

113 J. Sager, 'Just Stories', in S.E. Browne, D. Connors and N. Sterne (eds) *With the Power of Each Breath: A Disabled Women's Anthology*, Pittsburgh, PA: Cleis Press, 1985, pp. 191–98. She writes (at p. 198): "It's hard to get close to people. I feel angry a lot. I am afraid to be made love to. I don't like my body. I'm ashamed of my body. I treat my deformed leg as an 'it,' not a real part of me. My curved back is something to be hidden by my long hair."'

114 See C. Hardesty, 'Pain' in M. Saxton and F. Howe (eds) *With Wings: An Anthology of Literature by and about Women with Disabilities*, New York, NY: The Feminist Press, 1987, pp. 19–23; L.A. Donovan, 'For a Paralyzed Woman Raped and Murdered While Alone in Her Own Apartment' in Saxton, M. and Howe, F. (eds) *With Wings: An Anthology of Literature by and about Women with Disabilities*, New York, NY: The Feminist Press, 1987, pp. 31–32; B. Ruth, 'In My Disabled Women's Group' in M. Saxton and F. Howe (eds) *With Wings: An Anthology of Literature by and about Women with Disabilities*, New York, NY: The Feminist Press, 1987, pp. 32–33.

115 R. Cepko, 'On Oxfords and Plaster Casts' in M. Saxton and F. Howe (eds) *With Wings: An Anthology of Literature by and about Women with Disabilities*, New York, NY: The Feminist Press, 1987, pp. 56–59.

116 D. Driedger, *Living the Edges: A Disabled Women's Reader*, Toronto: Inanna Publications and Education, 2010.

117 But see Dossa, op. cit., n. 111 (writing about immigrant muslim women). Driedger's anthology is also a partial exception. See Driedger, op. cit., n 116.

118 M.G. Mason, *Working against Odds: Stories of Disabled Women's Work Lives*, Boston, MA: Northeastern University Press, 2004.

119 Mason, ibid, p. 5.

120 See C. Lewiecki-Wilson and J. Cellio (eds) *Disability and Mothering: Liminal Spaces of Embodied Knowledge*, Syracuse, NY: Syracuse University Press, 2011.

121 Anne Finger is one of many authors of disability memoirs we could have selected for commentary, but space precludes a comprehensive discussion. Other notable memoirs include N. Mairs, *Waist-High in the World: A Life among the Non-Disabled*, Boston, MA: Beacon Press, 1996 (narrative of woman with multiple sclerosis); K. Fries, *Body, Remember: A Memoir*, New York, NY: Dutton, 1997 (narrative of disabled poet and academic); J. Hockenberry, *Moving Violations: A Memoir: War Zones, Wheelchairs and Declarations of Independence*, New York, NY: Hyperion, 1995 (narrative of disabled journalist).

122 A. Finger, *Past Due: A Story of Disability, Pregnancy and Birth*, Berkeley, CA: Seal Press, 1990.

123 Finger, *Elegy*, op. cit., n. 52.

124 Finger, *Elegy*, op. cit., n. 52, pp. 169–70.

125 G. Reaume, *Lyndhurst: Canada's First Rehabilitation Centre for People with Spinal Cord Injuries, 1945–1998*, Montreal and Kingston, McGill-Queen's University Press, 2007.

126 Reaume, ibid, pp. 113–14. See also M. Tremblay, A. Campbell and G.L. Hudson, 'When Elevators Were for Pianos: An Oral History Account of The Civilian Experience of Using Wheelchairs in Canadian Society. The First Twenty Five Years: 1945–1970' *Disability and Society*, 2005, vol. 20, pp. 103–16 (discussing barriers faced by disabled civilians after the Second World War).

127 G. Reaume, *Remembrance of Patients Past: Patient Life at the Toronto Hospital for the Insane, 1870–1940*, Toronto: University of Toronto Press, 2000. Particularly ironic is the use of patient labour to build the wall which incarcerated them. Reaume now offers tours of the site.

128 D.J. Connor, *Urban Narratives—Portraits in Progress: Life at the Intersections of Learning Disability, Race & Social Class*, New York, NY: Peter Lang, 2008, p. 60. Another example of narrative analysis in the context of special education is Ellen Barton's study of a parent advocate support group discussing integration of disabled students. See E.L. Barton, 'Disability Narratives of the Law: Narratives and Counter-Narratives' *Narrative*, 2007, vol. 15, pp. 95–112.

129 Barton, ibid, p. 63.

130 Barton, op. cit., n. 128, pp. 62–63.

131 Barton, op. cit., n. 128, pp. 59–61.

132 Barton, op. cit., n. 128, pp. 64–65.

133 Barton, op. cit., n. 128, pp. 65–67.

134 Barton, op. cit., n. 128, p. 191.

135 Barton, op. cit., n. 128, pp. 376–78.

136 Barton, op. cit., n. 128, pp. 371–76 (noting the racial disparities in services to American learning disabled students).

137 D. Galer, 'Disabled Capitalists: Exploring the Intersections of Disability and Identity Formation in the World of Work' *Disability Studies Quarterly*, 2012, vol. 32, no. 3, available online at http://dsq-sds.org/article/view/3277/3122 (last accessed January 12, 2013). See also Ignagni, op. cit., n. 52 (qualitative study of physically disabled young people).

138 Galer, ibid.

139 We elaborate on grounded theory in Chapter 2.

140 Galer, op. cit., n. 137.

141 Galer, op. cit., n. 137.

142 Galer, op. cit., n. 137.

143 Galer, op. cit., n. 137.

144 Galer, op. cit., n. 137.

145 Galer, op. cit., n. 137.

146 R. O'Brien (ed.) *Voices from the Edge: Narratives about the Americans with Disabilities Act*, Oxford: Oxford University Press, 2004.

147 R. O'Brien, 'Introduction' in R. O'Brien (ed.) *Voices from the Edge: Narratives about the Americans with Disabilities Act*, Oxford: Oxford University Press, 2004, pp. 4–5. Unlike Delgado and other CRT scholars, however, this volume separates the legal commentary from the narratives.

148 J. Aleshire, 'Eye of the Beholder' in R. O'Brien (ed.) *Voices from the Edge: Narratives about the Americans with Disabilities Act*, Oxford: Oxford University Press, 2004, pp. 29–39.

149 R. O'Brien, 'Defining Moments: (Dis)ability, Individuality and Normalcy' in R. O'Brien (ed.) *Voices from the Edge: Narratives about the Americans with Disabilities Act*, Oxford: Oxford University Press, 2004, pp. 40–52.

150 C.G. Basas, 'The New Boys: Women with Disabilities and the Legal Profession' *Berkeley Journal of Gender, Law & Justice*, 2010, vol. 25, pp. 32–124.

151 Basas, ibid, pp. 32–36.

152 While one of the authors (Malhotra) attended Harvard Law School at the same time as Professor Basas, he did not register for the class so described.

153 Basas, op. cit., n. 150, p. 35.

154 Basas, op. cit., n. 150, pp. 59–60.

155 Basas, op. cit., n. 150, pp. 80–81.

156 Basas, op. cit., n. 150, pp. 90–93.

157 R.D. Dinerstein, '"Every Picture Tells a Story, Don't It?": The Complex Role of Narratives in Disability Cases' *Narrative*, 2007, vol. 15, pp. 40–57.

158 Dinerstein, ibid, p. 43.

159 Dinerstein, op. cit., n. 157, p. 43.

160 Dinerstein, op. cit., n. 157. The same issue has arisen in many US States in the context of making arguments relating to intellectually disabled defendants when the defendant is facing the death penalty.

161 G.T. Couser, 'Undoing Hardship: Life Writing and Disability Law' *Narrative*, 2007, vol. 15, pp. 71–84. See also G.T. Couser, *Signifying Bodies: Disability in Contemporary Life Writing*, Ann Arbor, MI: University of Michigan Press, 2009.

162 Couser, 'Undoing', ibid, p. 73.

163 Couser, 'Undoing', op. cit., n. 161, pp. 73–74. Asch went on to become a well-known scholar on disability issues.

164 Couser, 'Undoing', op. cit., n. 161, pp. 74–77. Couser apparently did not take into account the 2008 amendments of the ADA which broaden the definition in response to unduly restrictive Supreme Court jurisprudence. See Chapter 4 for further discussion.

165 Couser, 'Undoing', op. cit., n. 161, pp. 77–79.

166 Couser, 'Undoing', op. cit., n. 161, pp. 79–81.

2 Methodology

This chapter discusses the methodology of Engel's and Munger's original study and the current study upon which this book is based. It considers not only the differences between the studies but also the implications those differences have for the development of our theoretical framework. By first examining Engel's and Munger's methodology in *Rights of Inclusion*, we hope to provide context for the discussion of our methodology in the study at hand. We also examine the different legal contexts in which the two studies took place, which not only has implications for the results documented in this book but was also one of the sources of inspiration for conducting this study within a disability rights system significantly different from that of Engel's and Munger's. Lastly, we discuss the development of the theoretical framework, using a Grounded Theory (GT) qualitative research methodology for data analysis. This includes discussion of how the specific participant population analyzed may limit the universality of the conclusions we have drawn, but enhance our ability to conduct detailed analysis and provide room for each participant's own voice in telling their narratives.

Methodology in the rights of inclusion

Rights of Inclusion: Law and Identity in the Life Stories of Americans with Disabilities documented the results of Engel's and Munger's ground-breaking study in the field of disability rights. Over many years, Engel and Munger conducted interviews with 60 Americans with physical or learning disabilities, none of whom had engaged in litigation under the ADA, to gather information on their attitudes towards disability rights, legal consciousness, and identity.[1] Engel and Munger had been inspired to conduct this study by the 1990 passage of the ADA, which prohibited discrimination against disabled people,[2] and hoped to observe how these historic rights mattered, or did not matter, to the law's intended beneficiaries.[3]

Engel and Munger began by contacting employers for interviews and conducting focus group sessions with disabled people. From these initial interviews, they produced a list of 180 participants who participated in telephone interviews.[4] The list was then further reduced to 60 participants with whom they conducted in-depth interviews over a period of several years, followed by a second round of follow-up interviews with six participants.[5] Participants were sampled selectively to balance gender and to incorporate three distinct age categories and work experience levels: high school seniors, individuals in their early twenties who had gained some experience in employment, and people in midlife with substantial employment narratives (or lack thereof).[6] The authors used this method of sampling to ensure they received a wide variety of viewpoints and experiences. It was not their intention, however, to seek a representative sample of the American population or the American disability community.[7]

Two methodological aspects of Engel's and Munger's study warrant particular attention and had specific influence upon the design of our study. First, they crafted a dynamic, open-ended approach to data collection. Rather than ask participants to respond to a set of pre-fabricated questions, the authors used a life-narrative methodology, allowing the participants to tell their own biographical narrative, including early childhood experiences, family life, educational environments, the timing of the onset/diagnosis of disability, work experiences, the relationship to mentors and overall problems and achievements.[8] Biographical data was gathered, and questions about the impact of law in the participant's life and her or his willingness to invoke legal rights were deferred until the end.[9] This allowed the researchers to focus on how a disability identity is shaped over a lifetime, with the possibility of legal rights being activated through the crystallization of legal consciousness, at different points on the life span continuum.[10] Consequently, no two interviews were alike. This methodology is relatively unusual, departing from more structured, question-template approaches applied in most other qualitative research,[11] and is in keeping with the best of the narrative paradigm discussed in Chapter 1. It maximizes empowerment of the participant and allows the researcher to collect richer data, including topics and themes that were not anticipated at the outset.

A second innovation was Engel's and Munger's willingness to provide their analysis to the participants for commentary during the second in-depth interview, thereby explicitly acknowledging that ethnographic narrative research is a dialogue between the participant and the researcher.[12] Engel and Munger solicited comments from their participants on the written analysis of their individual interviews, and these comments were then included in italics throughout the text of *Rights of Inclusion*. This process is somewhat akin to the principles of Participatory Action Research (PAR) that seeks to empower research subjects by allowing them to shape the research questions and the study's design. This approach has become particularly popular among disability studies scholars because of the frequent power differentials between disabled participants and researchers.[13] It has also been viewed as a means of breaking from traditional research into disability issues, which have treated disabled people as the objects of the professional researcher,[14] rarely focused on issues of relevance or use to the individuals themselves,[15] and done little to "have a positive impact on their material wellbeing and quality of life."[16]

Traditional research has also been criticized for too often resulting in supposedly objective descriptions of the life experiences of disabled people, intended for non-disabled audiences, which had little to say and less to advocate in regards to changing mainstream policy and societal structures to ensure greater equality.[17] PAR, as an approach falling under the larger umbrella of emancipatory research,[18] is intended to challenge these traditional problems by ensuring that research participants are full participants: involved in and able to provide feedback and commentary on all stages of the research process.[19] The importance of a PAR approach has become widely recognized since it was first developed. In fact, the 1992 amendments to the American Rehabilitation Act implicitly mandate the use of PAR by encouraging principles of community involvement. Similarly, the National Institute of Disability and Rehabilitation Research (NIDRR), an American agency that promotes research to improve the quality of life for disabled people, has promoted the use of PAR.[20]

Methodology

This study was adapted from Engel's and Munger's basic life-history framework to take into account Canadian conditions, particularly the gradual recognition of disability rights in general anti-discrimination legislation such as the Charter and provincial human rights codes, in contrast to the more specific disability rights legislation found in the American experience. It was also necessary to design around limited funding, which dictated a smaller sample size. The objective of the study was not simply to replicate Engel's and Munger's work within a different country, however, but to examine what impact, if any, a different legal, institutional, and social context had on the recursive relationship Engel and Munger identified between rights and personal identity for disabled people. A qualitative grounded theory (GT) approach was employed to analyse the collected data, selected for its ability to examine the "dynamic, holistic, and individual aspects of human experience and attempts to capture those aspects in their entirety, within the context of those who are experiencing them."[21]

The participants and the research design

In all, interview data was collected from interviews with a dozen post-secondary students with mobility impairments from three post-secondary academic institutions in a large Canadian city during 2007 and 2008, after obtaining approval from the Research Ethics Board of each institution.[22] The participants were recruited primarily through the administration-run disabled students' service offices at each of the institutions and the student-run disabled students' centres where such centres existed. A listserv operated by a national advocacy group, the National Educational Association of Disabled Students, was also approached as a potential alternative avenue for recruitment but without success. Inclusion criteria for participation in the study required only that the individual have a physical impairment of some kind, providing one commonality across all participants. Further demographic variables such as age and gender were not considered as criteria for exclusion or inclusion as it was expected that the role these factors played in influencing experiences with identity and rights would become clear with analysis of the data. Nonetheless, seven women and five men between the ages of 18 and 57 were recruited as participants. Although a large majority of participants were between the ages of 18 and 24, a small number of older students were included. The mean age of 27 is consequently misleading. It is more useful to think of our sample as composed of a younger and older cohort. The mean age among the nine younger students was 20.5 and the mean age of the three older students was nearly 47. These participants also displayed a range of different physical impairments, including several invisible impairments; different times for onset of impairment, and different experiences with additional impairments, such as learning disabilities, hearing restrictions, and depression. A significant number, five of 12, used attendant services for activities of daily living such as bathing, dressing and toileting. As will become clear, the relative youth of our sample and the fact many must rely on attendant services to participate in activities of daily living has certain implications for their insights into topics such as employment.

Participants were interviewed at locations of their choice, usually on campus but occasionally at their parents' home, in residence rooms or even at coffee shops. Following the approach used by Engel and Munger, the interview format was crafted to be open-ended and flexible, based loosely on a biographical timeline meant to begin with early childhood and move towards the present day. Where participants spontaneously raised other issues or chose to present their narratives in a different order, this was pursued through further questions. In doing so, we moved back and forth between the interview typologies that Alex Jakle classifies as "the Reporter," asking open-ended questions about static topics in order to describe a participant's experiences, and "the Detective," asking open-ended questions about flexible topics in order to discover the "how or why" behind a participants' belief and actions.[23] This style of interviewing also prevented the development of theory from coming ungrounded[24] early in the process through the pre-determination of the issues to be discussed.[25] Topics discussed included childhood experiences and friendships, barriers in driving and using public transit, integration in the public school setting, relationships with siblings, work and/or volunteer experiences, post-secondary experiences, accessing the social assistance program for disabled people in Ontario known as ODSP,[26] experiences at summer camps, involvement in sports and other extracurricular activities, and the formation of an identity as a disabled person.

Although we approached the interviews with specific interest regarding the intersection between class background and the ability to articulate disability identity, this was not reflected in the interview design, and the control given to each participant to steer the discussion, combined with the open-ended format, prevented external theory from being forced upon the data within the interview process itself.[27] Each initial interview lasted between one and two hours and was audio-recorded. To protect confidentiality, the participants were assigned pseudonyms which have been used throughout the process of analysis and the writing of this book.

GT methodology was formally adopted as the approach to data analysis only after the interview process was completed. However, this choice was made after an examination of the steps taken to ensure that they complied with GT requirements. For example, in a melding of the PAR approach to this study and the search for theoretical saturation under GT methodology,[28] preliminary analysis was conducted upon finishing each interview. Constant comparisons were made between new interview data and those which had already been conducted to discover the reoccurring themes and issues raised by the participants and to discover gaps in the data. The participants were provided with a copy of the transcript of their interview and the preliminary analysis memo by email for feedback. They were invited to participate in focus groups, divided by sex, to provide their responses to the preliminary findings and to further discuss the areas which had not yet become fully saturated.[29] Fifty per cent of the original 12 participants, four women and two men, took part in the focus groups in 2008. This data was then further analyzed using the GT methodology.

Data analysis: using the Grounded Theory methodology

As a methodology, GT, a qualitative research methodology, provides a systematic, operationalized approach to analyzing and developing theory from qualitative data.[30] Glaser and Strauss originally developed GT[31] as a process that would step away from what they saw as a growing emphasis within sociological research on the verification of already established theory, rather than the discovery of new theory.[32] GT allows a researcher to approach the phenomena under study critically, flexibly and creatively in a way which is designed to ensure that the resulting theory closely resembles reality[33] and is able to predict, explain and be relevant to the behaviour under study, or what Glaser and Strauss termed a theory's ability to "fit" and "work."[34] Strauss and Corbin defined a grounded theory generally as one that:

> is inductively derived from the study of the phenomenon it represents. That is, it is discovered, developed, and provisionally verified through systematic data collection and analysis of data pertaining to the phenomenon. Therefore, data collection, analysis, and theory stand in reciprocal relationship to each other. One does not begin with a theory, then prove it. Rather, one begins with an area of study and what is relevant to that area is allowed to emerge.[35]

GT was founded in the symbolic interactionism tradition,[36] which makes it a methodology particularly well-suited to developing theory related to the development of personal identity through societal and personal interaction. The basic premises of symbolic interactionism are that: (a) the meaning individuals give to things determines how they will act towards them; (b) meaning arises from social interaction with others; and (c) meanings are processed through and modified by the individual's way of interpreting them and examining their own interactions.[37] GT builds on this basis to enable the researcher to look deeply into "meaning, self, social context, and social actions" and to develop theory on these foundations,[38] essentially focusing on the interpersonal interactions found in symbolic interactionism to develop a theoretical view of the experiences and phenomena being studied.[39]

Beyond the advantages of choosing a method rooted in symbolic interactionism, GT was chosen as the method of data analysis for a number of reasons. The desire to ensure that this study went beyond simple verification of Engel's and Munger's original study and instead captured the actual processes at work within a different legal system was paramount. Given this, the inherent goal of GT, to discover theory grounded within the data through a process that is both inductive and deductive rather than attempting to fit the data to any external theory,[40] was a distinct advantage.

Additionally, we wished to remain mindful of the criticisms levelled against many traditional qualitative research methodologies, as noted above, and particularly the charges that traditional methodologies often disenfranchise participants and result in findings that have little relevance to the participants or communities involved in the study. One of the fundamental characteristics of PAR research is thus to counter this disenfranchisement by allowing the problems and issues to be defined by the participants and community under study rather than through prior definition by the researcher.[41] Given GT's focus on allowing key issues and concerns to emerge from within the interviews rather than defining them beforehand,[42] we felt that adopting this methodology would strongly support the other elements of PAR implemented during the research process and aid us in the researcher's inherently difficult task of "'telling the narrative' from the point of view of the research participants, and unpacking the narrative in some way such that the broader meanings can be elicited."[43]

GT and narrative analysis have also developed a strong partnership over the past two decades. As one of the more popular approaches to sociological ethnographic research[44] and the philosophical "parent" of narrative methods such as the narrative psychology perspective,[45] GT has demonstrated its ability to meld well, both theoretically and practically, with analytical narrative approaches. As a result, a number of studies have now been conducted which employ a combination of narrative and GT methodologies.[46] Questions have naturally arisen about the compatibility of classic Glaserian GT and narrative approaches but even in those instances, strong arguments have been made that the two models may work in tandem without compromising either model.[47] As Denzin and Lincoln observe on topic of combining methodological paradigms:

> Is it possible to blend elements of one paradigm into another so that one is engaged in research that represents the best of both worldviews? The answer, from our perspective, has to be a cautious yes. This is especially so if the models (paradigms) share axiomatic elements that are similar, or resonate strongly between them . . . Commensurability is an issue only when researchers want to "pick and choose" among the axioms of positivist and interpretivist models, because the axioms are contradictory and mutually exclusive.[48]

While Glaserian GT, from the positivist/objectivist tradition, and narrative analysis, from the constructivist/subjectivist tradition, come from apparently opposing schools of thought,[49] Bryant and Lasky argue that they have many axiomatic similarities which make them compatible. These similarities include an understanding of reality that is "multi-layered" and a primary interest in the symbolic undercurrents behind social acts and experiences.[50]

This compatibility becomes even more pronounced when one considers Charmaz's constructivist take on GT, which is the theoretical perspective that we have generally preferred in the analysis and writing of this book. Charmaz rejects the objectivist prescriptions of orthodox Glaserian GT.[51] Instead, she proposes a GT approach that falls between positivism and post-modernism[52] and puts aside the idea of a single, objective, discoverable reality to embrace the concept of multiple social realities:

> [T]he primary aim of this methodological strategy is to study experience from the standpoint of those who live it, but with a full and explicit acknowledgement that the final analyses represent only *one* interpretation of *a* reality as it was articulated by the participant during the interview(s) . . . It is the pluralities of experiences, which are related through their resemblances to the experiences of various others, that allow for a credible and reflexive accounting that links the personal with the socio-political.[53]

A constructivist GT approach thus has additional significant levels of methodological compatibility with narrative work, as it also recognizes that a reality is "created by 'an interaction between [a participant's] beliefs, goals and activities, and the constraints and possibilities of the physical, socio-historical and linguistic background and context'"[54] and by the interaction between participant and researcher.[55] This ability to meld the theoretical and analytical development strengths of GT with the emancipatory and sensitivity-based goals of narrative models was another attraction of this particular method of data analysis.

Lastly, we were intrigued by work done by previous scholars to develop GT frameworks that embrace and support critical perspectives.[56] Malagon *et al* particularly have argued that GT is not incompatible with theoretical positions such as critical race theory.[57] Although Glaserian GT holds that approaching data with predetermined theoretical positions is likely to cloud analysis and distort the data in order to force it to fit the position,[58] Strauss and Corbin have since acknowledged that a researcher's theoretical positioning, like his or her prior knowledge and experiences, are themselves components of the data and useful in analysis.[59] Malagon *et al* thus argue that theoretical positioning can inform a GT analysis and capitalize on the shared strengths of GT and critical perspectives – such as the common goal of better understanding and elucidation of the life experiences of participants[60] – while moving GT in a direction that more directly questions the structural and power relations at work behind phenomena.[61]

Again, Charmaz's constructivist approach to GT also goes a long way towards providing a GT framework that can support theoretical positioning. Constructivist GT recognizes that the researcher, his or her role in the research, and his or her interactions with the participants already form an intrinsic portion of the research "story."[62] As an additional inherent part of constructivist GT, Charmaz also believes that the researcher must explore:

> how, when, and to what extent the studied experience is embedded in larger and, often, hidden positions, networks, situations, and relationships. Subsequently, differences and distinctions between people become visible as well as the hierarchies of power, communication, and opportunity that maintain and perpetuate such differences and distinctions.[63]

This is of particular interest to us and was one of the principal reasons behind our selection of GT as we approached the design and analysis of this study from a perspective strongly influenced by the social model of disability.

Following the GT methodology developed originally by Glaser and Strauss[64] and further expanded upon by Strauss and Corbin[65] and Charmaz,[66] data analysis was primarily conducted by way of a line-by-line analysis of each transcribed interview. This allowed the development of a system of open codes, through highlighting different incidents and issues raised by the participants and generating names for each phenomena that attempted to address the deeper processes at work and fracture the data to encourage thinking about the phenomena from many perspectives.[67] Memo writing was an invaluable part of this process.

Memos, such as those in Figure 2.1, were written throughout the data analysis process to capture ideas and themes as they emerged and to further develop the relational links between ideas.

Reoccurring themes and relationships between ideas—especially those related to identity, advocacy and rights—emerged very quickly, sometimes addressed specifically by the participants within the interviews. Memos provided a means of capturing these relational links as well as allowing for the

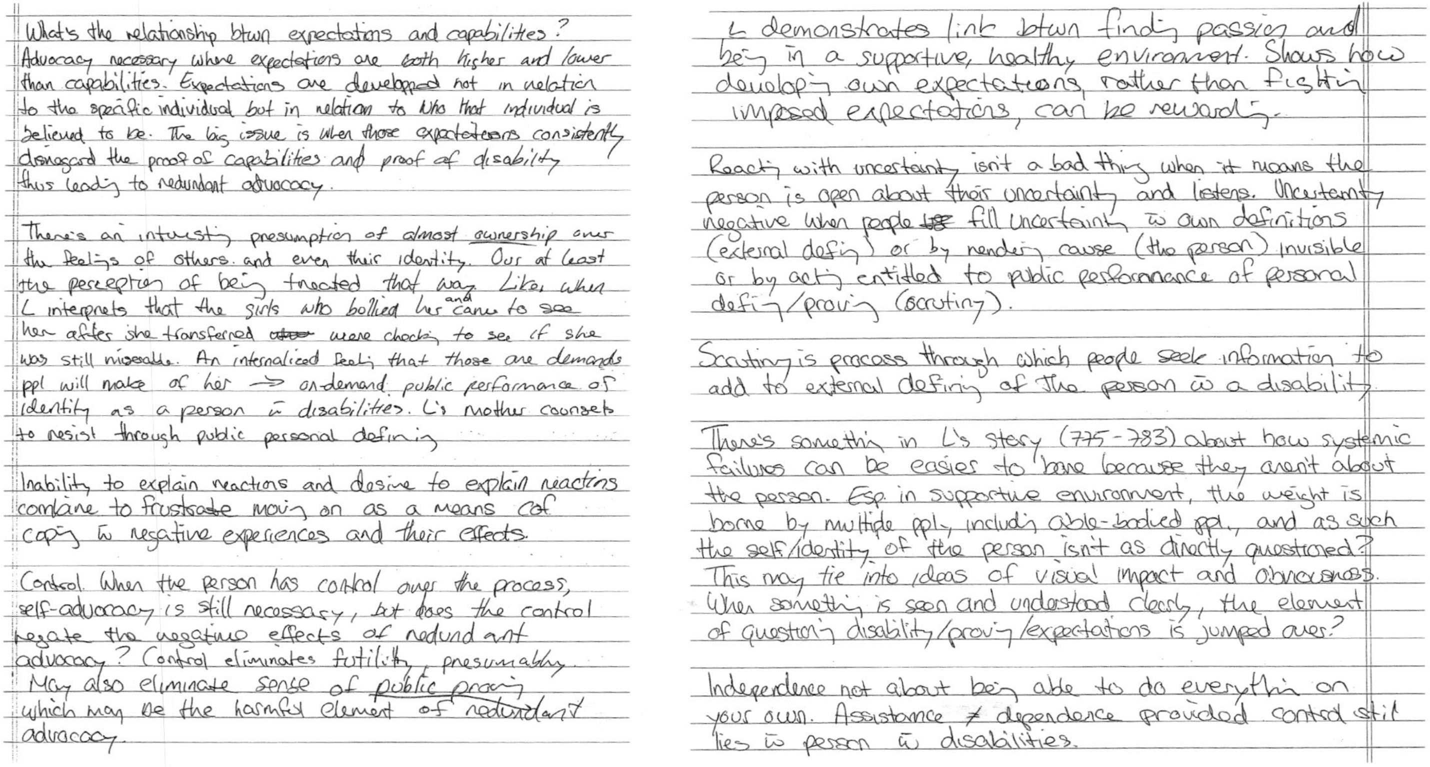

(a)

What's the relationship btwn expectations and capabilities? Advocacy necessary where expectations are both higher and lower than capabilities. Expectations are developed not in relation to the specific individual but in relation to who that individual is believed to be. The big issue is when those expectations consistently disregard the proof of capabilities and proof of disability thus leading to redundant advocacy.

There's an intrusive presumption of almost ownership over the feelings of others and even their identity. Or at least the perception of being treated that way. Like when I interpret that the sisters who bullied her came to see her after she transferred were checking to see if she was still miserable. An internalised feeling that those are demands ppl will make of her → on-demand public performance of identity as a person in disabilities. L's mother counsels to resist through public personal defining.

Inability to explain reactions and desire to explain reactions can combine to frustrate moving on as a means of coping to negative experiences and their effects.

Control. When the person has control over the process, self-advocacy is still necessary, but does the control negate the negative effects of redundant advocacy? Control eliminates futility presumably. May also eliminate sense of public proof which may be the harmful element of redundant advocacy.

(b)

L demonstrates link btwn finding passion and being in a supportive healthy environment. Shows how developing own expectations rather than fighting imposed expectations can be rewarding.

Reacting with uncertainty isn't a bad thing when it means the person is open about their uncertainty and listens. Uncertainty negative when people fill uncertainty to own definitions (external defin) or by random cause (the person) invisible or by actn entitled to public performance of personal defin/proxy (scripting).

Scripting is process through which people seek information to add to external defin of the person is a disability.

There's something in L's story (775-783) about how systemic failures can be easier to bare because they aren't about the person. Esp in supportive environment the weight is borne by multiple ppl, includ able-bodied ppl, and as such the self/identity of the person isn't as directly questioned? This may tie into ideas of visual impact and obviousness. When something is seen and understood clearly, the element of question disability/proxy/expectations is jumped over.

Independence not about being able to do everything on your own. Assistance ≠ dependence provided control shift lies in person to disabilities.

Figure 2.1 Examples of memos

necessary constant comparison between incidents and interviews on which GT methodology is founded.[68] Further questions, points-of-interest, ideas and areas requiring further consideration and elucidation were also annotated in memo form so that they could be returned to and incorporated into the emerging framework as further data allowed. Upon completion of coding the interview with a participant named Tracy, no new codes were found, all of the data could be related back to the central code[69]—"advocacy identity"— and thus data saturation was judged to have been reached.[70]

As has been frequently noted with respect to GT methodology, the different "stages" of coding are not truly independent, linear stages but instead co-exist, with the researcher continually moving between different approaches to coding and different levels of abstraction.[71] Consequently, the first stages of axial coding began during the open coding process, once codes began to be grouped within larger parent categories. The purpose of axial coding, as defined by Strauss and Corbin, is "to begin the process of reassembling data that were fractured during open coding" by "relating categories to sub-categories along the lines of their properties and dimensions" to determine how categories link and interrelate.[72] The paradigm model approach to axial coding was employed in order to determine the causal and intervening conditions, contexts, interactional strategies and consequences of the different phenomena identified during open coding.[73] While some of this process was completed through memoing responses to questions such as "What conditions gave rise to this category?" and "What were the consequences of the interactional strategies used to handle it?"[74] the majority of the paradigm process was completed through the use of small diagrams which were combined into larger diagrams as further categorical relationships were discovered.

As can be seen in Figure 2.2, during the axial coding phase of data analysis, codes began to be grouped into larger parent categories in order to express and define the properties and dimensions of the categories as well as further exploring the interrelationships between categories.

From this paradigm approach, the central code of "advocacy identity" as well as the three major axial code categories—rights, identity and advocacy— were discovered and linked to all other categories and codes. All previous memos and diagrams were referenced in order to write a conceptual narrative of the central code and major code categories, as Strauss and Corbin suggest for the integration of data and the refinement of the theory.[75] The result is the theoretical framework discussed below. This theory fits Glaser's and Strauss's definition of substantive theory, as a theory which is developed to relate to and explain a particular area of inquiry, in this case disability rights and identity. Although Glaser encourages researchers to take the final step and generalize their substantive theory further, to make it applicable in other areas of study,[76] we have declined to do so, as our study is concerned with the particular life experiences of disabled people and thus is not served by generalizing beyond this substantive area.[77]

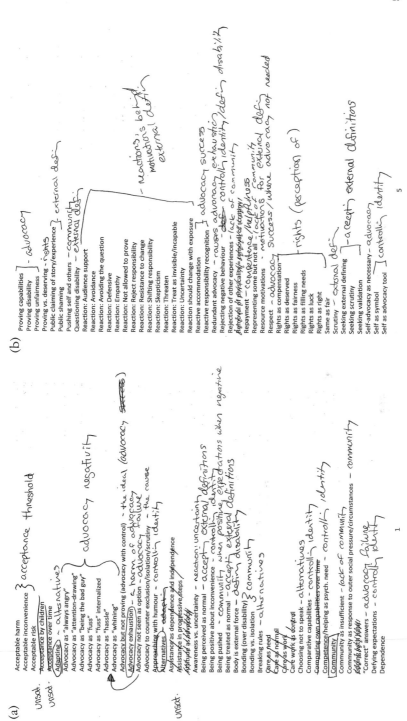

Figure 2.2 Axial coding phase of data analysis

As already noted, the majority of axial coding was completed through the paradigm model approach and through the use of diagrams capturing causes, conditions, contexts, interactional strategies and consequences. Figures 2.3 to 2.6 demonstrate both small diagrams and the incorporation of smaller diagrams into ever-expanding webs of larger diagrams.

Ensuring rigour

Although GT methodology and qualitative analysis in general both stress the importance of taking a creative and imaginative approach to research data, this does not lift the requirements for ensuring that resulting findings and theories have been checked to ensure they are thorough and reliable.[78] Strauss and Corbin noted that often the best method for judging the quality of research is by allowing the findings to speak for themselves and be judged by others.[79] Nonetheless, they also provide a number of general factors which can be used to compare and evaluate qualitative research.

Table 2.1 A summary of Strauss and Corbin's factors for evaluating qualitative research[80]

Criterion	Definition
Fit	Do the findings resonate with the study participants and the professionals in the field of study? Can participants see themselves in the broad scheme of the findings?
Applicability	Do the findings add new explanations or insights to the field of study? Are they "useful"?
Concepts	Concepts are intended to provide a common understanding and language for discussing the findings. Do the findings have substance that move the audience beyond trying to make sense of unanalyzed data?
Contextualization of concepts	Has the researcher provided context for the concepts that permit the audience to answer questions such as why events occurred and why certain meanings were ascribed to those events?
Logic	Is there a logical flow to the ideas and findings? Is the methodological approach made sufficiently clear so that the audience may judge its appropriateness?
Depth	Depth refers to the description and detail which provides "richness and variation and [lifts] the findings out the realm of the ordinary."
Variation	Have variations in the data been built into the findings? Have the researchers provided and explained examples which display differences or do not fit a theme or pattern?
Creativity	Are the findings new and original? Do they posit new ideas or new formulations of old ideas?
Sensitivity	Did the findings result from research driven by the data or was the data collection affected by preconceived ideas or theories?
Evidence of memos	Does the final report show evidence of memo work? Memos are important to the development of theory with a high degree of depth and abstraction as it is hard to impossible to achieve when relying on memory alone.

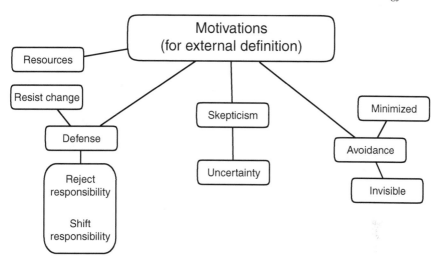

Figure 2.3 Motivations (for external definition)

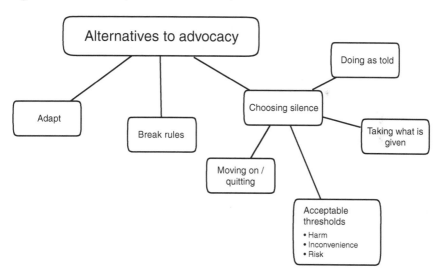

Figure 2.4 Alternatives to advocacy

By applying these factors to the research at hand, we can not only be reflective about our own research and our roles within the research process but may also provide others with better tools by which to assess this study.

Fit

Following other GT scholars who have observed that it is essential for a good theoretical framework to give rise to "an immediate recognition that

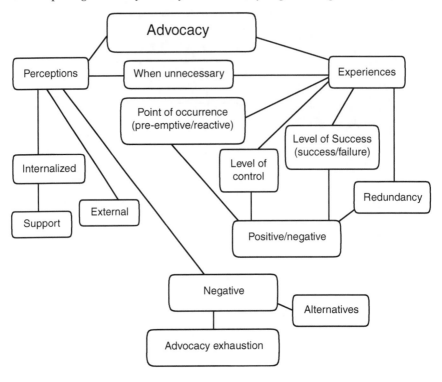

Figure 2.5 Advocacy

this theory, derived from a given social situation, is about real people,"[81] we sought feedback from the participants to ensure the fit of theory to real experiences. The theory developed from the data has been tested for fit by discussing it with others, including both scholars studying within the area of disability rights and other disabled individuals, to evaluate the degree to which it may genuinely reflect life experiences of disabled people. Additionally, the use of a PAR-aligned approach which allowed the participants themselves to provide feedback on the initial analysis has helped contribute to ensuring that the theory fits the reality of the experiences described.

Applicability

This study, while based on Engel's and Munger's original study and supportive of many of their findings, adds to the discussion by examining how the key findings of *Rights of Inclusion* manifest or are modified within a different legal context where a single, emblematic disability rights document like the ADA does not exist. Specifically, the study highlights the importance of advocacy and advocacy experiences in how the participants form their personal identities and come to understand their rights.

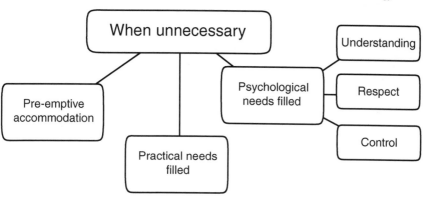

Figure 2.6 When unnecessary

Concepts

The theory developed from the interviews is based on concepts drawn out of the data through the GT methodology processes explained above. Open coding, axial coding and selective coding created a long list of concepts describing and theorizing different elements of the incidents described by the participants. To promote greater understanding of our theoretical perspective, the key concepts—identity, rights and advocacy—and their interrelationships are illustrated in greater detail below.

Context

The researchers have endeavoured to present their findings in a way that describes the political, legal and social context within which they arise. Particularly in cases where a topic is the subject of controversy and debate, we have provided an overview of different perspectives in order to provide context for our findings and the participants' experiences and viewpoints.

Logic

The findings are discussed below, including specific consideration of how the theoretical model builds off and modifies the theory adopted by Engel and Munger in *Rights of Inclusion*. Once the framework and the relationship of the key concepts has been outlined, the subsequent chapters then discuss and further explain how the theory operates in relation to everyday experiences and problems in areas such as transportation, education, and employment.

Depth

The importance of providing depth to the findings through the use of descriptive details is particularly recognized and embraced in this study. As noted in Chapter 1, the use of narratives is a key goal of this study, both in telling the larger, biographical narratives of the participants and providing a forum for their own observation, thoughts and explanations of their narratives. As much as possible, we have provided the narratives upon which the findings are based in the participants' own words.

Variation

Variations in the experiences of the participants, particularly regarding how they defined their identities in relation to their impairments, proved to be sources of great theoretical richness and were treated as such. Rather than seeing variations as instances that contradict theory, they were incorporated into the framework to ensure that the theory explained the widest possible range of experiences.

Creativity

We have attempted to approach the question of the interaction between rights and identity for disabled people from a creative perspective by proposing that perceptions and experiences with advocacy play an important, additional role in how identity is constructed and how rights are perceived and approached. This builds on the theoretical findings of Engel and Munger while providing a new way of looking at the complex relationship between rights and identity and how they interact on a day-to-day level.

Sensitivity

Theoretical sensitivity towards the participants and data was a high priority. Certain areas, such as early childhood experience, educational experiences and issues relating to transportation, were specifically raised in all interviews. The interviews were generally unstructured, allowing the participants to move the conversation in directions that were of most importance and relevance to their perspectives and experiences. This helped to prevent the imposition of preconceived theories onto the data within the interview process and also returned some of the power in the research relationship back to the participants. Equalizing the power between researcher and participant was also expanded upon later in the research process by seeking feedback and input from the participants on the early results of analysis to ensure that the ideas the researchers were generating felt realistic and relevant to the participants.

Evidence of memos

The processes of data analysis and theory development were accompanied by extensive memo-writing and diagramming (see Table 2.1). These mid-process memos and diagrams were then drawn upon and incorporated in order to create the theoretical framework that is applied throughout this book.

Differences in legal context

As noted above, one of the motivations for conducting an adapted version of Engel's and Munger's study was the desire to see what, if any, difference would be made by examining life narratives within a different legal context. Although both the current study and *Rights of Inclusion* aspire to look more broadly at the interaction of disabled people and the law, both are, at least in part, a product of the legal system in which they take place. Compared to American disability law, the development of Canadian disability rights law is younger and has progressed in an often slow, piecemeal fashion. In part, this is attributable to Canada's federalized system, with a number of different pieces of human rights legislation existing at both the federal and provincial levels. Most prominently, the Canadian Charter of Rights and Freedoms exists as an entrenched constitutional set of rights for people in Canada. It includes the section 15(1) guarantee of equal protection and benefit of the law without discrimination on a number of listed and analogous grounds, including "mental or physical disability."[82] When section 15 came into force, it was the first constitutionally entrenched right to equality for disabled persons in the world.[83] However, the application of the Charter is limited only to legislation and acts of government and state actors. A separate tier of human rights legislation exists, both federally and provincially, to address discriminatory action by private actors, such as schools and employers. Combined, these two tiers represent the bulk of legal protections for disability rights in Canada, and they have developed together over the years, sharing elements of interpretation as the courts have grappled with disability issues in case decisions.[84] Only one province, Ontario, has passed legislation specifically designed to address disparate treatment of individuals with disabilities,[85] but it is thus far unclear what the substantive impact of this law will be within the province.

The development of disability rights law through decisions, particularly decisions by the Supreme Court of Canada in section 15(1) cases, has been a complex mixture of positive and negative from the perspective of disability rights advocates. Starting in 1985, not long after section 15(1) came into force,[86] the court considered the application of a mother to have her daughter, Eve, a 24-year-old woman with a mental impairment, sterilized to prevent future pregnancy. The Court of Appeal had approved a hysterectomy, but the Supreme Court overturned this decision, refusing to authorize the procedure because it was medically unnecessary.[87] Although the court accepted the lower courts' perception of Eve as incompetent and incapable of expressing her own opinion or choice, despite substantial evidence to the contrary,[88] it nonetheless recognized the long history of discrimination against disabled people in Canada and held that its *parens patriae* power to make decisions on behalf of people under an incapacity could only be exercised for the protection and benefit of the person themselves. As the court stated, "non-therapeutic sterilization could never be said to be a decision for the benefit of a person who is incapable of consenting themselves."[89]

Throughout the 1990s, the court continued to address issues that touched directly and indirectly on disability rights. The 1999 decision in *Meiorin*, which involved a claim of sex discrimination in the job qualification requirements placed on forest firefighters, established the approach for questioning rules, such as job requirements, for both direct and adverse effects discrimination.[90] This approach was then applied to disability in *Grismer*, which challenged the mandated automatic denial of a driver's license to individuals with a field of vision less than 120 degrees. The Supreme Court held that this breached British Columbia's human rights legislation as it was based on generalized, stereotypical assumptions about individuals with a specific disability, rather than on an individualized assessment of needs and capabilities.[91]

For many, the 1997 decision in *Eldridge* represents the high watermark in Canadian disability law jurisprudence.[92] *Eldridge* sought to challenge the failure of British Columbia's government to provide sign language interpretation for deaf individuals in relation to medical services. The Supreme Court upheld the challenge and adopted a strong social model approach to disability, recognizing that disabled people "have been subjected to paternalistic attitudes of pity and charity, and their entrance into the social mainstream has been conditional upon on their emulation of non-disabled norms."[93] The court held that the duty to accommodate may require positive action on the part of government and service providers "to ensure that members of disadvantaged groups benefit equally from services offered to the general public."[94] At the same time, however, the *Eldridge* decision broadcast some of the problems that the next decade of disability jurisprudence would see. Particularly, the court's use of comparison to determine the needs of the deaf claimants was done in such a way that non-disabled needs remained the baseline default while the needs of individuals with disabilities were presented as extraordinary.[95]

In *Granovsky v Canada*, for example, the Supreme Court dismissed a challenge to the Canada Pension Plan (CPP) after the claimant was denied a disability pension due to having not made sufficient contributions to the plan over a sufficient number of years to be eligible. Granovsky argued that his rights under section 15(1) of the Charter were violated by this requirement as it was his impairment that prevented him from working and paying into the program as regularly as a non-disabled person. The court, however, held that this was not a case of discrimination. They compared Granovsky's treatment, as a person with a temporary disability, to the treatment of individuals with permanent conditions under CPP and found that the comparative difference in treatment was not demeaning to Granovsky's human dignity and, as such, not discriminatory.[96] To many, this represented a great step back from the decision in *Eldridge* because, as Rosenbaum and Chadha note, it exposed "the Supreme Court's misunderstanding of the multitude of disability experiences and [revealed] the Court's inclination to rank disabling conditions in a hierarchical manner."[97]

The decision in *Auton* completed the withdrawal from the seemingly optimistic promises of *Eldridge*.[98] *Auton* dealt with a challenge to British Columbian health care which failed to provide funding for specialized treatments for children with autism. The families of a group of children argued that this was in violation of the children's section 15 right to equality, but the Supreme Court found that there was no discrimination in the province's decision not to fund such treatment. In so finding, the Court held that the Canadian health care scheme was intended to provide funding for "core" medical services and that the autism treatments sought by the claimants could not qualify as core due to their novelty, recent development, and cost.[99] The decision in *Auton* has been roundly criticized by disability rights scholars in Canada; as Pothier notes, "This analysis [in *Auton*] is circular. A challenge to under-inclusiveness is met with the answer that what is claimed is not included . . . The court did not even address the argument . . . that a health system privileging services provided by doctors and hospitals is geared to the typical needs of the non-disabled population."[100]

The legal context in which this study takes place is thus significantly and inherently different than that of Engel's and Munger's study. As has been observed, the ADA represents a particularly striking, emblematic victory for disability rights within the United States that has not generally existed in Canada. More substantively, differences have become apparent in the interpretation and impact of the two disability rights schemes. With its specific requirement for environmental accessibility, the ADA has proven to be an effective document for ensuring the ability of individuals with a wide range of disabilities to access physical spaces in the United States.[101] Except for the fledgling Accessibility for Ontarians with Disabilities Act, comparable legislation does not exist within Canada, and general human rights documents at the federal and provincial level have done little to ensure similar environmental accessibility.[102]

In other areas, however, the presence of some social model reasoning at the Supreme Court level in Canada, and filtered down through the various other levels of court and tribunal decisions, has been somewhat advantageous for Canadian disability rights. The biomedical approach applied to the employment sections of the ADA, particularly, has resulted in strict scrutiny of the impairments of individual complainants, the barring of many claims, and few substantive victories as a result.[103] Comparatively, Canadian courts and tribunals have been less restrictive and less hierarchical than their American counterparts and have shown a greater willingness to examine issues relating to disability from the perspective of individuals with disabilities.[104] Overall, however, these more social model-oriented decisions have resulted in few widespread, practical changes.[105] As the following chapters explore, the practical effects of disability rights law in Canada remain mixed.

Differences in theoretical development

The core finding of *Rights of Inclusion* was the valuable insight that there is a recursive relationship between rights—both legal rights as discussed above and the more general concept of rights—and disability identity. In other words, identity and rights are mutually constitutive and contingent, altering as circumstances change over time and constantly being renegotiated by the disabled person. The acquisition or rejection of a disability identity can determine the context in which rights become active but the emergence of rights can also shape a person's development of her or his identity regardless of whether or not the person actually seeks legal enforcement of the right.[106]

Engel and Munger postulate three ways in which this occurs. First, the enactment of disability rights laws can transform individuals' self-perceptions. Some participants in their study clearly regarded themselves as entitled to disability accommodations such as accessible washrooms which enabled them to succeed in careers. Not only did an appreciation of rights encourage those participants to challenge obstacles that might stunt their careers but it also transformed their interactions with friends, family and colleagues.[107] Second, Engel and Munger suggest that enactment of rights spawns cultural and discursive shifts that alter how others regard disabled people.[108] Employers, for instance, increasingly become aware of responsibilities with respect to accommodation in the workplace even without specific complaints from employees. This comes about as everyday language and media reporting about disability rights increasingly incorporate key concepts of disability rights. Lastly, rights may generate institutional transformations such as adaptations in the workplace. The growth in public representations of wheelchair users, for instance, generates a cultural shift that eventually leads to changes in policies, infrastructure and day-to-day practices in educational and workplace settings.

This is not to suggest that Engel's and Munger's interpretation of their data is without concerns. As specialists in the sociology of law rather than specifically disability law scholars, they seem to suggest at times, clearly influenced by Goffman's *Stigma*, that the more successful participants in their study achieved goals because they were able to distinguish their disabilities from their sense of self:[109]

> . . . [t]he capacity to distinguish disability from self [is] a key to opening a space in which rights must become active. For the individual who perceives and describes herself as a "disabled person," it is less likely that exclusion from mainstream activities will appear to be notable or unfair treatment. Such an individual is unlikely to consider using rights

to change a situation that strikes her as normal and appropriate. On the other hand, to the individual who perceives and describes herself as a person with many attributes and capabilities, of which the disability is but one, there is a greater chance that exclusion will appear unfair, because it precludes her participation on the basis of one aspect of her identity while ignoring the many others that make her similar to people who participate freely in mainstream activities and settings.[110]

This perspective poses two difficulties. First, it conflates impairment and disability, a distinction that is central to understanding the social model of disablement. It is important to recognize that structural barriers in society are the sources of disabilities and to clearly distinguish between physiological impairment, such as an inability to travel without a wheelchair, and disability due to the interaction of that impairment with structural barriers, such as a lack of wheelchair ramps.[111] Second, it implies that disability is inherently a negative characteristic that successful disabled people manage to overcome by effective psychological adaptation. This omits the reality that there are many successful disabled people for whom disability is a major yet cherished part of their lives.[112]

Similarly, some scholars have critiqued *Rights of Inclusion* for analyzing the narratives of the study participants without fully considering the larger institutional issues in play and the effects they had on the individual and the individual's sense of identity. Jerome Bruner, for example, notes that many of the narratives described the stigmatizing and belittling experiences of special education classes and that Engel's and Munger's analysis focused largely on the effects these experiences had on the individual. Doing so left unquestioned and invisible those decisions that led to special education being established, being conducted in such a detrimental fashion, and being poorly funded.[113] In part, this is because Engel and Munger chose to focus their study on personal narratives of experiences, not on the wider societal context surrounding those personal narratives; however, from a social model perspective, it is far more difficult to separate the personal from the structural when discussing experiences with disability.[114] It may also be part of a second critique of the original study, which noted that Engel and Munger conducted their analysis with an understanding of formal equality but without expanding on experiences relating to substantive equality. As Dianne Pothier noted in her review of *Rights of Inclusion*, "Engel and Munger seem not to fully appreciate that the radical transformation is not to erase difference (the route of formal equality) but to embrace difference (the route of substantive equality). For the ADA and other rights-constituting measures to effect a radical transformation, the negative conception of disability needs to be understood as an inappropriate social construction."[115]

Keeping these issues in mind, the theory generated from our data nonetheless largely supports Engel's and Munger's key original finding on disability identity and rights, with a few differences. Like Engel and Munger, we found that a recursive relationship exists between rights and identity. Engel and

Munger described this recursive relationship as fundamental, since the recognition of rights depends first on how an individual defines him or herself: "The perception of boundaries wrongly marked is inseparable from the sense of self. The perception that exclusion is appropriate or inappropriate, indeed the *awareness* that exclusion has occurred, hinges on the way in which individuals and those around them define their identity."[116] As scholars working in areas related to personal identity have frequently noted, personal identity is not static; it develops and changes throughout an individual's life in response to how the individual sees herself or himself and how others perceive her or him.[117] Engel and Munger observed that one of the main means for constructing identity out of personal experience was through creating narratives that addressed and attempted to combine internal and external definitions of who the individual was into a single narrative of their identity.[118] As noted above, those narratives could then loosely be divided into categories: those who established clear divisions between their sense of self and their disability and those for whom the divisions were blurry or non-existent.[119]

We noted a similar process of narrative as a means of telling the narrative of identity; however, among our participants, this was often a means of resisting external definitions. These definitions attempted to label the participants as strange and different, placed expectations on them that could be either beyond their physical capabilities or far lower than what they could actually accomplish and otherwise attempted to hijack their ability to define their own sense of self in order to tell a different narrative from an outside perspective about who they were as disabled people.

The idea that the ability of disabled people to tell their own narratives is complicated by the presumptions of non-disabled society about those narratives—particularly that they are narratives of loss, suffering, dependency, and weakness[120]—is not new. As others have observed in regards to personal story-telling for disabled people:

> . . . when it comes to narrating one's life, norms constitute intelligibility. Thus, to tell one's narrative and to be understood, one is inevitably caught within webs of meaning informed by normative assumptions. Unfortunately, the normative view of disability is not a particularly positive one . . . Yet, as Butler explained, even when we are resisting dominant scripts, we still must engage with them to be rendered intelligible.[121]

Total rejection of the external defining of their identity and experiences is thus not possible. Disabled people will still find their personal perceptions of themselves are shaped by others and that they must engage with other people in order to make their experiences, perspectives, and needs known and to avoid exclusion from society. Personal narratives of identity thus include both internal and external components, reflecting how the individual sees himself or herself both independently from and in comparison with how society sees him or her.[122]

The participants often found that being a disabled person seemed to inherently open up their personal narrative of identity to scrutiny by those around them; others would question it, discuss it together, and theorize about it. When a participant was seeking accommodations, he or she found that professors, employers and others had the power to demand to hear the narrative in order to decide whether it fit the requirements for accommodation. For many participants, this was a frustrating process which further complicated the already complicated process of developing a personal identity.

Interestingly, we found that the personal identity narratives developed by the participants to explain their sense of self could not be as easily divided as the narratives of Engel's and Munger's participants. The idea of multiple, flexible selves emerged from many of the interviews. Unlike Engel's and Munger's findings, these participants neither divided their sense of self from their disability nor blurred the line. Instead, they described identifying their self with their impairment and experiences of disability as something that changed depending on the social context they found themselves in and was often influenced by how they were treated and perceived by others. When the participants felt scrutinized or when they faced barriers, their identities as disabled people became more pronounced but in other circumstances, their impairment was often seen as largely irrelevant, something that contributed to who they were over their life but did not comprise the entirety of their identity within the specific moment. As one participant, Lisa, put it:

> If somebody told me tomorrow that they could rewind the clock and I could start from the beginning and not have a chair I would politely decline because I would be a completely different person. I wouldn't know any of the people that I know, any of the friends that I have, and I wouldn't have the life that I have. I would be completely 100% different and I am not prepared to entertain that idea, but at the same time if somebody came up to me with a medical cure and said, "We can do this for you and if we do this for you, you will be able to be disability-free," then I would accept that because I would be able to keep the identity that I've built and keep the people in my life that are in my life.[123]

Lisa's explanation presents one way in which the participants were able to reconcile the feeling that being a person with a disability was an essential ingredient of who they were but, at the same time, largely irrelevant as well. It could be both a sometimes unpleasant or painful experience and also a source of pride. The extent of these multiple selves varied greatly amongst the participants. Some almost always identified their self with a disability identity and found great pride and motivation in that identity while others wished to distance themselves from disability and felt that their impairment was more often something that prevented others from seeing their true, "core" selves than something which contributed positively to who they were.[124]

As Engel and Munger noted, rights play a strong role within the development of personal narratives of identity, providing a baseline conception of what fair and equal treatment looks like and supporting the sense that disabled persons are entitled to such treatment and should not be excluded. This effect on personal perception could also spread to the perceptions of other people and institutions around the individual with a disability, and this was observed as well within the narratives of our participants. Strikingly, however, the idea of "rights" was often understood, observed, and expressed in largely informal, rather than legalistic, ways. Participants drew attention to incidents that they saw as unfair, ignorant, and hurtful, often without any direct reference to legal rights. This accords with theories of legal consciousness[125] which have observed that giving personal meaning to things like law and rights is a repetitive process that people engage in when trying to understand the world; once repeated often enough, the law or rights becomes internalized into the individual's own meaning system which is then used to give meaning and to understand other aspects of the world.[126] Thus, while the participants could easily identify situations in which they felt they had been treated in a discriminatory manner, their reference point for defining what was discriminatory was through an internalized, informal sense of what their rights were rather than through a formal, legal document.

Whether rights awareness is more formal or informal may be affected by a number of factors in addition to disability, including age, race, class, gender and education level.[127] Within the context of this study, awareness may also be one of the most directly observable results of the difference in legal systems. Within the American context, with its single, landmark legal instrument for protecting the rights of disabled people, the discussion of rights among Engel's and Munger's participants frequently circled back to the ADA as the touchstone for both those seeking to have their rights enforced and those from whom rights were sought.[128] In legal contexts, such as that of Canada and comparable systems, where the rights of disabled people are protected through a variety of different legal documents and often in concert with rights protections for other marginalized groups, it may be that while awareness and expression of rights is high overall, flowing as a common basis for understanding themselves and the reactions of others, rights take on a far more informal, internalized nature within such systems.

This has substantial implications for advocacy, which was the last element we identified as having a recursive relationship with both rights and identity. Used in this context, advocacy refers to all the processes and interactions in which disabled people might engage in order to ensure their rights are respected and to remedy discriminatory treatment. On a formal level, this can include engaging in legal proceedings, as one of our participants had, but less formally and more commonly, it can include such things as seeking accommodations and devising what accommodations should be or simply speaking up when a stereotypical opinion is voiced. For the participants, experiences with different forms of advocacy, of varying levels of formality, were daily occurrences and as their narratives quickly illustrated, these experiences with advocacy in themselves had profound effects both on how the participants felt about rights and how they constructed their own identity narratives.

For the participants, advocacy was a lifelong and often daily process, necessary in order to combat the stereotyping, negative interpersonal interactions and systemic barriers they encountered in many different areas of life. In many cases, however, the participants framed advocacy not as a formal assertion of legal rights in the face of discrimination but as a more informal assertion of who they are and what their needs are in the face of perceived attempts by others to define, incorrectly, their life experiences, needs and how best to accommodate those needs. From this perspective, then, advocacy becomes yet another process of identity formation, albeit one specifically intended to react to situations in which personal identity is challenged. Advocacy may, in fact, be seen as a point of intersection between identity and rights, presenting an opportunity for the individual to tell her or his personal narrative to ensure that her or his rights are respected and to resist the effects of stereotyping which may seek to transform the narrative along more stereotypical lines.[129]

Advocacy, however, was not a solely, or even largely, positive process from the perspectives of the participants. The majority of the participants found advocacy to be wearing, exhausting, and unpleasant at times. Thus, whether advocacy takes place and how it takes place depended on the individual's perceptions of advocacy, past experiences with advocacy, and how they saw themselves in relation to the role of advocate. For many, certain levels of treatment and behaviour that they consider unfair, harmful, risky or inconveniencing may be deemed acceptable in order to avoid having to advocate for better treatment or accommodations; only when treatment or behaviour fall below acceptable levels would the participants feel the need to advocate to fix them, even if they remain frustrated and hurt by actions they otherwise deem acceptable. In situations of "acceptable" unfairness, participants would more often look for alternatives to advocacy, including adapting to the situation, finding partial solutions they could institute on their own, breaking the rules that created barriers in the first place, moving on from or quitting the situation that gave rise to the issue, or choosing to accept the situation and the barriers that came with it. While some of these tactics can be seen as forms of advocacy in their own right and can lead to substantive change, the participants spoke of them specifically as means of avoiding advocacy or as the road they would take when other advocacy efforts failed.

Part of this desire to avoid having to engage in advocacy comes from the overall negative perceptions of advocacy, which resulted both from personal experiences with advocacy and from internalizing the perspectives of others regarding advocacy. While most participants noted that their family, particularly their parents, were very supportive of advocacy and often advocated on their behalf as well, some nonetheless felt negatively about advocacy. They characterized it as "whining," "a hassle," or "drawing attention," reflecting both the exhausting effect of repetitive advocacy and some stereotypical perceptions of advocacy efforts by marginalized groups.

The more difficult issue, however, is the often extremely negative past experiences with advocacy. These affect not only the individual's desire to advocate in the future but their feelings towards the law, legal rights and their own identity narratives, such as whether they find rights effective or ineffective protections from discrimination and whether they can consider themselves successful individuals after failed or negative advocacy experiences. A variety of factors were found to contribute to whether an experience with advocacy was seen as negative or positive, including the point of occurrence (i.e. whether advocacy was pre-emptive to a future issue or reactive to a present one), the level of control given to the individual both within the advocacy process and in crafting a solution, the attitudinal approach to the process and the individual, and the degree to which the solution resolved the issue at hand. Of particular importance, while the need to repeatedly advocate and the preponderance of negative experiences led participants to feel exhausted—or, as one participant phrased it, tired of being constantly angry—positive experiences did exist and did not have the same negative, exhausting effects as less positive advocacy. These experiences, particularly those that gave a large amount of control to the individual to direct the process and craft the solution, resulted in feelings of happiness and satisfaction. From an identity and rights perspective, this is important as the participants also expressed feeling as though they were respected, in control of their own lives, and treated equally as a result.

This theoretical framework should be kept in mind throughout the following chapters as we explore in greater detail the barriers that arise in the lives of the participants and particularly analyze how the participants manage these barriers. The interconnected and recursive web of rights, identity, and advocacy falls over a wide range of experiences within the participants' narratives, including their interpersonal relationships and their interactions with institutions such as schools, transportation systems, and employers. For disabled people, constructing a personal identity narrative is a constant balance between personal perceptions of one's own characteristics, strengths and weaknesses, personality traits, histories and the often negative presumptions held by society at large. Rights, whether formally or informally understood, play an important role in this process by affecting how individuals and institutions perceive and treat the individual with a disability while simultaneously providing a tool for the individual to define her or his own entitlements. Advocacy operates to give voice to both rights and identity, challenging presumptions about identity and the ways of fulfilling rights that otherwise ignore or conflict the individual's own perspective. These relationships are cyclical and recursive. The use and perceptions of rights come to define the contents of the law.[130] Personal identity affects whether an individual believes advocacy is necessary in a given situation, and it is affected by negative and positive experiences in advocacy. Together, these factors create the shifting landscape of personal identity that affects how and when disabled individuals access rights and advocate for change and how they perceive and manage barriers even when they do not.

Implications and limitations of the participant sample

The participant sample has potential implications both for the theoretical framework and for the ways in which that model differs from the one proposed by Engel and Munger. For example, Engel's and Munger's framework specifically incorporated recognition of work and employment as central to the development of adult identity.[131] As our study focused specifically on the narratives of individuals who were students at the time, the importance of work in their lives to that point varied widely. Some had extensive work experiences either concurrently with their schooling or prior to returning to school, while others had only limited or no experience. Work thus did not play the same central role that Engel and Munger noted for many of their participants and was often subordinate to interpersonal relationships and experiences within educational settings. In addition, given the strong emphasis on employment within Canadian disability law, this may reflect why the participants' understandings of rights were less formal and less connected with legal rights: most had only limited experiences with the area in which disability rights have become the most formalized and effectively advocated. It is interesting to note, thus, that Tracy, one of the participants with the most prior work experience, was also the one who spoke most directly and forcefully about the need to push for recognition of legal rights.

There are additional implications to consider in relation to sample size. The relatively small number of individuals interviewed limits the ability to draw specific and generalized conclusions from the data. This is also true given that the sample was not chosen in a way that was meant to be representative of the demographics of the disability community or Canadian society, beyond ensuring roughly even proportions of female and male participants. As the participant sample was entirely individuals who were post-secondary students at the time, this sample inherently reflects only a particular range of experiences and does not deal directly with the narratives of individuals who were unable to attend post-secondary education or who began post-secondary education but did not graduate, both of which, though on the decline generally, remain frequent experiences for disabled people.[132] The focus on post-secondary students also likely had inherent effects on the socioeconomic backgrounds of the different participants as well as the types of impairments found in the sample.

A final important implication of the sample is that, given the nature of the study and the participants' recruitment through centres for students with disabilities, it is unsurprising that all of the participants identified themselves in some way as individuals with disabilities and displayed at least some interest in and awareness of issues affecting disabled individuals in general. Had it been possible to recruit participants for the study without relying on self-identification, there may have been more variation in these two characteristics. Specifically, the study may have included more individuals who had acquired an impairment during adulthood and whose experiences, particularly with rights and identity, would possibly have had substantial difference. Those participants in the study who had acquired an impairment later in life had already lived with it for a period of years or decades at the time of the interview and had come to identify as individuals with disabilities as a result.

Nonetheless, the participants involved in this study are far from a homogenous group. In addition to the approximately even numbers of male and female participants, the participants were a wide range of ages, from those just entering their first year of post-secondary education to those approaching graduation to individuals who had returned to school after a long period in the workforce. Although the study was restricted to individuals with mobility impairments, this still gave rise to a significant variety of diagnostic conditions, including cerebral palsy, spina bifida, and injuries acquired in motor vehicle accidents. Moreover, during the interviews, several participants disclosed that they had learning disabilities and/or psychiatric disabilities as well and discussed the impact these conditions had, particularly on the accommodation advocacy process. The disabilities of the participants were obvious to all in most cases; however, some of the older participants used wheelchairs only in certain contexts, and their mobility impairments were less obvious or, at times, invisible otherwise. The participant sample also includes a number of individuals who have lived part of their life abroad in other countries, from the United States to Qatar, and thus under different legal rights regimes as well. This wide range of different characteristics and life experiences has led to life narratives that contain a similarly wide range of experiences with and perspectives on issues relating to disability and rights.

The above limitations of the sample, both in terms of size and constitution, must be acknowledged; however, in light of the wide variety and great richness of experience that does exist within our participant sample and the discussion of the advantages of the narrative approach within Chapter 1, we believe that there are many advantages to working with our sample. The similarities in demographic background make comparison easier, and the smaller sample size allows us to put forward a richer, more in-depth portrait of the individual participants in the following chapters. Just as Engel and Munger chose a few life narratives as the focus of their analysis, grounding this study in the lives of a dozen individuals allows the narratives that follow to more fully convey the experiences and perspectives of the participants, which may be quite different and otherwise difficult to understand for the reader if these could only be conveyed in short anecdotes or generalized summaries. It also allows us to give greater effect to our titular goal of providing a platform for the voices of the participants by allowing them, as much as possible, to recount their narratives in their own words.

Conclusion

In this chapter, we have demonstrated the development of our theoretical perspective through the use of a grounded theory methodology. Our work owes a great debt to Engel's and Munger's preceding work on the interaction between rights and identity for disabled individuals. Growing from the basis of their insightful study, we have conducted an ethnographic study of the narratives of our study participants which examines how rights and identity interact specifically at points in which the participants have been called on to advocate for accommodation and how this interaction has led to the development of identity narratives and, in turn, advocacy identities. We have also highlighted the legal contexts in which Engel's and Munger's study and our research took place to provide a better foundation for the analysis to follow. Lastly, we have taken advantage of the opportunity to engage in reflective practice to consider some of the limitations and advantages of our methodology. From here, we proceed to the substantive discussion of the narratives of our participants, beginning in Chapter 3 with an exploration of their experiences in education.

Notes

1 D.M. Engel and F.W. Munger, *Rights of Inclusion: Law and Identity in the Life Stories of Americans with Disabilities*, Chicago, IL: University of Chicago Press, 2003, pp. 7–9.

2 For a good review of the contradictory motivations and ideological social movements that led to bipartisan backing of the ADA in Congress, see S.R. Bagenstos, 'The Future of Disability Law' *Yale Law Journal*, 2004, vol. 114, pp. 14–18.

3 Engel and Munger, op. cit., n. 1, p. 1; E. Berrey and L.B. Nielsen, 'Integrating Identity at the Bottom of the Dispute Pyramid' book review of *Rights of Inclusion: Law and Identity in the Life Narratives of Americans with Disabilities* by D.M. Engel and F.W. Munger, *Law & Social Inquiry*, 2007, vol. 32, pp. 233–60 at p. 235.

4 Engel and Munger, op. cit., n. 1, p. 7.

5 Engel and Munger, op. cit., n. 1, pp. 7–9. The authors had originally intended to conduct follow-up interview with eight participants but for reasons that are not fully provided, only six were completed.

6 Engel and Munger, op. cit., n. 1, p. 8.

7 Engel and Munger, op. cit., n. 1, p. 7.

8 Engel and Munger, op. cit., n. 1, p. 8.

9 Engel and Munger, op. cit., n. 1, p. 9.

10 Engel and Munger, op. cit., n. 1, pp. 10–11.

11 R. Atkinson, 'The Life Narrative Interview' in J.F. Gubrium and J.A. Holstein (eds) *Handbook of Interview Research: Context & Method*, Thousand Oaks, CA: Sage, 2002, pp. 130–31.

12 Atkinson, ibid, p. 9. See also D.J. Connor, *Urban Narratives—Portraits in Progress: Life at the Intersections of Learning Disability, Race & Social Class*, New York, NY: Peter Lang, 2008. pp. 57–59; C.K. Riessman, *Narrative Analysis*, Newbury Park, CA: Sage, 1993, p. 15.

13 K. Heyer, 'A Disability Lens on Sociolegal Research: Reading *Rights of Inclusion* from a Disability Studies Perspective' book review of *Rights of Inclusion: Law and Identity*

in the Life Narratives of Americans with Disabilities by D.M. Engel and F.W. Munger, *Law and Social Inquiry*, 2007, vol. 32, pp. 277–88. Connor also attempts to involve participants directly in his research. See generally Connor, ibid. See also A. Shaffer *et al.*, 'Changing the Food Environment: Community Engagement Strategies and Place-Based Policy Tools that Address the Influence of Marketing' *Loyola of Los Angeles Law Review*, 2006, vol. 39, pp. 675–76 (discussing PAR).

14 J. Morris, 'Personal and Political: A Feminist Perspective on Researching Physical Disabilities' *Disability, Handicap & Society*, 1992, vol. 7, pp. 157–66 at p. 159.

15 P.S. Duckett and R. Pratt, 'The Researched Opinions on Research: Visually Impaired People and Visual Impairment Research' *Disability & Society*, 2001, vol. 16, pp. 815–35 at p. 827.

16 R. Norway, 'Ending Participatory Research?' *Journal of Intellectual Disabilities*, 2000, vol. 4, pp. 27–36 at p. 28.

17 V. Williams, *Disability and Discourse: Analysing Inclusive Conversation with People with Intellectual Disabilities*, Hoboken, NJ: John Wiley & Sons Ltd., 2011, p. 13.

18 Norway, op. cit., n. 16.

19 Norway, op. cit., n. 16.

20 Heyer, op. cit., n. 13, 281.

21 D.F. Polit and C.T. Beck, *Nursing Research: Principles and Methods*, 8th edn, Philadelphia, PA: Lippincott, Williams & Wilkins, 2008, p. 17.

22 To preserve confidentiality, the institutions will be referred to as Institutions A, B, and C respectively throughout. Institutions A and B are universities while Institution C is a community college. The participants are also referred to using pseudonyms.

23 A. Jakle, 'Surveyors, Reporters, and Detectives: A Typology of Qualitative Interviews' paper presented to the 2012 Law & Society Association Conference, June 2012, unpublished.

24 Theory can become ungrounded when preconceived ideas or theories are allowed to affect the collection of data and thus what data is available for analysis and integration into a final theory.

25 B.G. Glaser and A.L. Strauss, *The Discovery of Grounded Theory: Strategies for Qualitative Research*, Chicago, IL: Aldine Publishing Company, 1967, p. 4.

26 This stands for the Ontario Disability Support Program. Details may be found at http://www.accesson.ca/mcss/english/pillars/social/odsp/ (last accessed July 10, 2009).

27 Glaser and Strauss, op. cit., n. 25.

28 Theoretical saturation is defined by Strauss and Corbin as the point at which no new, relevant data emerges in relation to the different categories of study and the relationship between the categories is well-established in the data collected. This is considered the point at which further data collection is unnecessary. A.L. Strauss and J. Corbin, *Basics of Qualitative Research: Grounded Theory Procedures and Techniques*, London: Sage, 1990, p. 188.

29 The use of focus groups as a good means of reaching theoretical saturation has been recognized by other GT scholars. See P.N. Stern, 'On Solid Ground: Essential Properties of Growing Grounded Theory' in A. Bryant and K. Charmaz (eds) *The SAGE Handbook of Grounded Theory*, London: Sage, 2007, p. 117.

30 J. Green and N. Thorogood, *Qualitative Methods for Health Research*, London: Sage, 2004, p. 180.

31 Glaser and Strauss, however, later developed opposing perspectives on GT. Glaser refined his perspective into what is now known as orthodox or classic GT. This version of GT is objectivist, in that it assumes that there is a single, objectively ascertainable truth which the researcher may discover through the GT analysis. The

researcher is also considered an objective, neutral observer rather than a participant in the construction of theory (L.R-M. Hallberg, 'The "Core Category" of Grounded Theory: Making Constant Comparisons' *International Journal of Qualitative Studies on Health and Well-being*, 2006, vol. 1, pp. 141–48 at p. 144). Strauss and his collaborator Corbin, conversely, rejected some of the objectivism inherent in Glaser's approach by acknowledging that the "reality" created in data is subjective and the result of the interaction between researcher and participant (Hallberg, ibid, p. 145). They also argue that the theory generated by GT is verified within the process of theory construction itself, whereas Glaser argues that further verification is required (Hallberg, ibid, p. 143).

32 Glaser and Strauss, op. cit., n. 25, p. 223.
33 A. Strauss and J. Corbin, *Basics of Qualitative Research: Techniques and Procedures for Developing Grounded Theory*, 2nd edn, London: Sage, 1998, pp. 12–13.
34 Glaser and Strauss, op. cit., n. 25, pp. 3–5.
35 Strauss and Corbin, op. cit., n. 28.
36 V.L. Olesen, 'Feminist Qualitative Research and Grounded Theory: Complexities, Criticism, and Opportunities' in A. Bryant and K. Charmaz (eds) *The SAGE Handbook of Grounded Theory*, London: Sage, 2007, p. 422.
37 Y. Jeon, 'The Application of Grounded Theory and Symbolic Interactionism' *Scandinavian Journal of Caring Science*, 2004, vol. 18, pp. 249–56 at p. 251.
38 D.L. Crooks, 'The Importance of Symbolic Interactionism in Grounded Theory Research on Women's Health' *Health Care for Women International*, 2001, vol. 22, pp. 11–27 at p. 18.
39 T. Bradshaw, *Canadian Forces Military Nursing Officers and Moral Distress: A Grounded Theory Approach*, MS thesis, University of Ottawa, Ottawa, 2010.
40 Green and Thorogood, op. cit., n. 30, p. 180.
41 M. Brydon-Miller, 'Breaking Down Barriers: Accessibility and Self-Advocacy in the Disabled Community' in P. Park *et al.* (eds) *Voices of Change: Participatory Research in the United States and Canada*, Westport, CT: Bergin & Garvey, 1993, p. 135.
42 J. Reichetz, 'Abduction: The Logic of Discovery of Grounded Theory' in A. Bryant and K. Charmaz (eds) *The SAGE Handbook of Grounded Theory*, London: Sage, 2007, p. 215.
43 Green and Thorogood, op. cit., n. 30, p. 175.
44 I. Tavory and S. Timmermans, 'Two Cases of Ethnography: GT and the Extended Case Method' *Ethnography*, 2009, vol. 10, pp. 243–44.
45 S. Edwards and M. Gabbay, 'Living and Working with Sickness: A Qualitative Study' *Chronic Illness*, 2007, pp. 155–66 at p. 157.
46 See e.g. S. Shapiro *et al.*, 'Identity and Meaning in the Experience of Cancer: Three Narrative Themes' *Journal of Healthy Psychology*, 1997, vol. 2, pp. 539–25; D.F. Hones, 'The Transformational Power of Narrative Inquiry' *Qualitative Inquiry*, 1998, vol. 4, pp. 225–48 at p. 225; J. Floersch, J.L. Longhofer and D. Kranke, 'Integrating Thematic, GT and Narrative Analysis: A Case Study of Adolescent Psychotropic Treatment' *Qualitative Social Work*, 2010, vol. 9, pp. 407–25 at p. 407.
47 See e.g. J. Bryant and B. Lasky, 'A Researcher's Tale: Dealing with Epistemological Divergence' *Qualitative Research in Organizations and Management: An International Journal*, 2007, vol. 2, pp. 179–93.
48 N. Denzin and Y. Lincoln (eds) *The Landscape of Qualitative Research,* 2nd edn, London: Sage, 2003, p. 267.
49 As noted, Glaserian GT takes as a starting point the assumption that a single reality is objectively discoverable and that the researcher stands outside the researcher as a neutral observer who does not impact, only discovers, the present theory. Strauss's and Corbin's reformulated GT and, to an even greater degree, Charmaz's constructivist GT both adopt more subjectivist perspectives, in that they recognize that the

reality discovered through GT is only one of multiple possible realities, constructed by both participants and researchers.

50 Bryant and Lasky, op. cit., n. 47, p. 191.
51 K. Charmaz, 'Grounded Theory: Objectivist and Constructivist Methods' in N. Denzin and Y. Lincoln (eds) *Handbook of Qualitative Research*, London: Sage, 2005, pp. 510–11.
52 Hallberg, op. cit., n. 31, p. 146.
53 Edwards and Gabbay, op. cit., n. 45, pp. 157–58.
54 L. McMahon, C. Murray and J. Simpson, 'The Potential Benefits of Applying a Narrative Analytic Approach for Understanding the Experience of Fibromyalgia: A Review' *Disability and Rehabilitation*, 2012, vol. 34, pp. 1123–30 at p. 1124.
55 Hallberg, op. cit., n. 31.
56 See Olesen, op. cit., n. 36; M.C. Malagon, L.P. Huber and V.N. Velez, 'Our Experiences, Our Methods: Using Grounded Theory to Inform a Critical Race Methodology' *Seattle Journal of Social Justice*, 2009–2010, vol. 8, pp. 252–72 at p. 253; N.K. Denzin, 'Grounded Theory and the Politics of Interpretation' in A. Bryant and K. Charmaz (eds) *The SAGE Handbook of Grounded Theory*, London: Sage, 2007, p. 454.
57 Malagon, Huber and Velez, op. cit., n. 56, p. 263.
58 B.G. Glaser, *Theoretical Sensitivity: Advances in the Methodology of Grounded Theory*, Mill Valley, CA: Sociology Press, 1978.
59 Malagon, Huber and Velez, op. cit., n. 56.
60 Malagon, Huber and Velez, op. cit., n. 56, p. 260.
61 Malagon, Huber and Velez, op. cit., n. 56, pp. 262–63.
62 Hallberg, op. cit., n. 31, p. 146.
63 K. Charmaz, *Constructing Grounded Theory: A Practical Guide Through Qualitative Analysis*, London: Sage, 2006, pp. 130–31.
64 Glaser and Strauss, op. cit., n. 25.
65 Strauss and Corbin, op. cit., n. 33.
66 Charmaz, op. cit., n. 63.
67 Green and Thorogood, op. cit., n. 30, p. 181. Coding in GT is different from coding in other forms of qualitative research methodologies, such as thematic analysis, because it progresses inductively rather than deductively. Codes are not standard-ized and arise as the researcher attempts to identify and describe the different social actions, relationships, and meanings at work in each phenomenon. While inevitably the researcher's perspectives and ideas will contribute to what codes are generated— and as such the researcher's ideas and perspectives are themselves data—the purpose of codes is to capture, as succinctly and organically as possible, the elements of a phenomenon as described by a participant. As a result, codes often mirror the exact words used by participants.
68 L.B. Lempert, 'Asking Questions of the Data: Memo Writing in the Grounded Theory Tradition' in A. Bryant and K. Charmaz (eds) *The SAGE Handbook of Grounded Theory*, London: Sage, 2007, p. 251.
69 The central code or core category is the concept into which all other codes and cat-egories can be integrated. It "determines and delimits the theoretical framework." (Hallberg, op. cit., n. 31, pp. 143–44).
70 Strauss and Corbin, op. cit., n. 33.
71 Strauss and Corbin, op. cit., n. 33.
72 Strauss and Corbin, op. cit., n. 33.
73 Green and Thorogood, op. cit., n. 30, p. 182.
74 Green and Thorogood, op. cit., n. 30, p. 182.
75 Strauss and Corbin, op. cit., n. 33, pp. 148–49.

76 B.G. Glaser, 'Doing Formal Theory' in A. Bryant and K. Charmaz (eds) *The SAGE Handbook of Grounded Theory*, London: Sage, 2007, pp. 98–99.

77 Malagon, Huber and Velez, op. cit., n. 56, p. 261.

78 Green and Thorogood, op. cit., n. 30, p. 174.

79 Strauss and Corbin, op. cit., n. 33, p. 305.

80 A. Strauss and J. Corbin, *Basics of Qualitative Research: Techniques and Procedures for Developing Grounded Theory*, 3rd edn, London: Sage, 2008, pp. 305–7.

81 Stern, op. cit., n. 29, p. 114.

82 Canadian Charter of Rights and Freedoms, s.15, Part I of the Constitution Act, 1982, being Schedule B to the Canada Act 1982 (UK), 1982, c. 11 [Charter].

83 P. Rosenbaum and E. Chadha, 'Reconstructing Disability: Integrating Disability Theory into Section 15' *Supreme Court Law Reports*, 2006, vol. 33, p. 343.

84 D. Pothier, 'Legal Developments in the Supreme Court of Canada Regarding Disability' in D. Pothier and R. Devlin (eds) *Critical Disability Theory*, Vancouver: University of British Columbia Press, 2006, p. 305.

85 See Accessibility for Ontarians with Disabilities Act, S.O. 2005, c. 11.

86 Pothier, op. cit., n. 84.

87 *E. (Mrs) v Eve, Supreme Court Reports*, 1986, vol. 2, p. 388 at para 86 [*Eve*].

88 Rosenbaum and Chadha, op. cit., n. 83, p. 352.

89 *Eve*, op. cit., n 87.

90 Pothier, op. cit., n. 84, p. 308.

91 Pothier, op. cit., n. 84, pp. 308–9.

92 Rosenbaum and Chadha, op. cit., n. 83, p. 356.

93 *Eldridge v British Columbia (Attorney General), Supreme Court Reports*, 1997, vol. 3, p. 624 at para 56.

94 *Eldridge*, ibid, at paras 78–79.

95 Rosenbaum and Chadha, op. cit., n. 83, p. 358.

96 *Granovsky v Canada (Minister of Employment and Immigration), Supreme Court Reports*, 2000, vol. 1, p. 703 at para. 79.

97 Rosenbaum and Chadha, op. cit., n. 83, p. 361.

98 Whether the Supreme Court's recent decision in *Moore v British Columbia (Education)*, 2012 SCC 61 signals a return to the promise of *Eldridge* is not yet clear.

99 *Auton (Guardian ad litem of) v British Columbia (Attorney General), Supreme Court Reports*, 2004, vol. 3, p. 657 at paras 32–33.

100 Pothier, op. cit., n. 84, p. 311.

101 M.D. Lepofsky, 'The Long, Arduous Road to a Barrier-Free Ontario for People with Disabilities: The History of the *Ontarians with Disabilities Act*—The First Chapter' *National Journal of Constitutional Law*, 2004, vol. 15, pp. 125–33.

102 Lepofsky, ibid, pp. 125–33.

103 R. Malhotra, 'The Legal Genealogy of the Duty to Accommodate American and Canadian Workers with Disabilities: A Comparative Perspective' *Washington University Journal of Law and Policy*, 2007, vol. 23, pp. 1–32.

104 Malhotra, ibid.

105 Lepofksy, op. cit., n. 101.

106 Engel and Munger, op. cit., n. 1, pp. 241–42.

107 Engel and Munger, op. cit., n. 1, p. 243.

108 Engel and Munger, op. cit., n. 1.

109 Engel and Munger, op. cit., n. 1, p. 46. E. Goffman, 'The Stigmatized Self' in C. Lemert and A. Branaman (eds) *The Goffman Reader*, Malden, MA: Blackwell Publishing, 1997, p. 75.

110 Engel and Munger, op. cit., n. 1.

111 See M. Oliver, *The Politics of Disablement*, London: Macmillan, 1990; J.E. Bickenbach, *Physical Disability and Social Policy*, Toronto: University of Toronto Press, 1993.

112 If anything, this sentiment is far more common in the United States, where there is a stronger disability rights movement, than in Canada. See J. Shapiro, *No Pity: Disabled People Forging a New Civil Rights Movement*, New York, NY: Times Books, 1993, pp. 99–104. See also Pothier, op. cit., n. 84, pp. 142–43 (making essentially the same point by noting how many disability rights activists have rejected "people first" language to emphasize their disability pride).

113 J. Bruner, 'Identity as Inclusion' *Buffalo Law Review*, 2005–2006, vol. 53, p. 347.

114 B.A. Ferri, 'Disability Life Writing and the Politics of Knowing' *Teachers College Record*, 2011, vol. 113, pp. 2267–82 at p. 2271.

115 D. Pothier, 'Book Review of *Rights of Inclusion: Law and Identity in the Life Narratives of Americans with Disabilities* by D.M. Engel and F.W. Munger' *Social and Legal Studies*, 2008, vol. 17, pp. 139–43 at p. 143.

116 Engel and Munger, op. cit., n. 1, p. 40.

117 Engel and Munger, op. cit., n. 1, pp. 44–45 (summarizing J. Bruner, *Acts of Meaning*, Cambridge, MA: Harvard University Press, 1990; G.C. Rosenwald, 'Conclusion: Reflections on Narrative Self-Understanding' in G.C. Rosenwald and R.L. Ochberg (eds) *Narratives Lives: The Cultural Politics of Self-Understanding*, New Haven, CT: Yale University Press, 1992, p. 265; Goffman, op. cit., n. 109).

118 Engel and Munger, op. cit., n. 1, p. 44.

119 Engel and Munger, op. cit., n. 1, p. 68.

120 R. Garland-Thomson, 'Shape Structures Narrative: Fresh and Feisty Narratives of Disability' *Narrative*, 2007, vol. 15, pp. 113–23 and p. 114.

121 Ferri, op. cit., n. 114, p. 2269.

122 Other studies into identity and narrative among disabled people have noted similar combining of external and internal perceptions, especially as relates to the body. See e.g. J. Scott, 'Stories of Hyperembodiment: An Analysis of Personal Narratives of and through Physically Disabled Bodies' *Text and Performance Quarterly*, 2012, vol. 32, pp. 100–20.

123 Lisa, personal interview, 2007–08, p. 47.

124 Even in the latter cases, however, this did not amount to a "spoiled" identity in the same way that Goffman, Engel and Munger describe it. Even though the individual's impairment may be a constant, unforgettable presence in her or his life, it remained only one of the many elements that made up the individual's life and not a particularly important one, either. It was seen as more likely to spoil the perceptions of others than the individual's perception of herself or himself. See Engel and Munger, op. cit., n. 1, p. 46; Goffman, op. cit., n. 109, p. 75.

125 That is, theories relating to how law is experienced and understood by the people it affects, including law as a concept and the "gaps" in which law fails to operate or be understood as originally conceived (S.S. Silbey, 'After Legal Consciousness' *Annual Review of Law and Social Sciences*, 2006, vol. 1, pp. 326–27). The related concept, "rights consciousness," examines similar questions within the narrower field of human rights.

126 P. Ewick and S.S. Silby, 'Conformity, Contestation, and Resistance: An Account of Legal Consciousness' *New England Law Review*, 1992, vol. 26, pp. 731–49 at p. 741.

127 Ewick and Silby, ibid, p. 747.

128 For example, see the narratives of Raymond Militello, who largely felt negatively towards rights, and Jill Golding, who felt positively. Despite their differing perspectives on the value of rights, both connected the idea of rights closely to the legal rights contained in the ADA (Engel and Munger, op. cit., n. 1, pp. 34, 74, 146–47).

129 For example, by turning functional needs into dependencies or signs of helplessness or by turning personal success into narratives of overcoming adversity, both staples

of the stereotypical depiction of individuals with disabilities. See Ferri, op. cit., n. 114, p. 2268.

130 Ewick and Silby, op. cit., n. 126, p. 737.

131 M.A. Stein, 'Under the Empirical Radar: An Initial Expressive Law Analysis of the ADA,' book review of *Rights of Inclusion: Law and Identity in the Life Narratives of Americans with Disabilities* by D.M. Engel and F.W. Munger, *Virginia Law Review*, 2004, vol. 90, p. 1167.

132 A. Katsiyannis *et al.* 'Postsecondary Education for Individuals with Disabilities: Legal and Practice Considerations' *Journal of Disability Policy Studies*, 2009, vol. 20, p. 35.

3 Educational barriers

In high school, Lisa's school was considered wheelchair accessible. Yet, the school only had one elevator, and it was consistently broken. Long stretches of time would pass where Lisa was unable to access the top floors of the school and her classes located there. The school office rejected suggestions from Lisa's teachers to move the classes to the ground floor. Eventually, frustrated with the school's inaction, Lisa decided that she would attempt to climb the stairs to her classes. But even then, the school required Lisa to prove to the principal, vice principal, and school board physiotherapist that she was capable of climbing the stairs before she would be allowed to do so:

> My parents were there, and my dad kept saying to me, "Let me support your hips. Let me do this." And I said, "No, because if you touch me and if you let me use you as support, they are going to see that as sufficient reason to not allow me to do this if I need to. Yeah, it breaks your heart because you're my father, and you don't want to see me stumble on a flight of stairs, but this could be the difference between me getting the credits I need to graduate or not. So just, unless I start falling, just please, I have to do this. It's going to hurt, and I'm going to feel it for days, but I need to prove to them that I'm not unable."[1]

The advocacy of Lisa and her parents ultimately led to a number of Lisa's classes being moved to the ground floor. The elevator, however, continued to break down on a consistent basis, and no alternative was ever put in place.

The most central and formative experiences in the lives of many of the participants were those related to education. As an institution of socialization and one of the first settings in which children with disabilities may encounter formalized exclusion and the need to advocate for accommodation,[2] education plays a key role in the formation of personal identity and opinions on advocacy. The stories of the participants reflect how, even within a modern education system, navigating the barriers which continue to exist in schools can be a frustrating, exhausting, repetitive and personally damaging process. This chapter examines how, despite the protections of Canadian human rights legislation and court decisions regarding accommodation within schools, the participants continued to find themselves challenged by physical and attitudinal obstacles to their full inclusion. This chapter begins and ends with an examination of the debate surrounding segregated versus inclusive education. This debate will first be analyzed by looking at education as a whole and later in the specific case of summer camps for children with disabilities. The participants' experiences with barriers—in primary, secondary, and post-secondary institutions—are explored to examine the role that these experiences play in shaping how individuals feel about advocacy and its effectiveness as well as how these feelings influence their thoughts about rights and their own identities.

Inclusive education

When considering the experiences of disabled people in the education system, the initial question implicates one of the most basic elements of education: in what classroom should teaching take place? It remains contentious whether the needs both of children with disabilities and the education system as a whole are better met by placing children with disabilities in regular classroom settings or by segregating them in special schools and classrooms.[3] Historically, the policies of governments and schools in Canada and other Western countries have segregated children with disabilities into a separate stream of "special education" classrooms and institutions, regardless of the specific needs of the child.[4] The philosophical basis behind the early dominance of segregated education lay in the belief that students with disabilities needed to be protected from a potentially hostile and unwelcoming school environment and from educational expectations and demands which, it was believed, they would be unlikely to meet.[5] At the same time, governments and schools were also concerned with protecting the education and safety of non-disabled children, and the inclusion of children with disabilities in regular classrooms was seen as running counter to this goal due to the perception that children with disabilities would be disruptive or otherwise limit the pace of learning within the classroom.[6]

Since the 1970s and 1980s, however, running parallel with the introduction of the Charter in Canada, a shift away from segregated education and towards inclusion has occurred in most Western countries.[7] Segregation had come under criticism for encouraging stereotypes, exclusion, and suspicion between disabled people and non-disabled people[8] and for limiting the capacities of disabled people by lowering the expectations and opportunities they experienced early in their educational careers.[9]

In Ontario, Canada, for example, 1980 saw the introduction of Bill 82, which amended the provincial Education Act to require school boards to provide education services to children with disabilities.[10] Before this, public education of students with disabilities was becoming increasingly common but as it was not mandated, it still required parents to advocate for their children in order to receive any formal education at all.[11] Bill 82 also provided parents with mechanisms to appeal a child's placement in a potentially inappropriate environment. [12] Canadian laws such as the Education Act, however, stopped short of creating a legal presumption in favour of inclusive education.

In 1997, the parents of Emily Eaton, a child with cerebral palsy who was unable to speak or otherwise communicate at the time, relied on the Bill 82 appeal mechanisms to contest their daughter's placement in a segregated classroom. At the Ontario Court of Appeal, Arbour J.A., as she then was, held that segregated placement should be a last resort and that the Charter and Education Act required the placement of students in the least exclusionary environment that could accommodate their needs, unless parental consent to segregation was given. [13] The Supreme Court, however, reversed this decision. In holding that the segregated placement decision was not discriminatory, the Court ruled that creating a legal presumption in favour of integration would prevent proper consideration of student needs and potentially disadvantage those students for whom segregated education would be most beneficial. [14]

Educational policy has since adopted a presumption in favour of inclusive education regardless. Ontario's 2000 *Standards for School Boards' Special Education Plans* requires school board plans for students with disabilities to "acknowledge that placement of a student in a regular classroom is the first option considered." [15] More recently, the Supreme Court of Canada's decision in *Moore v British Columbia (Education)* [16] has made a significant leap in the approach of Canadian courts to the accommodation of disability in schools. In this appeal, the main question was whether British Columbia's Ministry of Education had discriminated against students with learning disabilities by failing to accommodate their disabilities within its educational services. In the particular case of Jeffrey Moore, who had dyslexia, the allegation was that the Ministry had failed to identify Moore's disability early enough and had failed to provide him with the necessary supports to access educational services. On November 9, 2012, the Supreme Court of Canada allowed the appeal from the Court of Appeal's decision and restored the finding of discrimination. The Court noted that defining the service as special education and comparing Moore only to other children with disabilities risked developing a "separate but equal" system that would allow the province to cut all disability support services without running afoul of human rights provisions. The Court held that because the school district was aware of Moore's needs, nonetheless chose to cut the support services available to him, and informed his family that other services could not be provided, a *prima facie* case of discrimination had been made out.

In the United States, the shift from segregation to inclusion took the form of the Individuals with Disabilities Education Act (IDEA), which succeeded the 1975 Public Laws 94-142, the "Education for All Handicapped Children Act." [17] The current law enshrines the right of all students to "Free Appropriate Public Education" and requires the placement of students in the "Least Restrictive Environment" for their education, creating at least a weak presumption in favour of inclusion. [18] Following the passage of the ADA, rights-based arguments for inclusive education have been bolstered by courts' willingness to view the ADA as supplementary to the IDEA.[19]

UK law has also shifted towards inclusion, albeit even more incrementally. The Disability Discrimination Act 1995 made it unlawful to discriminate against individuals with disabilities in employment and service provision but was roundly criticized for adopting a view of disability that focused on individual "deficit," rather than structural, societal barriers.[20] Educational institutions were also generally exempted from the original provisions of the law.[21] The 2001 amendment, the Special Education Needs and Disability Act 2001 (SENDA), focused specifically on discrimination in the education sector. It made it unlawful to discriminate against students with disabilities in application, admission, and enrolment processes or in the provision of education services once a student was enrolled.[22] The SENDA, however, was weakened by its reactive formulation; although institutions were expected to take proactive measures to avoid discrimination,[23] in practice it required individuals to complain about individual acts of discrimination in order to receive the benefit of the law.[24] The 2006 Disability Equality Duty amendment to the Disability Discrimination Act 1995 continues the shift towards positive inclusion in education. It requires institutions to take on a positive duty to include individuals with disabilities, to incorporate cultural aspects of disability communities, and to include disabled people in design and implementation of measures under the new duty.[25]

Despite legal evolution, inclusive education had only variable practical success initially, as it was often implemented only partially or without the supports in place to enable full participation by disabled children within the regular classroom.[26] In the decades since, the concept of inclusive education has grown and solidified. Inclusion now entails both a physically accessible classroom that fully accommodates students with mobility impairments and a welcoming environment wherein teachers, peers and educational aides actively remove barriers.[27] Mere physical presence in the classroom is insufficient; inclusive education requires immersion and involvement in the classroom setting.[28] According to Katarina Tomasevski, for any right to education to be meaningful, whether for non-disabled or disabled students, it must be available (free with adequate infrastructure and teachers), accessible (non-discriminatory and accessible to all), acceptable (comprised of content that is relevant and non-discriminatory) and adaptable (capable of evolving to meet changing needs and challenging inequality).[29] As Winnie Dunn observes, "[This] might not mean that all children will learn the same things, but it does mean all children will participate to the extent possible in learning tasks."[30]

Inclusive education is now often regarded as a practical outgrowth of the social model of disability. Whereas segregated education was based on the medical model which views disability as a "within-child phenomenon . . . to be treated with special procedures, which are sometimes best implemented in separate placements, in order to remediate the deficit or impairment,"[31] inclusive education has embraced the view that the environment, such as a classroom setting, can exacerbate the social construction of disability.[32] It has also found a place in international treaties with strong social model perspectives, such as the United Nations Convention on the Rights of Persons with Disabilities (CRPD), which came into force in 2008 and attempts to promote equality for disabled people in a wide range of areas.[33] Article 24 of the CRPD, which focuses on education, has been seen as mandating a commitment to inclusive education on the part of states[34] and, indeed, the Convention describes the education to which students with disabilities must have access as "inclusive, quality and free."[35]

Recently, a similar and parallel line of discussion has evolved in relation to higher education. Within the already highly individualized educational streams of colleges and universities, the concept of universal design—proactively designing spaces and teaching approaches to ensure accessibility for all—has taken greater hold than the standard inclusion versus segregation debate.[36] In the United States, the concept of universal design has received legal support from the provisions of the ADA which require private and public spaces to be physically accessible to individuals with disabilities.[37] However, universal design in education is seen to extend beyond the physical to touch on other areas of learning as well. It may include in and out of class reforms such as untimed tests,[38] assisted note-taking[39] and closed captioning on video presentations.[40] Universal design approaches the inclusive education debate from the perspective that designing for inclusion from the beginning prevents the drawn-out, exhausting process of demanding accommodation later on.[41]

Despite the growing acceptance of inclusive approaches and the social model in wide swathes of international education policies,[42] sharp divisions remain between proponents of inclusive education and individuals and groups who believe that segregated education remains the better model. For those critical of inclusive education, concerns arise that fully inclusive education has been sought and implemented on the basis of philosophical ideals that do not necessarily reflect or even consider what is best, educationally and socially, for individual children.[43] The presumption in favour of the most inclusive educational arrangement is seen to mask the fact that some disabled children do better in other settings, such as pull-out classes[44] and special education.[45] Other critics, especially advocates on behalf of children who are blind or Deaf, have argued that the emphasis on inclusion can limit interaction between disabled children, which in turn may prevent disabled children from forming connections and a sense of belonging with people who share similar life experiences.[46] This is thought to be necessary to combat the isolation and alienation that takes place when disabled children are included in regular classrooms.[47]

The ongoing search for inclusion and greater participation, as well as the internal struggle over whether segregated or inclusive education better serves the child, can be seen in many of the narratives of the participants. The majority of participants were educated in a regular classroom setting with their non-disabled peers and were satisfied with the overall experience of inclusive education. Yet, even well after the passage of the Charter and the amendment of the Ontario Human Rights Code to prohibit disability discrimination, this inclusion was not always immediate or easily obtained. Tom remembers how, as a child, he was quiet and rarely talked around other people, perhaps leading rehabilitation experts to underestimate his intelligence. He recounts:

> So they wanted to put me in the special needs class. And my mother stood up and said to the school board, very angrily, that I was perfectly fine, I was as intellectual as any four year old and as capable as any four year old or five year old being in the integrated classroom, [and] all I needed was an educational assistant to basically be my arms and legs . . . So eventually after a couple of what she says were gruelling meetings with people who don't know what they're talking about at school boards, she was able to get me into a fully integrated classroom.[48]

Similarly, Lisa's eventual inclusion in regular classrooms would likely not have happened without advocacy by her parents. In describing her experience, Lisa comments:

> They started school at a segregated school at the [segregated school for disabled children], and those were segregated classrooms, and I was there from junior kindergarten to first grade. When I was in first grade at [the segregated school], my parents decided to sort of pilot a bit of a . . . something I don't think many people have done. What happened was that Monday to Thursday I was at [the segregated school], in my segregated class, and then Fridays I went to my neighbourhood Catholic school, which was an integrated environment. They hadn't had a student with a disability at that school prior to me, because my parents knew that they didn't want me to have an entirely segregated school experience. My parents have always believed that there is no firm red line between me and the rest of the world because I'm in a wheelchair, and they didn't want to foster the idea of "She has to be treated differently all the time, and that she's special kind of in that way." . . . Then in Grade 2, at the age of 7, I went to my neighbourhood Catholic school full time.[49]

Tom and Lisa's experiences highlight the continuing tension between inclusive and segregated education, wherein the desire remains to place disabled children in segregated settings regardless of their capabilities. They also illustrate the important role that parental choice and advocacy can play in determining a child's classroom. Like Tom and Lisa's parents, many individual parents and parent organizations have been instrumental in pushing for greater opportunities for inclusion and fighting against resistance to inclusion from within schools.[50] In many cases, this means doing as Tom's mother did, achieving inclusion through lobbying the school board and refusing to accept the recommendation that Tom be placed in segregated education when she knew he would thrive in a regular classroom. In more extreme cases, advocating for inclusion has meant taking schools and school boards to court[51] or lobbying for changes to education legislation.[52] Lisa's parents, meanwhile, opted for an approach based less in advocacy and more in creative alternatives to advocacy, which may not have challenged the segregated education system directly but which achieved the ultimate goal of placing Lisa in inclusive education without the need to engage in a fight.[53] The participants, including Tom and Lisa, employ both of these tactics—direct advocacy and seeking alternatives—throughout their educational experiences.

One disadvantage of the importance of parental advocacy, however, is that reliance on advocacy to secure inclusion may mean that decisions about a child's placement are made on the basis of the parents' abilities to advocate rather than on the needs of the particular child. A number of studies have drawn attention to how parents' education-levels and their ability to take time off in order to advocate can have an impact on the education decisions made for children with disabilities, who may be placed in segregated classrooms despite being capable of learning effectively in regular classrooms simply because their parents, unlike Tom and Lisa's parents, were unable to effectively articulate the arguments for inclusion or take the time necessary to perform advocacy.[54]

At the same time, differing parental opinions on the segregation versus inclusion debate clearly influence the decision of where a student is placed, such that "two students with the same learning profile and disability classification would be placed in entirely different programs," depending on parental preference.[55] Like Lisa, Nancy began her education in a segregated preschool for disabled children before transitioning to inclusive education in kindergarten. Unlike Lisa, however, Nancy characterizes this early experience of segregated education not as something her parents had to work against but as something which was voluntarily chosen:

> Interviewer: Were you enrolled in integrated classroom settings from kindergarten onward, or if not, what age were you integrated at?
>
> N: Actually I started school when I was two. I started preschool. I had, I'm from [omitted], and there was, at the time, a school in the treatment centre for children and youth with disabilities. They had a preschool there that was just disabled children but when I made it into the mainstream, like kindergarten and onward, I've always been integrated, yes. I had [Educational Aides] to help me with my scribing and whatnot.
>
> Interviewer: So did your parents want you to go to that special school? Or were you placed there against their wishes?
>
> N: No, my mom said that it was the best thing she's done, she did for me, because I was able to get a lot of one-on-one attention and it gave me

the opportunity to get used to being at school and things like that. No, I believe it was totally voluntary.[56]

Nancy's comments reflect the important role her mother's opinions on segregated education played in early decisions about placement; from Nancy's description, it seems that placing her in segregated preschool was a choice made on the belief that it offered a better setting for Nancy at the time and would best prepare her for entering kindergarten. It should also be noted, however, that Nancy later describes how her mother raised Nancy on her own and how the family was often in a precarious financial position.[57] It is possible that time and resources also influenced the decision of where Nancy would be placed. Nancy's own memories of her time in segregated education are positive.[58]

Perhaps the most striking long-term effect of these early battles over segregation versus inclusion are not in how they translated into academic success—as all participants achieved a level of academic success and have been admitted to university and community college programs—but in the opinions that form about identity, rights and advocacy as a result. Tom, Lisa, and Nancy regard their parents as supporters and advocates who have worked on their behalf at various points in their lives. All three are also able to identify moments in their education, in primary, secondary and post-secondary institutions, in which they feel they have been treated unfairly or inadequately accommodated.

Tom and Lisa's exposure to early parental advocacy and engagement with education as an institution have had long-term effects on them. They both seem to have embraced the idea that educational decisions are inherently political and that the status quo of an institution is not an inflexible, unquestionable or unalterable arrangement.[59] They express strong social model perspectives on education and an awareness of their rights within the educational system. They also both recognize the importance of parental and self-advocacy for accommodations in school, although Lisa particularly expresses frustration at the constant need to fight for the supports that she needs. While both are prepared to fight for accommodation and recognition of their rights within the educational sphere, Tom has built the idea of being an advocate in education, for himself and others, into a foundational element of his identity narrative, insulating himself somewhat from the negative effects of advocacy because he sees it as his role to fill. Lisa, meanwhile, is determined to secure fair and respectful treatment for herself but continues to wish for a system in which fighting for equal treatment is not a constant necessity.

Nancy is just as aware of the barriers and unequal arrangements she encounters within education. In fact, she far more readily and openly associates unfair treatment in education with violations of her legal rights than either Lisa or Tom and is one of the few participants to have become involved in legal proceedings to ensure that her rights are respected. However, Nancy does not seem to view herself as an advocate. While she feels that other disabled students often give up too easily, she also expresses that she often feels frustrated and overwhelmed by the need to fight for the necessary classroom supports. She recalls an instance in which she felt her university refused to implement accommodations she needed. After insisting on her needs but not seeing results, she notes:

> I ended up dropping my classes anyway because I wasn't getting the supports and by this time I was—I felt like I was drowning. It was bad because I was so frustrated, and I basically said to my mom, "Maybe I should just quit school and write a book" because I just feel like so much goes wrong for me in education, and I don't know why, but it just happens that way.[60]

Nancy's perspective on the ability of advocacy in education to affect change is significantly more pessimistic than Lisa or Tom's perspectives. Rather than fighting unfair or discriminatory treatment, she seeks alternatives instead, choosing to adapt herself as much as possible to the situation in order to avoid another stressful and invasive advocacy experience.

The importance of parental choice, advocacy and opinions on education in affecting educational placement and longer-term opinions on education has important implications. As noted, these factors can draw attention away from the needs and best interests of the child, the criteria for educational decisions that both inclusive education and special education proponents consider most important.[61] Scholars such as Suanne Gibson argue that one of the largest continuing barriers to substantive and meaningful inclusion in education is an unwillingness to listen to the experiences and opinions of the children about whom educational decisions are being made.[62] Instead, decisions are made regarding placement, whether to accommodate and how to accommodate, often without regard for the needs of the individuals most affected. Michael, for example, discusses how he considered seeking accommodation in university to assist with his computer work, only to find that the sole accommodation of this sort offered was a specific program to translate spoken words into written text, software which was of little use to someone in computer programming. He was left frustrated and with the sense that "my reasons [for needing accommodation] aren't good enough."[63]

Despite barriers and inadequate accommodations, which remain the reality in many inclusive classrooms, the participants largely valued their inclusive educational experiences. This perspective dominated despite the fact that many noted that they were excluded and isolated by classmates due to their impairments during early grades. For many reasons, however, including the sense of normalcy available by being included and the opportunity to grow up with, rather than removed from, many of their peers, the participants paint a picture of inclusive education as a difficult but rewarding process that ultimately placed them in a better position to succeed in life. As Charles explains:

It's kind of a bit of a conflict of interest there. I mean, the fact of the matter is the entire intent of school, the pedagogical intent of school, as I see it, right, is to kind of integrate students into the world. Well, into this whole notion of values, and so on and so forth, that will allow them to succeed in the adult world, right? And the fact of the matter is that, well, unfortunately, the adult world is not always accessible and so on and so forth. So, I believe that it's best to learn how to deal with those challenges from an early age, rather than be integrated into a more adaptive setting, so to speak . . . I think it would be great to have other students in the environment who had physical disabilities as well because, I mean, I think that would have provided someone for me to identity with and so on but nonetheless, I'd have to say that I would prefer that setting.[64]

Physical barriers

The right to be physically present in the classroom, whether in the regular classroom envisaged by inclusive education or an alternative arrangement, is only the first step towards substantively fulfilling the educational needs of disabled individuals. Full access to education and academic success still requires accessible environments or the accommodation of students to assist them in bypassing the physical barriers that continue to exist within the school system. Yet, despite the fact that access to a level of accommodations is guaranteed by law in Canada and many other countries, seeking accommodations in education remains a process laden with frustrations and stigmatization for disabled students,[65] as many participants in our study experienced firsthand in their own academic lives.

The right to be present in the classroom is, for example, often limited by physical barriers which prevent or make difficult physical access to the classroom, even in otherwise relatively accessible schools. After difficulties with harassment, insufficient accommodation and unsupportive teachers during her primary school years, Lisa was significantly happier with her high school experiences. Yet, Lisa's account of the walking test, noted above, paints an image of a school largely unprepared to reliably maintain the accessibility of its facility. It also shows an inversion of the social model in relation to physical barriers, where Lisa was required to physically demonstrate that she was worthy of inclusion in an inaccessible environment. The public gaze surveillance and evaluation of Lisa's ambulatory functions are reminiscent of numerous medical narratives in the disability studies literature where disabled children and teenagers are made to ambulate, often partially or totally nude, so that medical students and other health care professionals can assess their physical abilities and use them as teaching tools, occasionally including photographing or videotaping the examinations.[66] Perhaps most revealing is the fact that Lisa observes how the test was not even realistic because she was ordered to climb multiple flights of stairs and immediately descend whereas, in a normal school day, she would never climb up and then down without a lengthy period in between to rest. Consequently, in a real world example of how the medical model in practice is often misleading, her tested performance did not reflect her actual abilities.[67]

Lisa's experience is not the only one which demonstrates the continuing physical inaccessibility of educational institutions. Others told stories about buildings without ramps, narrow doorways which wheelchairs could not fit through, and residence rooms with shelving that was too high to reach unaided. Even on campuses that were otherwise considered to be accessible and which actively sought to market themselves to disabled students on this basis, major obstacles were present, causing disabled students to miss class, sometimes for weeks in a row, or to arrive late consistently. Nancy, who was otherwise content with her accommodations, noted that she nonetheless commonly encountered physical barriers that prevented her from fully accessing important elements of the institution, such as professors' offices:

> There's some parts where there needs to be improvement. Especially the doors. I think it's called the Social Sciences building or something. My prof's office is there . . . and there's not a wheelchair button on the door, which is really dumb because there is a ramp on the other side of the door. It doesn't make sense . . . When I've spoken to one of the coordinators at [the student-run disability centre], they have told me that basically the school has no more money and aren't able to put the buttons on the doors.[68]

Accessibility measures, such as those described by Nancy, which are present but incomplete or which respond to a single accessibility issue while missing or further complicating others was a reoccurring theme raised by the participants. Cheryl, for example, found herself forced to choose between an accessible residence room or a room in one of the buildings that would allow her to opt out of the meal plan, a necessity since the school's cafeteria food was unsafe due to her serious food allergies.[69] The school had not provided an arrangement such that Cheryl could be accommodated both for her mobility limitations and her allergies. As a result, it was left to Cheryl to decide which accommodation was most important to her. Similarly, Tracy found that her college had seemingly not fully considered the practical needs of their disabled students when designing their accessibility measures. While the building in which she took classes was itself accessible and had accessible washrooms, there were no automated doors for any of the washrooms when she first arrived. She found herself required to advocate for more accessibility because, while she could access the washrooms herself, it was clear that others with different mobility impairments would not be able to:

> I got a hold of the centre for students with disabilities counsellor, and I'm like, "What can be done about this?" Like, these doors are impossible to get cranked open. And then like, okay, I don't have great arm strength,

and I'm standing at the right leverage point. What about people in wheelchairs in this building? Well, their accommodation was they put in automatic door openers on the first floor and the third floor. Okay, so if I'm busting a bladder and I'm on the [second] floor, I have to take an elevator down. It was just like, "Okay."[70]

Interactions such as this demonstrate how securing even basic physical access to educational institutions remains not only a physically taxing process, as students with disabilities attempt to navigate inaccessible or only inconsistently accessible environments, but psychologically taxing as well, as they are required to engage in repetitive advocacy to secure full and equal access to classrooms and other educational services. Many, perhaps most, educational institutions in countries such as Canada, the United States, the United Kingdom and Australia, now have policies and support services in place to address issues of physical accessibility for students with disabilities, bolstered by the legal rights in place.[71] Responses under these policies, however, are often based on perceptions of needs that are incomplete or unrealistic. They are designed by individuals who may have no or limited experience with accessibility issues and without substantial input from the students they are meant to serve.[72] The result is often situations like those described by Tracy, Nancy and Cheryl, where accommodations do not address all needs or are themselves inaccessible. At the same time, these accommodations remain reactive, more often than proactive,[73] requiring disabled students to advocate on an ad hoc basis for the accommodations they need[74] and to constantly prove and reprove their entitlement to such accommodations.[75] As Hibbs and Pothier note, this preponderance of reactive, ad hoc accommodation:

> ... places the onus on disabled students to initiate and maintain the process through to completion, despite the university's recognition of its responsibility to "provide reasonable accommodation, up to the point of undue hardship, to qualified students with a disability" ... This places disabled students in an adversarial position vis-à-vis the university, such that their objective – to complete a course, to win a scholarship, or to earn a degree – may be thwarted if they are unable or unwilling to identify themselves as disabled, if they cannot provide acceptable documentation that proves the legitimacy of their claim, or if they are unable to reach agreement with an instructor over an accommodation.[76]

Advocacy exhaustion and the other ill-effects of the repetitive need to advocate, including increased stress and lowered feelings of self-worth, are cited by many of the participants in relation to advocacy. These examples become particularly striking in the education context, given how enthusiastic most of the participants are about education and learning in general. For some, education, particularly post-secondary education, is an area in which they have felt that their presence and right to be fully included and participate is less subject to constant scrutiny than in other areas of their lives. As Henry observes:

> I don't feel like I need to prove myself. For example, in university, I'm obviously here because I'm able to be here academically. So there's a reason why I'm here. The school didn't let me in just because I applied and they said I was disabled and they didn't want to insult me by denying me entrance.[77]

The feeling of being recognized for his academic abilities is an important one for Henry as it involves both an external recognition of strengths that Henry sees in himself and bolsters his confidence in those strengths, confirming for him that he deserves to be included within the institution he is attending. Yet despite this feeling, Henry has experienced the stress of constant advocacy for accommodations within the educational section, particularly with regards to consistently securing the assistance of an educational assistant (EA). Up until high school, when he entered a school with a specialized physical disability support unit, he recalls that the stress of advocating constantly had a negative impact on both his grades and his physical health.

While sometimes the most inherently excluding, preventing access to education at the most basic level, physical barriers can be less personally harmful and have fewer direct impacts on the identity narratives of disabled individuals than barriers that arise because of the attitudes of people in positions of power, discussed below. Because they are pre-existing, often impact all individuals with mobility impairments, and are clearly based within the physical environment of the school, it can be easier for a given disabled individual to distance himself or herself from the fight for accommodation while still engaging in advocacy. Because the fight is less personal, individuals can access their legal rights without drawing as much scrutiny towards themselves and their personal narratives of identity and disability, as they are often required to do in more individualized accommodation situations. Lisa, for example, found her experiences with the broken elevator at her high school to be extremely frustrating but not as tiring or personally damaging as other, more personal accommodation issues:

> It was all sort of big, wide school issues that had an effect on me and had negatives effects on me, but I knew that it was nothing that I personally did, and it wasn't necessarily a vendetta against me, so the sorrow or the depression that I would feel because the elevator constantly broke was not the same as being left in the bathroom for two hours [during fire drills] because no one cared.[78]

As physical barriers are often the result of old facilities and issues relating to the management of scarce resources by schools, students may find accommodations needs placed lower on the list of priorities due to their impact on a smaller number of students. In this regard, disabled individuals may, as Lisa did, find such barriers less harmful in a personal sense. These barriers do not as frequently reflect the same stereotypical perceptions of the worth of the person with a disability as more attitudinally based barriers.

At the same time, the lack of personal identification with the issues can strongly affect how they are seen in relation to rights as well. Barriers and failures of accommodation that are more directly aimed at the capabilities and needs of the individual can raise strong feelings of unfairness or the specific identification of the situation as one in which legal rights have been ignored. Yet many physical barriers, because they are less personal, fall into the realm of acceptable inconveniences, which can be borne or worked around at the individual level to remove the necessity of advocating for accommodation. Michael, who used a walker when he was younger, described his elementary school as inaccessible, with multiple levels and no elevator. However, neither he nor his parents advocated for accommodations; instead, Michael says, "I just suffered. Well, not really. I just took the time to walk up and down the stairs. I just took forever."[79] This continues to be true through to university, where Michael accepted the long walks between his classes instead of requesting that classes be moved. He was, in fact, unaware of the option to request that classes be moved. His approach to these sorts of physical barriers is one that recognizes them as inconvenient but does not connect them with rights issues: "You definitely think about [the difficulty of long walks between classes] but in my head, it's like, 'What can I do about it?'"[80]

Attitudinal barriers

Thus, often the most difficult barriers to overcome are not physical but attitudinal. Because attitudinal barriers are invisible, pervasive, and imply fundamental perspectives on whether disabled students should be accommodated to begin with, the participants generally highlighted events involving attitudinal barriers as more frustrating and harmful than those involving physical barriers. Attitudinal barriers in education encompass specifically the attitudes of teachers, administration and other school staff, which can impact upon the treatment and accommodation of disabled students within the school. Attitudes can include both how educators and staff feel about disabled individuals generally, as well as how they feel and what they believe about inclusive education and the duty to accommodate.[81]

A number of studies internationally have examined the ways in which the attitudes of educators can affect the implementation of inclusive education policies and reforms. They have found that teachers with positive attitudes towards inclusive education "more readily change and adapt the ways they work in order to benefit students with a range of learning needs."[82] These same teachers may also influence co-workers and peers to have more positive attitudes towards students with disabilities and inclusive education as well.[83]

At the same time, however, similar studies have shown that many teachers remain concerned about the inclusion of disabled students within mainstream classrooms.[84] The majority support inclusive education conceptually but worry about the practical impacts of having disabled students within their own classrooms.[85] Frequently cited concerns include the need for individualized attention, the potential effect on the education of the other students in the class, and the lack of training and preparation specifically oriented toward supporting inclusive education.[86] As Slee observes:

> Teachers often feel at a loss and are personally distressed about the difficulties experienced by disabled children in their classrooms . . . Unreasonable policy impositions, competitive targets and narrowing notions of educational purpose restrict creativity, innovation and the attention required to educate children rather than teach to tests . . . Teachers are overtly and covertly encouraged by prevailing cultures and circumstances to enter into a condition of collective indifference.[87]

In addition, teachers and other school staff often feel that insufficient training places them in a position where, despite being inherently involved in the need to accommodate disabled students, they often have little knowledge of how to go about accommodating.[88] Whether due to stereotypical beliefs about disabled children or simply uncertainty as to how to proceed, attitudinal barriers, and particularly resistance to accommodation, can be as great an impediment to inclusion in education as physical barriers.

Henry recalls that he encountered attitudinal barriers early in his educational experiences. He was never placed in a segregated education environment, which he was glad of because inclusion in regular classrooms allowed him to interact with and befriend other students, both with disabilities and without. Due to his mobility restrictions, Henry was accommodated with an EA who assisted him with activities such as note-taking. However, as a child, Henry's family moved a number of times, and he was required to begin again in new school settings with new EAs after each move.

One time, Henry says that he and his family encountered strong resistance from a school principal who Henry feels did not want to allow him to attend the school: "My principal didn't want to let me in, and so he thought that if he made life as hard as possible for me that I would leave."[89] In the circumstances, this meant refusing to hire an EA for Henry, which would have prevented Henry from being able to learn and participate within the classroom. Regardless of the motivations of the principal—whether based in a direct desire to exclude Henry from his institution or a more indirect resistance to accommodation—the result was a substantial physical as well as attitudinal barrier that Henry had to overcome in order to continue his education and see his rights respected. Happily, Henry's mother was able to serve as his EA while the family fought and advocated for accommodation, eventually winning when the principal agreed to hire an EA. However, it is easy to see how a child in a similar position, whose parents could not afford to take the time necessary to serve as an EA or advocate for accommodation, might indeed have been required to give up and leave or might have been irreparably damaged by a long, institutionally constructed exclusion from the classroom.

Lisa also encountered a number of attitudinal barriers during her primary school education and on into high school. Like Henry, she required an EA to assist with the schoolwork and activities her impairment prevented her from doing on her own. Her EA, however, was frequently given other duties by teachers, which prevented her from being able to assist Lisa when she needed it. These other duties included assisting students in English-as-second-language programs and doing laminating and photocopying for teachers. This resulted in a large fight between Lisa's parents and the school:

> My parents understood that there were a few other students who maybe were a little behind and needed her assistance, but what they didn't take kindly to was that instead of helping me, she was busy laminating photographs, and she was busy doing photocopying or this or that instead of assisting me. And it was a big battle not only with the classroom teacher but also the main office for not juggling responsibilities properly because it wasn't fair to me as a young child to have to take responsibilities for things that, based on medical and professional testing, I was not supposed to be doing.[90]

When this initial fight had been resolved, however, it was necessary for Lisa and her parents to continue to advocate repeatedly over the same issue. As Lisa says, the situation would "fluctuate," with the teacher and school withdrawing the additional requests on the EA's time only to replace them again after time had passed. Lisa and her parents were required to constantly return and complain.[91]

What Lisa eventually came to believe was that there was very little interest among most teachers or school staff to listen to what she or her parents had to say about her needs and what was required to accommodate them. While some teachers would admit to her that they did not understand how to accommodate her, she felt that many others were resistant to any need to change and assumed that, because they were professionals and she was a student, they had a better understanding of how to fulfill her needs than she did. She found this to be particularly true as she entered high school:

> They heard the word "accommodation," and they freaked out because they thought, "I'm going to have to change everything. It's going to be really difficult to work around." But if they had a suggestion that didn't work, and I, as a student, tried to tell the teacher, "This doesn't work, I think this is what we need to do," they became very firm in their ground ... So it was a different kind of wall that I was coming up against. It wasn't closed-mindedness. It wasn't "I refuse to budge." It was, as a

student, as somebody who was younger, they wouldn't listen to me. And as a teacher, they kind of thought, "Well, I came up with it, so therefore it's gotta work because I'm a teacher."[92]

As noted above, even teachers who embrace the concept of inclusive education often find the idea of accommodation alarming when applied to their own classrooms because they believe, as Lisa feels her teachers did, that accommodation will require a complete change from the method of teaching they have developed over several years.[93] However, Lisa's story demonstrates a second concern: the paternalistic, professional-knows-best approach taken by some of her high school teachers towards her as a disabled student. While partially based on her age and comparative status as a student, this story may also suggest a tendency among some teachers to adopt the view that they are better positioned than the disabled individual to judge what is good for her or him, a perspective that has long been an issue for disabled people in their interactions with professionals.[94] Attitudinal barriers like this are thus often based on stereotypical presumptions about disabled students—such as that they are dependent and helpless without professional care—even in individuals whose intentions are good and whose feelings about inclusive education are generally positive.

This demonstrates part of what makes attitudinal barriers more difficult to navigate for disabled students than physical barriers: where physical barriers are often the result of carelessness or a lack of thought given to the needs of disabled people, attitudinal barriers reflect views about the individual and the individual's identity as a disabled person that are stereotypical and negative. As Lisa found, accommodations may be harder to secure in a permanent or lasting way when the difficulty to overcome is a perception held by teachers and staff regarding the individual or disabled people in general, leading to the need for repetitive advocacy and the risk of advocacy exhaustion.

In university, Nancy experienced a particularly stark example of this sort of attitudinal barrier. She found highlighting her textbooks to be a particularly physically challenging activity which left her with sore muscles. She approached a staff member of the university about finding a volunteer to assist her:

I was falling way behind, and I was like, "I need help to catch up on this reading," and he basically told me that I wasn't going to get that and then he went on and told me this story about how when he went to school he didn't get everything he wanted either, and I hate it so much when people compare me to other people. It's like, "I'm not that person." Why? It's to compare me to the other students. And I'm like, "I'm not her . . . I'm Nancy."[95]

Attitudinal barriers such as Nancy encountered directly implicate the personal narratives of disabled people because they reflect attempts by school staff to redefine the seeking of accommodations along stereotypical lines. What Nancy saw as fulfilling her needs and asserting her rights, this staff member seemed to have interpreted as laziness or an unwillingness to work as hard as other students. The refusal to accommodate did not only result in Nancy's need for assistance going unfulfilled, it directly questioned her capabilities and worth as a student in comparison to other, perhaps non-disabled, students.

At the same time, however, the deeply personal impact that educational professionals and staff's attitudes bring to accommodation may also be seen in a positive sense as well, in that a single teacher, for example, who approaches accommodation with respect and an interest in learning from the student may have a substantial, and possibly life-long, effect on the individual, his or her feelings about himself or herself, and his or her feelings towards education. Sarah's experience in post-secondary education was one of the most positive experiences in her life, in terms of the approach taken towards accommodation. While she recognizes that the efforts of many people went into this, she credits the attitude of one particular professor for making the difference:

> She is just a dynamo for respecting human dignity, and it is just her absolute commitment everywhere, in every instance, showing respect for human dignity. She has been at that college for a number of years, and it sort of has permeated throughout the college, and that's the way things are handled . . . It wasn't "What are we going to have to do for you?" It was "What can we do for you?" And it was obvious that I was not felt to be a burden, and my disability was not to be a burden for others. The whole atmosphere was "What can we do to help you make your experience more positive, better, and work for you?"[96]

This was a positive and unexpected change for Sarah, who was used to both having to fight for accommodation and having the accommodation process directed towards changing her to fit the institution, rather than changing the institution to fit her. By treating accommodation not as a burden, approaching the need to accommodate proactively rather than reactively, and involving Sarah in the planning of her accommodation, one professor made a tangible difference in Sarah's experience of education, transforming something that could have been exhausting and frustrating into something pleasant and mutually satisfying instead.

Despite Lisa's difficult experiences with the educational system through primary and high school, she nonetheless encountered a few teachers who also stood out and changed her perspective on school and on what she could achieve. In high school, she approached both her English and philosophy teachers in order to talk to them personally about her accommodations and found both willing to admit that they were not well-prepared to design accommodations for her themselves. The key difference between these two teachers and others Lisa had interacted with, however, was that they were also willing to listen to her suggestions and opinions on her needs. Lisa found that their willingness to listen and to give her control over the accommodation process changed her experience of accommodation advocacy, from one which had been about struggle to one which was about collaboration and which did not require her to constantly defend and explain her requirements. This experience had a life-long and far-reaching impact:

> It went a long way in terms of realizing I don't have to be ashamed for the fact that I need help. I don't have to be worried that people are going to judge me, and the fact that I need to do things a little differently doesn't really affect how far I can go. Between the two of them, they kind of taught me that, "Okay, you need help. Does that mean that without help you can't climb a mountain? No." So really, they kind of burst the doors wide open, and they made me realize that as long as I have a passion for something, and I want to do it, and I realize there may be challenges, I can do whatever I want.[97]

Lisa's experience with her English and philosophy teachers thus had greater significance than the immediate result of ensuring she was accommodated. Like Sarah, meeting teachers who approached accommodation positively showed Lisa that accommodation and self-advocacy could take place in a way that did not feel like fighting. It was also the experience that helped Lisa reconcile the fact that she requires assistance at times with her own sense that she was not a dependent or weak person. Because assistance was offered here in a way that did not link it to dependency or inadequacy, Lisa was able to reconcile both parts of herself into a single identity story that made sense to her. The importance of this experience on Lisa's ongoing attitudes toward education and her own identity cannot be overstated. In the future, Lisa aspires to go into teaching in the hopes of playing the same role in the lives of other disabled children and to prevent the sort of attitudinal barriers she experienced from other teachers from reoccurring.

The post-secondary setting

Although many of the observations made by the participants regarding physical and attitudinal barriers carry over to post-secondary education, universities and colleges also represent a unique set of circumstances in which old concerns may become exacerbated and new concerns may arise. In part, this is because the move from secondary to post-secondary education can result in major changes to both the life situations of disabled students[98] and the methods they have developed for navigating educational systems and securing necessary supports.[99] While efforts to expand post-secondary educational opportunities for students in many countries have led to rising levels of participation in university and college programs across the globe, disabled students still have lower rates of retention and graduation from post-secondary institutions than their non-disabled peers.[100]

Organizationally, post-secondary education is a very different institution from primary and secondary schools, both generally and in how universities and colleges have developed their approaches to accommodation. Primary schools and high schools in countries such as Canada and the United States have largely adopted individual education planning, often after gentle nudging by legislation, which requires students, parents and educators to meet annually to assess and discuss the needs of the student and what accommodations will need to be in place within the school and classroom.[101] Post-secondary institutions, however, have generally not adopted this approach,[102] instead relying on institutional policies, which can vary widely in content from school to school; specialized accommodation co-ordinators and offices, and the faculty itself to ensure that disabled students are accommodated and supported.[103] The result is that accommodation in post-secondary institutions often becomes fractured. While accommodations may be arranged with the accommodations office, implementation on the campus and in the classroom requires the student to secure individual co-operation from a wide variety of faculty and administrators, not all of whom are necessarily aware of their legislative responsibilities or even their own institution's policies on disability accommodation.[104] The result, thus, is an increase in the number of times a student must advocate to ensure both the approval of and then implementation of accommodations. This situation can become even more complex when the issue that needs to be accommodated or altered is not a general feature of the school but something specific to the classroom or instruction practices of particular professors who are often caught off-guard by or resistant to the suggestion that their teaching might be inaccessible.[105]

All of this takes place within a situation of increased independence for the student, a reality which can be both daunting and freeing. With variable class times, longer periods of unsupervised study and work, and a much smaller role for parents in securing accommodations,[106] post-secondary education can be a shock to the system for disabled students who have become proficient at navigating the barriers of the primary and secondary school environments and now find themselves dropped into a significantly different situation. For some of the participants, the impact of this change in environment was immediate and largely positive. Andrea, who had found her high school to be very supportive and accommodating towards her through its provision of a physical support unit, nonetheless found that she enjoyed the independence of university more because it was not something she had not experienced in high school where there was always an EA around to assist her. She also found the social environment to be more accepting: "I have not encountered one person who was, like, stand-off-ish or not willing to talk . . . It's very nice not to be questioned all the time, where you don't sort of have to answer for yourself, you know?"[107] Henry expressed a similar sentiment regarding his own feeling that the university environment did not place the same pressure on him to prove that he deserved to be there as other educational situations had.[108] Both Andrea and Henry felt that they were not regarded as abnormal within the university setting, as they had sometimes felt when they were younger. Because they had been judged and admitted to the school on the same standards as other students, whether non-disabled or disabled, this served as proof that they belonged and removed the sense that their presence was constantly under question.

Mary also experienced a positive change in the transition to post-secondary education, which may specifically highlight the important role that accommodation offices and co-ordinators can play. She had attended adult high school in her thirties and struggled with writing the final exams. The requirement that she write by hand for long periods of time without breaks caused her hands to become too sore to continue writing. Although the school was aware of her impairment and its effects, the possibility of accommodations during test-writing, such as being able to write on a computer, was never raised with her, and Mary assumed, as a result, that the school was resistant to providing that form of accommodation. When she entered college, however, a number of test-taking accommodations were provided for her by the college's accommodation co-ordinators, and the effects of being appropriately accommodated were striking: "[In late high school,] I would end up failing or getting low grades. So I went from a C student in high school to an A student in college when I was getting accommodations, like longer time to do exams and, you know, the ability to do it on computer."[109] While staff and teachers in primary and secondary schools may become familiar with certain accommodation possibilities due to interactions with disabled students, post-secondary accommodation offices and staff are far better equipped to spot where issues may arise and to work with individuals to ensure that they are aware of the accommodations available and receive those they need.

Despite the generally positive view of post-secondary education held by the participants, however, attitudinal and physical barriers remain within modern university and college institutions. Faculty reluctance to accommodate or lack of awareness regarding the requirement to accommodate remained a substantial issue for many. Tracy, who, in addition to her mobility impairment, also experiences some difficulty hearing, found that one of her teachers in college refused to wear the device she needed to hear during class and seemed unaware that accommodating her disability was required by both the institution and the law:

> He wouldn't wear this. He refused to wear it. It took a month and a half of me chasing him around and finally sitting there and saying, "Look, under the Accessibility for Ontarians with Disabilities Act, this is an accommodation under the law." I had to read him the riot act on it. And he still tries to screw around with it. I got told by someone in my division, "Don't you dare take this to the [accommodations co-ordinator]. It

will be very bad for you at the College." How do I protect myself from something like that?[110]

In Tracy's experience, even though the school itself may be more accessible and accommodations more readily provided than in secondary education, staff and faculty outside the accommodation office often do not understand or respond well to requests for accommodation. As most university services are provided by offices outside the accommodation office, this means that the need to advocate remains as pressing and frustrating in post-secondary education as in all other educational institutions. Tracy discovered that she could often not ensure that an accommodation such as a classroom change was actually implemented, despite support from the accommodations office, unless she first threatened the college with legal action.

Tracy also experienced difficulty with the in-class arrangements of some professors, which often reflected what was most convenient for the professor or the majority of students and failed to take into account the needs of students with specific types of impairments. These sorts of arrangements could include restrictions on eating and drinking during class or skipping the mandated break time in long lectures to end class early instead. For Tracy and a number of other students in her classes, these arrangements presented particularly difficult problems to circumvent:

> Some instructors get right cranky if you're eating in the classroom and you've got a coffee cup . . . I went back to college, and I went from completely managing my blood sugar levels – I'm hypoglycaemic – managing my levels and being able to step out for a bite whenever. If I'm like, "My sugar's taken a plunge, I need to go grab something," I can't do that. Or I have to get up and leave class and miss lecture and get a teacher getting cranky at me for getting up and disrupting class, even though it's on my accommodation sheet: "For medical reasons, I may have to leave the class suddenly."[111]

Tracy's experiences with reluctant or oblivious instructors are extreme but not unusual, and her frustration at having to constantly resort to threats of legal action are even more common. As noted, the arrangement of university and college accommodation processes to be reactive rather than proactive place Tracy, and others in similar situations, in a position where she must be adversarial towards people who hold power over her ultimate success in her program. As Hibbs and Pothier note:

> In the accommodation policy, power is seen to be reasonably balanced by the process of accommodation: the documentation requirements purportedly take discretion regarding the nature of the accommodation out of the hands of the instructor and balance it against the opportunity for the student to have a role in suggesting appropriate accommodations.

But how can there ever be a genuine balance of power when the student is ultimately dependent on the professor as evaluator? How can there ever be a genuine balance of power between an individual student and a university bureaucracy, especially a resistant one?[112]

Without advocacy, Tracy is concerned that she will be placed in a position where she is unable to perform to the full extent of her capabilities but, with advocacy, she may earn retributive action from an instructor or the institution generally. This is a particularly stark example of how advocacy within the educational system can be a double-edged tool. The institutional arrangement of post-secondary schools relies on advocacy to replace the default assumption that accommodation is unnecessary;[113] however, these same arrangements can operate, directly and indirectly, to convince disabled students not to advocate, even when they recognize that their rights have been ignored and their personal sense of fairness offended.

The implications of segregated summer camps

The debate over segregation versus inclusion has not been limited to academic education alone. Summer camps have proven another arena in which the need to determine what best serves the needs of disabled children has played out. Like physical education, sport and nature-based educational programs,[114] summer camps present additional obstacles for proponents of inclusion due to perceptions that these sorts of activities require greater costs, time, staffing and accessibility measures to allow the participation of disabled children.[115] There also continue to be widely held beliefs that camp activities, particularly outdoor activities, may be beyond the abilities of many disabled children and may present safety risks.[116] A social model approach to summer camps, however, draws into question these perceptions. As Nadia von Benzon observes in relation to outdoor leisure activities, "None of the barriers . . . are direct results of impairment but rather products of social reactions, or non-reactions, to impairment which lead to stigma, exclusion, inappropriate facilities or resources and environmental barriers to access."[117]

Nonetheless, the debate surrounding summer camp experiences for disabled children often centres around physical ability and whether inclusive or segregated summer camps are better positioned to allow disabled children to feel "normal" and accepted. As in general education, the argument in favour of inclusive summer camps rests on the idea that all children have a right to participate as equals in regular camps and camp activities and that accommodations must be put in place where impairments disrupt the ability to participate.[118] This accords with von Benzon's view that, even in the supposedly less accessible realm of outdoor activities, many barriers are caused by facility design and lack of accommodation rather than being inherent and immutable elements of the activities themselves.[119]

Unlike the general educational sphere, however, inclusion has not achieved the same wide acceptance as a governing principle in relation to summer camps. Strong proponents of the segregated camp experience continue to argue that such camps are not only necessary to allow disabled children to participate in camp activities they would otherwise be excluded from but segregated camps are also important to provide a space in which disabled children can relax and not feel subject to scrutiny or competition.[120] This argument is premised on the often-true belief that so-called inclusive camps are, in practical terms, camps for non-disabled children which disabled children are allowed to attend. These few inclusive camps[121] often reflect a more general trend in physical education programming. Inclusion in these instances generally means attempting to fit disabled children into physical education programs designed for non-disabled children; when impairments disrupt the ability to fit, disabled children are segregated into specialized activities within the so-called inclusive setting to allow non-disabled children to continue with the planned program.[122]

The advantages of segregated summer camps were voiced by many of the participants, even those, like Lisa, who otherwise strongly believed in and advocated for their right to inclusion within mainstream classrooms. For Lisa, the experience at segregated summer camp was not comparable to other life situations, in which she expected and would fight for inclusion, for two primary reasons. First, she did not see the choice as being one between segregated summer camp and inclusive summer camp but rather between segregated summer camp and no summer camp at all. Second, rather than approaching summer camp as another sphere in which to advocate for herself, Lisa seemed to feel that summer camp was an opportunity to take a break from the constant need to re-prove her rights:

> I liked it mainly because it was ten days where you could check all your baggage at the door and not really have to care, and the biggest worry that you had was what they were making for dinner because it did not matter how involved you were or weren't or how independent you were or weren't. Everybody was equal and had the same opportunities to do the same activities. It was just completely accepting and very free.[123]

Lisa enjoyed the camp because she felt that she was seen for herself, without stereotypes distorting the perceptions of those around her, and, as a result, was treated with respect and in a way that accorded with her perception of herself.

Nancy similarly found segregated summer camps to be a rewarding experience. Having attended segregated summer camp from the age of seven to 19, she describes these times as some of the best experiences of her life.[124] For her, their greatest value lay in providing an accessible environment with accommodations already built in to allow disabled children to participate in activities they otherwise would not have been able to. Her favourite activity was sailing in a flat-bottomed pontoon boat which had been equipped with a ramp to allow children in wheelchairs to wheel on and off. She also recalls, however, that a wide range of activities were available, including some that did not seem possible or safe at first glance:

> They implemented – I'm not sure why I never did this – but they implemented a program where you could actually go white-water rafting. They were taking children with special needs in the raft, and my mom was like, "Are you crazy? Kids that don't have very much balance, and they are taking them on rafts?" They're like, "Oh yeah, we're in the boat with them. We hold onto them." But a lot of kids did it, and they loved it.[125]

While the experiences of participants who attended segregated summer camps were mostly positive, others voiced some reservations about them. Andrea, for example, had been unable to attend segregated summer camp because her condition required specific training to accommodate. The general accommodations available at the camps were targeted largely at providing accessibility for individuals with mobility impairments and did not provide the sort of care services that Andrea's impairment required.[126] This echoes one of the criticisms raised regarding segregated summer camps, which often espouse social model ideas but operate and plan their accommodations around medical model diagnostic generalizations, assuming that all or most disabled campers will have "identical needs, interests, and abilities; they are looked on as mechanized robots from an assembly line."[127]

Michael also never attended segregated summer camps or any other form of summer camp. Until he turned 16 and began working through the summer, Michael spent his breaks from school with friends around his home. Like Lisa, he seems to operate under the assumption that the only summer camp experience that would have been available to him would be within a segregated camp. Though he says he never wanted to go to a summer camp, he seems to have conflicted feelings on the topic. On the one hand, he recalls that he was reluctant to put himself in a position where the greater needs of other campers might become limitations on him as well. On the other, however, he seems to regret, at least slightly, the missed opportunity to form friendships with other disabled people:

> It's hard to say. I want people at my level, so if I'm with someone that would need more or that requires more dependence than I would, it's like, "Why can't you do it?" You know? So at that age, it was like, "No, I'm me. That's all I need." I preferred friends with – That are just, to a certain case, normal, that didn't have any disability. Then it pretty much screws you over to a certain extent because they are not as good friends as you could have made with people with a disability 'cause they are like you, they know what you went through, and stuff like that. It kind of screwed me over, but that's okay.[128]

This seems to suggest that Michael felt that a crucial piece of his identity—his experiences with disability—was not fully understood by the friends he spent time with during his childhood summers. But while he recognized that other disabled children might be better positioned to understand those experiences, he was still reluctant to form friendships with them out of the sense that it could compromise other elements of his personal identity that he valued, notably his independence.

Michael is not the only participant to have raised this concern. A number of the participants who had attended segregated summer camps noted that they often had difficulty identifying with the other campers. While Nancy was able to make at least one lifelong friendship at camp,[129] individuals like Lisa and Tom found that they related better to their often non-disabled counsellors.[130] In particular, Tom found that he was sometimes asked to take on quasi-counsellor roles of entertaining and leading the other campers. Henry, who also attended and enjoyed segregated summer camp, explained that from his perspective the lack of connection between himself and other campers was often intellectual. Though he felt he had to attend segregated summer camp to receive the attendant care he required, his needs and interests were often not the same as the other campers around him:

> In terms of intellectual level, I found that sometimes . . . I found it challenging to relate to some of the campers that attended, but I still found it amazing to go to camp with some of these people. They're all such amazing individuals once you got to know them, and these camps gave you an opportunity to see their true capabilities. And also, just on a side note, because I couldn't really relate to the campers that also gave me the ability to relate more so to many of the camp counsellors. Because of my intellectual level, the counsellors felt that they knew that they could talk to me on a normal level because I was a young adult and often times, I was pretty close in age to many of the camp counsellors.[131]

Again, this illustrates the difficulty that segregated camps, like other educational institutions, may encounter when they assume that disabled children will form a common community simply by virtue of having a disability, regardless of the realities of their individual impairments and individual experiences. While Henry's approach to feeling disconnected from some of his fellow campers is ultimately more optimistic than Michael's, both nonetheless reflect a desire to be seen for themselves and their own abilities rather than to be grouped together with others in a single, generalized category.

Proponents of segregated camps argue that responses such as Michael's and Henry's demonstrate another reason to support segregated camp experiences. The desire to avoid other disabled individuals or to heavily identify with non-disabled peers has been noted as one response that many young disabled people have when they internalize negative constructions of disability identity.[132] Segregation proponents argue, as in relation to education generally, that participation in spaces intended only for disabled people reduces this reaction and promotes a sense of community amongst disabled people.[133] As Tom, Lisa and Henry's accounts show, however, this is frequently not the case in segregated summer camps, especially where the majority of counsellors are non-disabled people.

This view of segregated summer camps also accepts as inalterable the present state of inclusive camps. Like other physical education programs, summer camps have yet to be problematized in the same way or to the degree that other inaccessible services have. The current arrangement of mainstream summer camps is accepted as the necessary or only means of organizing such programs. When disabled children are included it is in programs that are not designed with their needs in mind and supervised by staff who have likely not received training regarding the needs of disabled campers. Although individuals like Lisa might describe positively the break from constant advocacy that a segregated camp represents, it is difficult to tell if these attitudes would remain the same if inclusive camps were viewed as genuine alternatives. At the moment, choosing to participate in inclusive summer camps and other forms of inclusive outdoor and physical education is rarely truly inclusive. Despite policies aimed at promoting inclusion in physical education curricula, more often disabled children and their parents must choose between segregation or segregation within a supposedly inclusive setting, where disabled children are shunted into programs and activities that are viewed as being lesser value by the children, their supervisors, and their peers.

Conclusion

This chapter has examined how participants have exercised their advocacy skills and developed their advocacy identities in response to the gaps and failings in the law's ability to address barriers in education. We note the immense sense of pride that many of the participants take in their educational accomplishments and the impact this has on their perception of educational failures to accommodate, which can seem more daunting or can provide an even greater motivation for advocacy efforts depending on the individual participant's own perspectives on advocacy and experiences in attempting to self-advocate for accommodation. We began by looking at the legal context in which disabled individuals must seek educational accommodation in Canada, the United States, and the United Kingdom, including the increasingly common presumption in favour of inclusive, rather than segregated, education. While all three of these legal milieus have seen great advancements in the development of accommodation law within the past decades, they still leave significant issues unaddressed and lack applicability to many of the practical problems faced by disabled students.

This is amply demonstrated within the narratives of our participants. To this end, we considered both the physical and attitudinal barriers faced by our participants as they transitioned from elementary school to high school and lastly to post-secondary education. We explored how both positive and negative experiences with seeking accommodation affected their views of education and the process of seeking accommodation as a whole. Lastly, we considered the special case of summer camps, which continue to buck the trend toward inclusivity demonstrated in more traditional educational institutions. However, we also explored how this was not seen as something to be challenged by the majority of the participants. Instead, summer camps were generally seen as spaces in which the participants could vacation from the otherwise everyday needs for advocacy. As we see further in Chapter 4 and issues relating to employment, this is an approach the participants rarely took to other areas of their lives.

Notes

1 Lisa, personal interview, 2007–08, p. 24.
2 T. Parsons, 'The School Class as a Social System: Some of Its Functions in American Society' *Harvard Educational Review*, 1959, vol. 29, pp. 297–318 at p. 297.
3 D.J. Connor and B.A. Ferri, 'The Conflict Within: Resistance to Inclusion and Other Paradoxes in Special Education' *Disability & Society*, 2007, vol. 22, pp. 63–77 at p. 64.
4 D. Lipsky and A. Gartner, 'Inclusion, School Restructuring, and the Remaking of American Society' *Harvard Educational Review*, 1996, vol. 66, pp. 762–96 at p. 763.
5 L. Pfhal and J.J.W. Powell, 'Legitimating School Segregation: The Special Education Profession and the Discourse of Learning Disability in Germany' *Disability & Society*, 2011, vol. 26, pp. 449–62.
6 Pfhal and Powell, ibid, pp. 449–62.
7 F. Polat, 'Inclusion in Education: A Step towards Social Justice' *International Journal of Educational Development*, 2011, vol. 31, pp. 50–58.
8 L. Barton, 'Inclusive Education: Romantic, Subversive or Realistic?' *International Journal of Inclusive Education*, 1997, vol. 1, pp. 231–42 at p. 235.
9 Lipsky and Gartner, op. cit., n. 4, p. 766.
10 In the Canadian federal system, education falls under the constitutional powers of the provinces.
11 P. Burge *et al.*, 'A Quarter Century of Inclusive Education for Children with Intellectual Disabilities in Ontario: Public Perceptions' *Canadian Journal of Educational Administration and Policy*, 2008, vol. 87, pp. 1–18 at p. 4.
12 Burge *et al.*, ibid, pp. 4–5.
13 *Eaton v Brant County Board of Education, Supreme Courts Report*, 1997, vol. 1, p. 241 at para. 57.
14 *Eaton*, ibid, at para. 79.
15 Ontario Ministry of Education, *Standards for School Boards' Special Education Plans*, Toronto: Queen's Printer for Ontario, 2000, p. 10.
16 *Moore v British Columbia (Education)*, 2012 SCC 61.
17 Lipsky and Gartner, op. cit., n. 4, p. 777.
18 Lipsky and Gartner, op. cit., n. 4, pp. 769–70. As Lipsky and Gartner note, however, this presumption has come under criticism for legitimating some restrictive/segregated classrooms, focusing too heavily on the physical elements of classroom accessibility, and assuming that many specialized services can only be provided in segregated classrooms.
19 Lipsky and Gartner, op. cit., n. 4, p. 775.
20 S. Riddell, T. Tinklin and A. Wilson, 'New Labour, Social Justice and Disabled

Students in Higher Education' *British Educational Research Journal*, 2005, vol. 31, pp. 623–43 and p. 626.

21   Riddell, Tinklin and Wilson, ibid, p. 627.

22   M. Madriaga, 'Enduring Disablism: Students with Dyslexia and their Pathways into UK Higher Education and Beyond' *Disability and Society*, 2007, vol. 22, pp. 399–412 at p. 399.

23   Riddell, Tinklin and Wilson, op. cit., n. 20, p. 628.

24   Madriaga, op. cit., n. 22.

25   Madriaga, op. cit., n. 22, p. 400.

26   Polat, op. cit., n. 7, p. 50.

27   W. Dunn, 'Best Practice Philosophy for Community Services for Children and Families' in W. Dunn (ed.) *Best Practice Occupational Therapy in Community Service for Children and Families*, Thorofare, NJ: SLACK, Inc., 2000, p. 1 at 4.

28   Dunn, ibid. See also N. Hansen, 'Spaces of Education: Finding a Place That Fits' *Review of Disability Studies*, 2005, vol. 1, pp. 22–36.

29   K. Tomasevski, *Human Rights Obligations in Education: The 4-A Scheme*, Netherlands: Wolf Legal Publisher, 2006.

30   Dunn, op. cit., n. 27.

31   H. Menzies and M.A. Falvey, 'Inclusion of Students with Disabilities in General Education' in T.C. Jiménez and V.L. Graf (eds) *Education for All: Critical Issues in the Education of Children and Youth with Disabilities*, San Francisco, CA: Jossey-Bass, 2008, p. 73.

32   Menzies and Falvey, ibid, p. 73.

33   R. Malhotra and R. Hansen, 'The United Nations *Convention on the Rights of Persons with Disabilities* and Its Implications for the Equality Rights of Canadians with Disabilities: the Case of Education' *Windsor Yearbook of Access to Justice*, 2011, vol. 29, pp. 73–106 at pp. 73–74.

34   Malhotra and Hansen, ibid, p. 82.

35   Convention on the Rights of Persons with Disabilities, 30 March 2007, 2515 UNTS 3, art. 24(2)(b) [CRPD]. At the same time, the CRPD also recognizes that in specific, limited circumstances, segregated education may be beneficial for some children; it highlights education for children who are blind or deaf as instances in which separate education may be appropriate (Malhotra and Hansen, op. cit., n. 34, p. 82).

36   J. McGuire, S. Scott and S. Shaw, 'Universal Design and Its Applications in Educational Environments' *Remedial and Special Education*, 2006, vol. 27, pp. 166–75 at p. 167.

37   P. Silver, A. Bourke and K.C. Strehorn, 'Universal Instructional Design in Higher Education: An Approach of Inclusion' *Equity & Excellence in Education*, 1998, vol. 31, pp. 47–51.

38   Silver, Bourke and Strehorn, ibid, p. 48.

39   Silver, Bourke and Strehorn, op. cit., n. 37, p. 48.

40   McGuire, Scott and Shaw, op. cit., n. 36.

41   Silver, Bourke and Strehorn, op. cit., n. 37, p. 47.

42   S. Gibson, 'Beyond a "Culture of Silence": Inclusive Education and the Liberation of "Voice"' *Disability & Society*, 2006, vol. 21, pp. 316–17.

43   J.P. Hall, 'Narrowing the Breach: Can Disability Culture and Full Educational Inclusion Be Reconciled?' *Journal of Disability Policy Studies*, 2002, vol. 13, pp. 144–52 at p. 148.

44   Pull-out classes are programs in which a child spends the majority of time in an inclusive classroom but will be occasionally "pulled out" to receive some education and assistance in segregated environments.

45   R. Colker, 'The Disability Integration Presumption: Thirty Years Later' *University of Pennsylvania Law Review*, 2006, vol. 154, pp. 789–862 at p. 796. See the rebuttal

by Mark Weber: M.C. Weber, 'A Nuanced Approach to the Disability Integration Presumption' *University of Pennsylvania Law Review Pennumbra*, 2007, vol. 156, pp. 174–87 (defending integration where it is done well).

46 Hall, op. cit., n. 43, p. 147.

47 Hall, op. cit., n. 43, p. 149.

48 Tom, personal interview, 2007–08, p. 1.

49 Lisa, p. 2.

50 Lipsky and Gartner, op. cit., n. 4, p. 773.

51 See e.g. *Eaton*, above, n. 13; *Greer v Rome City School* 950 F. 2d.

52 Connor and Ferri, op. cit., n. 3, p. 63 (commenting on the impact that parental lobbying had on the 1975 passage of the "Education of All Handicapped Children Act" in the United States).

53 Lisa, pp. 2–3.

54 D.J. Connor, *Urban Narratives—Portraits in Progress: Life at the Intersections of Learning Disability, Race & Social Class*, New York, NY: Peter Lang, 2008, pp. 26–28 (commenting on the documentation in American literature of how working class African American children are more likely to be classified as having intellectual disabilities and placed in segregated classrooms than middle class white children with similar learning issues).

55 Connor and Ferri, op. cit., n. 3, p. 71.

56 Nancy, personal interview, 2007–08, p. 1.

57 Nancy, p. 2.

58 Nancy, p. 2.

59 Barton, op. cit., n. 8, p. 231.

60 Nancy, p. 5.

61 Colker, op. cit., n. 45, p. 797.

62 Gibson, op. cit., n. 42, p. 322.

63 Michael, personal interview, 2007–08, p. 16.

64 Focus Group 2, Focus Group Interview, 2008, p. 4.

65 S. Field, M.D. Sarver and S.F. Shaw, 'Self-Determination: A Key to Success in Postsecondary Education for Students with Learning Disabilities' *Remedial and Special Education*, 2003, vol. 24, pp. 339–49 at p. 346.

66 See e.g. L. Blumberg, 'Public Stripping' in B. Shaw (ed.) *The Ragged Edge: The Disability Experience from the Pages of the First Fifteen Years of the Disability Rag*, Louisville, KY: Advocado Press, 1994, pp. 73–77; C. Frazee, J. Gilmour and R. Mykituk, 'Now You See Her, Now You Don't: How Law Shapes Disabled Women's Experiences of Exposure, Surveillance, and Assessment in the Clinical Encounter' in D. Pothier and R. Devlin (eds) *Critical Disability Theory: Essays in Philosophy, Politics, Policy and Law*, Vancouver: University of British Columbia Press, 2006, pp. 223–47.

67 Lisa, p. 24. This also underscores the social relations and profoundly political choices, such as enforcing a walking test, that underpin physical barriers. For a powerful theoretical account of physical barriers including the political decision to require cumbersome keys in accessible elevators, see R. Gorman, *Class Consciousness, Disability and Social Exclusion: A Relational/Reflexive Analysis of Disability Culture*, PhD Dissertation, Toronto: University of Toronto, pp. 98–102.

68 Nancy, p. 30.

69 Cheryl, personal interview, 2007–08, pp. 6–7.

70 Tracy, personal interview, 2007–08, pp. 11–12.

71 U. Sharma *et al.*, 'Impact of Training on Pre-Service Teachers' Attitudes and Concerns about Inclusive Education and Sentiments about Persons with Disabilities' *Disability & Society*, 2008, vol. 23, pp. 773–85.

72 Gibson, op. cit., n. 42, p. 322.

73 T. Hibbs and D. Pothier, 'Post-Secondary Education and Disabled Students: Mining

a Level Playing Field or Playing in a Minefield?' in D. Pothier and R. Devlin (eds) *Critical Disability Theory: Essays in Philosophy, Politics, Policy and Law*, Vancouver: University of British Columbia Press, 2006, p. 197.

74 P. Vickerman and M. Blundell, 'Hearing the Voices of Disabled Students in Higher Education' *Disability & Society*, 2010, vol. 25, p. 30.

75 Hibbs and Pothier, op. cit., n. 73, p. 197.

76 Hibbs and Pothier, op. cit., n. 73, pp. 196–97.

77 Henry, Personal Interview, 2007–08, p. 41.

78 Lisa, p. 26.

79 Michael, p. 1.

80 Michael, p. 10.

81 Sharma *et al.*, op. cit., n. 71, pp. 779–81.

82 Sharma *et al.*, op. cit., n. 71, p. 773.

83 Sharma *et al.*, op. cit., n. 71, p. 773.

84 J. Campbell, L. Gilmore and M. Cuskelly, 'Changing Student Teachers' Attitudes towards Disability and Inclusion' *Journal of Intellectual & Developmental Disability*, 2003, vol. 28, pp. 369–79 at p. 370.

85 Campbell, Gilmore and Cuskelly, ibid.

86 Campbell, Gilmore and Cuskelly, op. cit., n. 84.

87 R. Slee, *The Irregular School: Exclusion, Schooling and Inclusive Education*, London: Routledge, 2011, pp. 86–87.

88 Campbell, Gilmore and Cuskelly, op. cit., n. 84, p. 371. It should be noted that this situation has improved over the years, thanks to a greater emphasis on disability studies within teacher training; however, studies consistently note that even teachers who advocate on behalf of students with disabilities display a tendency to rely on negative imagery related to disability and the medicalization and individualization of disability issues in doing so (A.A. Broderick, D.K. Reid and J.W. Valle, 'Disability Studies in Education and the Practical Concerns of Teachers' in S. Danforth and S.L. Gabel (eds) *Vital Questions Facing Disability Studies in Education*, New York, NY: Peter Lang, 2006, p. 157).

89 Henry, p. 2.

90 Lisa, p. 4.

91 Lisa, p. 5.

92 Lisa, p. 15.

93 Campbell, Gilmore and Cuskelly, op. cit., n. 84, p. 370.

94 R. Wood, 'Care of Disabled People' in G. Dalley (ed.) *Disability and Social Policy*, London: Policy Studies Institute, 1991, p. 200.

95 Nancy, p. 13.

96 Sarah, personal interview, 2007–08, p. 14.

97 Lisa, p. 29.

98 J. Goode, '"Managing" Disability: Early Experiences of University Students with Disabilities' *Disability & Society*, 2007, vol. 22, pp. 40–41.

99 Field, Sarver and Shaw, op. cit., n. 65, p. 340.

100 A. Katsiyannis *et al.*, 'Postsecondary Education for Individuals with Disabilities: Legal and Practice Considerations' *Journal of Disability Policy Studies*, 2009, vol. 20, pp. 35–36.

101 Field, Sarver and Shaw, op. cit., n. 65, p. 340. While the participants certainly recognized that this process led schools to institute appropriate accommodations, such as EAs, they were often critical of individual education plans, noting that it was often a highly bureaucratic process that did not equip the classroom teacher themselves with the necessary knowledge or skills to accommodate in the classroom and that the need to re-prove the same needs annually to secure the same accommodation for a new school year was often a frustrating, invasive and exhausting process.

102 Field, Sarver and Shaw, op. cit., n. 65, p. 340.
103 Hibbs and Pothier, op. cit., n. 73, p. 197; Field, Sarver and Shaw, op. cit., n. 65, p. 340.
104 Katsiyannis *et al.*, op. cit., n. 100, p. 36.
105 S.B. Thomas, 'College Students and Disability Law' *The Journal of Special Education*, 2000, vol. 33, p. 248.
106 Field, Sarver and Shaw, op. cit., n. 65, p. 340.
107 Andrea, p. 5.
108 Henry, p. 17.
109 Mary, personal interview, 2007–08, p. 9.
110 Tracy, p. 15.
111 Focus Group 1, Focus Group Interview, 2008, p. 3.
112 Hibbs and Pothier, op. cit., n. 73, p. 200.
113 Hibbs and Pothier, op. cit., n. 73, p. 199.
114 J.E. Lord and M.A. Stein, 'Social Rights and the Relational Value of the Rights to Participate in Sport, Recreation, and Play' *Boston University International Law Journal*, 2009, vol. 27, pp. 251–52; N. von Benzon, 'Moving on from Ramps? The Utility of the Social Model of Disability for Facilitating Experiences of Nature for Disabled Children' *Disability & Society*, 2010, vol. 25, pp. 622–23.
115 von Benzon, ibid.
116 von Benzon, op. cit., n. 114.
117 von Benzon, op. cit., n. 114, p. 618.
118 D.L. Goodwin and K. Staples, 'The Meaning of Summer Camp Experiences to Youths with Disabilities' *Adapted Physical Activity Quarterly*, 2005, vol. 22, pp. 160–78 at p. 161.
119 von Benzon, op. cit., n. 114, pp. 622–23.
120 A.J. Withers, *Disability Politics and Theory*, Halifax: Fernwood Publishing, 2012, p. 75.
121 Goodwin and Staples report that in 2005 only approximately 40 out of 200 camps in Ontario requested a listing on the Integrated Camp List. Goodwin and Staples, op. cit., n. 118.
122 A. Smith, 'Disability and Inclusion Policy Towards Physical Education and Youth Sport' in H. Fitzgerald (ed.) *Disability and Youth Sport*, London: Routledge, 2009, p. 32.
123 Lisa, p. 29.
124 Nancy, p. 8.
125 Nancy, p. 8.
126 Andrea, p. 5.
127 Information and Research Utilization Center in Physical Education and Recreation for the Handicapped, *Involving Impaired, Disabled and Handicapped Persons in Regular Camp Programs*, Washington, DC: American Alliance for Health, Physical Education, and Recreation, 1976, p. 7.
128 Michael, p. 6.
129 Nancy, p. 9.
130 Lisa, p. 29; Tom, p. 6.
131 Focus Group 2, p. 24.
132 Goodwin and Staples, op. cit., n. 118, pp. 161–62.
133 Goodwin and Staples, op. cit., n. 118, p. 162.

4   Employment barriers

When Mary attempted to use a job counsellor to obtain employment, she found that her counsellor lacked the requisite knowledge about how her impairments periodically affected her energy level and prevented her from consistently being able to work full-time. The counsellor also expressed skepticism that Mary was sincere about the impact that her impairments had on her:

> The counsellor didn't treat me like there was anything wrong. Because she works with [people on welfare], so she is sort of used to working with people, but I think because she saw me as healthy she's pushing for full-time. And one of the things she said is oh, you've been working with kids for 30 years. Do you want to go work with young ones again? I said no I don't. I said I don't want to baby-sit anymore. Well why not? I said, because I don't have the energy or the patience anymore for them. She says: Oh come on. What's the big deal? I've got a job here for someone to do crafts with the young ones. And so I stopped and said well, I don't want it. And she said, well, it's only preschoolers. When she asked me why, I said, if I remember clearly she had a ten or 11 year old daughter right now, I said, do you forget how much energy a four or five year old takes? They are just a bundle of energy. I don't have that energy anymore. I would love to. Eventually I hope to have at least some of it back, but not right now I don't.[1]

Mary continued to struggle to obtain suitable employment in light of her impairments.

Employment constitutes a core part of most people's identities and contributes to one's sense of citizenship, self-fulfillment and community.[2] Despite the fact that a large majority of participants in our study were under the age of 24 and all were students, the individuals interviewed reported a wide range of employment and volunteer experiences. As we explore in this chapter, the advocacy identity developed in challenging barriers in the educational system may well prove to be useful and effective in securing employment. At the same time, the more explicit goal of productivity and profitability expected by many employers poses significant and different challenges to disabled job applicants who are often perceived, rightly or wrongly, as inefficient and a burden. This chapter explores how despite the fact that Canadian human rights law mandates that employers provide accommodation for disabled workers up to the point of undue hardship, the lived reality is often a world of obstacles and red tape that makes securing employment difficult and the risk of a life on welfare a very real one. This must be situated against the background reality that a large majority of disabled people in Western countries, particularly those with severe impairments, do not participate in the labour market and are more likely to live in poverty than their able-bodied counterparts.[3] Yet survey data also clearly indicates that disabled people want to enter the labour market[4] and statisticians point to labour market shortages in many countries as the Baby Boom generation retires.[5]

In recent years, one has seen the emergence of a transformative set of public policies throughout the Western industrialized countries that may collectively be characterized as neo-liberalism or globalization and constitutes one framework for understanding the experiences of the participants. Neo-liberalism entails a shift away from well-remunerated full-time employment to flexible employment standards where employees typically have more autonomy but are also poorly paid and work longer hours; part-time work with few or no benefits is also commonplace, frequently in sectors of the economy that have been dominated by women.[6] While this set of policies is occasionally mistakenly regarded as a withdrawal of the State in economic intervention or deregulation, it might be more accurately regarded as reregulation: a transformation of the role of the State from one focused on economic redistribution to one that is focused on facilitating profitability through contract enforcement and the protection of property rights.[7] They also feature an attempt to reduce reliance of all groups, including disabled people, on welfare wherever possible.[8] Neo-liberalism has also seen a growth in income inequality and declining unionization rates.[9] While flexible employment presents both genuine opportunities and challenges for disabled workers, we suggest that the experiences of our participants are cause for worry as the economic well-being of disabled workers may suffer in the more flexible New Economy.

Including disabled people in the labour market

With the rise of industrial capitalism and a shift away from agriculture to factory based production, workers were increasingly judged on their ability to conform to set standards of agility, defined body movements, speed and co-ordination.[10] While disabled workers might well have been productive in slower-paced agricultural settings,[11] the rigorous requirements of factory production in frequently squalid conditions for brutally long hours so eloquently described by Marx in Volume 1 of *Capital* often precluded the participation of many disabled people in the urban, industrial labour market.[12] Simultaneously, an array of workhouses, asylums and institutions arose in which workers who could not conform to workplace standards were increasingly institutionalized as the Enlightenment encouraged both a positive movement away from demonizing disabled people as divine punishment and a negative tendency to use scientific rationality to classify and distinguish various kinds of impairments.[13] Ironically, one of the reasons why asylums were regarded as especially efficient by policymakers is because unpaid patient labour offset the costs of running them.[14]

Conditions in the workhouses and asylums were typically extremely oppressive.[15] The English Poor Law Amendment Act 1834 marked an attempt to create a modern competitive labour market by regulating a distinction between those disabled people who were expected to work and those deemed to be a burden and consequently entitled to charity because of the severity of their impairments. This distinction, which could be altered depending on changing socioeconomic conditions, continued to be a foundational concept in the construction of welfare programs for disabled people in Canada, the United States and Britain. Physicians have emerged as gatekeepers to welfare programs and disability pensions by using the medical model to determine who is or is not eligible for a disability pension.[16] This underscores the capricious dimension to defining disability as disablement rates vary widely among Western countries depending on the level of benefits provided, the manner in which impairments are assessed and the character of regulations governing alternative programs such as unemployment insurance.[17] Workers in the nineteenth century responded to these harsh conditions in a variety of ways, including the formation of fraternal societies to promote financial security through insurance premiums that would generate income benefits if a worker became injured or died. In Victorian Ontario, fraternal societies formed to offer compensation for workers who experienced workplace injuries at a time when workplace injuries were growing in a rapidly industrializing economy. However, the original impulse of solidarity became bureaucratized over time as significant numbers of prospective members were rejected to ensure the financial viability of the fraternal society. The fraternal societies were caught between a commitment to helping their fellow workers and using invasive medical testing to exclude those who might have pre-existing conditions.[18]

A central intellectual legacy of the nineteenth century is the idea that the market is a self-regulating mechanism as distinguished from the public sphere of governmental regulation. Accordingly, contract law and property law were regarded as the core of the system, while other areas of legal doctrine, such as family law, were deemed marginal because they were based primarily on statutory interpretation rather than the interpretation of case law and precedent.[19] This had the effect of justifying massive differences in wealth and power because the market was regarded as efficiently allocating resources through contract and property law in a scientific manner.[20] In the context of disablement, this encouraged the belief that the built environment and workplace rules such as work schedules and dress codes are natural. Disabled workers were expected to adapt to the job as it existed or face exclusion even where the rule might arbitrarily preclude employment of a physically or mentally disabled person who requires, for instance, a more flexible schedule due to transportation barriers or periodic breaks due to a mental health concern.[21] In many Western countries, sheltered workshops, which tragically continue to this day, were established by statute that paid sub-minimum wages to disabled people who were regarded as incapable of competitive employment to perform monotonous tasks such as stuffing envelopes.[22] Employing as many as 500,000 employees across 17 European countries as recently as the mid-1990s,[23] these have been widely criticized by disability rights advocates who see them as degrading and exploitative, especially because they rarely innovate over time since they have no economic incentive to do so. Consequently, the employees are typically not provided with new job skills over time.[24]

Spurred by returning and often politicized disabled veterans at the end of the two World Wars and the Vietnam War in the United States, a disability rights movement has coalesced and has fought for the development of vocational rehabilitation programs, labour market integration and dignity for disabled workers to perform fairly remunerated work with accommodations. This has taken the form of political lobbying, education and, at times, demonstrations and civil disobedience.[25] Although the trade union movement has been historically slow to embrace disability rights, trade unions in Canada, the United States and Britain have increasingly established committees and conferences that periodically discuss issues of concern to disabled workers.[26] A number of policies have been contemplated or proposed, including the provision of appropriate accommodations, tax credits, wage subsidies and the adoption of employment equity or work preferences for disabled job applicants in both the public and private sector.[27]

As we discussed in Chapter 2, in Canada, disability discrimination is prohibited by section 15 of the Charter of Rights and Freedoms,[28] Canada's constitutional document which applies to government, and by the human rights codes of the various provinces and territories which govern both the public and private sector and are accorded quasi-constitutional status in Canadian law.[29] Disability discrimination in employment is typically the most common form of disability discrimination alleged before provincial human rights commissions.[30] There is a duty on the part of employers to accommodate workers with disabilities up to the point of undue hardship using its best efforts.[31] In federal government employment, preference or equity for candidates with disabilities also applies.[32] The Canadian definition of disability in the employment context is extremely broad. It encompasses physical, learning, sensory and psychiatric conditions, whether permanent or temporary. It may also include perceived impairments that have no impact whatsoever on the employee's ability to perform the job.[33] While accommodation generally does not require an employer to create a new job, employers are expected to modify existing positions or assign a disabled employee to perform another job and provide the appropriate accommodations.[34]

In the landmark case, *Meiorin*, the Supreme Court of Canada examined the duty to accommodate in the context of gender discrimination and clarified the scope of the duty to accommodate where an employer claims that a workplace rule constitutes a *bona fide* occupational requirement.[35] A British Columbia firefighter who had been employed for a number of years, Tawney Meiorin, was laid off after she failed an aerobics test that required all firefighters to run 2.5 kilometers. Her union grieved this before an arbitrator who concluded that the vast majority of women were not physically capable of meeting this standard even after training and that such a requirement was not essential to perform safely as a firefighter.[36] Consequently, the grievance was upheld and Ms Meiorin's reinstatement was ordered. The arbitrator concluded that Ms Meiorin's human rights under the British Columbia Human Rights Code had been violated.[37] The British Columbia Court of Appeal reversed this decision because of the safety implications and because the grievor had been granted individual testing.[38]

On appeal to the Supreme Court of Canada, the Court, in a judgment by Justice McLachlin, as she then was, restored the arbitrator's decision for the grievor in a decision that embraces some key elements of social model thinking. The decision created a unified three-part test for evaluating workplace standards and thereby eliminated what was previously an arbitrary distinction between adverse effect and direct discrimination.[39] The first branch of the new test asks whether the standard was adopted for a purpose rationally connected to job performance. The second branch asks whether the employer adopted the standard in an honest and good faith belief that it was necessary for the fulfillment of that purpose. The third branch asks whether the employer can demonstrate that the standard is reasonably necessary to achieve the work-related purpose.[40] In meeting the third branch of the test, the employer must show that it is impossible to accommodate the employees with the characteristic of the claimant challenging the standard.[41] While litigated in the context of gender discrimination, the *Meiorin* test has been instrumental in allowing disabled workers and other equality seeking groups to challenge workplace standards that have the potential to create barriers for disabled workers.

Although there is no specific disability anti-discrimination statute in Canada at the federal level, the province of Ontario has adopted such a statute. Inspired by the ADA,[42] the Accessibility for Ontarians with Disabilities Act (AODA), 2005 was enacted in 2005 and includes standards on many disability rights issues including employment.[43] However, it will be some years before most of the regulations with respect to employment take effect and so it is far too early to judge its impact.

In the United States, Title I of the ADA prohibits employment discrimination by both public and private entities against disabled people whose impairments substantially limit them in one or more major life activity, have a record of impairment or are regarded as having an impairment.[44] It builds on section 504 of the Rehabilitation Act of 1973 which prohibits employment discrimination by entities receiving federal financial assistance.[45] It provides a duty to reasonably accommodate disabled people up to the point of undue hardship.[46] Some common examples of accommodations mandated by the ADA include altering existing facilities to make them accessible, job restructuring, introducing modified work schedules, reassignment to a vacant position, the acquisition or modification of equipment or devices, supplying qualified readers or interpreters, or other similar accommodations.[47]

One major difference between the United States and Canada is the fact that the original version of the Act was interpreted by American courts very narrowly, excluding large numbers of disabled Americans from ADA coverage because they were deemed not to be substantially limited in major life activities or because they failed to qualify after mitigating measures were considered.[48] Under the mitigating measures doctrine, a disabled person was judged by their physical state after they had used corrective measures such as eyeglasses, medications or prosthetics. This led to absurd results: many disabled people, including people with very serious health conditions, who obviously both required accommodations in the workplace and faced stigma by potential employers, were excluded from the Act's protection.[49] Disabled litigants under the ADA have also had a very poor success rate.[50] Congress amended the ADA in 2008 to make clear its intent that the law apply to disabled people without reference to the mitigating measures rule and to have the "substantially limited" definition applied more flexibly by the regulatory agency, the Equal Employment Opportunity Commission, charged with drafting such regulations. It also indicated that disabled people who had episodic conditions that fluctuated from day to day would be covered.[51] This brings ADA jurisprudence more closely in alignment with social model principles. Although job preferences for the federal sphere are mandated by section 501 of the Rehabilitation Act, Weber has cautioned that the lower courts often confuse affirmative action principles with a mere duty to accommodate.[52]

In Britain, the Equality Act 2010 (EqA) consolidates and expands upon rights accorded to disabled workers in the Disability Discrimination Act 1995 (DDA).[53] Sections 20 to 22 require reasonable adjustments and a failure to do so results in a finding of unlawful discrimination.[54] However, Lawson has criticized the narrow definition of disability contained in the EqA. The new legislation retains a rigid requirement from the DDA that an impairment must have a substantial and long term effect on day to day activities in order to qualify as a disability.[55] The concept of indirect discrimination in disability discrimination is also clarified in the EqA.[56] This was necessary because of a formalist 2008 House of Lords' decision concerning housing discrimination in *Lewisham v Malcolm*[57] that required the claimant to base legal arguments using a comparator group consisting of able-bodied people, making it much more difficult to demonstrate discrimination, and because of concerns regarding compliance with the European Equality Directive.[58] Indirect discrimination challenges neutral provisions, criteria and practices that have discriminatory effects and is analogous to what is known as adverse effect discrimination in other jurisdictions such as Canada.[59] This holds out hope that future cases will more vigorously challenge the structural dimensions of disability discrimination.

The same tensions surrounding inclusion that we identified in Chapter 3 in the context of education may be identified and analyzed in debates with respect to the inclusion of disabled people in employment. Policymakers prioritize the provision of vocational rehabilitation services to train disabled people to enter the labour market in order to become financially independent. The focus is accordingly on preparing the disabled person to hone her or his skills to better suit the existing labour market. Yet there may be no employment available after repeated attempts at vocational training and the disabled person is then deemed a failure and consigned to a life on social assistance.[60] More radical proponents of universal design, on the other hand, recognize that workplace practises need to be systematically altered to eliminate barriers that arbitrarily hold back disabled people from achieving their full potential.[61] An even more radical position is articulated by Taylor who cogently questions the notion of valuing disabled people for their ability to work when many disabled people outside the labour market make valuable contributions in a myriad of ways such as through volunteering, art and political activism.[62] One notable difference between the education and employment spheres is that it is generally acknowledged throughout the West that education of children, whether in segregated or inclusive settings, is provided to all citizens as a matter of right.[63] The notion of employment as a citizenship right, however, has been severely attenuated with the rise of a market society in recent years and the abandonment of the welfare state. Mass unemployment is now accepted as the new norm and competition for jobs is the default mechanism.[64] We begin our discussion of inclusion by contrasting the experiences of Nancy in fighting for suitable access to a workplace placement so that she can satisfy requirements in an educational program to graduate with Sarah's experiences in attempting to maintain her employment after a physical injury.

Nancy provides one dramatic illustration of barriers to inclusion in a workplace placement she did as a requirement for her studies in early childhood education:

> I was flourishing, I was doing great. But as part of the curriculum, you have to do placement in daycares . . . and they wanted to put me in the daycare on campus, but when I went to view the daycare it was just too small, it wasn't safe for me or the children to be there because once my wheelchair gets in the classroom it just wasn't safe. And so I approached them about it. I said, you know, can I find another placement in the community that's bigger and that's safer, that's more accommodating. And they basically gave me this song and dance about who do you think you are, no one gets to pick their own placement, why do you think that you should be any different . . .[65]

In this workplace placement, a commitment to formal equality, treating everyone alike, led to absurd consequences for Nancy, who simply could not fit her wheelchair into the tiny workspace not designed for wheelchair users. Consequently, inclusion was not achieved. Physical barriers in the day care were certainly a problem for a wheelchair user such as Nancy. Just as importantly, the attitudinal barriers created by the staff who were openly hostile to Nancy's participation demoralized her.

Yet this was by no means the only barrier Nancy experienced in her placement. Her school continued to block accommodations that Nancy required to succeed, such as the provision of a teaching assistant and assistance to find an accessible placement notwithstanding the fact that Nancy was one of the very few participants in our sample to consult legal counsel and bring formal legal complaints about the school officials' allegedly discriminatory treatment in her placement.[66] Given that such placements, although certainly a form of work, are typically requirements for graduation from many academic programs, this is particularly troubling, especially as the school employed placement co-ordinators whose very job description was to place students in workplace settings.[67] Moreover, Nancy was deprived of the practical work experience that is highly desired by employers and supposed to facilitate a transition to full-time permanent employment. Frustrated by the numerous barriers, Nancy quit her studies and transferred schools.[68] This raises questions about the limits of advocacy and the utility of an advocacy identity. As we noted in Chapter 3, Nancy does not regard herself as an advocate. She nevertheless in fact took more confrontational steps in challenging barriers than many other participants. It may well be that the experience of past discrimination proves more useful in honing the skills necessary to advocate for the accessibility and services one needs than fostering an explicit identity as an advocate.

Even where physicians have specifically indicated that a disabled person may not engage in certain physical tasks, it is not necessarily the case that the employer will comply, creating barriers that may not only preclude access to employment but force workers who acquire disabilities to leave the labour force. Sarah, one of the older participants who acquired a disability at the age of 29, experienced a motor vehicle accident which left her in a coma for days and with serious permanent physical impairments while she was still recuperating from a hysterectomy she had before the accident. Employed in the military as an office manager with more than a dozen people reporting to her, she noted how her employer required her to perform in ways that dangerously exacerbated her disability:

> I was posted and got to another base and got some quality PT (physical training) but by then most of the damage had been done and it was really quite too late, and then they mis-employed me and made me do things that were beyond my physical capabilities and did more damage to my foot and ankle, so I was left with instead of a mild disability, a slight you

know, limp maybe or whatever which, and eventual arthritis down the road, I had immediate osteoporosis and osteoarthritis and limited ability to the point where now I have maybe five percent in one direction only up and down, nothing sideways.[69]

Articulating a sentiment that would be echoed by other participants, Sarah comments that she would be more productive if employers appreciated that she must have periodic breaks when she gets up and walks around; she is physically unable to sit still without enduring pain that limits her ability to concentrate.[70] She stresses that if she is forced to do something that is beyond her physical capabilities due to an employer's inflexibility, it may take her days to recover.[71] Therefore, she emphasizes the importance of educating employers about the needs of disabled workers.

This underscores the fact that for many disabled people with significant impairments, managing both the disabilities and the impairment effects[72] that may result can be an exhausting task that constitutes another job in itself. Andrea comments:

> I think what really helps me to sort of get it across to some people is I say "taking care of myself, imagine you working at whatever job you do now and then having a second job on top of that. My second job is my body." It just takes that much to maintain and when I go home after work or class I go to my second job because I have to take care of myself, I have to eat the special foods that I eat, I have to take my medications, I have to do other treatments that I have to do. So it's a second job and most people, they go "oh geez, wow, I can't imagine having a second job." And I say "well, there you go." I don't have any choice . . .[73]

For both Andrea and Sarah, managing the medical professionals they consult in order to maintain a decent quality of life while trying to work is an enormous and time consuming challenge.

Nevertheless, struggling to meet the requirement of 20 years of service that would entitle her to a disability pension by staying on the job and facing an inhospitable workplace environment that was unaccommodating, Sarah felt that she had no choice but to risk her health by running and participating in parades to avoid being discharged without a pension even though her physicians had specifically advised her against such physical activities in light of her injuries.[74] Despite her willingness to comply with dangerous requests by her employer, Sarah still faced enormous roadblocks in securing the disability pension to which she was entitled. She situates it in the context of Canadian troops stationed in Afghanistan who will return with injuries that require accommodations:

> I should tell you I had to fight for four years to the highest level to get my pension, my veteran's pension, and the only way I got it was the

fact that they misemployed me. And so veterans are having to fight and go through legal battles to get a pension for injuries they receive, and I only get a small pension because they only admit to a small portion of responsibility for my injury. And that is something that to me is wrong, that is a backwards mindset, because if you had done what you were required to do, and especially for these people coming back from Afghanistan it should be automatic that they get the treatment that they need, that they get psychological treatment, they get physical medical treatment and that they get their needs taken care of from then on. It's just a responsibility I think that the country has for them. I don't get any medical help. I don't get any dental help, I don't get any help other than the pension, my stipend every month, and this rehabilitation program to help me back to work but I get nothing out of them as far as . . . other than chiropractic and massage therapy that's it, that's the only thing that, any kind of supplementary, holistic healthcare that I am entitled to, and that's wrong.[75]

While this workplace is unusually rigid and inflexible and subject to a unique legal framework in which Canadian military personnel are expected to be physically fit regardless of their role,[76] this underscores the vulnerability of many disabled people who fear that they will be forced into poverty if they lose their current employment. It is in turn reinforced by broader neo-liberal trends that are tightening access to disability pensions, medical services and welfare payments more broadly even as injured soldiers returning from conflicts such as Afghanistan require rehabilitation services.[77] Yet again, poor attitudes toward disabled workers play a role. Sarah initially faced barriers because of inflexible pension policies that will not allow her to terminate her military service earlier without a financial penalty. However, this was clearly compounded by the inflexible application of regulations by administrative decision-makers who in fact frequently have significant discretion in how pensions are awarded.[78] Despite not being particularly oriented toward disability activism or an advocacy identity as she had only recently acquired impairments, the dire situation she found herself in forced her into action. These narratives complicate the idea that a strong disability identity or a history of activism is a prerequisite for effective lobbying for disability rights. In some cases, the situation simply compels a person to engage in advocacy. At the same time, Sarah's years of work experience in the military entitled her to a disability pension that most participants in our study, having been born with disabilities, would never be entitled.[79]

Another aspect well worth considering is how disabled people are often made to feel by employers that they are burdens, especially when, like Sarah, they are already in a position which commonly does not employ disabled people. Disability scholars have commented how social attitudes and economic pressures can make disabled employees struggling to obtain accommodations feel like burdens. The burden narrative has a negative and degrading effect on both those who explicitly identify as disability rights advocates who are trying to transform the workplace and those who simply want the dignity and economic independence associated with paid employment.[80] Unlike some other participants, Sarah is less explicitly political about broad disability rights struggles but she still clearly rejects the disability burden narrative:

> Interviewer: To be called an administrative burden, when you are so emotionally traumatized, what was that like, I know that's probably the word they needed to use, but that's not what you need to hear?
>
> Sarah: No no. It's not and when you're getting, at least this was happening all at the same time. I was having trouble fighting my weight, they were telling me I was becoming an administrative burden because I was overweight they, my lawyer was trying to construct a case that seemed to me totally unrelated to me and my issues and my truth, and I couldn't take this anymore. Chuck this far away, I'm out of here.[81]

Sarah's alienation from the construction of the case and the narrative of her life as articulated by her lawyer is not uncommon and serves as another layer of oppression for her to navigate.[82] As Sarah was battling her inflexible employer over accommodations, she simultaneously was forced to sue her mother, the driver of the car in which she was a passenger, to secure financial compensation from the insurance company for the motor vehicle accident.[83] She describes this dark period of her life as one marked by sporadic depression and heavy drinking.[84] Like Nancy, Sarah was one of the very few in our sample to have direct experiences with lawyers as she attempted to win compensation, and she found the experience emotionally exhausting:

> every couple of weeks I'd be getting a letter from him wanting this information, wanting me to do this you know I had to go through, and you know I had to get the military hospital to account for every single hospital visit, to go through all my documents, to go through all my records, go through every physio visit, every hospital visit every doctor's visit every specialist, everything, every single second of my time that was spent not at work on this medical issue and so needless to say no one was happy with me, and I was experiencing a lot of personal difficulty, a lot of deep emotional difficulty and loneliness and really deep depression and you know I had never experienced that before.[85]

This minute regulation and surveillance of every aspect of Sarah's medical experiences is reminiscent of Lisa's walking test, described in Chapter 3, and is particularly striking because not only is every aspect of Sarah's impairment thoroughly documented but Sarah is herself conscripted in documenting her own body to the satisfaction of legal authorities.[86]

Work and globalization

As we noted in the introduction to this chapter, the changing nature of work is also having a significant impact on inclusion and the provision of accommodations. Approximately one-third of working age employees in Canada are in non-standard employment such as part-time work, multiple jobs, self-employment and temporary contract positions.[87] These jobs may well be regarded as precarious and exploitative positions. Wilton has observed how employers may be reluctant to provide accommodations for what they know is a short-term, part-time position with high turnover as a replacement may be easily secured.[88] As employment counselors face greater pressure to place individuals in jobs, commitment to fully accommodating a person is sometimes lost. In the case of Mary, quoted in the opening to this chapter, this resulted in pressure to accept a full-time job offer even though Mary has fibromyalgia, a condition that can sporadically flare up from time to time, which makes such work almost impossible for some.[89] Faced with depression, learning disabilities, a nervous breakdown she experienced at the age of 25 and her physical impairments, Mary was at the time of the initial interview 42 years old and largely unemployed for the last 15 years.[90] She observes how prospective retail employers would be open to hiring her when she initially walked into the store but when her fibromyalgia required her to take breaks, they would object to both the length of the break and simple accommodations, such as allowing her to use a stool while serving customers.[91] Mary tries to secure employment with the assistance of an employment counselor but is stymied by both physical barriers and attitudinal barriers. This is particularly true because, unlike many other participants in this book, Mary's impairments are mostly invisible, leading skeptical employers and even, as documented above, her employment counselor to misunderstand the complexity of her accommodation needs and her abilities because she appears healthy on the surface.[92] Mary's experience also highlights how, as corporations increasingly focus on maximizing productivity to ensure competitiveness, many jobs, particularly service sector positions, are subject to increasingly rigorous speed up and the satisfaction of customer preferences that cannot readily accommodate employees who may require breaks.[93] Yet in a focus group, Mary is adamant that she cannot work more than ten hours per week at her exhausting housekeeping and elder care jobs without aggravating her fibromyalgia.[94]

Tracy echoes many of the sentiments expressed by Mary. An older participant with a job waiting for her while she recovered from her accident and post-traumatic stress disorder, she nevertheless observes that after her injury, she faced hostility and harassment from one manager who was unwilling to make the necessary adaptations for Tracy to thrive. She notes how he used safety regulations as an excuse to avoid accommodation:

> . . . this guy was looking for a way to get rid of me and I was really glad to be pulled out of that group and get into a more positive situation. But

this guy would throw up road blocks left, right and centre. The insurance company provided me a scooter to get back and forth to work, so I'm [not] burning myself out. It's only a few blocks, but I'd rather not be all sweaty and burnt out from wheeling the four blocks each way. Well, he got it so that due to fire code, (I couldn't get the scooter in the door of my office, so I'd have to leave it out in the hallway) . . . I would have to leave it out in the foyer even though I'm down at the end of the hallway and it can go up against the window and there's no traffic there, nobody's going to be tripping over it. He got it so that the fire code put it so that that was the absolute letter of the law, nothing is allowed to be out in the hallway period even if it's not in a traffic area. I would have to leave it at the desk. So I brought my hospital chair and left it behind the desk and then I would wheel down and then hop the chair through the doorway. Well, that became an issue because I was scraping the doorframe and I was damaging the building. He brought stuff against me that I was damaging company property.[95]

Andrea also felt that she was harassed on the job because of her disability. Her manager did not believe that she was capable of working and kept assigning her extra tasks requiring overtime so that he could prove she was incompetent even though she, like many of our participants, required part-time employment as an accommodation while she simultaneously attended school.[96] While her workplace situation significantly improved once a new manager arrived, she highlights how she feels trapped between two unrealistic extremes which both reinforce ableism: employers who wrongly assume a disabled employee is completely unproductive and employers who unfairly insist on treating disabled employees identically to their able-bodied counterparts, without recognition of the need for legally mandated accommodations that would enable productivity.[97] In Andrea's case, this can be as simple as giving her the break she needs to take medication she requires to prevent pain.[98] Weber has documented disability harassment in the United States in a variety of contexts. Interestingly, in some cases, work colleagues harass disabled men by referring to them as women and challenging their masculinity, consequently reinforcing how both disabled people and women have historically been associated with dependency, emotional behaviour and immaturity.[99] As we discuss in Chapter 6, this places disabled women in the workplace in a particularly precarious position as it becomes challenging to defy stereotypes.

One effective way of challenging the power of employers is to unionize the workplace in order to redress the power imbalance and obtain equitable working conditions for workers. Although Canadian unions have historically had an ambivalent relationship to the struggles of disabled people despite the prominence of injured workers amongst their routine grievances, some disabled people have become union activists.[100] Tom was one of the few participants in our study to be an active union member as a result of his paid part-time position at his educational institution advocating for disabled students. Although he was unable to serve on the union local's bargaining team because of his multiple activist commitments, he clearly conveyed his passion and dedication to trade unionism:

> I was offered a position on the bargaining team, I turned it down largely because I have so many other things to do. And I said that whoever is on the bargaining team should be devoted a lot more to it than I could devote to the bargaining team. That and a position on the bargaining team would mean that my relationship between the . . . executive, all of whom I am very good friends with through various walks of life, would be significantly changed. And I wasn't comfortable . . . because I'll be working with these people all year, because if I was on the bargaining team and things went sour, [support for disabled students] could suffer or the student association could suffer, so I politely declined a role on the bargaining team. But I am definitely a supporter of the union, and will continue to be involved, will attend all union meetings from now on.[101]

When asked about a recent strike of support workers that occurred on Tom's campus, he expressed strong support for the striking workers, even though this affected both disability supports provided to disabled students and even transportation as unionized bus drivers would not enter the campus in solidarity with the strikers, leaving students to traverse a large distance. Tom remarks:

> There were definitely implications with regards to accessibility . . . the buses weren't allowed to come on campus so they had to stop [off campus], and then of course the big one, the [administration disability office staff] was part of [the local] who went on strike so they were not operating at full capacity or any capacity really . . . So there were definitely some implications. But having said that I was absolutely 110% behind the union, I said that this administration needed to start paying its staff. I was a supporter of what they were fighting for and eventually after a very painful two weeks a lot of me rolling the picket line, yelling out random cheers that we came up with at 2 am, you know we ended it. It was also big for us at the students association because we of course went on strike in solidarity, we closed our offices . . . in solidarity with that.[102]

Tom is one of the most passionate of the participants interviewed about disability rights and improving accessibility. His identity in many ways centres on his commitment to empowering disabled people in the world. It is who he is. Yet this interest in a disability identity also facilitates his passion for other social justice issues such as collective bargaining.

Volunteer work

Another dimension that warrants close attention is attempts by disabled people to volunteer. Particularly for younger adults with comparatively little work experience, who constitute the majority of our sample, volunteering provides an important way to gain experience that may later prove valuable for obtaining paid employment in terms of generating both contacts and skills. Volunteering allows people outside the labour market to increase their social capital by developing networks that may give them access to the hidden job market where many workers are hired for unadvertised positions. In some cases, the network itself may prove to be a desirable quality that makes a candidate desirable for an employer as it gives the employer access to potential customers or cultural groups to which it may not readily have access.[103] The skills used to address barriers encountered in volunteering may also be transferable to advocacy in a workplace situation. If disabled people face major barriers in volunteering, this may discourage paid labour market attachment. For others, volunteering may also be an end in itself that allows the volunteer to flourish and demonstrate her abilities. It has been suggested that volunteering is associated with a higher quality of life and increased mental and physical health.[104] At the same time, some scholars have warned that disabled people may be identified for an endless treadmill of volunteering as a training program which does not ultimately lead to paid employment.[105]

For Andrea, volunteering was in itself rewarding rather than a deliberate stepping stone for employment networking. She volunteered by assisting with crafts and other activities at a day camp operated by the paediatric hospital for disabled children where she was treated as a youth.[106] She also volunteered annually at a writers' camp for children where she was paired with an author whom she assisted with presentations.[107]

Cheryl too finds satisfaction in volunteering because of how it improves her sense of self-worth:

> I love helping people out. It really brings me joy to be able to help out. I'm probably one of those people that derives a certain amount of self worth, it's how I help society by volunteering because I really enjoy doing it. It makes me happy. And I really like having something to do in my spare time.[108]

Perhaps not surprisingly, for many of the participants, volunteering with disability organizations or paediatric rehabilitation hospitals that had assisted them in their own youth was often the focus or at the very least a part of their volunteer experiences. Cheryl recounts:

> I have done work on the [paediatric hospital] youth forum which was a once a month thing, which was when we talked about how to make . . . the children's hospital, more accessible to 13–18 year olds, how to make

it more youth friendly because it's really geared towards the younger children. And sometimes the really bright colours and fuzzy things really irritates teenagers. So we implemented different changes. We got them to change their menu for the inpatients so that way the inpatients . . . the older patients could get food that they might actually enjoy.[109]

Cheryl even answered telephones at a telethon to raise money for her paediatric hospital.[110] Clearly, Cheryl found this to be consistent with her conception of promoting the quality of life for disabled people. This is notable as telethons, particularly in past years, have been sharply criticized by many disability rights advocates for promoting pity and degrading portrayals of disabled people while promoting a sense of community.[111]

Lisa describes her volunteer work for her paediatric rehabilitation hospital as follows:

> But when I was at [the paediatric hospital] and I was their ambassador, I would go to the fundraisers they would host and different events that they would put on in order to bring awareness about the Centre. So I went to black tie dinners, I went to media junkets, I went to all kinds of different things, it was me and a boy actually who I went to preschool with so it was kind of fun to go with a guy I went to school with as a very young child. We're now seeing each other as 12 and 13 at all these different junkets and even when our year was up and they got different current ambassadors, a lot of the past ambassadors are invited to attend so I was attending these things from about the age of 11 or 12 all the way up to 16.[112]

She also noted with pride her volunteer work in training elementary school teachers on effective strategies to provide disabled students with accommodations by recounting her own barriers and successes.[113] It is easy to see how this kind of volunteering could foster an advocacy identity and help Lisa advocate in the future.

In some cases, however, the link with developing skills was more direct. Charles also spoke to corporate sponsors on behalf of the summer camp he attended for disabled children and believes that it enhanced his leadership abilities. He comments:

> I went to a leadership development camp that was sponsored by [redacted] not this previous summer but the summer before so preceding it. The program was called leaders of tomorrow, the camp was located in [redacted]. So that, it was a two day experience in August I believe which ultimately strove to well improve my personal leadership abilities and also to meet with other adolescents who had other similar disabilities to mine. However, after that weekend I was then obliged to participate in various speaking events for [redacted] over the duration of the next two

years, I guess this is . . . my second year of affiliation with the organization so to speak.[114]

Remarkably, despite Andrea's firm rejection of a disability identity, she also volunteered her time to give talks for her paediatric hospital on a variety of issues including the transition to adulthood, employment and training staff to more effectively serve their disabled clients.[115] Similarly, Nancy, who also largely rejected a disability identity, volunteered at disabled summer camps and a student-run centre focused on raising disability awareness at her university as well as in elementary schools.[116] This underscores the situational context of how identity may manifest. Although Andrea and Nancy reject embracing disability identity as a source of pride, they still find a sense of accomplishment in volunteering to benefit disabled people in the right context.

One important observation is that a recent policy change in Ontario, where most of our participants attended high school, requires all students to complete 40 hours of volunteer work in order to graduate from high school.[117] Engel and Munger documented how the passage of the ADA affected some disabled Americans who themselves had engaged in no litigation whatsoever in transforming their self-understanding, rendering them more confident and willing to advocate for their rights in contexts such as employment.[118] Similarly, the discursive shift that was fostered by the compulsory volunteer policy effectively mandated accessible volunteering opportunities. This was noted repeatedly by participants as one reason for volunteer activity, suggesting that the policy change, although enacted for pedagogical reasons completely unrelated to disability rights, may have had the inadvertent effect of making organizations that seek volunteers more accessible as well as leading to paid job opportunities.

Lisa described how her volunteer work required for high school graduation, at a camp for children with acquired brain injuries, led to paid summer employment as a counselor at the camp and "a glowing reference letter."[119] At the same time, she notes that barriers with accessible transportation for wheelchair users such as her made it challenging for her to engage in volunteer and other extracurricular activities.[120] Henry fulfilled the requirement for 40 hours by volunteering after school at a flu shot clinic, again apparently in part because of the convenience of work that could be completed at school itself.[121] Charles completed his volunteer requirement by working at a small second-hand bookstore where he stocked shelves and effectively ran the store on his own. He reported that he experienced no disability-related barriers from either the management or with respect to harassment from customers.[122] It is important to acknowledge these positive experiences. At the same time, this must be understood in the context of participants who have all been relatively successful in terms of educational attainment. It is quite conceivable that the impact of a volunteer experience would be less significant for a disabled person who chose not to pursue post-secondary education and needed to rely on that experience to secure a full-time job on a long-term basis.

In Chapter 3, we noted how socioeconomic class might affect accommodations in the educational context.[123] In some cases, well-connected families may be able to provide volunteer opportunities for their adult children that might not otherwise be available. This proved to be the case for some participants. Henry reports how he volunteered in an election campaign for a candidate who was a family friend.[124] He comments:

> I volunteered in the last federal election, I volunteered a lot at, for a guy who is running as a Liberal in [redacted]. I volunteer at his campaign office because he's a family friend. And I enjoyed that a lot, and politics is one of my passions. I was just loving that opportunity.[125]

Similarly, Lisa's mother's job as a nurse enabled her to use connections to find the volunteer position for Lisa at the camp for children with acquired brain injuries described above.[126] These examples highlight how social capital is not only increased through volunteering but a family's social capital may increase volunteering opportunities.

Social assistance

A very significant proportion of participants in our sample were in receipt of social assistance payments specifically designed for disabled people. The attitudes toward it varied widely among our participants. For some participants, it was more akin to extra spending money while essential expenses were covered by family members. Henry observes:

> Yeah, I am [receiving social assistance], and that honestly has been amazing, and I really don't, I mean I understand why I'm getting it and all that, and it's great for a lot of people, but for me, I don't, I find that I could live without it. Just because it's nice to have the extra money lying around, but I don't really get why, cause my parents cover so many of my expenses, like my tuition, and other stuff that you know, it's essentially giving me money for being me.[127]

In Henry's case, the social assistance funding is largely directed toward the hiring of attendants, which allows Henry to have a higher quality of life.[128] It seemed to have little effect on his self-conception as Henry seems perfectly happy to accept financial assistance from his family, who are able to generously provide for Henry's needs.

In other cases, however, participants either struggled to have a good quality of life because of the low level of payment or recognized that they would struggle but for the assistance they receive from family. They also seemed very aware of the stigma it carries for many and struggled to follow the complex array of rules required to receive social assistance. Cheryl observed:

my only complaint is that [social assistance] doesn't exactly make it easy to pay for your education because they won't allow you to have over five thousand dollars in your possession at any given time or else they will cut your . . . the money they give you. So it makes it really hard to pay for your education. It also makes it fairly difficult to get a job while you're on [social assistance] because if you're making above a certain amount of money they start taking away the money that they give you. So [social assistance] is not. I don't think it's supposed to be meant as a full-time for the rest of your life sort of thing, it's supposed to be meant as a way to get you through until you can find good employment. Which is what I plan on doing. I don't plan on being on [social assistance] forever. I couldn't LIVE on [social assistance] forever! But for right now it works because I'm a student, but for paying off my education it's a little bit of a pain in the butt![129]

For Nancy, however, the concerns are not hypothetical but immediate. Her family was not in a position to assist financially and so the social assistance payments were her lifeline. Unfortunately, they were so meagre that they left her with no money to spend on any kind of extracurricular activities after paying her essential expenses, making it very difficult for her to enjoy life on a daily basis. This in turn affected her emotional well-being, seriously impacting her academic performance.[130] She comments:

I get so much a month, and that's what covers me for the month, and once it's gone, it's gone. You know, I have no other source of income. So right now it costs me, for this room it costs me $1097 a month, because that includes my meal plan and my rent, and so my whole cheque goes to the school, so it leaves me with no other means of income.[131]

In Nancy's case, interlocking barriers make her life more difficult. While an able-bodied person in financial difficulty could easily choose to live in a cheaper apartment off-campus, Nancy requires attendant services for assistance with activities daily living that are provided in her university's dormitory. Consequently, she effectively has no option but to pay the higher rent on campus because of the chronically long waiting lists and bureaucracy for apartments which offer attendant services.[132]

Some participants pointed out how the seemingly inconsistent governance of social assistance in Ontario has led to arbitrary outcomes. As in the case of entitlement to a disability pension discussed earlier in this chapter, this underscores the discretion that bureaucratic actors have in implementing social welfare regimes.[133] Mary noted how she discovered through a friend that the welfare authorities were holding a workshop on how to access free bus passes, but had only invited selected recipients. As a result, she was able to save a significant amount of money but would not have even been aware of the program's existence had she not been informed by her friend of the workshop.[134] This also underlines the power of those who work in the professions relating to social welfare provision whose smallest actions can have an enormous impact on the lives of disabled people who rely on timely and accurate information on available services in order to make informed choices. The very manner in which services are provided creates dependency on the part of disabled social assistance recipients who risk alienating staff, and their entitlement to benefits, should they be regarded as difficult clients.[135] In other cases, the very rules contained in the social assistance program have a perverse effect of discouraging excellence. Tom notes how he had won a number of prestigious scholarships but withdrew from one because the scholarships income was collectively too high, making him ineligible for social assistance at a time when his parents had several other children who also required parental financial assistance with post-secondary education.[136] This also speaks to the particular challenges that large families face where one child has a disability.

Conclusion

We have shown in this chapter that an advocacy identity plays an important role in shaping employment outcomes for our participants. We began with a brief survey of the history of disability discrimination in the labour market and how the rise of capitalism facilitated the classification of disabled people into categories of profitability and efficiency. We then provided a brief synopsis of the state of the law relating to the employment of disabled people in Canada, the United States and Britain. We highlighted the advocacy experiences of Sarah's accommodations as a woman serving in the military who acquires impairments and Nancy's attempts to secure an accessible environment for her work placement. We then analyzed how our participants are coping with the dramatic changes to the labour market that have become widespread in recent years, marking a paradigm shift from full-time employment with benefits to a world where low-paid part-time employment is increasingly common. Mary and Tracy's labour market experiences vividly convey some of the stresses that disabled people face in a labour market where there is enormous pressure to increase hourly productivity. We concluded this chapter with a discussion of the experience of participants with volunteering and as recipients of social assistance. We now turn in Chapter 5 to explore the experience of our participants in accessing transportation.

Notes

1 Mary, personal interview, 2007–08, pp. 6–7.
2 V. Schultz, 'Life's Work' *Columbia Law Review*, 2000, vol. 100, pp. 1886–92.
3 For some recent American statistics, see F. Lipman, 'Enabling Work for People with Disabilities: A Post-Integrationist Revision of Underutilized Tax Incentives' *American University Law Review*, 2003, vol. 53, pp. 395–97; A.M. Smith, 'Persons with Disabilities as a Social and Economic Underclass' *Kansas Journal of Law and*

Public Policy, 2002–2003, vol. 12, p. 21. For Canadian statistics, see Canada, *2010 Annual Report on Disability Issues*, Ottawa: Government of Canada, p. 43; G. Brodsky, S. Day and Y. Peters, *Accommodation in the 21st Century*, Ottawa: Canadian Human Rights Commission, 2012, p. 2, available online at http://www.chrc-ccdp.gc.ca/proactive_initiatives/default-eng.aspx (last accessed September 19, 2012).

4   For data on disabled people expressing a desire to enter the labour market, see M.C. Weber, 'Beyond the Americans with Disabilities Act: A National Employment Policy for People with Disabilities' *Buffalo Law Review*, 1998, vol. 46, pp. 127–74 at p. 128.

5   D. Lero, C. Pletsch, and M. Hilbrecht, 'Introduction to the Special Issue on Disability and Work: Toward Re-conceptualizing the "Burden" of Disability' *Disability Studies Quarterly*, 2012, vol. 32, para. 3.

6   An avalanche of literature could be cited. See M.P. Thomas, *Regulating Flexibility: The Political Economy of Employment Standards*, Montreal and Kingston: McGill-Queen's University Press, 2009; J. Fudge and B. Cossman, 'Introduction: Privatization, Law and the Challenge to Feminism' in B. Cossman and J. Fudge (eds) *Privatization, Law and the Challenge to Feminism*, Toronto: University of Toronto Press, 2002, pp. 3–37; K. Banks, 'The Impact of Globalization on Labour Standards: A Second Look at the Evidence' in J. Craig and S.M. Lynk (eds) *Globalization and the Future of Labour Law*, Cambridge: Cambridge University Press, 2006, pp. 77–107; L. Vosko (ed.) *Precarious Employment: Understanding Labour Market Insecurity in Canada*, Montreal and Kingston: McGill-Queen's University Press, 2005; A. Supiot, 'Introductory Remarks: Between Market and Regulation: New Social Regulations for Life Long Security?' in P. Auer and B. Gazier (eds) *The Future of Work, Employment and Social Protection: The Dynamics of Change and the Protection of Workers*, Geneva: International Labour Organization, 2002, pp. 153–54. For an overview of neoliberalism and its intellectual roots, see generally D. Harvey, *A Brief History of Neoliberalism*, Oxford: Oxford University Press, 2005.

7   Fudge and Cossman, ibid, pp. 19–20; G. Albo, 'Neoliberalism, the State and the Left: A Canadian Perspective' *Monthly Review*, 2002, vol. 54, pp. 46–55.

8   See C. Ford, 'Disability Politics in a Time of Capitalist Crisis' *New Politics*, 2012, vol. 14, no. 1, pp. 10–15. For a discussion of the rise of workfare, or policies which require work for welfare, see, J. Peck, *Workfare States*, New York, NY: The Guildford Press, 2001.

9   M. Lynk, 'Labour Law and the New Inequality' *University of New Brunswick Law Journal*, 2009, vol. 59, pp. 14–41.

10 H. Hahn, 'Advertising the Acceptably Employable Image: Disability and Capitalism' in L.J. Davis (ed.) *The Disability Studies Reader*, New York, NY: Routledge, 1997, p. 176.

11 B. Gleeson, *Geographies of Disability*, London: Routledge, 1999, pp. 88–90 (examining 16th century census records). See also W. Turner, 'Preface: Abilities and Disabilities' in W. Turner and T. Pearman (eds) *The Treatment of Disabled Persons in Medieval Europe: Examining Disability in the Historical, Legal, Literary, Medical, and Religious Discourses of the Middle Ages*, Lewiston: The Edwin Mellen Press, 2010, p. xiv (commenting '[W]hether physically or mentally *challenged* in a day-to-day sense, the medieval person who could carry out the tasks associated with her lot in life meant that she was a fully functioning member of society').

12 K. Marx, *Capital, vol. 1*, London: Penguin, 1976, pp. 592–99 (describing the horrors of child labour employed in brick making for 17-hour days).

13 D. Braddock and C. Parrish, 'An Institutional History of Disability' in G.L. Albrecht, K.D. Seelman and M. Bury (eds) *Handbook of Disability Studies*, Thousand Oaks, CA: Sage, 2001, pp. 17–18, 25. For an interesting account of the expansion of asylums in Quebec and the initiatives by asylums to actively recruit patients, see A.

Cellard and M. Thifault, 'The Uses of Asylums: Resistance, Asylum Propaganda and Institutionalization Strategies in Turn-of-the Century Quebec' in J.E. Moran and D. Wright (eds) *Mental Health and Canadian Society: Historical Perspectives*, Montreal and Kingston: McGill-Queen's University Press, 2006, pp. 97–116.

14 On this point, see G. Reaume, 'Patients at Work: Insane Asylum Inmate Labour in Ontario, 1841–1900' in J.E. Moran and D. Wright (eds) *Mental Health and Canadian Society: Historical Perspectives*, Montreal and Kingston: McGill-Queen's University Press, 2006, pp. 69–96; J. Abbas, 'A Legacy of Exploitation: Intellectual Disability, Unpaid Labor and Disability Services' *New Politics*, 2012, vol. 14, no. 1, pp. 22–26. Abbas notes how a 1904 book entitled *Mental Defectives* was allegedly typed by intellectually disabled inmates.

15 K. Soldatic and H. Meekosha, 'Disability and Neoliberal State Formations' in N. Watson, A. Roulstone and C. Thomas (eds) *Routledge Handbook of Disability Studies*, London: Routledge, 2012, p. 199. See also B. Gleeson, 'Disability Studies: A Historical Materialist View' *Disability & Society*, 1997, vol. 12, pp. 179–202 at p. 195.

16 K. Polanyi, *The Great Transformation: The Political and Economic Origins of Our Time*, Boston, MA: Beacon Press, 1944, p. 82; Soldatic and Meekosha, op. cit., n. 15, p. 195; D. Stone, *The Disabled State*, Philadelphia, PA: Temple Press, 1984, pp. 3–14.

17 Organisation for Economic Co-operation and Development, 'Disability Programmes in Need of Reform' in B. Marin, C. Prinz and M. Queisser (eds) *Transforming Disability Welfare Policies: Towards Work and Equal Opportunities*, Aldershot: Ashgate, 2004, pp. 21–22. Impairment rubrics, that assign a value to the loss of a particular bodily function, are hardly scientific for the simple reason that they do not consider the impact of the structural environment.

18 D. Galer, 'A Friend in Need or a Business Indeed? Disabled Bodies and Fraternalism in Victorian Ontario' *Labour/Le Travail*, 2010, vol. 66, pp. 27–30.

19 R. Malhotra, 'The Implications of the Social Model of Disablement for the Legal Regulation of the Modern Workplace in Canada and the United States' *Manitoba Law Journal*, 2009, vol. 33, pp. 1–41 at p. 3.

20 See J. Singer, 'Legal Realism Now' *California Law Review*, 1988, vol. 76, pp. 478–82.

21 For an excellent analysis of such regulation by geographers, see H. Parr and R. Butler, 'New Geographies of Illness, Impairment and Disability' in R. Butler and H. Parr (eds) *Mind and Body Spaces: Geographies of Illness, Impairment and Disability*, London: Routledge, 1999, pp. 9–10.

22 Abbas, op. cit., n. 14, pp. 24–25.

23 E. Samoy, 'Activation Through Sheltered Work? Not *If* But *How*' in B. Marin, C. Prinz and M. Queisser (eds) *Transforming Disability Welfare Policies: Towards Work and Equal Opportunities*, Aldershot: Ashgate, 2004, p. 207.

24 Abbas, op. cit., n. 14, pp. 24–25.

25 For an account of the political activism of blinded war veterans in Canada, see S. Durflinger, *Veterans with a Vision: Canada's War Blinded in Peace and War*, Vancouver: University of British Columbia Press, 2010. For accounts of the activism of radicalized and disabled Vietnam war veterans, see D.Z. Zames and F. Zames, *The Disability Rights Movement: From Charity to Confrontation* updated edn, Philadelphia, PA: Temple University Press, 2011, pp. 53–56; J. Shapiro, *No Pity: Disabled People Forging a New Civil Rights Movement*, New York, NY: Times Books, 1993, pp. 64–69.

26 The Canadian Labour Congress, for example, has issued a report. See Canadian Labour Congress, *Toward Inclusion of People with Disabilities in the Workplace*, Ottawa: Canadian Labour Congress, 2008.

27 Weber, op. cit., n. 4; Lipman, op cit., n. 3. Quotas have been popular in Europe.

See S. Bagenstos, 'Comparative Disability Employment Law from an American Perspective' *Comparative Labor Law and Policy Journal*, 2003, vol. 24, pp. 653–55.

28 Part 1 of the Constitution Act, 1982, being Schedule B to the Canada Act 1982 (UK), 1982, c.11, s. 15. Note that although the Charter was adopted in 1982, section 15 did not take effect until 1985 and disability rights advocates had to campaign to have disability included as a prohibited ground in the Charter. See W. Boyce *et al.*, *A Seat at the Table: Persons with Disabilities and Policy Making*, Montreal and Kingston: McGill-Queen's University Press, 2001, pp. 49–65.

29 See e.g. Ontario Human Rights Code, RSO 1990, ch. 19, s. 5; Canadian Human Rights Act, RSC 1985, c. H-6, s. 3.

30 See e.g. Ontario Human Rights Commission, *Policy and Guidelines on Disability and the Duty to Accommodate*, Toronto: Ontario Human Rights Commission, 2009, available online at http://www.ohrc.on.ca/en/policy-and-guidelines-disability-and-duty-accommodate (last accessed September 6, 2012).

31 M. Lynk, 'Accommodating Disabilities in the Canadian Workplace' *Canadian Labour and Employment Law Journal*, 1999, vol. 7, p. 191. The origins of the duty to accommodate in Canada lie in the accommodation of religious minorities and may apply to any ground. See R. Malhotra, 'The Legal Genealogy of the Duty to Accommodate American and Canadian Workers with Disabilities: A Comparative Perspective' *Washington University Journal of Law and Policy*, 2007, vol. 23, pp. 1–32.

32 Employment Equity Act, SC, 1995, c. 44. Recent amendments to the legislation may alter the requirement of federal contractors to comply with principles of equity.

33 *Quebec (Commission des droits de la personne et des droits de la jeunesse) v Montréal (City) [Montréal]*; *Quebec (Commission des droits de la personne et des droits de la jeunesse) v Boisbriand (City)*, 2000 SCC 27, *Supreme Court Reports*, 2000, vol. 1, p. 665 [*Boisbriand*].

34 Lynk, op. cit., n. 31, p. 191.

35 *British Columbia (Public Service Employee Relations Commission) v BCGSEU (Meiorin Grievance)*, *Supreme Court Reports*, 1999, vol. 3, p. 3; *Dominion Law Reports*, 1999, vol. 176 (4th), p. 1 [*Meiorin* cited to *Supreme Court Reports*].

36 *Meiorin*, ibid, p. 13.

37 *Meiorin*, above, n. 35, pp. 13 and 44–45.

38 *Meiorin*, above, n. 35, pp. 13–14.

39 *Meiorin*, above, n. 35, pp. 31–35. Under earlier Canadian jurisprudence, a duty to accommodate absurdly only arose in cases of adverse effect discrimination (i.e. a neutral rule inadvertently disadvantages members of a group covered by a protected ground) and not direct discrimination, leading employers to argue that they did in fact engage in direct discrimination.

40 *Meiorin*, above, n. 35, pp. 32–33.

41 *Meiorin*, above, n. 35, pp. 32–33.

42 Pub. L. No. 101-336, 104 Stat. 327.

43 SO 2005, c. 11. An important history of the social movement that eventually led to the AODA is M.D. Lepofsky, 'The Long, Arduous Road to a Barrier-Free Ontario for People with Disabilities: The History of the *Ontarians with Disabilities Act*—The First Chapter' *National Journal of Constitutional Law*, 2004, vol. 15, pp. 125–333 (outlining the political mobilization for disability rights legislation in Ontario between 1994 and 2003).

44 42 USC § 12102(2) (1994) (ADA).

45 R. Colker, 'Winning and Losing under the Americans with Disabilities Act' *Ohio State Law Journal*, 2001, vol. 62, pp. 241–42.

46 Colker, ibid, p. 242.

47 42 USC 12111(9); 42 USC 12111(2) (1994).

48 J. Cox, 'Crossroads and Signposts: The ADA Amendments Act of 2008' *Indiana*

Law Journal, 2010, vol. 85, pp. 201–2. See, e.g., *Sutton v United Air Lines, Supreme Court Reporter*, 1999, vol. 119, p. 2139 (petitioners with severe myopia correctable through use of glasses did not have substantial limitations as to qualify under the ADA); *Murphy v United Parcel Service, Supreme Court Reporter*, 1999, vol. 119, p. 2133 (petitioner commercial driver with hypertension did not constitute a substantial limitation as to qualify under the ADA); *Albertsons, Inc. v Kirkingburg, Supreme Court Reporter*, 1999, vol. 119, p. 2162 (truck driver's visual impairment did not constitute a substantial limitation as to qualify under the ADA).

49 A. Long, 'Introducing the New and Improved Americans with Disabilities Act: Assessing the ADA Amendments Act of 2008' *Northwestern University Law Review Colloquy*, 2008, vol. 103, pp. 220–21.

50 Colker, op. cit., n. 45, p. 240 (noting 93% of plaintiffs under Title I of the ADA lost in American trial court decisions).

51 Long, op cit., n. 49, pp. 219–21.

52 Weber, op. cit., n. 4, pp. 150–59. See also M.C. Weber, *Understanding Disability Law*, 2nd edn, New Providence, NJ: LexisNexis, 2012, p. 49 and pp. 161–63 (noting the majority of the Seventh Circuit's holding in *Fedro v Reno*, 21 F.3d. 1391 (7th Cir. 1994) that there is no elevated duty to accommodate a marshal whose impairments prevented him from returning to his previous job classification).

53 DDA, 1995.

54 EqA, ss 20–22.

55 A. Lawson, 'Disability and Employment in the Equality Act 2010: Opportunities Seized, Lost and Generated' *Industrial Law Journal*, 2011, vol. 40, pp. 359–83 at p. 363.

56 Lawson, ibid, p. 375.

57 [2008] UKHL 43.

58 Office for Disability Issues, *Consultation on Improving Protection from Disability Discrimination*, London: Office for Disability Issues, 2008, pp. 19 and 32. In *Lewisham*, a schizophrenic man was evicted from his house after he sublet it in violation of his tenancy agreement during a period when he had stopped taking his medications. A majority of the House of Lords concluded that Lewisham was justified in evicting him notwithstanding his disability because the appropriate comparator group was able-bodied people who sublet their homes.

59 Lawson, op. cit., n. 55, p. 375; R. Craig, *Systemic Discrimination in Employment and the Promotion of Ethnic Equality*, Leiden: Martinus Nijhoff, 2007, p. 30.

60 A. Roulstone, 'Disabled People, Work and Employment: A Global Perspective' in N. Watson, A. Roulstone and C. Thomas (eds) *Routledge Handbook of Disability Studies*, London: Routledge, 2012, p. 213.

61 See e.g. A. D'Aubin, 'Working for Barrier Removal in the ICT Area: Creating a More Accessible and Inclusive Canada' *The Information Society*, 2007, vol. 23, pp. 193–201 (describing initiatives advocating for inclusion in the Information and Communication technology industry in Canada).

62 S. Taylor, 'The Right Not to Work: Power and Disability' *Monthly Review*, 2004, vol. 55, pp. 30–44.

63 Roulstone, op. cit., n. 60, p. 215.

64 Of course, when employment was widely regarded as a citizenship right in the boom era between the 1950s and 1970s, it generally excluded disabled people as well as others such as women. For an account of the relationship between the development of unemployment insurance and gender in Canada, see A. Porter, *Gendered States: Women, Unemployment Insurance, and the Political Economy of the Welfare State in Canada, 1945–1997*, Toronto: University of Toronto Press, 2003.

65 Nancy, personal interview, 2007–08, p. 15.

66 Nancy, p. 16.

67 Nancy, p. 16.
68 Nancy, p. 16.
69 Sarah, personal interview, 2007–08, p. 2. See also Women's Focus Group, September 20, 2008, p. 21.
70 Women's Focus Group, September, ibid, p. 22.
71 Women's Focus Group, September, above, n. 69, pp. 22–23.
72 See our discussion of impairment effects in Chapter 5.
73 Women's Focus Group, September, above, n. 69, p. 27.
74 Sarah, p. 7.
75 Sarah, p. 16.
76 This is known as "Universality of Service." See 'Defence Administrative Orders and Directives: Minimum Operational Standards Related to Universality of Service', May 19, 2006, available online at http://www.admfincs.forces.gc.ca/dao-doa/5000/5023-1-eng.asp (last accessed December 11, 2012).
77 For a discussion of problems with pensions for disabled veterans in Canada, see A. Aiken and A. Buitenhuis, 'New Veteran Charter Shortchanges Our Disabled Soldiers' Toronto *Globe and Mail*, August 24, 2010, available online at http://www.theglobeandmail.com/commentary/new-veterans-charter-shortchanges-our-disabled-soldiers/article1213169/ (last accessed September 24, 2012). For a commentary on the serious delays in processing disability claims by veterans in the United States and the backlog of some 650,000 claims, see R. Riley, 'Preservation, Modification or Transformation? The Current State of the Department of Veterans Affairs Disability Benefits Adjudication Process and Why Congress Should Modify, Rather than Maintain or Completely Redesign the Current System' *Federal Circuit Bar Journal*, 2009, vol. 18, pp. 8–9. For a discussion on a policy shift to encouraging disability pension beneficiaries in Canada to return to work in the non-veteran context, see N. Lawand and R. Kloosterman, 'The Canada Pension Plan Disability Program: Building a Solid Foundation' in M. McColl and L. Jongbloed (eds), *Disability and Social Policy in Canada*, 2nd edn, Concord, Ontario: Captus University Press, 2006.
78 See L. Pottie and L. Sossin, 'Demystifying the Boundaries of Public Law: Policy, Discretion and Social Welfare' *University of British Columbia Law Review*, 2005, vol. 38, pp. 147–87 at p. 152 (noting that in the context of welfare applications, empirical interviews showed that decision makers typically consulted guidelines rather than the governing statute or regulation).
79 See D.G. Duff, 'Disability and the Income Tax' *McGill Law Journal*, 2000, vol. 45, pp. 873–74 (noting distinction between disability pensions based on past work experience and contributions and disability supports for those disabled people with little or no labour market experience in the Canadian context). The identity of injured veterans, even when not acquired during combat, is also one that has particular salience in popular culture and is likely to mobilize public support. See Durflinger, op. cit., n. 25.
80 D. Galer, 'Disabled Capitalists: Exploring the Intersections of Disability and Identity Formation in the World of Work' *Disability Studies Quarterly*, 2012, vol. 32, no. 3, available online at http://dsq-sds.org/article/view/3277/3122 (last accessed January 12, 2013).
81 Sarah, pp. 7–8.
82 For an illustration of this process in a historical context, see Barbara Young-Welke's construction of narratives of disabled railway passengers engaged in tort litigation in the nineteenth century: B. Young-Welke, *Recasting American Liberty: Gender, Race, Law and the Railroad Revolution, 1860–1920*, New York, NY: Cambridge University Press, 2001, pp. 128–36.
83 Sarah, pp. 4–5.
84 Sarah, p. 6.

85 Sarah, p. 6.

86 C. Frazee, J. Gilmour and R. Mykituk, 'Now You See Her, Now You Don't: How Law Shapes Disabled Women's Experiences of Exposure, Surveillance and Assessment in the Clinical Encounter' in D. Pothier and R. Devlin (eds) *Critical Disability Theory: Essays in Philosophy, Politics, Policy and Law*, Vancouver: University of British Columbia Press, 2006, p. 238. Grievance arbitrators in Canada have also upheld invasive requests by employers that employees requesting disability accommodations be subjected to Independent Medical Examinations to ensure that employers have a full understanding of their disabilities. See *Complex Services Inc v Ontario Public Service Employees Union, Local 278*, 2012 CanLII 8645 (ON LA, Surdykowski), available online at http://canlii.ca/t/fq9vg, (last accessed December 30, 2012). See also Chapter 3.

87 R. Wilton, 'Working at the Margins: Disabled People and the Growth of Precarious Employment' in D. Pothier and R. Devlin (eds) *Critical Disability Theory: Essays in Philosophy, Politics, Policy and Law*, Vancouver: University of British Columbia Press, 2006, p. 131. For a recent discussion of non-standard employment in the European context, see G. Schmid, 'The Future of Employment Relations: Goodbye "Flexicurity"—Welcome Back Transitional Labour Markets?' Working Paper 10-106, Amsterdam: University of Amsterdam, 2010, available online at http://www.uva-aias.net/uploaded_files/publications/WP106-Schmid.pdf (last accessed February 1, 2013).

88 Wilton, ibid, p. 145.

89 Mary, pp. 1, 6. For a moving narrative of life as a young woman with fibromyalgia, see A. Chow, 'This is Not Going to Control My Life: Young and Living with Fibromyalgia' in D. Driedger and M. Owen (eds) *Dissonant Disabilities: Women with Chronic Illnesses Explore Their Lives*, Toronto: Canadian Scholar's Press/Women's Press, 2008, pp. 99–108.

90 Chow, ibid, pp. 1, 6.

91 Chow, op. cit., n. 89, p. 8.

92 Chow, op. cit., n. 89, p. 6.

93 Wilton, op. cit., n. 87, pp. 144–45.

94 Women's Focus Group, September, op. cit., n. 69, p. 19.

95 Women's Focus Group, October 18, 2008, pp. 18–19.

96 Women's Focus Group, September, op. cit., n. 69, pp. 23–24.

97 Women's Focus Group, September, above, n. 69, p. 24. This echoes a long tradition of sexism in the workplace where women were accepted provided they did not make demands relating to parenting.

98 Women's Focus Group, September, above, n. 69, p. 24.

99 M.C. Weber, *Disability Harassment*, New York, NY: New York University Press, 2007, pp. 4–6.

100 See D. Galer, 'Building an Accessible House of Labour: Work, Disability Rights and the Canadian Labour Movement' in R. Hanes and N. Hansen (eds) *Untold Stories: Disability History in Canada*, Winnipeg: University of Manitoba Press, forthcoming, for a good overview of the tensions between unions and disability rights advocates.

101 Tom, personal interview, 2007–08, p. 12.

102 Tom, p. 12.

103 See B. Potts, 'Disability and Employment: Considering the Importance of Social Capital' *Journal of Rehabilitation*, 2005, vol. 71, pp. 20–25 at p. 21.

104 S. Balandin *et al.*, 'Older Disabled Workers' Perception of Volunteering' *Disability and Society*, 2006, vol. 21, p. 680. Although the authors' study is specifically about elderly disabled volunteers, they note that these conclusions apply to all age groups.

105 Roulstone, op. cit., n. 60, pp. 213–14. Human Rights Tribunals in Canada have held that employers may not discriminate on prohibited grounds, which would

of course include disability, in volunteering experiences. See *Rocha v Pardons and Waivers of Canada*, 2012 HRTO 2234, at para. 23 (finding age discrimination in volunteer experience that would lead to paid employment to be violation of the Human Rights Code).

106 Andrea, personal interview, 2007–08, p. 9.

107 Andrea, p. 9.

108 Cheryl, personal interview, 2007–08, p. 13.

109 Cheryl, p. 11.

110 Cheryl, p. 12.

111 P.K. Longmore, 'Conspicuous Contribution and American Cultural Dilemmas: Telethon Rituals of Cleansing and Renewal' in D. Mitchell and S. Snyder (eds) *The Body and Physical Difference: Discourses of Disability*, Ann Arbor, MI: University of Michigan Press, 1997, pp. 134–58.

112 Lisa, personal interview, 2007–08, p. 32.

113 Lisa, p. 30.

114 Charles, personal interview, 2007–08, p. 7.

115 Andrea, pp. 9–10.

116 Nancy, p. 6.

117 Deputy Minister of Education, 'Policy/Program Memorandum No. 124a' available online at http://www.edu.gov.on.ca/extra/eng/ppm/124a.html (last accessed September 27, 2012).

118 D.M. Engel and F.W. Munger, *Rights of Inclusion: Law and Identity in the Life Stories of Americans with Disabilities*, Chicago, IL: University of Chicago Press, 2003, p. 95.

119 Lisa, p. 32.

120 Lisa, p. 33.

121 Henry, personal interview, 2007–08, p. 11.

122 Charles, p. 9.

123 See Chapter 3.

124 Henry, p. 9.

125 Henry, p. 9.

126 Lisa, p. 32.

127 Henry, p. 9.

128 Henry, p. 9.

129 Cheryl, pp. 10–11.

130 Nancy, pp. 10–13.

131 Nancy, p. 10.

132 For a recent account, see J. Lord and P. Hutchison, 'Individualized Funding in Ontario: Report of a Provincial Study' *Journal on Developmental Disabilities*, 2008, vol. 14, pp. 44–53 at p. 46 (discussing funding limitations in the context of clients with developmental disabilities).

133 See Pottie and Sossin, op. cit., n. 78.

134 Mary, pp. 14–15.

135 M. Oliver and C. Barnes, *The New Politics of Disablement*, Basingstoke: Palgrave Macmillan, 2012, p. 133.

136 Tom, p. 10.

5 Transportation barriers

When Tracy attempted to take a bus to travel between cities, she encountered a litany of problems relating to accessibility despite planning well in advance:

> I called and reserved to make sure. What time is your wheelchair accessible bus coming through? I have to go to Kingston. I need a wheelchair accessible . . . bus. If you take this bus we will make sure. I called them three days ahead. This bus will be wheelchair accessible. It will have the lift and everything. I'm going ok fine. I'm out there waiting for a bus, guess what? No lift. I have to break down my own wheelchair and stow it because the bus driver won't. Then he sits there and decides that he's going to bitch at me about the fact that well he can't guarantee that my wheelchair will be intact when we get to our destination. And then I have to get up the stairs myself. I've got crutches but you know how narrow those things are. And I've just said you're kidding. Then he wouldn't tell people sitting in the front seats to move. So I didn't have to. I finally get up to the top of the stairs and I said can you please move? Why? Because I'm handicapped and I can't get very far please. Begrudgingly they gave me the front seat.[1]

Transportation remains one of the key barriers facing disabled people. It is essential to have affordable and accessible barrier-free transportation in order for disabled people to participate equally and independently in education, employment and leisure. It is also essential in order for disabled people, in an increasingly urbanized world, to be equal citizens and achieve what the French radical intellectual, Henri Lefebvre, has famously characterized as the right to the city.[2] This contemplates a right of participation in society through everyday practises such as work, transportation, and recreation.[3] Yet modern cities pose significant barriers for disabled people. This is particularly true in a country like Canada which is cold and snowy for many months each year, making travel by wheelchair alone difficult or impossible. Time and again, disabled people have collectively organized to protest inaccessible bus, rail and taxi transportation which require people to conform with physical attributes such as mobility and agility in order to participate.[4]

Urban transportation systems implicitly have been designed for economically productive bodies, thereby creating an array of barriers that exclude and marginalize those regarded as deviant and inefficient.[5] As Imrie notes, spatial structures reproduce dominant power relations which marginalize disabled people and leave unaddressed barriers that make life challenging for disabled people.[6]

These barriers encompass both physical barriers such as steps that preclude disabled people from participating in a transportation system and attitudinal barriers by transportation staff and management that make transportation challenging.[7] In this chapter, we explore the interviews of our participants to explore how our participants cope with accessibility barriers and how an advocacy identity facilitates or does not facilitate an improvement in accessibility in transportation.

One of the central debates in transportation policy has been whether to advocate for higher quality door to door bus services for disabled people, frequently known as paratransit services in North America, which provide seamless transportation from origin to destination, or to demand the integration of disabled people in regular barrier-free bus transportation. This parallels debates in educational policy concerning the integration of disabled students in regular classroom settings. The debate about integration in transportation has had particular symbolic importance in the United States because of how racial desegregation of buses, spearheaded by a combination of rank and file activism on the part of African Americans in Montgomery, Alabama, such as Rosa Parks and by strategic litigation, was so crucial to the emergence of the American civil rights movement.[8] Not surprisingly, the United States is in many respects a world leader in transportation accessibility even though public transportation in general remains undeveloped in many areas of the United States compared to Europe or Canada, as the private automobile has enormous cultural significance as the primary form of transportation.[9]

While the chief advantage of paratransit service is that it provides door-to-door service, a feature that may be essential for some disabled people, it often comes with an array of disadvantages including limited service hours, advance booking requirements that stymie spontaneity, chronic delays, restrictions on companions, eligibility for service to only customers with certain types of impairments, higher fares than comparable integrated transportation, cancellation fees and even prioritizing of rides by purpose of trip.[10] Moreover, it has been estimated to be as much as 75 times as expensive to operate on a per ride basis compared with fixed route service.[11] In larger cities, especially where the city straddles multiple provinces or states, a trip may well require use of more than one paratransit service which requires a considerable level of co-ordination with multiple service providers.[12] Barriers with one mode of transportation may force a disabled person to rely on a less desirable or convenient mode of transportation and driving one's own vehicle, as we shall see, is not an option for some disabled people for many reasons, including affordability and barriers to obtaining a driver's license and an accessible vehicle. One fundamental difference between educational or employment accommodation for disabled people and transportation, however, is that the potential market—and possibilities for durable political alliances—is not limited to younger disabled people but includes large numbers of elderly people who use assistive devices for mobility. This segment of the population is expected to grow dramatically in Britain, the United States and Canada in the coming years,[13] and some commentators have suggested that the transportation sector has lost significant revenue by not becoming more accessible.[14]

Just as neo-liberalism resulted in significant changes to the structure of the labour market, neo-liberalism in transportation policy has also resulted in dramatic change. In Canada, where local transportation is a provincially regulated matter, sharp budgetary cuts in some Canadian provinces have created a shortfall in available funding for paratransit even though the Ontario Human Rights Commission has recognized that the provision of paratransit service is a part of the legal duty to accommodate the needs of disabled people.[15] As a result, the issue has been offloaded to municipal governments to fund whatever paratransit services, if any, they are able to afford.[16] This not only creates barriers for disabled people. It also means that there is no standardization of services within a Canadian province. A wheelchair user may find dramatically different policies if she were to visit or relocate to another community. In some cases, she may find herself ineligible for paratransit in one community even after relying on it in another.[17] Subsidies for train service are also limited and rail services have found it challenging to turn a profit while top managers mandate a greater emphasis on efficiency and economic viability.[18] In Britain, passenger rail service has been privatized, while Canadian passenger rail service has been repeatedly subjected to cutbacks and service reductions, leading to a situation where the vast majority of trains arrive late at the station.[19] Surveys of disabled people in Britain have documented that a significant percentage have difficulty in reaching their physicians, places of work, and leisure activities as a result of barriers.[20]

Canada

Disabled people and paratransit

In Ontario, Canada's most populated province, an early policy decision was made in the 1970s that the needs of the disabled community would be best addressed by funding of municipal paratransit systems.[21] Municipalities were required to indicate how they would meet their accessibility goals.[22] However, budgetary cutbacks to provincial funding of municipalities in the 1990s meant that this system become increasingly less reliable and, in some cases, would not necessarily continue to operate.[23] In other cases, municipalities have introduced in person interview screening to verify eligibility using tests that very much embodied a medical model approach.[24] Yet this means that a disabled person could easily qualify for paratransit service in one municipality and be ineligible simply because she moved to another town. Obtaining access to medical appointments may also be challenging in larger cities when the paratransit system's boundaries are smaller than the metropolitan area, requiring pre-booking and co-ordination of transit rides with two distinct paratransit systems.[25] While each of the problems identified earlier remains a barrier with paratransit, it is important to bear in mind that the lived reality is one of chronic delays and alienation for disabled people as each individual problem is magnified by the systemic nature of the issue: a disabled person who chooses to use a wheelchair for paratransit may find no way of returning home if her evening commitments extend beyond the relatively early evening cut off time of many paratransit systems. This has a real impact on the ability of disabled people to participate in the labour market and in the life of the community. ARCH, a disability rights legal clinic, worked with disability rights advocates to secure an order from the Ontario Human Rights Commission declaring that paratransit was not a special service, as service providers wanted so as to exclude them from liability to human rights complaints.[26]

More recently, there has been a gradual introduction of wheelchair accessible buses in Ontario.[27] However, public funding for transportation in Ontario is relatively stingy, accounting for only approximately 25 per cent of revenues, compared to 60 per cent in the United States.[28] Whether recent legislation setting out provincial accessibility standards for transportation, the Accessibility for Ontarians with Disabilities Act, has a genuine impact remains to be seen as enforcement dates are staggered over a lengthy time period stretching into 2021.[29]

The International Year of Disabled Persons

As in other policy areas, the International Year of Disabled Persons proclaimed in 1981 by the United Nations was a significant turning point in the transformation of attitudes toward disabled people. The Canadian government established at the federal level the Special Parliamentary Committee on the Disabled and the Handicapped which issued the landmark *Obstacles Report*, making a number of recommendations for increased accessibility in many areas including transportation.[30] Recommendation 83 proposed a National Policy on Transportation for Disabled Persons which was eventually developed and mandated the removal of physical and attitudinal barriers for disabled people in federal transportation.[31] One foundational case was *Kelly v Via Rail*, concerning a law student named Clarris Kelly who was a wheelchair user. The case established the principle that a disabled person had the right to decide whether or not she required an attendant to travel on a train.[32] After some years of progress, a shift after the 1993 federal election toward a policy of voluntary codes of compliance by the transportation industry rather than enforceable requirements marked a setback for disabled people.[33]

Via Rail

A more recent positive if hard-won development was a landmark Supreme Court of Canada decision in 2007, *Council of Canadians with Disabilities v Via Rail*,[34] which restored by a narrow five to four margin a decision of the Canadian Transportation Agency (CTA) finding that various physical barriers on newly purchased railway cars, known as the Renaissance cars, constituted undue obstacles in violation of Part V of the Canadian Transportation Act[35] and thereby endorsed a vision of substantive equality for disabled people.[36] In 2000, Via Rail purchased 139 Renaissance cars at minimal cost in a move that the company regarded as efficient, given reduced government funding.[37] This was the first major purchase of railway cars since the adoption of accessibility standards.[38] However, these cars posed significant barriers for disabled people and were not acceptable to the British government because of their poor accessibility standards. Wheelchair users, for example, were unable to independently access washrooms using their own wheelchairs or access meals and would have to rely on the assistance of Via Rail staff.[39] The Council of Canadians with Disabilities (CCD), Canada's leading cross-disability advocacy organization, filed a complaint to the CTA, which has jurisdiction over federally regulated transportation systems such as railways, identifying some 46 barriers that they argued constituted undue obstacles under the Canadian Transportation Act, such as the lack of access to the sleeper cars, barriers to assistance animals and a lack of appropriate washrooms for wheelchair users.[40] The CCD in part relied on the fact that Via Rail had voluntarily reached an agreement in 1998 on accessibility known as the Rail Code and the Renaissance cars were in breach of this Code, in particular the requirement of wheelchair access.[41] This evolved into a seven year epic battle that eventually led to the Supreme Court and nearly caused the bankruptcy of the CCD.[42]

The CTA undertook what were clearly intensely acrimonious and confrontational proceedings. Some 70 decisions and orders were issued over the course of the proceedings.[43] After a lengthy series of hearings, the CTA issued a Preliminary Decision in March, 2003. The CTA concluded that there were numerous barriers and ordered Via Rail to demonstrate within a specified time frame why complying with accessibility would constitute undue hardship.[44] The CTA eventually had to secure a court order due to a lack of co-operation from Via Rail. Ultimately, Via Rail took the position that it simply did not have adequate funding to comply with orders to provide financial estimates of accommodations and it would refuse to further cooperate with the hearing.[45] As a result, the CTA issued a Final Decision in October, 2003 in which it ordered Via Rail to install accessible washrooms, widen doorways and implement other physical changes at a cost it estimated at well under one million dollars.[46]

On judicial review, the Federal Court of Appeal quashed the decision of the CTA and remitted it to the agency for reconsideration. The majority of the Court found that while the CTA did have jurisdiction to proceed with the CCD's complaint under section 172 of the Canadian Transportation Act, the Agency wrongly failed to consider accessibility provided by the network as a whole as well as the interests of other stakeholders, such as non-disabled people and those disabled people who do not use wheelchairs.[47] In other words, the Court of Appeal reasoned that one had to consider the fact that a wheelchair user might be able to travel from Montreal to Edmonton without using the inaccessible Renaissance cars, even though she wanted to actually travel from Montreal to Toronto where in fact her only option is the inaccessible Renaissance cars.[48] This betrays a shockingly impoverished vision of equality and one that is simply inconsistent with a social model vision. The Court espoused divergent views on the standard of review with respect to the administrative agency in question but unanimously concluded that the CTA had breached the procedural fairness rights of Via Rail.[49] The CCD appealed this decision to the Supreme Court of Canada.

At the Supreme Court of Canada, a five person majority, speaking through Justice Abella, restored the decision of the CTA. As Baker and Godwin have commented, the Court majority reached six key conclusions. First, it concluded that the Canadian Transportation Act must be interpreted in light of human rights principles which promote the full inclusion of disabled people and respects their independence, dignity and safety.[50] The reliance on staff for assistance for meals and toileting clearly was not consistent with this principle. Second, there is a duty to prevent new barriers.[51] Third, it is the burden of the respondent to demonstrate that a given accommodation constitutes undue hardship.[52] This responds to the highly evasive tactics of Via Rail in this case. Fourth, the term "undue obstacle" is equivalent to "undue hardship" in other human rights contexts.[53] Fifth, in evaluating whether a particular accommodation is undue, factors to consider include costs that can be shifted or attributed to issues unrelated to accommodation, tax credits, and any revenue that may be generated by increased accessibility.[54] Sixth, undueness is only reached when all reasonable means of accommodation are exhausted and the costs would threaten the survival of the organization.[55] Collectively, these principles serve as an important basis for equality for disabled people in transportation although the narrow margin of victory in a sharply divided court does give one pause as to the future of disability rights as the Court's composition changes over time.

The United States

In the United States, one has seen significantly greater political mobilization by disabled people on the streets in concert with a litigation strategy to ensure that regular transit is wheelchair accessible. This effectively replicates the strategy adopted by the civil rights movement in the 1960s to desegregate public buses in the American South: even unsuccessful litigation raises awareness as demonstrators use the opportunity to publicize discrimination against disabled people. As early as 1978, disability rights advocates from the

Paralyzed Veterans of America, the National Council of Senior Citizens and the American Coalition of Citizens with Disabilities demonstrated for accessible low floor buses that would enable accessibility for wheelchair users to regular transportation, following unsuccessful litigation by a coalition of 13 disability rights organizations.[56] The cross-disability character of the demonstrations is striking, as blind people and senior citizens also participated in the mobilization.

While it would take some years to raise awareness, lobby legislators and achieve victory, in 1982, the Second Circuit in *Dopico v Goldschmidt*[57] ruled that section 504 of the Rehabilitation Act mandated accommodation of disabled people in public transit, even when it required millions of dollars in expenditures to make newly purchased equipment accessible.[58] Nevertheless, disability rights activists in cities such as New York continued to mobilize against continued barriers such as broken wheelchair lifts and poor training of drivers who were unaccustomed to wheelchair users, including through such tactics as blocking buses when wheelchair users were denied entry.[59] The passage of the landmark ADA also gave new impetus for increased accessibility in transportation in a wide range of settings as policy makers hoped that increased transportation access would lead to a decline in welfare rates amongst disabled people.[60] In 1997, American Disabled for Accessible Public Transportation (ADAPT), an organization that has become famous for its creative in your face direct action tactics, campaigned vigorously against Greyhound's inaccessible intercity buses in dozens of cities and explicitly referenced the African American freedom struggle by chanting, "at least Rosa Parks could get on the bus."[61] Eventually, pressure by disability rights advocates from below convinced New York transit authorities to fund the retrofitting of key subway stations for wheelchair access, move to a policy of making 100 per cent of buses wheelchair accessible, and establish a committee to design an effective paratransit system.[62] The combination of litigation and political protest by disabled people has resulted in a comparatively high level of accessibility on regular transit, both locally and intercity.

Britain

In Britain, the grassroots advocacy group, the UPIAS, raised transportation discrimination against disabled people in one of its earliest documents.[63] Serious efforts to improve accessibility on railways date back to at least the 1980s in the form of the creation of advisory groups of disabled people.[64] Under the Railways Act 1993, train operators had to take into account the needs of disabled people, produce a policy guideline and comply with a statutory Code of Practice.[65] In accordance with the DDA, train operators were not to discriminate against disabled people and new trains were required to meet accessibility standards.[66] This legislation also marked a shift from voluntary compliance to a set of enforceable standards for accessibility of buses and coaches serving more than 22 passengers and railway systems, although the dates by which accessibility was required were often very far in the future.[67] The DDA established a deadline of 2020 for accessibility for all rail vehicles.[68] In 2006, the government released a policy paper committed to increasing rail accessibility. Some of the issues that are to be addressed include information, ticketing and reservations; station buildings and platforms; train carriages; and the quality and reliability of staff training.[69] The EqA mandates specific accommodations for taxis, public service vehicles carrying more than eight individuals, and rail.[70] According to disability rights lawyer and advocate David Baker, some 90 per cent of buses in the Greater London area are now accessible.[71] However, it is too soon, as in Canada, to tell what the long-term impact of the EqA on accessibility will be.

Accessibility barriers and buses

In the opening epigraph to this chapter, Tracy describes many of the frustrating barriers in transportation that make life so cumbersome for disabled people. Her story is revealing because of the interlocking layers of oppression it identifies that encompass both structural and attitudinal barriers. First, to take the intercity bus in a wheelchair, Tracy must arrange for accessible transportation days in advance.[72] This contrasts with other passengers who can simply take any bus. Tracy is denied this spontaneity of scheduling events at the last minute. In a just-in-time world built on flexibility, productivity and the ability to respond quickly to turbulent change, this can mean the difference between obtaining or not obtaining employment.[73] Then the pre-booked wheelchair lift-equipped bus fails to arrive.[74] When she demonstrates a willingness to be adaptable by dismantling and stowing her own wheelchair in order to reach her destination, she receives no assistance from the bus driver who, instead, complains that he cannot guarantee her wheelchair will survive the journey, leaving her flabbergasted.[75] Given the repeated calls in the literature by Canadian, British and American disability rights advocates for better training of bus drivers on accessibility issues,[76] this is hardly a surprise. To make matters worse, the bus driver refuses to make other passengers move from the front seats when Tracy finally boards while using her crutches. The gendered nature of disability oppression also manifests itself. It appears that while her original barrier was a failure of the wheelchair accessible bus to arrive, the hostility of the bus driver is most likely in part a sexist reaction to a woman who is perceived as being unduly demanding and confrontational in a manner inconsistent with traditional gender roles and the need to demonstrate gratitude.[77] It should also be noted that Tracy has some choices in how she deals with transportation barriers as someone who can climb stairs with crutches. She broke and dislocated her ankle and broke her leg and pelvis after a head-on collision with a double tractor trailer transport truck.[78] Others who lack this mobility may feel more intimidated and reluctant to complain.

Other participants repeatedly raised concerns about municipal bus transportation, both regular and door-to-door paratransit service, regardless of whether they identified as advocates or not. In analyzing the experiences that follow, we incorporate their experiences in the community they lived at the time of the interview and all other communities. As many were younger adults attending school while away from home, they often faced barriers when visiting family during holidays. The chronic tardiness, the rigidity of having to book at least a day in advance and unreliability of paratransit was a common theme. Andrea observed:

> You have to book them a day in advance first of all, so you can't decide, oh I'm going to go to the movies, I'm going to go to the store. And it's basically like their schedule, it's not yours. Let's say you have a ten o'clock class you have to get to. They can show up at like anywhere between eight o'clock and eleven o'clock. And you can't really complain. So I would have this ten thirty to eleven thirty class and they would be showing up at like eleven, and I would be like, no no. Come on! So after first year university I switched.[79]

In this remark, Andrea highlights how she gave up using paratransit despite the advantages of door-to-door service because of the chronic tardiness and instead, when the weather was suitable, used her scooter to go to her university classes.[80] She not only bemoans the lack of spontaneity but implicitly alludes to what is in fact a genuine rule on many paratransit systems: a scheduled pick-up is typically allocated to a window and consequently a pick-up of a passenger within the window would paradoxically still be classified as having been on time even when it was late.[81] Of course, many paratransit trips arrive beyond even the window, rendering chaos to the user's schedule that day. This could cumulatively have a devastating impact on a student's ability to keep up with her courses, particularly if the professor were to require attendance and penalize those who were absent. Faced with the reality of long Canadian winters when her scooter could not cope with snow and when regular transit is presumably impractical even if accessible due to the snowy barriers along the route to the bus stop, Andrea was left, as a person without a driver's license at the time of her interview, with no alternative but to rely on rides from her parents.[82] Since the original interview, Andrea has acquired a driver's license after becoming exhausted with the tardiness of the system and the rudeness of staff.[83]

Tom also decries how paratransit, which typically must be booked at least a day in advance, deprives him of the opportunity to be spontaneous, which is such a valued commodity for people his age. He observes:

> I'm not a big fan of [paratransit]. Largely because it makes my life very, very structured. As in you know if I have to set a pickup time so I can't really stay out or fly by the seat of my pants which is kind of what I like to do.[84]

The dysfunctionality of paratransit was a repeated theme in our study. Cheryl, when asked what she thought of the system, responds:

> Annoying. Really annoying! I can list off a whole bunch of reasons why I don't like [paratransit]. I find it's really, really useful if you need to get somewhere, but the half hour window is annoying.[85]

She also elaborates on a little known aspect of paratransit systems: the fact that they often pick up and drop off multiple passengers in a manner that greatly lengthens what would otherwise be quite a short trip even if the ride is not late. Cheryl explains:

> Once you're on the vehicle, you could potentially be dropped off at your location, or somebody else could be on the vehicle and be dropped off before you, or potentially somebody else could be picked up and dropped off before you! So I've been on the [paratransit] and a trip that should have taken me like half an hour has taken almost two hours. So that's why I'm not exactly fond of [paratransit].[86]

Given that the ride itself often begins late, this factor compounds the delay and creates significant hardship, raising questions about how trip routes are designed and whether a more efficient system could be implemented. As Mary notes, while there are often significant delays, the disabled person is expected to patiently wait during the entire pick up window and could easily miss a ride if she leaves even to use the washroom for a moment.[87] Cheryl also expresses irritation at the lack of respect she felt from some drivers who would refer to passengers as wheelchairs while discussing bus operations on their radios:

> Like getting onto a bus. I will hear the bus driver make a comment to somebody on the radio, "We have a wheelchair." I'm like, "Ugh, ok . . ." Which I guess gets the point across. But it's not all that much more effort to say, "We have a person in a wheelchair" or "a person who uses a wheelchair."[88]

This repeated disrespect and dehumanization by people in a position of power over disabled people can have a disempowering effect over time and shape how disabled people regard themselves.[89]

Another issue that was raised is the fact that despite all these restrictions, it is entirely possible that no ride will be available at the desired time due to the fact that the limited supply does not meet demand. In fact, it may be that there are no rides available at all or one simply cannot get through the busy signals to reach an operator. Charles comments:

> . . . I generally use [regular transit] to bus everywhere most days and I find, like you said, most of the time it's practically impossible on a given

day, especially during the winter to book [paratransit] because often times I'm on hold for literally anywhere from ten minutes to a half an hour. So it's extremely impossible to get a booking.[90]

Ironically, some paratransit systems, which in many Canadian cities over-whelmingly serve elderly people who require door-to-door service but are ambulatory, are not always accessible to wheelchair users who have larger chairs. Nancy reported how in her home town, she had avoided using paratransit at weekends for some time because they used vans that would cause her wheelchair to tip backwards.[91] This indicates the need to ensure that all segments of the disability community are receiving equal treatment.

Unlike some other participants, however, Cheryl has taken advantage of the fact that the regular bus system in her city is now wheelchair accessible and uses it for most trips apart from medical appointments:

> There is a ramp, an accessible ramp lift thing that it folds up, and then they use a control once you get inside the bus to lower it and raise it and whatnot. Then they tie down your wheelchair, make you wear a seatbelt and all that.[92]

However, some participants faced barriers because bus drivers refused to pull the switch to allow for low floor access or parked too far from the curb, underscoring the reality that physical accommodations alone are inadequate but need to be followed with appropriate training.[93] These sorts of barriers seemed to be particularly the case with those participants whose impairments were less obvious because they had some mobility with the use of canes. This undermined the ability of even those who articulated a strong advocacy identity to travel on the regular buses. Mary observes:

> I hadn't made it to the stop yet so I said, "Come on. Let me in please." And he was like, "No, go to the stop." And I didn't have my cane that day, but I was really sore. Because I was supposed to get a ride back home but that fell through so I said fine. So I took my time. Of course it took a while for him to stop. The driver looks at me and goes, "Can you walk any slower?" And I said, "Excuse me, I happen to have arthritis in both knees." You know sometimes it helps to lie. It's not far from a lie. And he went, "Well, whatever. You could have went faster."[94]

As with Tracy's experience on intercity buses, Mary also reports drivers who would not make people move even though she required a seat due to her impairments:

> Another one there was a driver, I come in, I had my cane, I was pulling my stuff in a dolly, I walked in, flipped them the card, and said, "I'm

going to need a seat." He looks at me and says, "I'm not making people move for you" . . . It was packed, but in the front only type of thing. They could have moved back. He goes, "Why don't you just wait for the next one?" I look up and say, "I really can't stand." So I told him where to go, and then said, "I'll f'ing take the next bus." I showed the cane, and the people in the front seat were like, "My God! He had no right to talk to her like that." So I called [the bus company] to tell them what happened, and they say that should not have happened.[95]

In the case of those with mobility impairments who do not use wheelchairs, distance to bus stops can also pose a barrier, particularly during cold Canadian winters where snow and ice pose significant obstacles for those with limited mobility. While one might regard this as a neutral policy, in fact bus routes have been the subject of budget cuts. Charles indicates that he has had to walk up to three kilometers because evening service is not available in his suburban neighbourhood where he still lives with his parents.[96] Tracy notes how in the past, train services had significant staff who would assist passengers to board, transfer and with carrying luggage.[97] They were simply reduced or eliminated over time as budget cuts to trains mounted. Interestingly, even those participants like Charles who generally disliked advocacy often would advocate on transportation issues. This may well be because transportation is so foundational to activities of daily living such as education and employment and because, unlike in other areas, it is not easy to find an alternative solution to such an essential service.

It should be noted that some participants either identified no problems with paratransit or praised the service. A positive experience with certain drivers may have left a lasting impression of good will on the part of some of the participants. Tracy, a determined activist on many issues including transportation where she feels she is facing discrimination, praises the efforts of some paratransit drivers:

I couldn't get a reliable driver to get me from [a nearby town] down to my appointment here, so they sent [paratransit] from here up to there to come get me and come back and the guy gave me his pager number. To sit there and get hold of him so I didn't have to go through and everything. [Paratransit] driver—excellent. Even when we were driving back up we were heading through [another town] and he asked if I needed to stop over at [a coffee shop] or anything so yeah, I could really use a good snack. No problem. The fact that he asked, that was a major good with them.[98]

Nevertheless, she eventually preferred the autonomy and freedom of driving her own vehicle.[99]

Other participants note how the local light rail system enabled accessibility. Lisa commented:

. . . it was kind of a happy accident that I realized, oh, I can get around the city and I can go out and I can go where I want and there's very little imposition in my way. I can go do groceries for the first time in my life completely by myself. I remember a friend phoning me and I said, "Well, I'm going to do groceries tomorrow," and she said, "Well, how are you going to manage that," and of course I was a smartass and said, "Well, I'm going to get on the . . . train, I'm going to go to [redacted]. I'm going to go in the lobby of Loblaws, check off the items on my list, and then come back," and she goes, "You're very smart," and I said, "Yeah, I know."[100]

This illustrates both the promise of accessibility as the regular transportation system becomes more wheelchair accessible and the continued dysfunctionality of paratransit.

Accessibility has multiple dimensions that work collectively to create a welcoming and inclusive transportation system for all. One that should not be forgotten when analyzing the experiences of disabled people is the financial accessibility of bus transportation. This was raised by some participants and not surprisingly it was often those participants on fixed incomes who were concerned. Nancy comments that while her roommate often went off campus to shop at the local mall, this basic activity of daily living was simply impossible for her because of her dire financial situation.[101] Mary recounts how, as someone who has both a physical disability and had experienced a nervous breakdown, she was dependent on social assistance. She noted that until a year before we conducted our interview, bus passes were not included as part of the social assistance payments except for individuals with frequent medical appointments, leading to people who were trapped at home due to the high cost of transportation.[102] We noted in Chapter 4 that Mary had discovered a workshop for social assistance recipients on how to access free bus passes.[103] This illustrates the important relationship between access to transportation and economic well-being.

Certain participants highlight more subtle accessibility issues. At the time of the original interview, Henry apparently made no efforts to use a wheelchair accessible regular bus because of concerns by his parents that he would not be able to handle it on his own.[104] This underscores the importance of the challenging issue surrounding changing attitudes about disability, including on the part of family members. Interestingly, by the time we conducted a focus group some months later, Henry commented that he was in fact using regular transit.[105] This indicates how for most of our participants, these are in many ways their formative years as they attempt to try different forms of accommodation and determine through trial and error what best suits their needs as young adults enrolled in undergraduate programs. Cheryl observes that the local bus company does not consider her eligible for a student-discounted bus pass, an enormous benefit to any student, because she only attends school on a part time basis to accommodate her learning disabilities.[106]

Tom, perhaps the participant with the most explicitly advocacy-oriented identity, noted that the local light rail system, a new and as noted above otherwise highly accessible transportation network, had ticket vending machines that were not accessible because they were too high for wheelchair users to reach. While this was not an issue in the past because the municipality in which Tom lived had a policy to allow disabled people to use public transportation for free, when the policy was terminated, a barrier was created. He comments:

> What they didn't realize was the . . . ticket machine was not accessible. I can't reach it if I'm sitting in my chair. So I said to them, "What do you want me to do? Because . . ." and they said, "Well, can't you just get someone to get a ticket for you?" And I said "Excuse me, sir, but I'm not going to get someone I don't know to go into my wallet to get money to put it in for the sake of a three dollar ticket. You get me an accessible ticket machine, and I'll start using it, but until that point I am not going to pay, and I want you to know that."[107]

At the same time, Tom conveyed an attitude of simply going on with his life regardless of the access barriers, consistent with his advocacy identity. He remarks:

> I mean, I get stuck a few times, I laugh about it, it's no big deal to me, I deal with it. I've never been severely wounded yet, and I'm just going to keep living my life. Transportation can get in the way but whatever, you work around it much like you work around everything else in life. As I said before, I don't get intimidated by problems. They just come up.[108]

He even notes the ways in which access barriers occasionally benefit him. For instance, due to barriers on the intercity train system,[109] he is regularly placed in first class which is wheelchair accessible:

> And to get home to [redacted] I'm big on the Via Rail trains because the Via Rail . . . there's only one wheelchair spot, and it's in first class. Which means that I'm paying student economy fare, and I get first class including dinner and wine and liquors and all sorts of other good stuff. Chocolates. The chocolate is very good.[110]

Yet this good fortune is ultimately rooted in the fact that significant barriers preclude disabled people from accessing all classes of the train system. It seems that Tom's commitment to consistent assertion of his disability identity leads him to downplay what are significant barriers in transportation.

Accessibility barriers and taxis

While the cost of taxis may simply be prohibitive for many disabled people, they allow disabled people to reach their destinations with flexibility. Indeed, they may well be the only option when travelling at night while paratransit or even many regular bus systems no longer operate. As the commentary below indicates, having an active social life into the late evening is a core part of the identity of many young adults. Unfortunately, participants reported a variety of problems with taxis, including availability of accessible taxis, extra fees and attitudinal barriers on the part of some drivers. Tracy comments:

> Sitting there and asking for a wheelchair accessible taxi. And they would send me a Crown Vic. This is really hard to get into, especially when, ok, I'm up on crutches and I've got to get down there? As in they are trying to clue the taxi cab driver that you are going to have to take the wheelchair, bring it around so I can get into it.[111]

The reluctance of the driver to provide even minimal assistance with assistive devices creates a very real barrier that may preclude many disabled people from travelling, suggesting the need for better training of taxi drivers on the needs of disabled people and to transform the discourse surrounding disability away from pity and toward rights. In Britain, a disability advocacy rights group, Democracy, Disability, and Society, has created an information and training package to educate taxi drivers on the issues facing disabled people.[112] Tracy notes that community colleges were operating programs to teach accessibility etiquette to taxi drivers including the fact that individuals with invisible disabilities may still require accommodation.[113] It will likely take some time before the effects are visible to the public.

Unfortunately, at least one participant reported that she had to hide her manual wheelchair in order for drivers to pick her up. Andrea comments:

> I visited my boyfriend in [a large Canadian city] earlier, and . . . I'm pretty sure it would be the same situation here – we would go to [redacted] as we were attending a convention there. And everyday, after it ended we would go out on the sidewalk to try to get a taxi and sometimes – I have a manual wheelchair and when I don't want to have to lug this thing around, I use my manual chair – and the only way that we could get a taxi to stop and pick us up was if I stood up (I can stand and walk for short distances) and we sort of hid the chair behind us. They would not pick me up while I was sitting in the chair.[114]

Mary, who from time to time escorts elderly disabled people as employment, reports how an elderly friend of hers experienced rude and insulting treatment from a taxi driver.[115] These blatant forms of discrimination suggest that physical accessibility will not improve services for disabled people until training is performed to transform the attitudes of drivers.

A more systemic issue is pricing and availability policies with respect to wheelchair accessible cabs. Lisa recounts how in her home town, wheelchair accessible taxis had to be pre-booked days and even weeks in advance due to a shortage of wheelchair accessible cabs, and the taxi meter started at more than 25 dollars.[116] She reflects on her experience:

> But in terms of [a large Canadian city], for a wheelchair cab, first of all you can't just phone for one because they are all prebooked by [paratransit], they are all pre-owned by the [paratransit] company. So if you're booking a wheelchair cab, unless you're booking it privately, and even if you book it privately, they need 24 to 48 hours of notice, and that's only if you're under the wire. Typically you phone and book weeks ahead. When I am coming home, and I have my power chair my mother will phone the cab company weeks before I come home saying, "My daughter is coming, she's in a power chair, we need a thing." And also the meter because the very tricky thing, as soon as a wheelchair gets into a cab the starting point jumps up to 25 dollars so for me to get from the train station to my home typically a 20 to 25 dollar affair is up around 50 dollars for me. To get from [the airport] to my home . . . again, typically maybe 30 dollars, it's like 60 dollars so I can't afford, first of all, cabs aren't available. Second of all, I can't afford it because I'm not made of money.

Despite making complaints about the pricing, Lisa's concerns were ignored.[117] Tom also reports having to yell at cab drivers to make them aware of his needs. Consistent with his strong advocacy identity, Tom expresses what almost might be characterized as pleasure at the challenge of fighting for accessibility:

> Because after midnight the [paratransit] stops running but as a university student my life doesn't stop at midnight, in fact sometimes it doesn't start until 11 pm. And so I've had to get wheelchair vans which has been a fun experience in the past. You know, but I'm a person who doesn't mind getting on the phone and yelling at people, in fact I get a certain exhilaration out of it.[118]

Similarly, Henry appreciates the spontaneity that taxis provide but notes how he has been stranded late at night because he has been unable to find an accessible cab.[119]

Price gouging by taxi drivers operating accessible taxis has in fact been covered by the Canadian media.[120] While no doubt there are additional operating expenses for wheelchair accessible taxis, such as insurance costs, policy and legal mechanisms can alter the situation. A rule allowing wheelchair accessible taxis to pick up able bodied passengers when they are not otherwise engaged would allow taxi drivers greater revenues from fares and make an accessible taxi system more viable.[121] Some Canadian municipalities have begun voucher programs to provide partial subsidies to disabled people for taxis so that a more flexible option is available.[122] Interestingly, living in a more accessible community for school with convenient transportation options, as in Lisa's experience, may well heighten awareness of the need for advocacy when a disabled person returns home and faces barriers.

Accessibility barriers and driving

The issue of driving is a complex one for disabled people. On the one hand, some disabled people do not possess the ability to drive in a safe manner. A balance must clearly be struck between providing accommodation to disabled people and public safety.[123] However, it is also clear that there are numerous barriers to driving even where a person has the physical ability to drive, with or without adaptations such as hand controls to operate the pedals. Driving has become a rite of passage to adulthood despite the fact that studies are showing young people in Canada, the United States and Britain are delaying the acquisition of a driver's license.[124] It is in many cases the quickest and most convenient mode of travel, and it often forms a key part of a person's identity. Indeed, one participant, Tom, who does not believe he can drive, has nonetheless considered obtaining a learner's permit for driving solely so that he can have another piece of identification.[125] This underscores the importance of driving as a sign of adulthood in modern society and the lack of alternatives for those who cannot or chose not to obtain a driver's license. In other cases, the pressures of coping with school, particularly when some participants are dealing with barriers as a result of both physical and learning disabilities, mean that there simply is not time to invest in driving lessons for those, like the majority of our participants, who were born with disabilities. In Cheryl's case, she has been told by educational experts that she should not be taking more than three classes per semester in order to maximize her academic potential because she needs additional time for studying and exam preparation. She therefore attends school on a part time basis. She recounts:

> I was told I had a learning assessment done by . . . an educational psychologist. Basically I have been told numerous times, "If you take more than three classes you're dooming yourself to failure and poor grades!" Ok, so I'll just take it a little bit more slow.[126]

It is consequently not surprising that given her physical and learning disabilities and the associated barriers, she has found little time for driving lessons.
On the question of driving, Cheryl remarks:

> I am perfectly capable of driving a vehicle; I just don't have a lot of . . . I can't exert enough pressure with my feet in order to push the gas above 60. I have enough reflexes to stop a vehicle, that is, slam on the brakes, but my reflexes are a couple seconds too short for it to be legal. My family has made the one car, – we own three vehicles – that has hand controls so that the minute I do get my licence, my family is completely supportive. I just haven't found the time to write my [learner's permit test]. And

then I have to be on a wait list because there's very few places in [town] that actually have hand controlled vehicles that you can practice with.[127]

This raises two distinct issues. Apart from her busy schedule, Cheryl faces structural barriers in that those who require hand-controlled vehicles do not necessarily have sufficient access to adapted vehicles that they need to practice while learning to drive. This can serve as a discouragement to learning to drive, especially as many disabled people, like Cheryl, have waited until their 20s when they have moved away from home and no longer have constant access to parental vehicles. Second, Cheryl notes that she has the full support of her family but simply has not made the time to learn to drive. As in the case of Henry's parents who were fearful of his use of public transit, there are likely many parents of disabled young adults who in fact are not supportive of driving out of concern that it will pose a serious danger to their child or others.

A dramatic contrast is provided by the case of Michael. He obtained a learner's permit and is very much interested in acquiring a driver's license so that he can hang out with his friends more easily.[128] However, his parents have a policy that all their children must purchase their own vehicles.[129] In Michael's case, this would also mean paying for hand controls, which he estimates at a cost of $1,000. As a result, he has put off driving as simply beyond his current financial means.[130] A further illustration of the role of parental attitudes is the apparent belief on the part of Michael's father that his son should try to use his feet to drive despite his physical disabilities that limit his mobility.[131]

Some participants have coped with the inability to drive in creative ways. Henry, who has a relatively severe disability which affects all his limbs and prevents him from driving, uses attendants to drive him where he needs to go using his accessible van.[132] He is therefore in the anomalous situation of having access to a vehicle but no driver's license. This enables him to participate in recreational activities such as movies or going to a pub. Interestingly, Henry reports this is also popular with his friends as it allows them to drink without having to worry about driving later.[133] Unfortunately, this option is likely unavailable to most disabled people due to the financial constraints.

One has to bear in mind that the cost of an automobile is not restricted to either the initial sticker price or to adaptations for those disabled people who are unable to pedal. The regular operating costs of owning a vehicle, including gasoline and insurance, may be prohibitive for many disabled people on limited incomes. Hence, Mary whose fibromyalgia did not fully manifest itself until she was in her 20s, has a driver's license but does not own a car because of the cost as someone who receives social assistance.[134] This suggests the interlocking nature of the themes that participants discussed with us. If someone is unable to obtain well-remunerated employment, that in turn affects their transportation choices. Yet the limited transportation choices may well impact their ability to obtain employment, leading to a vicious circle.

In other cases, however, driver's licenses were acquired at the conventional age of sixteen. Maxime owns his own car and learned to drive within a few months of his sixteenth birthday using adapted equipment to accommodate the paralysis in his legs.[135] Interestingly, he grew up, unlike most other participants, in a very small town.[136] One has to wonder whether the lack of feasible alternatives such as paratransit in his community actually encouraged him to drive.

Perhaps the most interesting experiences are among the small number of older participants in our study who acquired disabilities as adults and who possessed driver's licenses at the time of their disablement.[137] While one would think that barriers would be minor since they already demonstrated an ability to drive, Tracy notes that there are barriers in the process of re-licensing with an adapted vehicle due to the ignorance of driving examiners towards accommodations:

> I was told a lot of the examiners, if you have anything that is even slightly off of the strict norm, they can't deal with it . . . if you've got a totalitarian examiner, it's got to be by the letter or else no. I know a few people that have hand controls and number one the examiner's getting all freaked that "what are you doing with a vehicle already if you haven't got a licence" especially if it's got all these adaptations. And they don't know how those adaptations work, and they're not willing to take the time to find out so they know you're operating it properly. And the examiners get really uptight.[138]

Tracy recounted how a friend of hers who is an amputee was not permitted to use his adapted motorcycle during a road test.[139] She also observed that a small disability fund established by automakers was administered in a highly bureaucratic way that prevented her from applying the funds toward the accommodations that she really needed in order to drive. She wanted to use the fund to partly finance the purchase of an automatic vehicle because she was unable to use the clutch due to her impairments.[140] However, the automaker insisted that the fund could only be used for specified purposes:

> So I talked to [the automaker] and basically said, "Well can I apply the $500 disability fund toward the fact that I have to get an automatic?" No. That is only for the tailgate lift or the wheelchair automatic entry or the removing of the driver's chair and the docking mechanism for the wheelchair but it's not meant for that.[141]

She also noted that another automaker would not provide transportation from her remote location in a rural town to the car dealership so that she could take the merchandise for a test drive. They also tried to pressure her to purchase a model of car in which she was not interested. She consequently decided not to do business with them.[142]

Andrea, who was in the very unusual situation of acquiring a driver's license during the course of our study but was under the age of 24, indicated that while she had no major problems with testing as she was able to use her own vehicle, she faced barriers in purchasing as she could not test drive vehicles. She was able to surmount this barrier only because her boyfriend accompanied her and assisted her by testing vehicles on her behalf.[143] She also has found she is unable to rent vehicles, but her boyfriend is able to share the driving.[144] This reminds us again of how contingent barriers can be. Someone who is single might not have had the options available to Andrea.

It is also important to recognize that, in some cases, a disability may have intermittent effects such as fatigue or pain, rendering a disabled person perfectly able to drive one day and completely unable to drive the next. In those situations, no amount of accommodation can completely address the question. Rather, what has been referred to by disability studies scholars such as Carol Thomas as impairment effects that cannot be fully explained by the social model of disablement may need to be carefully managed by the disabled person through a variety of mechanisms such as careful monitoring of daily activity.[145] As Thomas correctly observes, this in no way means that impairment effects do not have a social dimension. There is a profoundly political aspect to how much fatigue a person will have depending on such factors as their socioeconomic circumstances and parenting responsibilities.[146] Mary notes that when she does have access to a vehicle, her disability may mean she is in so much pain that she is simply unable to walk to her vehicle.[147] At other times, she will slow down if she finds herself getting tired or sore:

> . . . [I]f I'm sore and I can't get to the car I'm not going anywhere. If I'm tired I promised myself when I first got my license at 16 that I was not going to drive tired, drunk, stoned, or angry. So I had already made that promise before I got a license. I stick to it now. And even when we were moving, while I was still ok and agile and awake we booted back and forth on the [highway] no problem, but as soon as I was getting tired, the speed went down to 90. You have to adjust your speed because I'm not moving as quick as I normally would, so I'm not going to think of being stupid. Same as if I'm sore. Luckily I've had no sudden pains that have made the driving hazardous. I can't guarantee what is going to happen as I get old.[148]

Mary clearly has made attempts to manage the impairment effects that stem from her disability, but it is not clear to what extent she will be able to drive in the future.

Accessibility barriers and aircraft

Disabled people have long faced major barriers on airplanes with respect to boarding and deplaning as well as with services in airports. Some disabled people have been refused passage via aircraft or refused passage unless they are accompanied by an attendant even if they do not require one.[149] A number of failures have been identified in Canadian policy-making at the federal level, which governs air transportation, including a lack of expertise on accessibility in Transport Canada, the government department responsible for regulating transportation.[150] Other failures include allowing respondents, most notably in the *Via Rail* case, to make claims of undue hardship based on costs incurred because of their failure to comply with accessibility regulations in the first place.[151] Tragically, Canada's international reputation as a leader in equality for disability rights has suffered due to the massive problems in the transportation sector.

One exception is the successful campaign by disability rights advocates to obtain what has become known as a "one person one fare" policy. After a lengthy legal battle including an unsuccessful application for leave to appeal to the Supreme Court of Canada by several airlines, the CTA ruled that severely disabled individuals who require attendants to assist them during the flight or obese people who require two seats may travel at the cost of only one fare.[152] The policy was to take effect 2009.

Although air travel was not a common theme mentioned by participants, Henry was passionate in observing that he has not flown for years, at least partly because of the degrading manner in which he has been treated. He observes that wheelchair users are obliged to stow their wheelchairs and use special airplane chairs which he clearly regards as invasive.[153] As in the *Via Rail* case, it is critical to appreciate how much wheelchairs are customized to suit an individual person's needs and simply substituting another chair is not acceptable. In refusing to fly, Henry effectively embraces advocacy in a situation where he has very limited control. He cannot force airlines to transform their insensitive practices and so he undertakes the option available to him by refusing to fly.

Conclusion

In this chapter, we have explored how our participants use an advocacy identity to deal with the widespread physical and attitudinal barriers that are endemic in Western societies. These barriers are so common that even those participants who are relatively reluctant to engage in advocacy in other contexts find themselves defiantly demanding better treatment and accessibility in the barrier-filled world of transportation. We began with a discussion of paratransit policy and how the debates surrounding it mirror those amongst policymakers regarding inclusive education. Increasingly, Western countries have undertaken gradual steps to make regular public transit wheelchair accessible, with the United States clearly a world leader. We then examined disability policy and law as it relates to transportation in Canada, the United States and Britain. Turning to our narrative interviews, we focused on the experience of our participants in bus transportation, noting a shocking variety of problems ranging from the highly restrictive rules that govern paratransit to rudeness and ignorance on the part of bus drivers who operate the regular routes and are not accustomed to serving disabled customers. It is worth remembering that in many cases, paratransit faces so much demand that a disabled person who wishes such a ride may not be served at all. Even the most patient of advocates found themselves frustrated by the litany of barriers.

We then considered the barriers that disabled people experience using taxis including blatant discrimination from taxi drivers who refuse to pick up disabled passengers to discriminatory pricing policies and the sheer lack of accessible taxis for wheelchair users. The frustration and anger expressed by our participants paint a bleak picture of Canadian transportation barriers. We also explored the barriers faced when driving independently for disabled people. Considerable barriers exist which prevent disabled people who are born with impairments from acquiring licenses. We return to this theme in Chapter 7. Surprisingly, we found even here a range of barriers including restrictive policies on the funding of adaptive devices for driving to barriers in purchasing vehicles. Lastly, we concluded our study with a brief exploration of barriers in airline travel. While advocacy can certainly mitigate the worst of abuses, the narratives described in this chapter underscore how a structural framework for eliminating barriers is pressing if we are to truly achieve equality for disabled people. We turn now in Chapter 6 to explore those issues relating to gender.

Notes

1　Tracy, personal interview, 2007–08, p. 21.
2　See L. Gilbert and M. Dikeç, 'Right to the City: Politics of Citizenship' in K. Goonewardena *et al.* (eds) *Space, Difference, Everyday Life: Reading Henri Lefebvre*, New York, NY: Routledge, 2008, pp. 250–51 (analyzing immigration flows to cities in the context of Lefebvre's theory). This theme has been taken up by disability theorists, particularly geographers, in a variety of ways. See R. Imrie, *Disability and the City: International Perspectives*, London: Paul Chapman, 1996; B. Gleeson, 'Disability and the Open City' *Urban Studies*, 2001, vol. 38, pp. 251–65.
3　Gilbert and Dikeç, ibid, p. 259. For an insightful typology of cities and their implications for how class relations would operate, see L. Boltanski and E. Chiapello, *The New Spirit of Capitalism*, trans. G. Elliott, London: Verso, 2005, pp. 107–36.
4　For Canadian accounts of activism and litigation relating to train accessibility, see D. Baker and S. Godwin, 'ALL ABOARD!: The Supreme Court of Canada Confirms that Canadians with Disabilities Have Substantive Equality Rights' *Saskatchewan Law Review*, 2008, vol. 71, pp. 39–77; A. D'Aubin, 'We Will Ride: A Showcase of CCD Advocacy Strategies in Support of Accessible Transportation' in D. Stienstra and A. Wight-Felske (eds) *Making Equality: History of Advocacy and Persons with Disabilities in Canada*, Toronto: Captus Press, 2003, pp. 87–118. For American accounts of the battle for accessible public bus transportation, see D.Z. Fleischer and F. Zames, *The Disability Rights Movement: From Charity to Confrontation*, updated edn, Philadelphia, PA: Temple University Press, 2011, pp. 65–70, 82–83; J. Shapiro, *No Pity: Disabled People Forging a New Civil Rights Movement*, New York, NY: Times Books, 1993, pp. 129–29. See Gleeson, op. cit., n. 2, p. 256 for a discussion of the regulation of the disabled body in geographic contexts.

5 Gleeson, op. cit., n. 2, p. 258.

6 Imrie, op. cit., n. 2, p. 2 (citing Mike Davis' iconic work on this subject).

7 Some scholars have identified the barriers as physical, temporal, economic, spatial and psychological. See J. Hine and F. Mitchell, 'Better for Everyone? Travel Experiences and Transport Exclusion' *Urban Studies*, 2001, vol. 38, pp. 319–32 at p. 330.

8 C. Coleman, L. Nee, and L. Rubinowitz, 'Social Movements and Social-Change Litigation: Synergy in the Montgomery Bus Protest' *Law and Social Inquiry*, 2005, vol. 30, pp. 663–737.

9 In other words, if it exists, American transportation services tend to be accessible and are so required by law but they may not exist at all. See D. Baker, *Moving Backwards: Canada's State of Transportation Accessibility in an International Context*, Winnipeg: Council of Canadians with Disabilities, 2004, p. 58; M. Lewyn, '"Thou Shalt Not Put a Stumbling Block before the Blind": The Americans with Disabilities Act and Public Transit for the Disabled' *Hastings Law Journal*, 2001, vol. 52, pp. 1037–100.

10 E. Chadha, 'Running on Empty: The "Not So Special Status" of Paratransit Services in Ontario' *Windsor Review of Legal and Social Issues*, 2005, vol. 20, p. 1.

11 Ontario Human Rights Commission, *Human Rights and Public Transit Services in Ontario: Consultation Report*, Toronto: Ontario Human Rights Commission, 2002, p. 13.

12 Chadha, op. cit., n. 10, pp. 14–15.

13 See generally Organisation for Economic Co-operation and Development, *Ageing Populations: High Time for Action*, Paris: OECD, 2005.

14 B. Nelson and D. Stambrook, 'Economics of Accessible Transportation in Canada' paper delivered at the 12th International Conference on Mobility and Transport for Elderly and Disabled Persons (TRANSED 2010), 2010, available online at http://www.sortclearinghouse.info/cgi/viewcontent.cgi?article=1622&context=research (last accessed November 22, 2012). However, their analysis acknowledges that they are focused on a sub-set of the disability population with high disposable incomes.

15 Chadha, op. cit., n. 10, p. 2.

16 Chadha, op. cit., n. 10, pp. 9–10.

17 Ontario Human Rights Commission, op. cit., n. 11, pp. 20, 22–23. See also *Cannella v Toronto Transit Commission, Ontario Appeal Cases*, vol. 123, p. 123 (Ontario Superior Court of Justice) (finding eligibility test not discriminatory with respect to mentally disabled individuals).

18 *Council of Canadians with Disabilities v Via Rail, Supreme Court Reports*, 2007, vol. 1, pp. 773–74; *Dominion Law Reports (4th)*, 2007, vol. 279, p. 97 (*per* Deschamps and Rothstein JJ.) [*Via Rail* cited to *Supreme Court Reports*].

19 See B. Martin, 'British Rail Privatisation: What Went Wrong?' 2002, available online at http://www.publicworld.org/docs/britrail.pdf (last accessed October 22, 2012); M. Bird, 'Where is VIA Going? A Case Study of Managing a Commercial Crown Corporation' in A.M. Maslove (ed.) *How Ottawa Spends, 2009–2010: Economic Upheaval and Political Dysfunction*, Montreal and Kingston: McGill-Queen's University Press, 2009, pp. 267–69.

20 L. Wilson, 'An Overview of the Literature on Disability and Transport' Manchester: Disability Rights Commission, 2003, p. 6; B. Matthews, 'The *Disability Discrimination Act* and Developments in Accessible Public Transit in the U.K.' *World Transport Policy and Practice*, 2002, vol. 8, p. 42 (noting two-thirds of British disabled people surveyed said barriers in public transit was a reason they did not go out more).

21 Chadha, op. cit., n. 10, p. 4.

22 Chadha, op. cit., n. 10, pp. 8–9.

23 Chadha, op. cit., n. 10, pp. 1–2.

24 Chadha, op. cit., n. 10, p. 10.

25 Chadha, op. cit., n. 10, p. 15.

26 H. Lazar-Meyn, 'Paratransit Services Are Not "Special Programs"' *ARCH Alert*, June 13, 2006, available online at http://www.archdisabilitylaw.ca/sites/all/files/ARCH%20Alert%20-%20June%2013%2006%20-%20Text.txt (last accessed December 15, 2012).

27 'MTO 2011–2012 Accessibility Plan', available online at http://www.mto.gov.on.ca/english/pubs/access11/report-transport.shtml (last accessed Nov 10, 2012) (noting expectation that vast majority of buses in Ontario would be wheelchair accessible by end of 2012).

28 Ontario Human Rights Commission, op. cit., n. 11, p. 3.

29 Integrated Accessibility Standards, O Reg 191/11.

30 Baker, op. cit., n. 9, p. 21.

31 Baker, op. cit., n. 9, p. 22. See also D'Aubin, op. cit., n. 4, pp. 91–93.

32 A. D'Aubin, 'Making Federally Regulated Transportation Systems Accessible to Persons with Disabilities' in M.A. McColl and L. Jongbloed (eds) *Disability and Social Policy in Canada*, 2nd edn, Concord, Ontario: Captus University Publications, 2006, pp. 379–80.

33 Baker, op. cit., n. 9, p. 5.

34 *Via Rail*, above, n. 18.

35 SC 1996, c. 10.

36 See generally Baker and Godwin, op. cit., n. 4.

37 *Via Rail*, above, n. 18, p. 665.

38 Baker and Godwin, op. cit., n. 4, para. 18.

39 *Via Rail*, above, n. 18, p. 666; Baker, op. cit., n. 9, p. 7.

40 *Via Rail*, above, n. 18, p. 668.

41 *Via Rail*, above, n. 18, p. 669.

42 Baker and Godwin, op. cit., n. 4, para. 1.

43 *Via Rail*, above, n. 18, p. 749 (*per* Deschamps and Rothstein JJ., dissenting, but not on this point).

44 *Via Rail*, above, n. 18, pp. 675–76. This took the form of a show cause order, giving Via Rail another opportunity to demonstrate that the accommodations were not feasible or too costly.

45 *Via Rail*, above, n. 18, pp. 678–80.

46 *Via Rail*, above, n. 18, pp. 680–81. In contrast, Via Rail had estimated the accommodation to cost tens of millions of dollars.

47 *Via Rail*, above, n. 18, p. 683.

48 This example is supplied by the authors to illustrate the formalism in the Federal Court of Appeal's analysis.

49 *Via Rail*, above, n. 18, pp. 683–85.

50 Baker and Godwin, op. cit., n. 4, para. 43.

51 Baker and Godwin, op. cit., n. 4, para. 43.

52 Baker and Godwin, op. cit., n. 4, para. 43.

53 Baker and Godwin, op. cit., n. 4, para. 43.

54 Baker and Godwin, op. cit., n. 4, para. 43.

55 Baker and Godwin, op. cit., n. 4, para. 43.

56 Fleischer and Zames, op. cit., n. 4, p. 56.

57 687 F. 2d. 644 (2nd Cir. 1982).

58 Fleischer and Zames, op. cit., n. 4, p. 58.

59 Fleischer and Zames, op. cit., n. 4, pp. 61, 74.

60 P. S. Dempsey, 'The Civil Rights of the Handicapped in Transportation: The Americans with Disabilities Act and Related Legislation' *Transportation Law Journal*, 1990–91, vol. 19, pp. 330–33 (drawing link between increased transportation accessibility and increasing employment rates for disabled people).

61 Fleischer and Zames, op. cit., n. 4, pp. 84–85. In later years, ADAPT changed its acronym to mean Americans for Attendant Programs Today while continuing the same direct action tactics such as crawling up stairs of government buildings. See Gleeson, op. cit., n. 2, p. 259.

62 Fleischer and Zames, op cit., n. 4, pp. 62–63. This underscores the fact that even universal accessibility of regular transit does not mean one can marginalize paratransit services which will always be essential for some disabled people to access employment, medical services and recreation.

63 Union of the Physically Impaired Against Segregation, *Policy Statement*, Leeds: Union of the Physically Impaired Against Segregation, 1974, p. 1, available online at http://www.leeds.ac.uk/disability-studies/archiveuk/UPIAS/UPIAS.pdf (last accessed November 28, 2012).

64 Department for Transport, *Railways for All: The Accessibility Strategy for Great Britain's Railways*, London: Department of Transport, 2006, p. 5, available online at http://assets.dft.gov.uk/publications/railways-for-all-strategy/railways-for-all-strategy.pdf (last accessed November 28, 2012).

65 Department for Transport, ibid, p. 5.

66 Department for Transport, op. cit., n. 64, pp. 5–6.

67 Matthews, op. cit., n. 20, p. 45.

68 Department for Transport, op. cit., n. 64, p. 6.

69 Department for Transport, op. cit., n. 64, p. 6.

70 EqA, ss. 160–188.

71 Baker, op. cit., n. 9, pp. 10–11. As Baker produced his study in 2004, one would expect an even higher figure today.

72 Tracy, p. 21.

73 See R. Hubbard and G. Paquet, 'Design Challenges for the Strategic State: Bricolage and Sabotage' in A.M. Maslove (ed.) *How Ottawa Spends, 2009–2010: Economic Upheaval and Political Dysfunction*, Montreal and Kingston: McGill-Queen's University Press, 2009, pp. 89–112. For an interesting discussion on flexible labour management techniques in Italy, see R.M. Locke, 'The Political Embeddedness of Industrial Change: Corporate Restructuring and Local Politics in Contemporary Italy' in T.A. Kochan and M. Useem (eds) *Transforming Organizations*, Oxford: Oxford University Press, 1992, pp. 28–43.

74 Tracy, p. 21.

75 Tracy, p. 21.

76 On British bus drivers, see Hine and Mitchell, op. cit., n. 7, p. 328 (noting some disabled people have stopped using regular transit buses because of driver attitudes); J. Meikle, 'Minister Calls for Change in Attitude as Wheelchair User Takes on Bus Companies' *The Guardian*, July 11, 2012, available online at http://www.guardian.co.uk/society/2012/jul/11/row-wheelchairs-buses-minister-attitude (last accessed November 29, 2012). On American bus drivers, see Fleischer and Zames, op. cit., n. 4, pp. 60–61.

77 See Chapter 6.

78 Tracy, p. 1.

79 Andrea, personal interview, 2007–08, pp. 8–9. Some Canadian cities allow bookings several days in advance. Since available trips are finite, this places pressure on all users to plan trips several days in advance.

80 Andrea, p. 8.

81 However, to our knowledge, the window is typically shorter than three hours in Canadian cities.

82 Andrea, p. 8.

83 Women's Focus Group, September 20, 2008, pp. 8–9.

84 Tom, personal interview, 2007–08, p. 9.

85 Cheryl, personal interview, 2007–08, p. 9.
86 Cheryl, p. 9.
87 Mary, personal interview, 2007–08, p. 13.
88 Cheryl, p. 19.
89 See C. Rice *et al.*, 'Creating Community across Disability and Difference' in D. Driedger (ed.) *Living the Edges: A Disabled Women's Reader*, Toronto: Inanna Publications and Education Inc., 2010, p. 260.
90 Men's Focus Group, September 13, 2008, p. 6. See also Charles, personal interview, 2007–08, p. 5.
91 Nancy, personal interview, 2007–08, pp. 28–29. This policy was eventually changed.
92 Cheryl, p. 9.
93 Tracy, p. 30.
94 Mary, p. 18. She refers to lying because her actual impairment is a little known condition, fibromyalgia.
95 Mary, p. 18. The card refers to one issued to disabled passengers by the bus company indicating that they require a seat.
96 Men's Focus Group, September, op. cit., n. 90, p. 8.
97 Women's Focus Group, October 18, 2008, p. 15.
98 Tracy, p. 22.
99 Tracy, p. 22.
100 Lisa, personal interview, 2007–08, p. 37.
101 Nancy, p. 12.
102 Mary, p. 14.
103 See Chapter 4.
104 Henry, personal interview, 2007–08, pp. 20–21.
105 Men's Focus Group, September, above, n. 90, p. 7.
106 Cheryl, p. 15. It should be noted that even students with mobility impairments only may feel they are only able to attend classes on a part time basis due to barriers with obtaining attendant services and ironically paratransit.
107 Tom, p. 11.
108 Tom, p. 9.
109 See the discussion of the Supreme Court of Canada's decision in *Via Rail*, above, n. 18.
110 Tom, p. 9.
111 Tracy, p. 21.
112 Democracy, Disability and Society Group, 'Taxi Training Pack', available online at http://www.ddsg.org.uk/taxi/ (last accessed November 28, 2012).
113 Women's Focus Group, October, above, n. 97, p. 11.
114 Women's Focus Group, September, above, n. 83, p. 12.
115 Women's Focus Group, September, above, n. 83, pp.12–13.
116 Lisa, p. 36.
117 Lisa, p. 36.
118 Tom, p. 9.
119 Men's Focus Group, September, above, n. 90, pp. 7–8.
120 A. Broverman, 'Toronto Wheelchair Taxi Cabs Price Gouge Patrons with Disabilities' *Wallet Pop*, October 31, 2010, available online at http://www.walletpop.ca/blog/2010/10/31/toronto-wheelchair-taxicabs-price-gouge-patrons-with-disabilitie/ (last accessed November 28, 2012).
121 Broverman, ibid.
122 See e.g. J. Ruocco, 'Town to Cover Taxi Voucher Program Increase Until New Year' *Whitecourt Star*, October 3, 2012, available online at http://www.whitecourtstar.com/2012/10/03/town-to-cover-taxi-voucher-program-increase-until-new-year (last accessed November 28, 2012).

123 See e.g. *British Columbia (Superintendent of Motor Vehicles) v British Columbia (Council of Human Rights)* [1999] 3 SCR 868 where the Supreme Court unanimously upheld a human rights tribunal's finding that the British Columbia government discriminated against a man with a visual impairment when it failed to even give him an opportunity to try to pass a driving test.

124 W. Immen, 'Fewer Drivers Makes It Harder to Hire' Toronto *Globe and Mail*, December 10, 2012, available online at http://www.theglobeandmail.com/report-on-business/small-business/sb-managing/human-resources/fewer-drivers-makes-it-harder-to-hire/article6114058/ (last accessed December 10, 2012); C. Morris, 'Fewer Young Canadians Are Getting Their Driver's License' *Shine On*, April 9, 2012, available online at http://ca.shine.yahoo.com/blogs/shine-on/fewer-young-canadians-getting-driver-licence-184210177.html (last accessed November 28, 2012).

125 Tom, p. 9.

126 Cheryl, p. 15. Cheryl stresses that she is considered to be a part time student for some purposes but not others.

127 Cheryl, p. 8.

128 Michael, personal interview, 2007–08, pp. 5, 7.

129 Michael, p. 7. Of course, this is far less expensive for Michael's able-bodied sister than for himself.

130 Michael, p. 7.

131 Michael, p. 7.

132 Henry, p. 21.

133 Henry, p. 21.

134 Mary, pp. 1, 13.

135 Maxime, personal interview, 2007–08, p. 12.

136 Maxime, p. 5.

137 Indeed, Tracy and Sarah acquired disabilities as a result of car accidents.

138 Women's Focus Group, October, above, n. 97, p. 8.

139 Women's Focus Group, October, above, n. 97, p. 8.

140 Tracy, p. 20.

141 Tracy, p. 20.

142 Tracy, p. 20.

143 Women's Focus Group, September, above, n. 69, p. 16. We use the term "boyfriend" because this is the term chosen by the participant.

144 Women's Focus Group, September, above, n. 69, p. 18. Other participants like Mary, however, enjoyed renting cars, particularly expensive ones that had better access. See ibid, p. 17.

145 C. Thomas, *Female Forms: Experiencing and Understanding Disability*, Buckingham: Open University Press, 1999, pp. 42–44. See our discussion in Chapter 1.

146 Thomas, ibid, pp. 42–44.

147 Mary, p. 13.

148 Mary, p. 13.

149 D'Aubin, op. cit., n. 32, p. 91.

150 Baker, op. cit., n. 9, p. 82.

151 Baker, op. cit., n. 9, p. 82.

152 'Highlights of One-Person-One-Fare Policy Decision', available online at http://www.otc-cta.gc.ca/eng/highlights-one-person-one-fare-policy-decision (last accessed December 5, 2012).

153 Men's Focus Group, September, above, n. 90, pp. 9–10. See also M. Oliver and B. Omansky, 'Unmet Promises of Disability Law and Policy' in M. Oliver (ed.) *Understanding Disability: From Theory to Practice*, 2nd edn, Basingstoke: Palgrave Macmillan, 2009, pp. 58–63 (describing barriers for wheelchair users during transatlantic voyage to the United States).

6   Gendered expectations, the body and identity

Cheryl has grown used to people assuming that she's helpless. She finds that strangers will sometimes feel the need to comment on her appearance but will rarely do it directly to her face. When out with her mother, it is her mother who gets asked the question: "What does she have?" This behaviour Cheryl easily identifies as attaching to her disability; when people see her in a wheelchair, they assume she must have other impairments as well. Other times when she is treated as though she is helpless, it is harder to classify. For instance, when she goes to the store, she is inundated with unsolicited questions: "Can I help you with that?" "Can I reach that for you?" But whether this reaction is because she is a person with a disability, a woman, or a woman with a disability, Cheryl cannot say:

> That's the really hard thing. I've been to focus groups where you're supposed to talk about how it feels to be a woman and what kind of challenges and discrimination you face. I can't tell you. I can't really comment on it because I am not only a woman. I am a woman with a disability. So if somebody says "I'm sorry, we can't hire you," is it because I am a woman or because I am a woman with a disability?[1]

Gender and disability both impact the formation of personal identity and intertwine in the ways in which individuals are included in or excluded from society. In Engel's and Munger's study, gender can be seen working alongside and in tension with disability to affect how the study's participants view themselves, their role in the world around them, their future opportunities and their legal rights.[2] Gender does not operate on its own and, in combination with disability, how these factors affect life narratives and self-concept varies depending on other factors such as culture, race and class.[3] Like disability, gender is, in many ways, a social construction linked to differences in biology and physical condition, around which particular stereotypes and societal expectations have arisen.[4] These expectations and stereotypes form the standards to which individuals compare themselves when assessing their identities and to which they will likely be compared by others.

The narratives recounted in this chapter reflect how the participants in our study have experienced the demands of gender roles and gendered expectations and how this intersects with their experiences with disabilities. These stories demonstrate how gender roles and the "disabled" role conflict to prevent disabled people from being seen as acceptable men and women and how these roles may also work together to exacerbate stereotyping and exclusion. This chapter also briefly examines how the subversion of expectations relating to masculinity, femininity and disability can result in harassment, lack of agency in relation to important, practical life decisions and rejection from certain fields of study and work. The participants reflect on the effect that these experiences have had on their self-worth, their construction of personal identity and their awareness of rights. They also demonstrate means of working within and around gendered expectations and their status as disabled individuals. The strong and largely positive self-conceptions forged by many of the participants of the study suggest that these work-around mechanisms may be highly effective.

Gender roles

As Judith Butler famously posited, gender can be seen less as something one is or has and more as something that one does or performs.[5] From this perspective, gender is not directly concerned with biological differences between men and women but instead with the roles prescribed to men and women by broader society.[6] Rather than embodying or being these roles, men and women are expected to perform their assigned roles, whether through choosing appropriate dress, displaying the required social behaviours and mannerisms, or selecting a gender-appropriate occupation. An individual who fulfills his or her assigned gender role earns the approbation of society and acceptance into the social milieu. An individual who rejects his or her assigned gender role or otherwise fails to perform it is similarly rejected by the society and censured.[7] Due to the inflexibility of gender roles, their one-size-fits-all model, and their foundation in the unequal power relations between men and women, gender roles and gender role assignment reflect a profoundly difficult form of socialization that focuses on restricting the individual, reproducing both dominant stereotypes and the status quo, and further excluding individuals who are unable to fulfil their roles.[8]

The process of exclusion inherent within gender roles has strong effects on those who, like disabled people, already find themselves excluded by society. Gender is only one part of the larger performance of identity. Some theorists, such as Goffman, have suggested that individuals who are part of marginalized groups may feel that their identity has been spoiled by the characteristic that makes them part of that group.[9] Others observe that these individuals may feel the need to work harder at performing the positive parts of their identity to overcome negative stereotypes.[10] In terms of gender and disability, these feelings of spoiling and needing to work to overcome may gain additional weight as the personal qualities, behaviours and activities that make up gender roles find their basis in a non-disabled standard, creating idealized notions of men and women that often lie outside the concrete abilities of men and women with disabilities.[11] The lives, experiences, and identities of disabled people may have little to do with the expectations society has attached to either gender or to disability. As a result, disabled individuals must manage two connected sets of expectations: gendered expectations which anticipate abilities that the individual may not have and disability expectations which anticipate a variety of stereotypical, negative behaviours.[12]

Disabled men and the performance of gender

For men, these roles are often in direct conflict. Where the male gender role emphasizes strength, independence and assertiveness, the "disabled" role anticipates weakness, dependency and passivity.[13] Male physicality takes a central place in the definition of the male gender, where much of the emphasis is on the "toughness, competitiveness, and ability" of men's bodies.[14] A man with physical disabilities thus finds himself in a zone of competing identities, where the societal perception that he is unfit physically prevents him from fully establishing himself within the masculine gender role. At the same time, many other elements of the hegemonic male gender role remain open to disabled men. For individuals with mobility impairments, qualities such as courage, aggressiveness and emotional strength may find their basis in traditional ideals of masculine physical strength but can also be successfully divorced from the physical.

Fine and Asch noted this conflict in the mid-1980s and argue that disabled men can often remove themselves partially from the "disabled" role by emphasizing masculine qualities such as assertiveness and leadership skills, effectively recapturing the male gender role.[15] Similarly, Gerschick and Miller theorize that most disabled men seek to discard the "disabled" role and adopt a variation on the hegemonic role, which has a variety of options available for resolving the conflict in society's perception of these roles.[16] Rejection, the full renunciation of the traditional standards of masculinity and the formulation of a new definition of masculinity, is perhaps the most obvious approach but not, in their study, the most commonly adopted.[17] More frequently, disabled men seem to accept and espouse the qualities of the hegemonic male gender role but reformulate it and shift the emphasis to match their own personal strengths. Thus, they de-emphasize but do not eliminate those aspects of masculinity relating to physical strength and toughness and underline elements such as leadership and outspokenness instead. Gerschick and Miller dub this approach "reformulation."[18]

Tom, like most of the male participants in the study, seems to adopt the reformulation approach. He is aware that he has physical limits that many non-disabled men do not have, but this is largely unimportant and incidental to his self-perception and identity. The de-emphasizing of physical limitations, however, does not reflect full rejection of the hegemonic notions of male strength and toughness. Instead, Tom reformulates those qualities to match his own strengths. This is especially apparent when he speaks of his relationship with his siblings:

> They've always just kind of seen me as that brother. They don't pull any punches. They know that I can't walk and can't use my right arm, and they take full advantage of that in certain regards when they need to. But I mean I've always loved them for that. They don't treat me fragilely. They don't . . . They're not afraid to hurt me because any other brother wouldn't be afraid to hurt his younger brother. They know my limits. They know how far they can push me without actually hurting me.[19]

Tom values how his siblings and friends interact with him without particular regard or allowances made for his impairment, except an awareness of his limits. In describing the interpersonal relationships he has formed over his life, Tom describes his most positive and comfortable relationships, be it with family or friends, as those in which he is treated "normally."[20] Throughout the stories he relates, however, the conceptualization of "normal" is inextricably bound to ideas of physical fitness and resilience. "Normal" is being treated "as if I wasn't going to break."[21] Tom, thus, uses examples of positive interactions and examples of how he would like to be treated as a means of emphasizing that, despite the presumptions of physical vulnerability, fragility and weakness which attach to disabled people, he is capable of meeting the masculine ideal of physical fitness, if the standard is reformulated to take into account his own personal strengths and circumstances.

The process of reformulation not only involves redefining qualities of masculinity but also reshaping the masculine gender role along new lines, often placing greater emphasis on intellectual and psychological qualities and displacing the importance of physical strength.[22] Some theorists have argued that for disabled men to achieve a highly valued masculine gender role, they must be able to hide or mask their physical condition or craft a narrative in which living with it is a sign of heroism.[23] This form of heroism reinforces a person's place within the biomedical approach to disability by making it a great achievement to succeed "in spite of" an impairment.[24] While these are both methods of reformulation in a sense, as they still involve embracing the traditional male gender norms, reformulation seems to allow for a far wider variety of narratives which nonetheless meet the societal expectations of men.

A particularly attractive narrative is that of the leader. Tom displays no interest in masking his impairment or the fact that he uses a wheelchair nor does he embrace the heroism narrative. He does, however, see himself as a leader and advocate for other disabled people. When discussing his time at segregated summer camp, he draws particular attention to how the experiences and interactions with other disabled youth helped him to recognize leadership qualities in himself:

It also helped me to mature, to realize that because of my ability to speak and my ability to be relatively articulate, although that depends who you ask, I was going to have to take a bit of a leadership role for disability advocacy, or I wasn't going to have to, but I wanted to because doing stuff like that makes me feel good. I'm not going to lie. That's a very, very cheesy line. It sounds like it should be on Oprah, but it does. It's a rewarding experience.[25]

Tom presents himself as an outgoing, assertive advocate for others. He is someone who others can turn to for assistance and someone who even people in relative positions of power, such as the camp counsellors, identify as serving as a leader. While aligning his strengths with the traditional masculine quality of leadership, Tom's narrative also undoes some of the primary stereotypes attached to disabled men. As a leader, helper and advocate, Tom's story rejects the expectations of helplessness and dependency, diffusing the conflict between the male gender role and the "disabled" role by firmly embracing his gender role.

Tom's story of leadership also accomplishes a further objective. More so than the other participants, Tom embraces the identity of a disabled person, eschewing the more flexible, contextual approach to disability identity that others took. In large part, this seems to be because he has constructed a life narrative in which being a leader and an advocate is a central feature. Tom's advocacy narrative helps to counter some of the more difficult elements of advocacy exhaustion. Rather than become frustrated with or disillusioned by advocacy failures, Tom seems to accept them as part of what he, as an advocate, has to fight. As such, he can more readily look on difficult experiences with advocacy as future challenges, rather than as personal setbacks.

Maxime, meanwhile, frames himself as someone who pushes the boundaries of his condition. While not relying on the heroism narrative, per se, Maxime approaches his story as one of seeking out and overcoming challenges. His involvement in sports is a way for him to display his adventurous qualities and lack of fear, in addition to his physical skills and his ability to think around his limitations "Someone says, 'You know, this is a lot of fun. You should try it out,' or someone says, 'Well, I'm not too sure if you would be able to do it because it's not a disabled sport,'" he explains, "I take on that challenge, and I show them that I can and that there is a way to do it."[26] This plays into a larger narrative of independence that Maxime carries into his home and school life as well. For Maxime, situations in which he might have to rely on others are challenges which can be overcome by finding a way to achieve his goal that does not require relying on others. Even as a child, he notes, he would never ask his parents to get him things from high shelves; he would instead find a way to get them himself. Like Tom's story, this narrative serves as a way of reformulating the male gender role to fit the strengths Maxime sees in himself. Also like Tom, Maxime clearly rejects the expectations of the "disabled" role and finds an escape from it in embracing many of the classic qualities of masculinity which are open to him regardless of his impairment.

Disabled women and the performance of gender

Women face a different challenge in grappling with the dual expectations of the female gender role and the "disabled" role. Both roles often traditionally anticipate similar qualities such as physical helplessness and passivity, leaving disabled women with no socially sanctioned choices beyond that of the silent dependent.[27] Fine and Asch write, "By refining their adeptness at the 'male' role, [men] can escape some of the restrictions of the 'disability' role. Such an escape hatch is unavailable for disabled women."[28] Due to the fact that the anticipated qualities of masculinity and having a disability are in near direct opposition, disabled men can reject the expectations inherent in the "disabled" role by more fully embracing the male gender role. Due to the similarities between traditional femininity and the "disabled" role, however, disabled women are placed in a position where rejection of one role is rejection of both. As a result, Fine and Asch argue that disabled women are more likely to identify as having a disability first[29] or as all together "roleless."[30] Rather than seeing this as positive or freeing, such "rolelessness," especially when it comes about from lack of choice or lack of means to achieve a role, "can cultivate a psychological sense of invisibility, self-estrangement, and/or powerlessness."[31]

Tracy finds herself caught between her desire to separate herself from qualities such as helplessness and dependency and yet to also maintain a traditional sense of femininity, in keeping with the role she was raised to believe women should fulfill. She sees conflict between the female gender role and the help she sometimes needs due to her impairment, as it removes her from the role of caregiver and nurturer to her family. She places her husband, Otto, in that role instead:

> [It] bugs me to no end when I get into such bad shape that I have to depend on somebody. And [Otto] just sees me as – He'll know before I have to sit there and ask for help. He will take care of it. He sits there and jumps the gun. He's been really observant on things and then I wind up feeling a massive case of guilt going like you're doing this for me but what am I doing for you and he says, "Because you're appreciating it, that's good enough." But the guilt, I mean, I'm a good Catholic girl. I was raised that way.[32]

Although Tracy dislikes being defined or restricted by the expectations of femininity, she is also frustrated by exclusion and the resulting sense of rolelessness, guilt, and the inability to give back. On the topic of rolelessness, Fine and Asch observe that exclusion from the female role, combined with the lack of societal and institutional supports to enable achievement of that role, may result in the role becoming more attractive to disabled women than it otherwise would be.[33] Thus, while Tracy emphasizes her qualities which do not fit the hegemonic female ideal—such as assertiveness and aggressiveness—and prides herself on these qualities, her need to depend on her partner on occasion, thus, automatically triggers feelings of guilt because it places her partner in the more traditional feminine role of caregiver.

Lisa's experiences with role expectations are similarly ones that suggest both rolelessness and a conflation of gendered expectations and the "disabled" role. Lisa recalls that in high school she did not fit into what many people expected of a female teenager with a disability: "[It] becomes very difficult because a lot of people didn't know what to do with a disabled teen who knew about dating, who knew about sex, who could talk to boys without blushing, who had a number of male friends who weren't potential suitors, and who could make fun of herself."[34] The people Lisa encountered expected her to be "emotionally and socially stunted" and were surprised when she was not. Despite displaying these qualities which run against the stereotype of the person with disabilities, however, Lisa has encountered difficulties in fully removing herself from the expectations of that role. Although she explains that in university she has experienced far fewer assumptions of the kind she met in high school, she still finds that she is often not considered a viable romantic partner for the non-disabled men around her due to her impairment. At the same time, people frequently assume that she will become romantically involved with her disabled male friends due to the commonality of having a disability:

> I think the idea of an ambulatory person with a wheelchair-bound person is not something people are aware of as a possibility, so I think the questions I get with my ambulatory male friends is more – It's curiosity, but it's more they are trying to wrap their heads around that idea. And I think the questions that I get with my male friends who are disabled, it may be just because I'm very close to them, and it may be also because, to other people who are maybe also not as aware, that is what makes sense.[35]

While not treated as entirely outside the female gender role, it still seems that Lisa's identity, as perceived by those around her, is more heavily dominated by the "disabled" role than her femaleness. She is classified as a disabled person, regardless, and is expected to primarily interact with other disabled people, despite her demonstrated social skills and outgoing nature. She encounters a form of stigmatization and segregation experienced by many disabled women, rendered solely platonic in her interactions with non-disabled men, with whom she is not seen as a viable partner candidate, but romantically linked to disabled men, whose choices are seen as similarly limited to disabled women.[36] The emphasis Lisa has been able to place on characteristics that do not match with those expected of a disabled person have not been sufficient to remove her from that role and re-establish her within the female gender ideal.

The failure of the reformulation technique for Lisa, where it seems to have had some success for male participants such as Tom and Henry, may suggest that, as Fine and Asch hypothesize, escape for disabled women from the expectations of the "disabled" role may not be as readily achievable as for men. [37]

This observation has particular implications for the intersectionality of the "disabled" role and gender roles.[38] While the male participants approached discussions of societal perception and their own self-perception largely in terms of how to emphasize their masculine qualities over the stereotypes of disability, the stories of the female participants reflect far greater uncertainty as to how to maintain or even initially strike this balance. The female participants express similar frustration at the expectations society holds for them as disabled people and are less certain about how to separate the "disabled" role from the female role. This perspective plays a particular part, as well, in how disabled women express their rights consciousness. Where the male participants could express with some certainty when their treatment was based on perceptions and stereotypes relating to their disability, female participants could not make this determination as confidently, especially where the treatment reflected perceived qualities, such as helplessness, which are common to both sets of expectations.

Cheryl's experiences, of which one example is noted at the beginning of this chapter, also highlight that while disabled women may seek to emphasize their identity as women over their identity as disabled people, they also feel that their experiences are different from those of non-disabled women. Cheryl's insights into intersectionality arose in part through her participation in a focus group many years earlier. In the focus group, she was asked to speak about her experiences as a woman, a question she did not feel she could answer because of the intersectionality of sex, gender and disability in her experience. Disabled women may, as a result of this intersectionality, find themselves roleless even in comparison to more modernized definitions of what a woman should be. As Anita Silvers notes, the ongoing process of defining personal identity for disabled women is a complicated one: "To do so successfully and authentically, they cannot be expected to think of themselves as women who merely happen to be disabled. Such a construction of identity would be as self-alienating as considering themselves to be persons with disabilities who merely happen to be women."[39]

Body image

For disabled men and women, body image plays a unique role both in relation to gender roles and in the experience and establishment of personal identity more generally. The interaction between body image and identity is circular and self-informing. How a person views himself or herself is linked to the body and the perception of discrepancies between the individual's own body and the societally dictated ideal body.[40] Where these discrepancies are perceived to be great, a person's self-concept and self-worth worsen. At the same time, lowered self-esteem can impact on body image, causing the discrepancies between the actual body and the ideal body to be seen as even greater and the actual body even more inadequate.[41]

This process of comparison bears a strong resemblance to Foucauldian theories of normalization. Foucault's concept of docile bodies, bodies "that may be subjected, used, transformed and improved,"[42] suggests that discipline, which creates efficient machines out of docile bodies, operates both externally and internally. As Amanda Booher summarizes:

> Each individual must internalize the goal of control and discipline by comparing bodies, behaviours, and functions to one another and to minimum thresholds, and by shaping and establishing (un)acceptable frames of difference, in order to achieve the transformations and improvements of docility.[43]

It is through this comparison that the concept of normalcy and the ideal, normal body emerge. Foucault theorizes that a body's degree of normality not only dictates membership in wider society "but also play[s] a part in classification, hierarchization and the distribution of rank," with bodies that fall outside the social body or deviate too greatly from the normal ideal being of little value or rank.[44]

These issues may be compounded for individuals with disabilities. The body is often the first site through which a physical impairment is experienced and similarly the primary focus of external reactions to the impairment. The body is also a key part of hegemonic gender ideals. Masculinity is intertwined with concepts of physical strength and fitness, and femininity is grounded in physical attractiveness.[45] Given the level of importance placed on physicality, body image for disabled people plays a particularly profound role in self-image. As Susan Wendell writes:

> Most disabled people cannot even attempt to make their bodies fit the physical ideals of their culture. They may wish for bodies they cannot have, with frustration, shame, and sometimes self-hatred; they may reject the physical ideals as narrow, unimaginative, and/or oppressive; or, like myself, they may fluctuate irrationally between these points of view. In any case, they must struggle harder than non-disabled people for a self-image that is both realistic and positive, and this is made more difficult by other people's reactions to them.[46]

The experience of body image discrepancy is thus experienced internally, through the individual's own perception of the failure of their body to meet the ideal; externally, through the reactions of others; and through a combination of external and internal, through those thoughts and perceptions that are externally produced but then internalized by the individual as truths.[47]

Many of the participants choose to approach these external, negative reactions to their bodies through humour. The same tactic can also serve to diffuse the discomfort other people exhibit towards their bodies. Lisa notes that, for her, humour is a "mechanism to break down barriers."[48] By being the first to address her physical impairment and by treating it lightly, she hopes to help others to understand that "I'm different, and it's okay to ask, and it doesn't have to be 100 percent serious, 100 percent of the time."[49] Henry also uses humour but indirectly and more as a method of internally breaking down a negative reaction than as a means of setting the other person at ease:

> I have a bit of a joke with my friends and my family about how when I'm meeting someone for the first time I can gauge how comfortable they are with me and the fact that I am disabled by their handshake they give me. Because I can't extend my arm out to meet your hand halfway, because if you want to shake my hand you would have to come 90 percent of the way, and I would come the other ten percent, but a lot of people aren't comfortable with going into other people's space like that ... I joke around with my sister and my friend that I should say, when someone gives me a weak handshake—I should ask them, "Oh, are you disabled?" And then when they say, "No, why?" I'll say, "Well, you shake like you are."[50]

In both Lisa and Henry's stories, humour allows them to dismantle and avoid internalizing negative body-based reactions which could otherwise become harmful to their self-images. It provides a way for them to correct and draw attention to misapprehensions and misperceptions that are formed about their selves on the basis of their bodies. At the same time, it also enables them to avoid the more overt kinds of self-image advocacy which many participants identified as exhausting and undesirable, such as getting angry. Humour is not a perfect tool, however, because rather than rendering an unequal encounter equal, it places the burden for easing negative reactions on the disabled person.[51] They are placed in a position where it falls to them to reassure non-disabled people they encounter who are troubled by their bodies.[52]

Humour also has limits on its ability to deflect. As Henry's experience demonstrates, the repetition of the same negative reaction can cause frustration and can sometimes have longer-lasting impacts when some elements of the external reaction are internalized. Analogous to the concept of the male gaze found in feminist theory,[53] the scrutiny disabled individuals experience can be both an act of dominance, positioning them as objects which are acted upon by the scrutiniser, and a stigmatizing act, signalling that an individual is different and unusual and thus worthy of scrutiny.[54] If nothing else, the repeated exposure to these sorts of reactions leads to increased body consciousness, as the disabled person becomes aware of constantly being under the gaze and scrutiny of those around him or her.[55] Even when deflected by humour, the awareness of being a subject of curiosity, study and evaluation lingers, emphasizing the otherness of the person with a disability and their body's deviation from the ideal body.[56]

Andrea was a born with a rare, genetic skin condition which caused her skin to be particularly fragile and prone to blistering and breaking. As one of only approximately 200 to 500 people in Canada with this condition, Andrea frequently encountered people who were uncertain about—and even scared of—her physical condition and appearance. "People on airplanes have been like 'Oh, is it contagious? Can I sit next to you?'" she recalls, "and especially when I was a kid some people would freak out."[57] Her parents often treated such reactions with the type of humour-based deflection that Henry and other participants use to deconstruct similar reactions. When asked if the condition was contagious, for example, Andrea recalls that her mother would sometimes respond, "You've caught it five minutes ago!" For Andrea and her parents, however, it is clear that the repeated and persistent nature of these misconceptions took a toll. She became frustrated with the ignorance of other people and angry when the stories they made up to explain Andrea's appearance frequently assumed that it was the result of child abuse.[58]

Andrea's relationship with her body and particularly with her perceived image became complicated as she attempted to find ways in which to control how she was seen by others. Her desire to show herself as a disabled person or to not show her impairment as much as possible fluctuated. She and her body were linked, a fact that Andrea recognized as unavoidable even if it made her uncomfortable or unhappy. In her role as an advocate on behalf of people with the same condition, however, Andrea strongly believed in making her image public. Whenever approached by the media for interviews related to her impairment and advocacy work, Andrea made her participation conditional on the publication of her image:

> I want people to put the picture [in the media], and I want the public to know, not only to raise awareness but to try and raise money for research because it's so little known. Most of the research is taking place in the United States, so there's practically no money here. So I want people to know about it, and I want people to understand what it is. So you know, if you see someone on the street who looks like me, you know it's not always that they're burned. And it's not contagious, and it's not going to hurt you.[59]

Thus, it is clear that Andrea created a distinction between how she interacted with her body on a personal level and how she interacted with her body on a professional, public level, where she used her physicality as symbolic and a means of awareness-raising. Personally, she felt at odds with her body due to her lack of control over her impairment and its role in how she was perceived, or mis-perceived, by others.[60] Rather than incorporating her condition into her self-concept, she repeatedly emphasized that it was something she would get rid of if possible. As an advocate, however, Andrea was comfortable with using her appearance as a tool to better the situation of herself and others. In part, this comfort might have been due to the fact that the context of publicizing her image and, to some degree, the reception of it were more fully within her control within a professional setting. Conversely, this was rarely if ever true in personal or private contexts.

Intersectionality and body image

In some instances, however, external perceptions of the bodies of disabled people cannot be avoided, deflected or controlled. Societal standards relating to bodily fitness and beauty are often internalized and used as the basis of comparison for the ways in which the individual's own body is lacking or inadequate. Because of the link between body image and self-image, a poor perception of one's body can easily extend beyond the attitudinal relationship to the body and into other areas of self-concept.[61]

At the time of her interview, 22-year-old Cheryl had never had a partner. She was aware that men frequently saw her and other women who use wheelchairs as sexless and linked this perception to "violence or discrimination or mistreatment against women with disabilities."[62] Contending with this outside view of herself had an impact on Cheryl's relationship with her body. She sought out the opinions of male friends to confirm for her that she is not unattractive, although even then she remained somewhat ambivalent about their responses:

> I know I'm not the most good-looking person on the face of the planet, but I'm not the most ugly either. According to most of my guy friends' honest opinions of me, I'm not all that bad looking. I am quite decent looking. I am quite . . . nice looking or something like that. Which is not the most insulting thing I've ever heard but not the nicest thing I've ever heard![63]

While Cheryl appears to view this as a practical process for judging her physical attractiveness to others, she holds negative and uncertain feelings towards it as well. She seeks out the opinions of friends because, as she says, "it's not like I'm going to be horribly insulted by my friends" and feels that it is necessary to gather these opinions "because at least then I know."[64]

The implication seems to be that Cheryl anticipates negative opinions and has become resigned to them. As someone who has experienced desexualization in the past, Cheryl, like many young adults with disabilities, may still be developing her sexual identity as she moves into her mid-20s.[65] Her negative experiences have left her wary about her appearance and inclined to assume that others will perceive her as unattractive. As Carol Brooks Gardner notes, scrutiny of the body, which may feel objectifying and harassing to non-disabled women, is often interpreted differently by disabled women; this kind of evaluative interaction can "welcome them to a gender club, membership in which they were often denied."[66] Especially given the part that physical attractiveness plays within the hegemonic gender role of "real" womanhood,[67] the discrepancy between personal body image and the societal body ideal can contribute to the previously discussed rolelessness that many disabled women face. Disabled women and their bodies are frequently desexualized by society at large, and they must strive to reconcile their own perceptions of their bodies, society's perceptions, and their desire to be viewed as attractive.[68] In this process, the views of others become immensely important in the construction of body image, as women may seek out perspectives that support their own self-concepts and challenge the societally dictated standards.

It must be recognized that being perceived as physically attractive has a tangible effect on perceptions of competence and value as well and that, in turn, perceptions of competence and value affect social and economic success.[69] People who are capable of presenting a combination of high status cues—whether in terms of attractive physical presentation or attractive personal qualities like confidence—are more highly valued in society.[70] Disabled bodies, however, are inherently assigned a lower value within modern society, leaving those individuals to once again work harder to overcome the assumptions made about their worth.[71] Making her body into an object to be rated by others causes Cheryl anxiety at times and leads her to question her positive self-image;[72] however, given the lack of disabled women amongst the imagery of female beauty[73] and the devaluing of disabled bodies in general, Cheryl may have few other alternatives for gathering positive external receptions of her body to substantiate her own perception of herself as an attractive, sexual person.

Despite the above examples, many of the participants see their impairment as different from the ideal for male or female bodies but do not attach negative connotations to that difference. For the most part, the participants experience challenges to positive body image as external, in the reactions of others and the exclusion of bodies with disabilities from hegemonic ideals of beauty. They have learned to resist these external perceptions and avoid internalizing them as true.

Harassment

The subtle processes of social pressure and censure are not the only forces experienced by disabled people as they attempt to navigate defining their identity in relation to both their gender roles and their disability. Disabled people often find themselves targets of overt physical, verbal and emotional harassment and bullying which seeks to "impose stigma, to form and perpetuate stereotypes, and to enforce subordination on people with disabling conditions."[74] Harassment is both an effect of the exclusion of disabled people from societal norms and roles and a contributing cause.[75] Because they are seen as different and separated from society, as people who contravene the hegemonic standards of acceptable citizenry, disabled people are seen as targets for abuse and harassment. Because they are harassed, they are then further singled out for suspicion, fear and exclusion.

Harassment, however, also has a distinct gendered component. Men and boys remain far more likely to be the harassers in harassment situations[76] and until recently, the majority of scholarship that has looked at theoretical explanations for harassment has focused on the motivations of male harassers.[77] Harassment, in these considerations, is a way for the harasser to demonstrate that he meets the gendered expectations of society, unlike the disabled person, who he has harassed. As Carol Brooks Gardner theorizes, the public harassment of disabled women by men "perpetuates men's right to define the situation in other areas and demonstrates men's ability to impose strength and evaluate appearance."[78] Harassment as performed by men who harass is thus both an indictment of the disabled person for their perceived failure to meet societal standards and an assertion on the part of the harasser that they have met the standards themselves.[79]

Tracy, now 41, experienced a large amount of harassment during college that was directed at her both as a woman and as a woman with disabilities. She was enrolled in a program for electrical engineering and trade technology and was the only woman in her year and one of only two people with mobility and auditory impairments in the program. She felt ostracized from her classmates, predominantly men in their 20s, who would not only refuse to speak to her socially but would actively tell her that women did not belong in the program. The harassment reached a level where she did not feel comfortable using a wheelchair to get to class because she worried that this would further mark her as different from her classmates. Even without the visible marker of her impairments, however, her classmates and teachers in the program used knowledge of her sex and her impairments to attempt to convince her that she did not fit in and would not be able to work in her chosen field:

> I'm totally shut out. From the majority of guys in class. I just started breaking in this year. Second year repeats are doing their best to shut me out and slam me to give up and leave because the majority of them are of the opinion that women don't belong in this course. I've got an instructor who because of the auditory problem is telling me I wouldn't be capable of doing my job when all this is . . . I can't separate out conversation. I can hear noise just fine.[80]

Tracy's story exemplifies how gender-based harassment can be used to exert group dominance and can easily overlap with other forms of targeted harassment. The men in Tracy's classes used gender harassment as a form of gender role policing to directly sanction her for choosing a traditionally masculine field of occupation.[81] At the same time, they reasserted the appropriateness of their own presence in the program.

Tracy's disabilities also provided a basis for people in positions of authority to justify her exclusion. This harassment communicated that because she was a woman, she was not welcome in electrical engineering and because she had disabilities, she was incapable of performing the job and posed a safety risk to others, regardless of her actual capabilities. Both layers of harassment attempt to re-establish Tracy within what her perceived proper role as a disabled woman and to remove her from a role perceived as open only to non-disabled men. Tracy, however, challenged those attempts to exclude her from the group by openly calling attention to these attitudes and demonstrating that she could complete the same tasks as others, even if it required taking a different approach to do so. However, even though her advocacy efforts were partially successful, Tracy clearly looks back on these experiences negatively because the situation and the advocacy process necessary to secure accommodation were inherently disrespectful.

Resisting harassment through advocacy

The notion that women do not harass has been steadily drawn into question in recent years.[82] It is now understood that both men and women may harass others, though men remain far more likely to harass. Men who harass tend to target both men and women, while women who harass largely target other women.[83] Even when harassment is perpetrated by a woman, however, it serves as a form of role policing by attempting to coerce conformity to traditional notions of femininity and enforcing stereotypes relating to aspects of personal identity such as gender, race, and disability.[84] Women who harass may more frequently use tools of indirect aggression, such as threatening to withdraw support and friendship to ensure conformity, but they also use many direct forms of harassment.[85] In either case, women who harass validate their own sense of fitting within societal norms in the same way that men who harass do. As Brown observes of same-sex female harassment amongst teenagers:

> Throughout childhood, complaints about other girls are laced with the derogatory – girls are too, well, girly, too feminine, too wussy, weak, deceitful, catty, critical. These are not words girls come into the world with – they are, after all girls themselves. It would seem counterproductive to denigrate the very group they are naturally part of. But ironically, if they want to "make it" this is exactly what they have to do . . . Belonging gives girls the power to exclude those "others" who don't fit – and as we've seen, belonging has much to do with race, class, sexual identity, physical ability and appearance.[86]

During elementary school, Lisa experienced harassment from both male and female classmates. She recounts experiences in which she was called "cripple" by male classmates or accused of cheating when using school-sanctioned accommodations to complete assignments. In one of the latter cases, she remembers being told she was cheating by a teacher after a classmate complained about her use of a calculator during math quizzes, despite having attended a meeting that morning with the teacher to ensure that she received that accommodation. While Lisa feels that such treatment was unfair, she found the harassment instigated by her male classmates easier to manage than that instigated by her female classmates. Boys were straightforward about their rejection while girls seemed to offer her the opportunity of inclusion, only to abuse her later. Teachers intervened, but their intervention generally demonstrated a lack of understanding or support for Lisa:

> The solution was to put me in a classroom, alone in a classroom, with these two girls who were both physically larger than me, not to mention the whole dynamic of I'm in a chair, they're standing over me. They left me alone in an empty room with these girls and said "Work out your issues" and left. And there was no one to supervise us. And so what do you think happened? They were cursing at me. They spat on me. They called me names.[87]

Due to the harassment, Lisa transferred schools mid-way through Grade 7. The harassment was having a severe impact of her emotional well-being and academic success. By the age of 11, she was seeing a psychiatrist to help manage the psychological effects of behaviour aimed at increasing her stigma and exclusion and preventing her accommodation within the school environment.[88]

Harassment, as illustrated in these examples, is one of the most direct and most damaging methods of external defining used by members of non-disabled society in order to police the roles, and thus the identities, of disabled people. It is a tool that may be used, often very effectively, to punish individuals who assert an identity which falls outside what external perspectives consider to be their appropriate identity. For disabled people, this can include demonstrating personal self-concepts that emphasize self-reliance and assertiveness, as Tracy does, or even something as simple as acting on a right to be present in a particular setting, such as in Lisa's story. The ability to weather harassment thus becomes an important skill. Disabled individuals often receive little help from individuals in positions of authority such as teachers who fail to see the uneven balance of power in the "other"-ing of harassment.[89] Moreover, learning to reject the external defining power of harassment is identified by many of the participants as an important first step in establishing their own, positive self-identities.

The process of rejecting harassment is a difficult one. As Lisa's story illustrates, harassment on the basis of disability is sometimes combined with offers of inclusion, bearing the implied message that if the individual is able to align themselves with their societally dictated role sufficiently and is prepared to accept a certain level of harassment, he or she may be included within the group, at least some of the time.[90] Particularly for young girls, the desire for any sort of belonging and the fear of exclusion can be powerful forces that pressure girls to change themselves to fit the peer-defined standard of "normal" or, where change is not possible, to internalize and incorporate into one's sense of self the blame for the failure to change.[91] Thus, for disabled women, this can be a particularly difficult process to reject, as Lisa notes, because the reality of impairment places limits on how much they can change themselves to conform to particular aspects of "normal," such as the feminine body ideals discussed previously. The choice can quickly become one in which rejecting harassment and the negative effects of harassment on self-identity means rejecting the potential for inclusion as well. As Brown explains, "anxieties about being left out and alone are so powerful that children will put themselves in uncomfortable or painful situations to avoid them; rather than have no one, they will seek out friendships with people who do not love or validate them in kind."[92] This reflects Lisa's experience with her harassers, which often involved accepting some abuse in order to occasionally feel like she belonged:

> The girls would kind of decide, "Okay, Monday and Wednesday, we'll be your friends, but the rest of the week we won't be your friend," and, of course, at that point I was kind of like, "You know, if they are going to give me Monday and Wednesday, I'll take Monday and Wednesday."[93]

Rejecting harassment can also be difficult where rejection may require drawing attention to oneself in undesirable ways. Where the benefits of rejecting harassment are outweighed by the drawbacks—which can include increased scrutiny—some participants chose to withstand harassment in silence instead. During the ninth grade, while living in the United States, Charles experienced a particularly severe incident of harassment when he was attacked by a group of fellow students who identified themselves as neo-Nazis and targeted Charles due to his disability. Charles was injured as a result of the attack but chose not to tell anyone about what had happened. Nonetheless, his gym teacher noticed that Charles's mood had changed and that he was limping during class and phoned Charles's parents. The students who had attacked him were eventually expelled, which Charles agrees was the appropriate response. However, he notes that having to draw attention to the attack gave him the sense that others, particularly his father, saw him differently afterward:

> Well, my mother didn't think anything in kind to what I thought my father might have thought. Well, after Grade 9, after that instance, I don't know. I think my father saw me in a bit of a different light because in that situation, I mean, I feel that he would have defended himself and I didn't do that.[94]

Although Charles did not believe that the attack was justifiable and felt that the school was right to take measures to punish the students responsible, the necessary process involved in getting this result placed him in a position where he was subjected to scrutiny that was, in itself, difficult to reconcile with his self-concept. Charles made the decision that the scrutiny and potential damage to self-image that could be done by advocating for himself in this instance outweighed the importance of securing measures against his attackers. Part of his reluctance to involve his parents arose out of the sense that it would encourage them to be overprotective, as the incident could easily feed into the view that he was helpless and dependent, two qualities that undermine his identity narrative. However, Charles's concerns about his father's opinion illustrate once again how gender roles and the "disabled" role can become entangled and how difficult it can be to separate them. Charles's worry suggests that beyond emphasizing undesirable elements of the "disabled" role stereotype, the incident may have also left Charles concerned about his ability to fulfill the masculine role. In this context, what Charles's father actually thought about the incident and his son following the incident are less important than Charles's impressions. Charles himself judges that he failed to live up to his father's ideals. This failure not only emphasized undesirable qualities like dependency, but it also exposed the gap between the classic tough, aggressive masculine role and Charles's ability and desire to fill that role.[95]

Harassment can have far-reaching consequences for the individual and for individual identity because it disrupts how disabled individuals view their identities in relation to their impairments and their chosen gender roles. The participants in our study all learned, eventually, how to reject the overt social pressure to normalize—or to be censured for failing to normalize—inherent in harassment. Lisa, for example, still encounters the women who harassed her occasionally: "Every time I see them I kind of chuckle to myself because it seems like it was so long ago, and that was probably one of the lowest points in my life, and everything from there just got better."[96] Their abilities to resist harassment became important parts of their identity narratives as well, as emblems of their perseverance, resilience, and ability to assert themselves. For others, however, who internalize, even just in part, the perspectives represented in harassing behaviour, harassment can do long-lasting damage to feelings of self-worth, resulting in depression and increased anxiety.[97] Experiences with harassment in school, particularly at young ages, can be formative. As a result of harassment, disabled students with disabilities "suffer low academic achievement, stop attending school, make few attempts to seek gainful employment, and sometimes drop out of the workforce altogether."[98]

Caregiving

Identity narratives and self-advocacy also play a role in positive interpersonal relationships. Caregiving is a concept with particular connotations in terms of both gender and disability. Care work is still inherently intertwined with images of femininity as it remains relegated to the private sphere of the domestic, the home and the family and has close connections to the view of women as nurturing wives and mothers.[99] There is also a close connection between the physical work of caring and the provisions of emotional sensitivity and support, which is the traditional domain of women.[100] A failure or disinclination to fill these needs and to take up the duties of the caregiver are met with strong reprobation from society, as seen in the narratives of bad mothers that circulate in society,[101] or from within, such as the guilt that Tracy expresses when she perceives herself as unable to give back traditional "care" to her partner.

The relationship of disabled people to the concept of caregiving likewise has a long history. Disability theorists from the early 1960s on have critiqued the concept of care and the practical structures of caregiving as oppressive.[102] Traditional caregiving practices often took a form that reinforced the idea that disabled people were incapable of making decisions regarding themselves and their own care: "the practices and discourses of paid (particularly professional) and unpaid carers have maintained disabled and older people in a position of, at worst, unwanted dependency, abused and stripped of their dignity, and at best, patronised and protected from exercising any agency over their lives."[103] As Richard Wood states, "Disabled people don't want care"[104] because care, as a concept, has frequently been used to justify the domination and management of the lives of disabled people by people who are considered carers.[105]

Redefining relationships of assistance

Given that caregiving dynamics were often unequal in this way and generally reinforced the inequality of disabled people in society, disabled people have moved away from the notion of caregiving—and its connections to mothering, the family, and private-sphere relationships—and toward notions of "assistance," in which the personal attendant (PA) is an employee of the disabled person.[106] Unlike traditional carers, the PA responds to the instructions of the disabled person and provides assistance neutrally, without framing the interaction as a form of benevolence or volunteerism.[107]

Many of the participants in this study use or have used PAs—whether privately employed or engaged by their schools. Lisa considers herself someone with minimal needs for assistance but during her time living in university residence, she used the school's attendant services for help in carrying heavy objects, preparing meals, or using the school cafeteria. Her experiences, generally positive, reflect the idea of PAs as service-providers for her, the client, rather than the outdated views of carers as parents or experts and of the relationship as one of dependency and inequality:

> All of the attendants will get to know your name eventually. It may take some time based on the number of staff they have and the number of clients they have to juggle. You may have to remind them of what you needed them to do but there is no constant "Ok, now we do this, now

we do this." There is a general idea of what each client needs. Sometimes we are asked to be part of hiring committees, if they are looking for new attendants, because they want to make sure that the people they are hiring are the people that we're ok with. Because of the nature of things that some of us need assistance with, it's important to have people that we are comfortable with.[108]

Although the employer of the attendants, in this instance, is the school rather than Lisa herself, the structure of the relationship is still such that Lisa has control of her own care. She decides when she needs assistance, may request and cancel assistance as necessary, and has a voice in who will be hired to work as attendants.

Henry has, on occasion, used the school-provided attendant program, but he generally hires private attendants to assist him. He requires more assistance services than Lisa and has had attendants live with him and his family in order to provide full-time services. He appreciates the freedom this gives him, as having a full-time attendant gives him more mobility in getting around and going out with friends. Having been involved in the hiring of many PAs over the years, Henry looks for respect and a willingness not to treat him as overly fragile when he assesses new candidates. Henry jokingly recounts that once "I actually hired an attendant basically just because he shook my hand well."[109] Once again, this represents a shift from the old structures of care in which the disabled person had little say over the care they received or who was hired to perform the care. Here, Henry may not physically perform many aspects of his own care, but he is both employer and client to those who do and has full say in who performs attendant duties, what those duties are and how they are performed.

Yet even with this advance in caring, notions of care as assistance and care as affective caring still become blurred at times. As noted, disability activists have attempted to promote a perspective that deconstructs care as a social relationship[110] in order to detach many of the paternalistic and "caring" connotations from personal assistance. For some of the participants, however, the practical distinction was not so clear-cut; it was not always straightforward to separate being assisted from being emotionally cared for. Nancy, who uses the attendant care services provided by her university, now values the services. However, she recalls that when her mother first began to hire PAs to assist in her care, she was opposed to the idea:

My mom used to have the attendant care come and help me with baths and to get me up in the morning and at first, I was really dead set against it because I felt like she was just passing me off. Like maybe she felt like I was a burden, at first.[111]

Nancy's story provides one example of how the emotional element of care remains a reality for many individuals, despite the decades of work done to divorce assistance and emotional care. She saw her mother's decision to employ PAs as a personal judgment of Nancy, as someone who was perhaps too dependent, and also as a rejection of the traditional mother-child roles. Through experience with personal assistance, however, Nancy's views have changed; she now understands and appreciates the decision her mother made:

> I'm glad we went that route because it gives me a chance to get to know how attendant care works and how to direct my own care, and it gives me a lot of opportunity to have that experience so that now that I am on my own I know how to work with that kind of thing.[112]

Participation in caregiving work

Concepts of caregiving and assistance, from traditional and feminist perspectives, have generally envisioned carers and the cared-for as distinct categories with no overlap. From this perspective, disabled people, as people who require care or assistance, cannot be included in the category of carers.[113] Instead, the dichotomy of carer and cared-for reinforces the perception of disabled people as passive, dependent recipients of care.[114]

This dichotomy between carer and cared-for, however, is false. It obscures the reality that many disabled people may require assistance in some areas of their lives while providing care for others in other areas. Charles has mobility restrictions due to his cerebral palsy and requires assistance with transportation and accessibility modifications to work areas. Nevertheless, Charles has been a caregiver as well, working for two summers with a youth camp. While he does not wish to work with children in the long term, he enjoyed the experience of looking after others during the camps. He enjoyed helping the children who, though curious about his impairment, did not seem to let it negatively affect their perception of him:

> I could probably only list one or two people off the top of my head who have ever actually directly and actually asked me what my physical limitation is. Whereas, in that particular setting, I would move from church to church on a weekly basis during the summer, without fail on the first day of every camp, at least half a dozen children would ask me, "What's wrong with your legs?" You know? And I would clear it up and kind of elaborate for them. I would have to kind of present it in comprehensible terms, if you help it. And once I did that they basically condoned it and life went on, so to speak . . . So I suppose I just felt relatively competent in that environment, which is an innate psychological need.[115]

Although the workplace itself, in the various churches Charles attended, was sometimes inaccessible, Charles does not feel that his ability to perform care work was ever in question and as a result, he felt a sense of psychological satisfaction in his work, which he hopes to be able to find in future jobs.

Despite experiences like Charles's, however, the dichotomy persists for many disabled individuals who seek employment in care work or who fill caring roles in a more personal capacity. Jenny Morris, a British feminist with disabilities, particularly explores the impact that this dichotomy has had on disabled women who frequently find themselves excluded from feminist discussions of caring and the traditional role of women as carers due to their status as disabled people. Tracing this issue back to the discussions in the late 1960s regarding community care,[116] Morris argues that many feminists of that time and later have been clear "that the term 'we' quite definitely does not include 'such people' [disabled people and elderly people]."[117] In response to that exclusion, Morris believes that caregiving relationships, whether formalized and professional or informal and personal, must be recognized as relationships in which the roles of the participants may shift and change over time:

> The failure of feminist researchers and academics to identify with the subjective experience of those who receive care has meant that they have studied caring situations where there are seemingly very clear distinctions between the person who cares for and the person who receives care ... However, a situation in which one party to a relationship has a clear identity as a carer while the other is clearly cared for can only represent one type of caring relationship – and may, in fact, not be the most common. If we focused not just on the subjective experience of those identified as carers but also on the other party to the caring relationship we may find that in some situations the roles are blurred, or shifting.[118]

Morris and others believe that by eliminating the false dichotomy between carers and cared-for, assistance relationships may move further towards power equality and will no longer prevent the recognition of caring work done by disabled men and women.[119]

Nancy has a long-held goal of working with young children. She had previously been enrolled in an early childhood teaching program, which she had enjoyed and excelled in academically. As noted in Chapter 4, a part of her program required her to complete a placement at a daycare. There, she was met with resistance. She recalls that the resistance ultimately focused on whether her cerebral palsy and wheelchair-use would leave her incapable of properly caring for children, a position which Nancy, who had been looking after her much younger sister for many years, firmly rejected:

> It used to be like, "Well, what if you fail at this, and what if you fail at that?" and then I just keep on saying, "Don't say that. Why is the word fail used before you're even giving me a chance to try?" And they are like, "Well, what happens if the kid is running and you can't catch them in time?" And I'm like, "I'm not the only one in the classroom. I can say,

'Hey, Bonnie, or whoever, that kid is running with scissors. Can you stop them?'" And they are not going to stand around and say, "Nancy didn't say anything, so we just let the kid go." So it didn't make any sense. And then they are like, "Well, what are you going to do if you need help setting up activities and you need to get something off a shelf or whatever?" And I was like, "I'll just ask one of the kids." Because I think it's an opportunity for kids to learn that even though adults are adults, sometimes we need help too. And I would just ask one of the kids, "Hey, can you pass me that bucket of markers or whatever," and they're like, "You can't do that. You can't ask a kid, that's not a kid's job."[120]

Nancy's request for a placement that would allow her to work safely with children was ignored. She indicates that she eventually brought the college before the Human Rights Tribunal where the college was ordered to put in place an accommodation plan. Even after this, however, Nancy says that her attempts to be matched with an accessible placement were stymied, and she eventually left the program, transferring into a university and majoring in psychology.

Nancy's experience reflects the perception that disabled individuals are frequently seen as incapable of caring for others because of their own assistance needs. While it seems apparent that Nancy's former college was not, at the time, set up to handle the accessibility needs of its disabled students, much of the difficulty that Nancy faced was not related to the accessibility of the day care but rather to the attitudes of the college staff and their belief that her status as a wheelchair-user left her unable to perform the caring work she was being trained for. Rather than being based on her actual abilities, these beliefs reflected presumptions that Nancy would fail without, as Nancy notes, even letting her try first. Rather than being prepared to accept or discuss other ways to provide caregiving, ways which did not conflict with Nancy's use of a wheelchair, the college fell back on the position that, as these ways would require the assistance of others in the classroom, they disqualified Nancy from being able to perform caring work.

Participating in care work can also have strong influences on personal identity construction. Mary has been performing care work in a personal rather than professional capacity since she was ten. She was the oldest of three children growing up and took over many of the childcare responsibilities because her parents were frequently absent for work or social activities. Mary characterizes her parents as "visiting" parents who were there on weekends while she was the primary caregiver to her siblings until she turned 21. In the midst of this, Mary was also managing her developing health condition. Although she cannot be certain when her fibromyalgia developed, she believes it has been a factor in her life since she was 16 or 17. When the impairment appeared, Mary found that her energy severely decreased. These days, she sometimes finds that she is too tired or in too much pain to play with her brothers' children, which frustrates and saddens Mary both because it is difficult to explain to the children and because it limits her ability to take care of them:

> They just don't understand. I would go – If I came over and they wanted to go to the park, well, if I'm having a bad day, it was like, "Oh, well, can we go?" And I would say, "I don't know. I really don't want to go down the elevator, walk all the way to the park, which may only be across the street, but it's all the way to the park, and then sit there and wait for you and then walk all the way back home." Where the worst part is you know 10 years before that I would have been like, "Let's go!" I would have been carrying them to the park. I would have raced them to the park. I would have gotten probably dirtier than they did.[121]

Mary clearly sees caregiving as a large part of her identity. Raising her brothers is something she feels she was forced into by her parents' absence and which put her life on hold; at the same time, it is also something she takes clear pride in. She frequently refers to her brothers as "my boys" and was adamant that her mother recognize the primary caregiving role she took in raising them, something her mother ultimately acknowledged. Claiming the role of "mother," like claiming the role of carer, requires resisting societal perspectives, which often define women and men with disabilities as incapable of real parenthood.[122] The situation between Mary and her mother was no doubt more complicated than that, given that Mary was challenging her mother's own self-perception as the mother-figure to Mary's brothers.

The participants' stories reflect a rich, multifaceted understanding of care. Unlike the monolithic rejection so often portrayed as the disability community's response to affective care and its historically oppressive traditions,[123] these stories demonstrate that "care" is seen both in its contractual, assistance and employment dimensions and in its emotional dimensions by the participants. The desire to control personal care and to have care valued as work exists simultaneously with emotional understandings and responses to the experiences of caring and being cared for. This supports an emerging body of literature which suggests that the tension that exists between contractual care work and affective care may be harmful to the long-term policy goals of the different groups involved in the debate and may also have little basis in the lived experiences of care.[124] What many scholars refer to as recognizing the importance of interdependence take a first step towards capturing this tension. This perspective recognizes that not all care work must include emotional caring but that all people engage in caring and being cared for, often with an emotional or relational component, throughout their lives.[125] This perspective also unwinds definitions of independence and self-determination that have arisen within disability literature which risk excluding individuals who experience need for greater or specific forms of personal assistance.[126]

Shifting to an understanding of interdependence that links affective care and personal assistance may promote positive developments in care work and assistance. Studies examining the satisfaction of individuals with disabilities regarding assistance note, for instance, that a relationship that involves some elements of relational or emotional care are often identified as more satisfying.[127] An interdependence-based perspective may also assist advocacy efforts, by helping to bridge debates that have placed feminist advocates and disability advocates on somewhat opposing sides in relation to issues such as welfare policy. Perhaps most importantly, by expanding the understanding of care to include the understanding that all people, both non-disabled individuals and individuals with disabilities, can be and frequently are both givers and receivers of care in different facets of their lives,[128] the concept of care becomes open not only to fuller definitions of who carers are but also to fuller definitions of what care work includes and how it may be accomplished.

Conclusion

More than many of the other topics discussed in preceding chapters, the participants' discussions of their experiences with gender roles and the "disabled" role most overtly evidence the ways in which the participants have constructed their identity narratives to both react to and reject stereotypical assumptions about their identities. In many instances, discussions of gender prompted the participants to openly and directly reflect on the ways in which they have formed their identities and the challenges they have had to navigate in so doing. While these stories have touched less on rights in the formal sense, the thread of informal rights—as fairness or unfairness, equality or inequality—is woven throughout. Particularly, this chapter illustrates many of the alternatives to direct advocacy that the participants have implemented in relation to gender and other aspects of their identities throughout the preceding chapters. In the highly personal world of negotiating gender roles, the participants have by and large seemed to prefer adopting creative solutions that work around the negative stereotypes still ingrained in wider society. While not advocacy in the traditional sense, these techniques have often proved effective in achieving the participants' goals and promoting positive self-identity narratives.

Notes

1   Cheryl, personal interview, 2007–08, p. 18.
2   D.M. Engel and F.W. Munger, *Rights of Inclusion: Law and Identity in the Life Stories of Americans with Disabilities*, Chicago, IL: University of Chicago Press, 2003, p. 213.
3   Engel and Munger, ibid, p. 213.
4   T. Shakespeare, 'Disability, Identity and Difference' in C. Barnes and G. Mercer (eds) *Exploring the Divide*, Leeds: The Disability Press, 1996, p. 99.
5   J. Butler, 'Performative Acts and Gender Constitution: An Essay in Phenomenology and Feminist Theory' in S. Case (ed.) *Performing Feminisms: Feminist Critical Theory and Theatre*, Baltimore, MD: Johns Hopkins University Press, 1990, pp. 270–71.
6   S.M. Whitehead, *Men and Masculinities*, Cambridge: Polity Press, 2002, p. 19.

7　Whitehead, ibid, p. 19.

8　Whitehead, op. cit., n. 6.

9　E. Goffman, 'The Stigmatized Self' in C. Lemert and A. Branaman (eds) *The Goffman Reader*, Malden, MA: Blackwell Publishing, 1997. For one of the many critiques of Goffman, see C.J. Gill, 'Divided Understandings: The Social Experience of Disability' in G.L. Albrecht, K.D. Seelman and M. Bury (eds) *Handbook of Disability Studies*, Thousand Oaks, CA: Sage, 2001, pp. 355–56 (observing how Goffman disregarded the possibility that disabled people may successfully reject the norms of the able-bodied world).

10　D.W. Carbado and M. Gulati, 'Working Identity' *Cornell Law Review*, 1999–2000, vol. 85, pp. 1259–308 at p. 1262.

11　S. Wendell, *The Rejected Body: Feminist Philosophical Reflections on Disability*, New York, NY: Routledge, 1996, p. 91; M. Fine and A. Asch, 'Disabled Women: Sexism without the Pedestal' in M. Deegan and N.A. Brooks (eds) *Women and Disability: The Double Handicap*, New Brunswick: Transaction Books, 1985, p. 11.

12　J. Lorber and L. Moore, *Gender and the Social Construction of Illness*, Walnut Creek, CA: AltaMira Press, 2002, p. 57.

13　Fine and Asch, op. cit., n. 11, p. 11; T.J. Gerschick and A.S. Miller, 'Coming to Terms: Masculinity and Physical Disability' in M.B. Zinn, P. Hondagneu-Sotello and M.A. Messner (eds) *Through the Prism of Difference: Readings on Sex and Gender*, Needham Heights: Allyn & Bacon, 1997.

14　Gerschick and Miller, ibid, p. 104.

15　Fine and Asch, op. cit., n. 11, p. 11.

16　Gerschick and Miller, op. cit., n. 13, p. 106.

17　Gerschick and Miller, op. cit., n. 13, p. 111.

18　Gerschick and Miller, op. cit., n. 13, p. 106.

19　Tom, personal interview, 2007–08, p. 4.

20　Tom, p. 5.

21　Tom, p. 5.

22　Gerschick and Miller, op. cit., n. 13, p. 106.

23　Lorber and Moore, op. cit., n. 12, p. 55.

24　P. Rosenbaum and E. Chadha, 'Reconstructing Disability: Integrating Disability Theory into Section 15' *Supreme Court Law Reports*, 2006, vol. 33, pp. 343–65 at pp. 347–48.

25　Tom, p. 6.

26　Maxime, personal interview, 2007–08, p. 4. For a critique of some of the problems with the Supercrip stereotype who overcomes through hard work in the context of jazz musicians with disabilities, see A. Lubet, *Music, Disability and Society*, Philadelphia, PA: Temple University Press, 2010, p. 48.

27　Fine and Asch, op. cit., n. 11.

28　Fine and Asch, op. cit., n. 11, p. 14.

29　Fine and Asch, op. cit., n. 11, p. 9.

30　Fine and Asch, op. cit., n. 11, p. 12.

31　Fine and Asch, op. cit., n. 11.

32　Tracy, personal interview, 2007–08, p. 22.

33　Fine and Asch, op. cit., n. 11, p. 13.

34　Lisa, personal interview, 2007–08, p. 27.

35　Lisa, p. 43.

36　Lorber and Moore, op. cit., n. 12, p. 64.

37　Fine and Asch, op. cit., n. 11, p. 8.

38　Intersectionality, or the idea that personal identity exists on multiple categorical axes concurrently, emerged out of the work of critical race theorists in legal studies. It challenged the tendency of courts, policymakers, and researchers to consider instances of discrimination from only one ground so that sex discrimination was considered in terms of white women only and race discrimination was considered in terms of black men only, further marginalizing black women who experienced both. The concept has since been broadened to become multi-disciplinary and to encompass other elements of personal identity. See e.g. K. Crenshaw, 'Demarginalizing the Intersection of Race and Sex: A Black Feminist Critique of Antidiscrimination Doctrine, Feminist Theory and Antiracist Policy' *University of Chicago Legal Forum*, 1989, pp. 139–67; K. Crenshaw, 'Mapping the Margins: Intersectionality, Identity Politics, and Violence against Women of Color' *Stanford Law Review*, 1991, vol. 43, pp. 1241–99. In the context of disability rights specifically, see D. Stienstra, 'Race/ Ethnicity and Disability Studies: Towards an Explicitly Intersectional Approach' in N. Watson, A. Roulstone and C. Thomas (eds) *Routledge Handbook of Disability Studies*, London: Routledge, 2012, pp. 381–82. An interesting reflection on how intersectionality is compatible with poststructuralist theorists such as Judith Butler because they both share an interest in "deconstructing categories, unmasking universalism, and exploring the dynamic and contradictory workings of power" may be found in K. Davis, 'Intersectionality as Buzzword: A Sociology of Science Perspective on What Makes a Feminist Theory Successful' *Feminist Theory*, vol. 9, 2008, pp. 67–85 at p. 74.

39 A. Silvers, 'Reprising Women's Disability: Feminist Identity Strategy and Disability Rights' *Berkley's Women's Law Journal*, 1998, pp. 81–116 at p. 100.

40 R. Freedman, *Beauty Bound*, Lexington Books: Toronto, 1986, p. 28.

41 Freedman, ibid, p. 28.

42 M. Foucault, *Discipline and Punishment: The Birth of the Prison*, trans. A. Sheridan, New York, NY: Vintage Books, 1995, p. 136.

43 A.K. Booher, 'Docile Bodies, Supercrips, and the Play of Prosthetics' *International Journal of Feminist Approaches to Bioethics*, 2010, vol. 3, p. 71.

44 Foucault, op. cit., n. 42, p. 184. Also relevant, Canguilhem has argued that the concept of the "normal" body only arises within the context of the environment within which a being exists. It is the relationship between the individual, his or her characteristics, and the environment that determines what is and is not normal. As such, "normal" is a concept with no fixed meaning; something which is not normal in one environment can become normal, or even better than normal, within a different environment or after changes to the original environment. G. Canguilhem, *The Normal and the Pathological*, trans. C.R. Fawcett and R.S. Cohen, New York, NY: Zone Books, 1991. This strongly echoes the core concepts of the social model of disability.

45 Freedman, op. cit., n 40.

46 S. Wendell, *The Rejected Body: Feminist Philosophical Reflections on Disability*, New York, NY: Routledge, 1996, p. 91.

47 K. Charmaz and D. Rosenfeld, 'Reflections on the Body, Images of Self: Visibility and Invisibility in Chronic Illness and Disability' in D. Waskul and P. Vannini (eds) *Body/Embodiment: Symbolic Interaction and the Sociology of the Body*, Burlington, VT: Ashgate Publishing Company, 2006, pp. 45–46.

48 Lisa, p. 43.

49 Lisa, p. 44.

50 Henry, personal interview, 2007–08, p. 16.

51 Charmaz and Rosenfeld, op. cit., n. 47, p. 46.

52 Wendell, op cit., n. 46, p. 91.

53 Laura Mulvey describes the male gaze concept, as it developed in feminist analysis of cinema, as follows: "In a world ordered by sexual imbalance, pleasure in looking has been split between active/male and passive/female. The determining male gaze projects its fantasy onto the female figure, which is styled accordingly." (L. Mulvey,

Visual and Other Pleasures, Indianapolis, IN: Indiana University Press, 1989, p. 19. See also K. Silverman, *Male Subjectivity at the Margins*, London: Routledge, 1992.)

54 R. Garland-Thomson, *Staring: How We Look*, Oxford: Oxford University Press, 2000, pp. 41, 44.

55 C.B. Gardner, *Passing By: Gender and Public Harassment*, Berkeley, CA: University of California Press, 1995, p. 234.

56 Gardner, ibid, p. 235.

57 Andrea, personal interview, 2007–08, p. 16. For a thoughtful commentary on how rare, genetic progressive conditions present significant challenges to the social model understanding of disablement, see S. Scambler, 'Long-Term Disabling Conditions and Disability Theory' in N. Watson, A. Roulstone and C. Thomas (eds) *Routledge Handbook of Disability Studies*, London: Routledge, 2012, pp. 145–47.

58 Andrea, p. 17.

59 Andrea, p. 19.

60 See e.g. T. Shakespeare, K. Gillespie-Sells and D. Davies, *The Sexual Politics of Disabilites: Untold Desires*, New York, NY: Cassell, 1996, p. 74.

61 Wendell, op. cit., n. 46, p. 91.

62 Cheryl, p. 18.

63 Cheryl, p. 19.

64 Cheryl, p. 19.

65 Shakespeare, op. cit., n. 60, p. 17.

66 Gardner, op. cit., n. 55, p. 236.

67 Freedman, op. cit., n. 40, p. 2.

68 Fine and Asch, op. cit., n. 11, p. 13.

69 Garland-Thomson, op. cit., n. 54, p. 37.

70 Garland-Thomson, op. cit., n. 54, p. 37.

71 Garland-Thomson, op. cit., n. 54, p. 38.

72 Gardner, op. cit., n.55.

73 Shakespeare, op. cit., n. 60, pp. 69–70.

74 M.C. Weber, *Disability Harassment*, New York, NY: New York University Press, 2007, p. 1.

75 Weber, ibid, p. 16.

76 See e.g. A. Pina, T. Gannon and B. Saunders, 'An Overview of the Literature on Sexual Harassment: Perpetrator, Theory, and Treatment Issues' *Aggression and Violent Behavior*, 2009, vol. 14, pp. 126–38 at p. 128 (examining the prevalence of male harassment across multiple studies).

77 L.M. Brown, *Girlfighting: Betrayal and Rejection among Girls*, New York, NY: New York University Press, 2003, p. 13.

78 Gardner, op. cit., n. 55, p. 237.

79 Brown, op. cit., n. 77, p. 10.

80 Tracy, p. 13.

81 C. Jones, 'Drawing Boundaries: Exploring the Relationship Between Sexual Harassment, Gender and Bullying' *Women's Studies International Forum*, 2006, vol. 29, pp. 147–58 at p. 154.

82 Brown, op. cit., n. 77, p. 13.

83 Jones, op. cit., n. 81, p. 152.

84 Brown, op. cit., n. 77, p. 5.

85 P. Chesler, *Woman's Inhumanity to Woman*, New York, NY: Thunder's Mouth Press, 2001, p. 37.

86 Chesler, ibid, p. 185.

87 Lisa, p. 9.

88 E.J. Meyer, *Gender, Bullying and Harassment: Strategies to End Sexism and Homophobia in Schools*, New York, NY: Teachers College Press, 2009, p. 1.

89 S. Bourke and I. Burgman, 'Coping with Bullying in Australian Schools: How Children with Disabilities Experience Support from Friends, Parents and Teachers' *Disability & Society*, 2010, vol. 25, pp. 359–71 at p. 368.

90 Brown, op. cit., n. 77, p. 69.

91 Brown, op. cit., n. 77, p. 69.

92 Brown, op. cit., n. 77, p. 69.

93 Lisa, p. 9.

94 Charles, personal interview, 2007–08, p. 18

95 Whitehead, op. cit., n. 6, p. 189.

96 Lisa, p. 10.

97 Bourke and Burgman, op. cit., n. 89, p. 360.

98 J.J. Holzbauer and C.F. Conrad, 'A Typology of Disability Harassment in Secondary Schools' *Career Development for Exceptional Individuals*, 2010, vol. 33, pp. 143–54 at p. 144.

99 S. Sevenhuijsen, *Citizenship and the Ethics of Care: Feminist Considerations on Justice, Morality and Politics*, London: Routledge, 1998, p. 132.

100 N. Watson *et al.* '(Inter)Dependence, Needs and Care: The Potential for Disability and Feminist Theorists to Develop an Emancipatory Model' *Sociology*, 2004, vol. 38, pp. 331–50 at p. 332. As discussed further in this section, the concepts of "care" as put forward by disability and feminist care scholars have been a source of much debate.

101 See e.g. E. Edwards and S. Timmons, 'A Qualitative Study of Stigma Among Women Suffering Postnatal Illness' *Journal of Mental Health*, 2005, vol. 14, pp. 471–81; M. Kelly, 'Regulating the Reproduction and Mothering of Poor Women: The Controlling Image of the Welfare Mother in Television News Coverage of Welfare Reform' *Journal of Poverty*, 2010, vol. 14, pp. 76–96 at p. 76; K. McCormack, 'Stratified Reproduction and Poor Women's Resistance' *Gender & Society*, 2005, vol. 19, pp. 660–79 at p. 660; L. Carlson, 'Cognitive Ableism and Disability Studies: Feminist Reflections on the History of Mental Retardation' *Hypatia*, 2001, vol. 16, pp. 124–46.

102 Watson *et al.*, op. cit., n. 100, p. 335.

103 F. Williams, 'In and Beyond New Labour: Towards a New Political Ethics of Care' *Critical Social Policy*, 2001, vol. 21, pp. 467–93 at p. 478. See also A. Bê, 'Feminism and Disability: A Cartography of Multiplicity' in N. Watson, A. Roulstone and C. Thomas (eds) *Routledge Handbook of Disability Studies*, London: Routledge, 2012, p. 365 (noting how the "activities of the disabled people's movement and the Independent Living Movement laid the groundwork for feminist thinkers in disability studies to redefine notions of dependency and care").

104 R. Wood, 'Care of Disabled People' in Gillian Dalley (ed.) *Disability and Social Policy*, London: Policy Studies Institute, 1991, p. 201.

105 Wood, ibid, p. 200.

106 Watson *et al.*, op. cit., n. 100, p. 336.

107 Watson *et al.*, op. cit., n. 100, p. 336.

108 Lisa, p. 40.

109 Henry, p. 16.

110 Watson *et al.*, op. cit., n. 100, p. 335.

111 Nancy, personal interview, 2007–08, p. 26.

112 Nancy, p. 26.

113 Wendell, op. cit, n. 46, p. 142.

114 Silvers, op. cit., n. 39, p. 90.

115 Charles, p. 6.

116 J. Morris, *Pride Against Prejudice: Transforming Attitudes to Disability*, London: The Women's Press, 1991, p. 148.

117 Morris, ibid, p. 154.
118 Morris, op. cit., n. 116, p. 167.
119 Wendell, op. cit., n. 46, p. 143.
120 Nancy, p. 17.
121 Mary, personal interview, 2007–08, pp. 5–6.
122 Morris, op. cit., n. 116, p. 161.
123 B. Hughes *et al.*, 'Love's Labours Lost? Feminism, the Disabled People's Movement, and an Ethics of Care' *Sociology*, 2005, vol. 39, pp. 263–64.
124 See Hughes *et al.*, ibid, p. 270; B.E. Gibson *et al.*, 'Consumer-Directed Personal Assistance and "Care": Perspectives of Workers and Ventilator Users' *Disability and Society*, 2009, vol. 24, pp. 317–30 at p. 319; C. Kelly, 'Making "Care" Accessible: Personal Assistance for Disabled People and the Politics of Language' *Critical Social Policy*, 2011, vol. 31, pp. 562–82.
125 Kelly, ibid, p. 576.
126 Kelly, op. cit., n. 124, p. 577.
127 Gibson *et al.*, op. cit., n. 124, p. 328.
128 Williams, op. cit., n. 103, pp. 486–87.

7 Toward an inclusive society

Narratives have the power to speak truth to power, to shape our understanding of the world and to identify new social developments and policy issues that ultimately lead to legal inquiry and, sometimes, to remedies. David Engel and Frank Munger have written passionately about the power of narrative. They persuasively comment: "We share the sense that narratives can help to breach the barriers of detachment, doctrinal technicality, skepticism, and even irony that often separate legal scholars from the actual life experiences on which they should draw when they write about disability."[1] In the previous chapters, we have shown how the narratives of the physically disabled people interviewed in our study powerfully illustrate the systemic barriers in education, employment and transportation that remain prevalent in Canadian society. We also devoted a chapter to discussing the performance of gender roles for disabled women and men, caregiving, body image and harassment. Throughout this book, we have linked our analysis back to the theme of advocacy identity that we discovered through the grounded theory methodology we explained in depth in Chapter 2.

In our concluding chapter, we begin with a discussion of our overall findings in each of these areas. Then, we turn to potential law reform proposals that might facilitate real change for disabled people in the areas of education, employment and transportation. Third, we consider ways in which we need to go beyond law—and the limits of law as a tool for social transformation—to build a truly accessible society for all. Lastly, we examine how the narratives suggest the need for a reworking of the social model, focusing in particular on the insights relating to gender.

Our findings

Education

Our participants generally expressed support for educational integration and inclusion despite frustration with a litany of barriers in the educational system at all levels. At the elementary school level, advocacy necessarily involves parents. Parental advocacy in public schools may take the form of direct lobbying for inclusion and accessibility for the disabled child or crafting alternatives that achieve inclusion without a combative stance against school administrators. However, as already noted, both socioeconomic status and the education level of parents impact their ability to advocate effectively on behalf of their children. Advocacy also affected how the participants regarded rights and identity. Some participants came to see the educational decision-making as inherently political and susceptible to change as a result of parental advocacy. Tom, in particular, has thoroughly embraced the idea of advocacy as a constituent and fulfilling part of his identity. Others, however, such as Nancy, are fully cognizant of their rights and the unfair treatment that they have experienced but find the barriers so overwhelming and the process so exhausting that they seek to avoid advocacy and disability rights activism rather than engage in it.

Physical barriers were reported in many cases in public high schools, universities and colleges. These ranged widely from elevators that do not work to washroom doors that cannot be independently opened, from narrow hallways to residence rooms with shelving that is too high for wheelchair users. In some cases, such as the notorious test of Lisa's ability to safely climb stairs at her high school, the measure indicates both a requirement that the disabled person adapt to fit her body into the existing structure and, more absurdly, does not even accurately evaluate what they were intended to determine. In other cases, disabled students are forced to choose between accessibility features: Cheryl could have a wheelchair accessible room or a meal plan that would accommodate her allergies but not both. However, many participants found that struggles for physical accessibility were less emotionally draining because they were less personal: the disabled person can typically launch advocacy efforts for an elevator or ramp without necessarily drawing unwanted scrutiny to her life history or the exact nature of her impairments.[2]

With respect to attitudinal barriers, we found that principals and teachers played a crucial role in creating either a welcoming or hostile environment. Some participants experienced bureaucratic inertia and opposition from principals who did not wish to welcome disabled students. The constant need to train EAs and their deployment on tasks unrelated to disability accommodations also proved frustrating for participants. Attitudinal barriers were often more challenging because professional educators attempted to redefine the particular needs of disabled students based on their stereotypes of what the experts thought was needed. On the other hand, teachers who were accommodating to disabled students and served as valuable role models left a powerful and lasting impression on participants.

The fractured nature of disability accommodations in the post-secondary environment merits attention. Disabled students are forced to spend considerable time dealing with multiple offices which have different mandates, while they are relatively free as adults to advocate for their rights how they wish. The post-secondary experience is thus simultaneously more bureaucratic and liberating. In many ways, the specialized disability offices that are commonplace in both Canadian and American campuses provide detailed expertise that improves the circumstances of disabled students. Yet many of our participants continued to face resistance from faculty members who blocked accommodations by declining to wear microphones.

Lastly, we examined the controversial issue of segregated summer camps for disabled children. They retain popularity amongst many parents and policymakers even in an integrationist world. By and large, our participants tremendously enjoyed their summer camp experience, and some saw it as a welcome break from exhausting advocacy for accessibility. However, participants also observed that they had difficulty in relating to fellow campers and related better to the generally able-bodied counselors. We suggest that this highlights the limited nature of inclusion in even mainstream camps that identify as accessible.

Employment

Although many participants had limited work experience, some participants expressed frustration with both physical and attitudinal barriers in the workplace. Nancy adopted an advocacy identity to challenge the physical and attitudinal barriers she experienced in a day care work placement that was a requirement for her degree. She was one of the few participants to turn to law for redress directly. Yet it left her extremely angry and ultimately she withdrew from the program. Sarah, who acquired her impairments in a motor vehicle accident at 29 while working as an office manager in the military, felt enormous pressure to conform to workplace standards even where it endangered her health in order to secure her entitlement to a pension. The spectre of the "burden" narrative, being regarded as a burden on her co-workers and employers, haunted her. Managing the impairment effects and the requirements of employment constituted two distinct jobs, indicating the toll that this took on many participants, especially when they were not adequately accommodated.

A second theme was how the changing nature of work has made entry into the labour market more challenging for many disabled people. Mary would be initially hired for retail positions only to discover that employers were unwilling to make the slightest deviation from their work routines, such as providing a break when her fibromyalgia flared up or a stool so that she could serve customers while seated. Having a less visible impairment than many other participants, she also faced skepticism from job counselors who tried to pressure her to accept employment that was inappropriate for her. At times, managers opposed the accommodations that would allow our participants to thrive or held disabled employees to higher standards, suggesting that advocating for change beyond physical access is that much more challenging.

We also explored how advocacy skills were strengthened by the fact that participants frequently engaged in volunteer work. This provided potentially valuable experience for the future. Interestingly, even those participants who strongly rejected a disability identity still frequently gave up their time to volunteer in disability organizations that they regarded as valuable. This suggests that identity may manifest itself in different ways depending on the context. The role of policy in influencing identity was also clear as the Ontario government has adopted a requirement that all high school students must commit to a certain number of volunteer hours in order to graduate. Lastly, we examined the experiences of participants with social assistance. Participants noted the meagre benefits, the seemingly random web of bureaucratic rules that lie at the root of the system and how it would be difficult to remain on it on a long-term basis.

Transportation

Participants expressed deep frustration with the accessibility of the key forms of public transportation including buses, taxis, personal cars and aircraft. Because it is so essential to participation in community life, even participants who did not particularly have a deep disability identity found themselves forced to advocate for transportation. Door-to-door paratransit services were almost universally criticized because of the chronic delays, rigid booking requirements and general lack of flexibility that denied people the right to be spontaneous. However, significant barriers were also reported with intercity bus transportation and regular local city buses. Beyond the physical inaccessibility of transportation systems, attitudinal barriers on the part of transportation staff were widespread. This was particularly a problem with bus drivers who did not believe participants had impairments where it was less visible.

Taxis were also a source of discrimination. Participants reported how taxi drivers refused to pick up passengers who used wheelchairs and how wheelchair accessible cabs charged exorbitant rates compared to other taxis. In some cases, participants reported being stranded at night because they were not able to get a cab. While in a few cases, such as Tom, the challenge of fighting for accessibility was an almost exhilarating feeling that enhanced his identity as an advocate, many others found having to constantly undertake the work of advocacy exhausting. Somewhat surprisingly, there were significant barriers with respect to driving including barriers to getting a driver's license, funding for appropriate technology and impairment effects that made driving difficult for those who had occasional pain associated with their disabilities. Some participants, however, tended to blame themselves for their lack of license rather than the structural barriers. Although few participants mentioned aircraft, one participant, Henry, refuses to fly because of the poor treatment he received.

Gender

Lastly, both male and female participants described how they grappled with the impact of disability on the performance of their gender roles. Men such as Tom and Maxime reformulated the traditional male role to accord with their identities as disabled men by emphasizing leadership skills, intellectual qualities or accomplishment in sports. Disabled women often have more difficulty than men because both their role as women and their role as disabled people are associated with vulnerability and helplessness. They consequently may feel as if they have no role. Tracy, for instance, expressed frustration at needing assistance to help with parenting at times due to her fluctuating impairments. Lisa found herself failing to conform to stereotypes of disabled females because of her maturity and sophistication, but also being excluded from a full female role on issues such as relationships. Tellingly, some female participants were not able to discern whether a particular incident reflected discrimination because of their impairments or their gender.

A second theme identified in our study was body image and its relationship to self-concept. Some participants reported using humour to deflect negative or awkward attitudes people had toward their bodies. However, humour as a tool of inclusion has definite limitations including the fact that it places the burden entirely on the disabled person and she or he may internalize the negative attitudes. Andrea, whose impairments result in visible skin blisters, was determined that her image be shown while she raised awareness of issues relating to her medical condition. At the same time, she did not identify with disability as a source of pride in the context of personal interactions, underscoring the complexity of her outlook.

Other participants regarded themselves as desexualized and appeared to partly internalize stereotypes about disabled bodies and the assumption that disabled people, particularly disabled women, are sexually unattractive. Cheryl, who had never had a partner at age 22, sought confirmation from her friends of her attractiveness and appeared anxious about her ability to conform to gendered expectations. Nevertheless, other participants developed strongly positive body images and rejected conventional conceptions of beauty.

A third theme we identified was harassment. Some participants, like Tracy, experienced harassment from fellow students on multiple grounds. In her case, she was harassed on the basis of her age as an older student, disability and gender. Her enrollment in community college classes in a traditionally male field made her a target for sexist bullying. The advocacy she had to undertake to challenge her experience left her feeling frustrated. Lisa experienced extreme bullying during elementary school from both female and male classmates, but found it more challenging to address female bullying and harassment. She was so traumatized that she had to change schools and undertake psychiatric therapy. Charles faced physical attacks but preferred to deal with it directly rather than risk being perceived as weak by involving his parents. Resisting harassment becomes a major challenge because students want to fit into their peer group even if it means accepting blame for being unable to change aspects of their identity, such as impairments, which cannot be changed.

Caregiving was another theme that participants raised in our interviews. While many disability rights activists have strongly advocated to separate the historically paternalistic delivery of caregiving from the provision of professional attendant services, participants in our study found the line more blurry in practice. Nancy originally was disappointed when her mother obtained attendant services to assist her with activities such as bathing and dressing. However, she eventually found the experience valuable as she learned how to manage her own attendant services. Others like Lisa and Henry enjoyed the independence that came with having control over their attendant services, while selecting different delivery options. Caregiving by disabled people has also been viewed with suspicion, even though a failure to do it contradicts the traditional identity ascribed to women. It was not always the case, however, that disabled women in our sample were accepted as caregivers or disabled men were rejected in the role. We report how Charles was successfully engaged in caregiving work as a summer job despite his mobility impairments. Nancy, however, was regarded as unsuitable for caregiving and her skills called into question. Mary experienced distress when her impairments rendered her unable to perform caregiving. We comment on gender further later in this chapter in our reflections on the social model but now turn to the articulation of law reform projects with respect to the themes of education, employment and transportation.

Law reform and the politics of disablement

How can the project of law reform assist in the project of eliminating structural and attitudinal barriers for disabled people so widely? We offer these suggestions in the spirit of legal scholar Roberto Unger's ambitious theory of radical change. Unger argues for transformative social change through what he calls democratic experimentalism with reforms. Unger advocates radical change through smaller policy shifts, such as amendments to existing inheritance law to secure better wealth redistribution, which can then percolate through the system and reinvigorate the polity toward greater democracy.[3] Highly relevant to a work based on interpreting and analyzing life stories, Unger eloquently comments that "[P]olitics should become little so that individuals may become big. The quest for the sublime—restless experimentation with the frontiers of experience—should take place on the scale of individual biographies."[4] We also stress that these policy proposals are reflected by the analysis of the qualitative interviews described in the previous chapters.

Education

With respect to education, one tangible legal project would be the provision of more efficient services by EAs for disabled students. What perhaps is most striking in studying the participant interviews is the dramatic inconsistency in the accommodations offered to disabled students across school boards and over time within the same school. A specific EA and teacher may be strongly committed to work collaboratively to provide accommodations and maximize the talents of a given disabled student, but this may all be abruptly altered due to staffing changes. Some school boards are more passionate and more committed about inclusion of disabled students than others and have had a longer history at practicing inclusion.[5] Moreover, many classroom teachers have unfortunately not had sufficient education in their teacher training about how best to include disabled students. There is also evidence that across Canada, there is insufficient ongoing training related to inclusion and accommodating disabled students. This makes the role of the EA all the more critical in order to move away from a deficit model paradigm where the disabled student is seen as deficient and needing to fit into the classroom.[6]

While students inevitably have new teachers each year and some school boards will always be more enthusiastic than others in a decentralized educational system, we believe that the proposal identified by the participants that would assign the EA to a student over a period of several years should be a cornerstone of accommodation policy. There is a particular bond that develops between EAs and students that warrants ensuring that the EA is assigned to the student, rather than the school. This also minimizes the risk of delivering sporadic and inconsistent accommodations. To expect a disabled student, often with more than one disability, who is coping with multiple barriers to re-adapt to a new EA every single year is neither realistic nor fair. A broader range of schools would also now be open to the student. Currently, the student must stay at the present school to keep the same EA. An EA that is more familiar with the student's needs would also be able to address the nuanced issues relating to teasing, bullying and harassment by fellow students that was so painful for some participants. They are also more likely to be trusted by the student.[7] This proposal has the added advantage of benefitting EAs by stabilizing employment and creating a progressive career ladder for EAs where seniority might be valued and the turnover minimized.[8] By looking at commonalities and the potential for coalition building that is plainly a possibility between unions representing EAs and disability rights advocates, this step transcends the unfortunate dynamic where unionized workers sometimes enter into unpleasant disputes with disabled people or their caregivers.[9] By delineating the employment responsibilities at the outset, having the aide follow the student may also significantly reduce the risk that students are not properly accommodated because school administrators are re-assigning unrelated tasks to the overburdened EA.

Although it is beyond the scope of this book to craft specific proposed regulatory language, a brief discussion of the legislative framework in Canada may be helpful to appreciate an effective strategy to translate the idea into reality. This would need to be adapted for other federal states such as the United States or unitary states such as Britain. Education is a matter of provincial competence under the Constitution Act, 1867.[10] Many provinces stipulate Individualized Education Plans (IEPs), as a regulation pursuant to the

provincial statute dealing with education, which govern the disability accommodations to be granted to each disabled student. IEPs are typically reviewed
on a regular basis.[11] In Ontario, decisions relating to identification and
placement of a particular disabled student, determined by the Identification,
Placement and Review Committee (IPRC), may be initially challenged at the
Special Education Appeal Board and then the Special Education Tribunal.[12]
Ultimately, they may be a matter for judicial review.[13] However, decisions
relating to specific programs and services may not be appealed.[14] Therefore,
any reform relating to stabilizing the relationship of EAs to students would
likely take the form of amendments to existing regulations issued under
the relevant provincial statute governing education. This would inevitably
be a long-term matter of painstakingly lobbying each provincial legisla-
ture. Accordingly, since there would be funding implications, it would be
a challenging project requiring investment of time and resources. However,
given the nature of Canadian federalism, such a decentralized approach is
unavoidable.[15]

An alternative approach might be to launch a challenge to the existing
statutory regulations of a particular province relating to IEPs, alleging that
the lack of specificity with respect to continuity of EAs violates the equality
rights of disabled students under section 15 of the Charter of Rights and
Freedoms, Canada's constitutional document.[16] It could also take the form of
a human rights complaint.[17] This could build political momentum toward
a legislative solution by calling attention to the dilemmas faced by disabled
students.[18] It might also help to create more long-term coalitions among
advocacy groups for disabled children that are divided along diagnostic lines
such as learning disabilities, spina bifida and cerebral palsy.[19] However, we
would suggest that such an approach is fraught with risks. While applying
Charter doctrine and values to provincial regulations relating to inclusion of
disabled children is certainly highly desirable, given that one would be asking
for more specific regulations rather than challenging an existing rule as discriminatory, it is questionable whether a court would be amenable to such a
claim. In *Auton (Guardian ad litem of) v British Columbia (Attorney General)*, the
Supreme Court of Canada unanimously rejected the argument that the failure
of the British Columbia government to fund applied behavioural therapy for
children with autism violated the equality rights of the children with autism
under section 15 because the benefit claimed was not provided by law.[20]

However, in a 2012 decision, *Moore v British Columbia (Education)*, the
Supreme Court of Canada unanimously held that a British Columbia school
district discriminated against Jeffrey Moore, a child with severe dyslexia, in
violation of the British Columbia Human Rights Code,[21] when it shut down
the specialized services relating to learning that he required due to funding
constraints without seriously contemplating alternatives.[22] While one might
try to argue that the case of educational assistance funding is less analogous to
Auton, where one was dealing with a relatively novel therapy,[23] than *Moore*, it
may be tactically best on this specific question to focus primarily on political

lobbying and building bridges amongst disability rights organizations, teachers' unions and EA unions for better continuity of services by EAs.

Employment

With respect to employment, an effective legal strategy would be the design of a system that facilitates seamless *transitions* without economic penalty to a disabled—or any other—worker. In our narrative interviews, we recall how Sarah struggled to deal with the effects of her impairments after a career in the military by maintaining employment in order to attain the all-important military pension without appropriate accommodations. We also observed how Nancy encountered particular physical barriers as a wheelchair user when she was placed in co-op settings that were poorly prepared to accommodate her needs.[24] These suggest a crisis during transitions that adversely impacts the lives of disabled people and can effectively force them to permanently exit the labour market involuntarily. Policymakers would agree that preventing labour market exit is far preferable, where feasible, to consigning disabled people to a life on social assistance benefits.

As one of us has previously argued elsewhere, one radical demand to prevent this would be the provision of disability supports across the lifespan that is neither means-tested nor linked to employment status in order to encourage labour market participation by disabled people.[25] Disability supports typically encompasses a range of services such as orthotic and prosthetic assistive devices, adaptive computer technology and interpreter/notetaking services.[26] This means that disability supports would continue without interruption despite any life transition, be it taking time away from work for parental leave or to pursue graduate studies or the rehabilitation necessary upon acquiring a disability (or an additional one) or simply choosing to engage in volunteer activities for some time. As should be apparent, while of particular salience to disabled people, a policy of seamless transition would also have significant implications in enhancing equality for numerous other groups including single parents and those with caring responsibilities for elderly parents. To the extent that there are many disabled lone parents or those with other caring responsibilities, the policy also enhances equality for disabled people.

Originating in the work of the French legal scholar, Alain Supiot, and the research team he led, one model for designing such a system is the establishment of Social Drawing Rights which attempts to place the development of human creativity and flourishing at the centre of the economic system.[27] Instead of evaluating an individual's relationship to the workplace on a weekly or monthly basis, the Social Drawing Rights model anticipates an extremely long time scale, such as a person's entire working life, in order to increase worker productivity in a world of globalization where an employee is expected to have many different employers over the course of her lifetime.[28] It anticipates the end of a linear career model and works to counter the negative impact of the dramatic growth in precarious employment by replacing *activity* as the foundational concept rather than the contractual relationship of employment. It thereby allows working people to share in the rewards of risk-taking in a flexible world.[29] Precarious employment, which would be neutralized by a focus on activity regardless of whether it involved wage labour, may be defined as work in which individuals engage in low wage, short-term work over which they have little control and minimal access to state benefits or collective bargaining.[30] An individual accrues credits over time which she may then allocate as she wishes. For instance, within a course of a lifetime, an individual could elect to distribute a sabbatical to upgrade her skills through training or volunteer for a year with gorillas in Africa. Involuntary job separation caused by the acquisition of an impairment would still be funded by the state with no loss of credits.[31] Income support and disability supports would continue throughout the person's life span. This could be funded by the state, the employer, trade unions, insurance companies, professional associations, social security agencies, the worker directly or some combination thereof.[32] In so doing, the Social Drawing Rights paradigm attempts to combine elements of security for workers with flexibility in recognition of the need for innovative employers to alter strategies quickly as market conditions change. It effectively focuses on *employment* security rather than job security.[33]

This is not a fanciful idea. Disability studies scholars are increasingly using the life cycle paradigm to espouse the analysis of disability policies from birth to death.[34] Such an approach already has echoes in the 2004 law in France allowing workers to accumulate training time capital that they accumulate regardless of their employer.[35] It also appears in skeletal form in the statutory response of some European Union countries to the economic crisis that gripped the West after 2008. In Germany, France, Belgium and the Netherlands, the metalworking, engineering and pharmaceutical sectors have adopted policies to reduce working time while supplementing the resulting lost wages from public unemployment funds. The worker consequently retains her employment and, to a large extent, her wages, while the employer benefits from both cost savings and the fact it retains its workers without having to go through the elaborate process of layoffs and hiring.[36] Provisions for training during the current economic crisis have appeared in both national and industry-specific agreements in a number of EU countries such as Italy, Spain, the Netherlands and France.[37]

Such an approach could easily be adapted to include disability supports. Germany has recently adopted measures to encourage the employment of disabled people. They are accorded the right to a job that enables them to use and develop their knowledge and abilities, special access to firm-specific training, access to external training, an accessible workplace, and an accessible work environment with the appropriate accommodations.[38] It will of course be more challenging to implement such policies in countries like the United States and Canada with a long history of highly decentralized bargaining and many unorganized workers.[39]

Transportation

Lastly, with respect to transportation, our proposal seeks to address transportation barriers for disabled people by ensuring: (a) that disabled Canadians who wish to obtain driver's licenses and are able to meet the legal requirements are able to do so; and (b) to improve the sorry situation relating to access in public transportation through better education of transportation workers of their responsibilities to disabled customers under human rights laws. The first issue is one that is rarely discussed as a matter of public policy or equality rights and yet is extraordinarily important if disabled people are to be able to exert their full rights as citizens. Bearing in mind the approach influenced by Unger of seeking smaller steps to serve as a catalyst for change, we think that any proposal has to work within the graduated licensing system that places dramatic restrictions on new drivers in Ontario.[40] While the extraordinarily lengthy process for obtaining a driver's license in Ontario known as graduated licensing may well save lives, the rules stipulating that an adult with years of driving experience accompany the learner in the vehicle at all times may have a disproportionately negative impact on disabled people who are trying to learn to drive while at university or college.[41]

However, given that this program requires that an additional driver be in the vehicle, we think that greater emphasis must consequently be placed on encouraging disabled teenagers to obtain driver's licenses while in high school. To the extent that many physically disabled students today are often in fully integrated environments where they are the only disabled student, this will require more initiative on the part of school boards and local high schools. School boards will have to be made aware of their duty to accommodate disabilities with respect to any driving instruction that they offer.[42] While certainly not all families will possess vehicles nor necessarily have time to assist their children with learning to drive, we would suggest that there is greater likelihood of success if high schools take pro-active measures to ensure disabled students have every opportunity to learn to drive before they leave home for university or college. The absolutely overwhelming number of participants in our sample who do not drive, while certainly not statistically valid, nevertheless suggests that public schools have not done all they can to educate disabled teenagers about their potential to drive. Systemic plans should be drawn up to ensure that all high schools are fully aware of the adapted vehicle resources in their communities and are prepared to liaise with the appropriate driving schools to ensure that no disabled student is left behind.[43] There is a symmetry to our policy suggestions in that the adoption of EA continuity that we advocate for would create a lower stress high school experience, allowing mobility impaired students more time to acquire driving skills as a teenager. To the extent that a driver's license means that a disabled person has a much greater chance of avoiding reliance on public transit, it goes a long way to resolving the more difficult problems relating to public transportation that we discuss presently and likely has a significant impact on the person's long-term employability.

With respect to public transportation, it is clear that there can be no long-term systemic solution without greater long-term funding commitments by provincial governments because there will always be a need for both wheelchair accessible public transportation—both door-to-door paratransit as well as regular public transit. Although the AODA[44] contains regulations for the implementation of accessible transportation with deadlines staggered until 2021,[45] the lengthy timelines for enforcement stipulated in the Draft Standard have been sharply criticized by Citizens with Disabilities-Ontario (CWD-O), Ontario's leading cross-disability advocacy organization for disabled people.[46] The funding and enforcement issues cannot be redressed immediately and will remain a matter of long-term political contestation; there is likely scope for both greater progress toward accessibility and for social justice struggles for transportation that transcend the boundaries of legal strategies as we discuss later. Perhaps what deserves more attention and is more manageable is rectifying some of the customer service issues that participants in this study recounted. Again and again, participants in our study related rude or inappropriate behavior on the part of local bus drivers, inter-city bus drivers and taxi drivers who would not wait until disabled customers were seated, overcharged customers or otherwise engaged in inappropriate behaviour.

We would suggest that this is an issue that can be fixed and that requires greater attention be focused on systemic mandatory sensitivity training for bus drivers, taxi drivers and other transportation workers. The CWD-O has written about the need for mandatory sensitivity training in the context of all front-line paratransit workers, including both booking agents and drivers. This includes training on the handling and storage of mobility aids and assistive devices and awareness of the impact of driving style and road conditions on various types of impairments.[47] Unions representing transportation workers in all sectors need to become part of a concerted and on-going tripartite dialogue including unions, management, and disability rights groups to ensure that disabled customers, including those whose mobility impairments are less visible at first glance, are treated with respect and dignity. Mandatory sensitivity training should be contained in the collective agreement in the case of unionized workers or a condition of a license in those cases where there is no union. There should be regular monitoring and an effective reporting mechanism for customer service issues that implicate the equality of disabled people analogous to those used in the reporting for compliance with the CRPD. Specifically, the work of the Committee on the Rights of Persons with Disabilities, a body of 12 elected independent experts which monitors compliance with the CRPD by reviewing initial submissions from each State Party and their periodic reports updating progress on improving accessibility, could serve as a template for logging the legion of customer complaints in the transportation sector.[48] Together, small steps forward for better transportation access can be made. We now turn to strategies for equality that go *beyond* law reform to strive for a more accessible society.

Beyond law reform: building an accessible society

The limits of law as a tool for social transformation, however, are well known. As noted by Byron Sheldrick, it contains both perils, such as co-optation, and possibilities.[49] He correctly reflects upon Marc Galanter's classic commentary on how corporate defendants, who are repeat players appearing numerous times in the courts, have systematic advantages when engaged in litigation with one-shot plaintiffs, such as disgruntled auto injury claimants.[50] Karl Klare famously wrote about how law deradicalized the left wing anti-capitalist labour movements of the 1930s that was mobilizing thousands of striking workers in the streets into the hearings of the National Labor Relations Board (NLRB) to reach compromises, some highly detrimental to the labour movement, with management.[51] Canadian legal scholars have questioned the efficacy of the Charter of Rights and Freedoms to achieve social transformation, regarding it as channeling political controversies to an unrepresentative judiciary where they are diluted.[52]

Like Sarah Armstrong, we agree that a dogmatic dismissal of the strategic role of law as simply reinforcing oppression is entirely misplaced.[53] Every effort should be made to pursue equality for disabled people through law. Law reform initiatives are particularly effective for the achievement of medium-term objectives. However, the experience of other social movements has amply demonstrated time and again the dangers of a reliance on law alone. It is simply one option in a tool kit that can be effective at times and counterproductive and distortive at others. A truly radical effort to transforming the lives of disabled people therefore ought to focus on grassroots organizing or what one of us has elsewhere referred to as disability rights struggles from below.[54] Such an approach may well question the constraining parameters of mainstream disability activism which has in many countries largely been dominated by non-profit organizations with ties to the state and increasingly the private sector on which they are dependent for funding.[55]

What might a strategy for social transformation in each of the areas identified above look like? In the case of education, we take inspiration from the work of David Connor and his colleagues. In articulating a radical vision of inclusion for disabled students, they provide the foundations for further development including a proposal for a disability studies curriculum.[56] While the provision of high quality EAs is an essential first step to equality for disabled students, we believe that a long-term commitment to disability studies and diverse ability as a critical component of the public school curriculum is crucial. This could easily be incorporated into existing subjects and would mark a radical change in an environment where disability has been seen, at best, as something to be tolerated and accommodated, and at worst, a shame and a tragedy that one should not discuss. Transforming the discourse around disability to include the perspective of the social model would have enormous impact on the lives of both able-bodied and disabled students. It would effectively employ narratives to instill the notion that disability is another facet of human diversity rather than accepting the predominant deficit model. An even more radical initiative would be to persuade summer camp administrators, particularly those who continue to operate segregated summer camps for disabled children, to implement age-appropriate disability studies content.

While disability studies is truly interdisciplinary and has made inroads in both the humanities and social sciences, perhaps one of the most obvious candidates for the public school classroom is disability history. There is vast potential for including disability history in both public school classrooms and in summer camp activities from a social model perspective.[57] Re-imagining disabled icons that are already discussed in classrooms, such as Helen Keller[58] and Franklin D. Roosevelt,[59] and introducing school children to new ones, such as double amputee E.T. Kingsley, a candidate for both the United States Congress and the Canadian House of Commons between 1896 and 1926,[60] has real potential to bring home the message of disability as a natural part of the human condition. We conclude that while disability history is not a panacea, many of the narratives recounted in earlier chapters regarding harassment and abuse would be mitigated if all students were explicitly taught about disability history and the rightful place of disabled people in Canadian society. Silence is no longer acceptable. It also cements the importance of narratives as a tool to educate in the minds of students.

In the case of employment, we think that one compelling starting point is Sunny Taylor's dazzling intervention on the value accorded to work in capitalist societies and its implications for equality for disabled people.[61] This issue is particularly salient because in recent years, as we noted in Chapter 4, there has been a convergence in the macroeconomic policies of most Western economies toward an emphasis on a neoliberal market society. In this model, one secures one's needs through the purchase of goods and services on the open market. The state is refocused on facilitating profitability of corporations through the vigilant protection of contract and property rights and the repression of dissent against corporate power, rather than serving a redistributive function.[62] The welfare state has been sharply curtailed. There has been a rise in income inequality, and union density rates in Britain, Canada and the United States have all declined.[63] The nature of work has also changed with a significant shift away from "Fordist" full-time jobs with benefits toward a massive expansion of "just in time," flexible but poorly paid part-time McJobs with few or no benefits, frequently held by women.[64] In this model, disabled people who are unable to compete on the market are cast aside and marginalized as social assistance recipients, or worse, commodified as sources of profit through institutionalization for the nursing home industry.[65]

Taylor makes the case that many disabled people make valuable contributions to society that cannot be monetized such as through art and participation in community life.[66] Given the profound structural barriers to employment for disabled people, she wants us to reconsider the value we place on wage labour as the current ethos of society devalues those who are unable to work.[67] We would at the same time campaign for accommodations for those who do wish to work. In so arguing for acknowledgment of the contributions of all disabled people, we would be consistent with Karl Marx's vision of a world where individuals are not exploited for their labour. One of Marx's many striking achievements was to demonstrate the relationship between the labour theory of value and the exploitation of the working class. The labour theory of value stands for the proposition that the value of a commodity is determined by the socially necessary labour time that workers have spent in producing it.[68] Marx showed that capitalist production is based on the exploitation of workers whose labour is commodified and then sold at a price lower than the price at which the capitalist charges for the product, thereby creating surplus value which is extracted from the workers' labour.[69] By refusing commodification, disabled people outside the labour market could in one sense be said to be truly facing reality, foreshadowing the workings of a new post-capitalist society free of exploitation.[70]

Lastly, in the case of transportation, we think that the disability rights movement would benefit enormously from a return to grassroots organizing and mobilization. For too long, disability rights advocates have engaged in a polite dialogue with the state. This is hardly surprising since disability organizations have frequently been funded by the state and such organizations are seldom willing to be so critical as to jeopardize their funding.[71] However, the effectiveness of this model of organizing has clear limitations, especially in a time of fiscal austerity across the industrialized countries. Disability rights advocates have a rich history to consider from both their disabled sisters and brothers in other countries and insightful lessons from the victories of other social movements.

The paradigmatic example of transportation struggles involving disabled people is, of course, the work of ADAPT and its long and ultimately successful struggle in the United States to make intercity bus transportation accessible to wheelchair users. On the one hand, ADAPT, founded in 1983, used highly creative and confrontational strategies to get its message about accessible transportation and its relationship to inclusion in the community heard. It would demonstrate at the conventions of the American Public Transit Association (APTA) and its members were entirely willing to engage in civil disobedience and be arrested in dramatic fashion to garner favourable media coverage and promote the struggle. It had an enormous strategic asset in that its members were largely social assistance recipients with little formal education who had formerly been residents of nursing homes or institutions.[72] Consequently, they have very little to lose and were willing to face jail time in order to make their point.[73] In an eloquent narrative, an ADAPT activist, Stephanie Thomas, vividly describes a militant action in Sparks, Nevada. She reports how wheelchair users were arrested when they failed to disperse:

> We tried to enter or block their hotel but the police were blocking us. They would pull us away, but we would simply wait till they left and then return to the building. Jerry Eubanks and Tim Baker, Julie Farrar,

Barb Toomer, ET, Lillibeth Navarro, Diane Coleman, Tom Olin and many more were there. It was like an act of sacrificing ourselves for the freedom and liberty of those who would come behind. We would just try again and again.[74]

When they learned that an African American member was given a much longer sentence than his fellow Caucasian protestors, the other demonstrators engaged in disruptive tactics in the courtroom to ensure that the judge would also give them lengthy sentences in solidarity.[75] Within two days, the jail authorities concluded that it was too much trouble to accommodate their impairments. After they were released, they returned to the convention site only to find the police had erected cement barricades. Those ADAPT members capable of crawling then crawled through the barricades to the consternation of the police authorities.[76] As Fred Pelka comments, some of the most marginalized disabled people in the United States felt a tremendous sense of empowerment as they realized that they were able to bring inaccessible buses to a halt through a simple act of civil disobedience.[77]

On the other hand, ADAPT simultaneously also used litigation strategies to transform legal discourse with respect to disability rights. In *ADAPT v Burnley*,[78] ADAPT joined numerous disability rights coalitions to argue that section 504 of the Rehabilitation Act and other federal statutes funding transportation required accessible public transportation.[79] This decision was vacated and replaced by *ADAPT v Skinner*.[80] In *Skinner*, a plurality of the Court held that these statutes do not require mainstreaming of disabled bus passengers and that local transit authorities could choose to focus on funding door-to-door paratransit.[81] Despite this loss, this coalition building was helpful in accelerating the momentum toward the 1990 passage of the ADA.[82] In so doing, ADAPT emulated the strategy of African American civil rights leaders who brilliantly combined litigation with direct activist struggle from below.[83] Their strategy was not always perfect or entirely consistent with a grassroots paradigm of struggle from below. At times, they made questionable strategic choices to rely on personal connections with politicians and to downplay criticism of those politicians, including conservative Republicans, whom they regarded as potentially sympathetic to their cause.[84] Nevertheless, their example is one that activists for accessible transportation in other countries should reflect upon closely.

Other radical social movements have also contributed theoretical and practical lessons that disability rights advocates from below can adapt for their own cause. Perhaps one of the most remarkable but largely ignored social movements in the United States was the small but highly innovative Sojourner Truth Organization (STO).[85] Active in workplace organizing and anti-imperialist solidarity movements from 1969 until the early 1980s and best known for producing a special issue of its journal devoted to the legacy of Black Trinidadian revolutionary socialist, C.L.R. James,[86] it was a champion of Puerto Rican self-determination[87] and its membership included many activist lawyers.[88] It argued for two principal ideas. First, it suggested, under the influence of Antonio Gramsci, that the working class exhibits dual consciousness: an acceptance of the status quo and an embryonic awareness of its transformative potential.[89] This idea has salience to the disability rights movement. In analyzing our narratives, we observed many participants for whom a disability identity, let alone disability rights struggles, was not important. Yet when it came to essential services such as transportation that are basic to survival, one saw glimpses of consciousness that disability oppression was simply not acceptable. Our participants perceived how they could change the world simply by speaking out, even if they largely accepted that barriers were endemic in other contexts. The STO's insights into dual consciousness warrant further serious attention from scholars of disability studies and may help to better understand organizing efforts such as ADAPT.

Second, the STO argued uncompromisingly for the idea of white skin privilege as conferring psychological and material benefits on white people long before theories of intersectionality had become widespread. In order to build multiracial unity of the working class, they sought to advocate that white people reject the benefits of white skin privilege, but argued this within a rigorous anti-capitalist political economy framework.[90] In so doing, they paralleled theories about racism developed by others including Theodore Allen and, earlier, the renowned Caribbean American theorist, Hubert Harrison.[91] For disability rights advocates, implanting the notion of abled privilege into community organizing at the outset would go a long way to raising awareness amongst activists of disability identity and oppression. Again, this is particularly salient in the context of transportation because in many countries, including Canada, the barriers to transportation for disabled people remain so profound that disabled people are precluded from participating in social justice causes. Making activists aware of abled privilege so as to dismantle ableist barriers more effectively would serve as a powerful impetus for social transformation from below.[92] At the same time, the disability rights movement badly needs to incorporate a commitment to anti-racism in all of its programming.[93] This is particularly true in the case of transportation where economically marginalized racial minorities in Canada, the United States and Britain are most likely to have difficulties in accessing public transportation.[94] In our closing section, we suggest how our narrative study implicates rethinking the social model.

Rethinking the social model of disablement

The traditional interpretation of the social model has rightly been criticized for its dogmatic insistence of explaining the oppression of disabled people entirely in terms of the structural barriers in society. While the social model has been enormously useful in shifting the debate away from the medical model and professionalism and creating the conceptual terminology for a disability rights movement to transform dialogue from a discourse of pity to one of rights, we would argue that the narratives we have discussed in this book suggest that a thorough reconsideration of the social model is warranted to better capture the complexity of the lived experience of disabled people. How can this be accomplished? First, as many other scholars have suggested,[95] it is imperative that more scholarly attention be given to thinking creatively about impairment effects and how policymakers can address this. As others have acknowledged, a social model theory that recognizes the corporeality of the body is needed.[96] Theorists of the social model need to accept that impairments have real effects on people's lives. Our narratives again and again signify that the disabled experience includes pain, exhaustion, and emotion. They cannot be reduced to structural barriers. By foregrounding impairment effects, we feel that we will be able to produce a richer understanding of disabled people. Most importantly, we would have a better understanding of the experiences of disabled women, whose life stories are often suffused with quite different understandings of disablement. Despite the protestations of Michael Oliver and Colin Barnes,[97] we believe that a social theory of impairment would have policy implications that would benefit disabled people in many areas from the accommodation of driving to learning in the classroom.

Lastly, we suggest the most basic point of all: those of us committed to the social model and the empowerment of disabled people, particularly when infused with a feminist lens, need to pay more attention to the life story narrative method so elegantly promoted by Frank Munger and David Engel and adapted in these pages. Narrative is far messier than the dry statistics of quantitative research. It is time consuming and requires much planning for scholars to do. Yet the rewards of narrative are rich. Counter-narratives destigmatize disability and give voice to those who have been marginalized for too long. Where do we go from here? A research agenda for the future includes narrative studies of disabled lawyers and the barriers they face, accounts of disabled people working in the health sector and the experiences of unionized disabled people. Do disabled people get promoted and move up the career ladder like their able-bodied peers? Are unions unequivocally beneficial to disabled people? The experiences of other marginalized groups raise significant doubts. We also need to know more about the life stories of disabled people in every industrialized country who live on social assistance payments. They constitute a large majority of disabled people and we owe it to them as scholars to make the tools of narrative available so that their stories may be heard. Building another world of accessibility and inclusion for disabled people is not only possible, it is necessary.

Notes

1 D.M. Engel and F.W. Munger, 'Narrative, Disability and Identity' *Narrative*, 2007, vol. 15, pp. 85–94.
2 Obviously, as Lisa's case illustrates, there may be exceptions.
3 R.M. Unger, *False Necessity: Anti-Necessitarian Social Theory in the Service of Radical Democracy*, Cambridge: Cambridge University Press, 1987, p. 64; R.M. Unger, *What*

Should Legal Analysis Become?, London: Verso, 1996, pp. 11–15. See also R.M. Unger, *The Critical Legal Studies Movement*, Cambridge, MA: Harvard University Press, 1983.

4 Unger, *What Should Legal Analysis Become?*, ibid, p. 143.

5 C. Crawford, *Scoping Inclusive Education for Canadian Students with Intellectual and Other Disabilities*, Toronto: The Roeher Institute, 2005, p. 8 (discussing pioneering inclusion efforts with respect to students with intellectual disabilities in Hamilton in 1969).

6 Crawford, ibid, pp. 53–57. See also D.J. Connor, *Urban Narratives—Portraits in Progress: Life at the Intersections of Learning Disability, Race, and Social Class*, New York, NY: Peter Lang, 2008; B.A. Ferri, 'Changing the Script: Race and Disability' in *Weights' International Journal of Inclusive Education*, 2008, vol. 12, pp. 497–509 at p. 498.

7 See Chapter 3. At the same time, we recognize the importance for an EA not to be excessively intrusive so as to undermine the development of potential peer relationships or prevent the fostering of quality teacher–student relationships. See Crawford, op. cit., n. 5, 52.

8 For evidence that turnover is reduced among attendants providing services with activities of daily living, see C. Howes, 'Upgrading California's Home Care Workforce: The Impact of Political Action and Unionization' *State of California Labor*, 2004, vol. 1, pp. 70–105.

9 One of us explores some of these issues in greater depth in a similar context: the conflicts between users of attendant services and attendants, in R. Malhotra, 'Empowering People with Disabilities' *New Politics*, 2006, vol. 11, no. 1, pp. 55–59.

10 30 & 31 Victoria, c. 3 (UK) s. 93.

11 See, e.g. R. Stack, 'Progress and Uncertainty: The Educational Rights of Special Needs Children in British Columbia' *Appeal*, 2001, vol. 7, p. 29 (discussing IEPs in British Columbia). This is no doubt influenced by the more systematic legislation in the United States stipulating accommodations for disabled children, the IDEA that was originally enacted in 1975. For a recent account of American debates surrounding integration of disabled students, see M.C. Weber, 'A Nuanced Approach to the Disability Integration Presumption' *University of Pennsylvania Law Review Pennumbra*, 2007, vol. 156, p. 174, available online at http://www.pennumbra.com/responses/10-2007/Weber.pdf. (last accessed January 22, 2013).

12 Crawford, op. cit., n. 5, p. 40. This assumes a parent has the time, money and resources to persevere through the lengthy administrative law process.

13 Crawford, op. cit., n. 5, p. 40.

14 Crawford, op. cit., n. 5, p. 40.

15 S. Torjman, 'Canada's Federal Regime and Persons with Disabilities' in D. Cameron and F. Valentine (eds) *Disability and Federalism: Comparing Different Approaches to Full Participation*, Montreal and Kingston: McGill-Queen's University Press, 2001, p. 154 (commenting "[t]here is no question that provinces act as delivery agents in the provinces of health, education, welfare and social services"). See also A.H. Puttee (ed.), *Federalism, Democracy and Disability Policy in Canada*, Montreal and Kingston: McGill-Queen's University Press, 2002.

16 Canadian Charter of Rights and Freedoms, Part I of the Constitution Act, 1982, being Schedule B to the Canada Act 1982 (UK), 1982, c. 11, s. 15 [Charter]. Laws must be consistent with the Charter.

17 See e.g. British Columbia Human Rights Code, RSBC 1996, c. 210, s. 8 (prohibiting discrimination in services). Unlike the Charter, the human rights codes of the various provinces and territories of Canada apply to both government and the private sector.

18 See S. Armstrong, 'Disability Advocacy in the Charter Era' *Journal of Law and Equality*, 2003, vol. 2, pp. 91–102 (suggesting that disability advocacy organizations need not see litigation and political advocacy as competing strategies).

19 Armstrong, ibid, p. 101. One reason for the emergence of coalitions is that the costs of litigation are so high.

20 [2004] 3 *Supreme Court Reports*, 2004, vol. 3, p. 657, 2004 SCC 78 [*Auton* cited to SCR].

21 RSBC 1996, c. 210.

22 2012 SCC 61. See Chapter 3. For a more detailed discussion of *Moore*, see R. Malhotra and R. Hansen, 'The United Nations Convention on the Rights of Persons with Disabilities and its Implications for the Equality Rights of Canadians with Disabilities: The Case of Education' *Windsor Yearbook of Access to Justice*, 2011, vol. 29, pp. 73–106.

23 Malhotra and Hansen, ibid, p. 62. A full discussion of *Auton* is beyond the scope of this book.

24 See Chapter 4.

25 R. Malhotra, 'The Implications of the Social Model of Disablement for the Legal Regulation of the Modern Workplace in Canada and the United States' *Manitoba Law Journal*, 2009, vol. 33, pp. 1–41.

26 This list is adapted from the rules governing the Ontario Disability Support Program but we would not endorse the highly bureaucratic and restrictive way in which these disability supports are provided. See 'Ontario Disability Support Program—4.3 Employment Supports Directives', available online at http://www.mcss.gov.on.ca/en/mcss/programs/social/directives/directives/ODSPDirectives/employment_support/4_3_ODSP_ESDirectives.aspx (last accessed January 25, 2013).

27 A. Supiot *et al.*, 'Possible Europes' *New Left Review*, May–June 2009, No. 57, pp. 59–60; A. Supiot, 'The Transformation of Work and the Future of Labour Law in Europe: A Multidisciplinary Perspective' *International Labour Review*, 1999, vol. 138, pp. 31–46 at p. 37. An earlier proposal with some similarities is K. Klare, 'Workplace Democracy & Market Reconstruction: An Agenda for Legal Reform' *Catholic University Law Review*, 1988, vol. 38, pp. 1–68.

28 A. Supiot *et al.*, *Beyond Employment: Changes in Work and the Future of Labour Law in Europe*, Oxford: Oxford University Press, 2001, pp. 56–57; L. Boltanski and E. Chiapello, *The New Spirit of Capitalism*, trans. G. Elliott, London: Verso, 2005, pp. 387–88. Supiot's 2001 book (published earlier in French) is also known in the literature as the Supiot Report. See also K.V. Stone, *From Widgets to Digits: Employment Regulation for the Changing Workplace*, New York, NY: Cambridge University Press, 2004, pp. 387–88; K.V. Stone, 'A Labor Law for the Digital Era: The Future of Labor and Employment Law in the United States' in K. Dau-Schmidt *et al.* (eds) *Labor and Employment Law and Economics*, vol. 2, *Encyclopedia of Law and Economics*, 2nd edn, Northampton, MA: Edward Elgar Publishing Ltd, 2009, pp. 713–14 (discussing social drawing rights in the American context).

29 Boltanski and Chiapello, ibid, p. 387; G. Schmid, 'The Future of Employment Relations: Goodbye "Flexicurity"—Welcome Back Transitional Labour Markets?' Working Paper 10-106, Amsterdam: University of Amsterdam, 2010, pp. 30–32, available online at http://www.uva-aias.net/uploaded_files/publications/WP106-Schmid.pdf (last accessed February 1, 2013); Supiot, 'The Transformation of Work', op. cit., n. 27, p. 36.

30 Hence, not all non-standard employment is necessarily precarious. A lawyer who works part time and commutes by aircraft hundreds of kilometres is likely not engaged in precarious work, whereas a maid who works part time for minimal wages and few or no benefits may well be. See R. Wilton, 'Working at the Margins: Disabled People and the Growth of Precarious Employment' in D. Pothier and R. Devlin (eds) *Critical Disability Theory: Essays in Philosophy, Politics, Policy and Law*, Vancouver: University of British Columbia Press, 2006, p. 131.

31 Law Commission of Canada, *Is Work Working? Work Laws that Do a Better Job*, Ottawa: Law Commission of Canada, p. 56, available online at http://dalspace.library.

dal.ca/bitstream/handle/10222/10307/Work%20Discussion%20Paper%20EN.pdf?
sequence=1 (last accessed February 1, 2013).

32 Law Commission of Canada, ibid, p. 56.

33 See generally Schmid, op. cit., n. 29.

34 See e.g. M. Priestley, *Disability: A Life Course Approach*, Cambridge: Polity Press, 2003.

35 Boltanski and Chiapello, op. cit., n. 28, p. 388.

36 V. Glassner and M. Keune, 'The Crisis and Social Policy: The Role of Collective Agreements' *International Labour Review*, 2012, vol. 151, pp. 354–58. But see Supiot, 'Possible Europes' op. cit., n. 27 (arguing that the EU's economic policies since 2000 have not adopted Supiot's ideas).

37 Glassner and Keune, ibid, pp. 358–59.

38 Schmid, op. cit., n. 29, p. 36. Of course, the implementation of such a measure will take time and will no doubt encounter resistance from employers.

39 On this point, see V. Marleau, 'Globalization, Decentralization and the Role of Subsidiarity in the Labour Setting' in J.D.R. Craig and S.M. Lynk (eds) *Globalization and the Future of Labour Law*, Cambridge: Cambridge University Press, 2006, pp. 119–20 (expressing concern about impact of globalization on Canadian decentralized bargaining); J. Fudge, 'The Gendered Dimension of Labour Law: Why Women Need Inclusive Unionism and Broader-Based Bargaining' in L. Briskin and P. McDermott, (eds) *Women Challenging Unions*, Toronto: University of Toronto Press 1993, pp. 231–48 (noting many female dominated industries were never unionized in the first place in Canada).

40 Given the obvious safety advantages of this initiative, we think it would both be morally problematic as well as politically unwise to simply oppose the development of Graduated Licensing tout court.

41 See 'Learning to drive: graduated licensing' available online at http://www.mto.gov.on.ca/english/dandv/driver/gradu/index.shtml (last accessed January 22, 2012) (describing the 20-month period to obtain a full driver's license in Ontario).

42 We recognize that due to funding cuts, driving instruction in high school in many jurisdictions is being eliminated entirely, making this a challenging, but in our view nonetheless, necessary proposal. See 'Driver Education is being Dropped from High School Programs' available online at http://www.virginiadrivertraining.com/news/driver-education-is-being-dropped-from-high-school-programs (last accessed March 10, 2013).

43 One recent initiative was productive discussions between the Ontario Human Rights Commission, the Canadian Hearing Society and Young Drivers of Canada (YDC), a major driving school, resulting in a commitment on the part of YDC to, *inter alia*, caption their training videos and provide sign language interpretation in their classes. See *Ontario Human Rights Commission Annual Report 2007–2008*, Toronto: Ontario Human Rights Commission, 2008, p. 18.

44 SO 2005, c. 11.

45 Integrated Accessibility Standards, O Reg 191/11.

46 See 'Feedback on the Initial Proposed Accessible Transportation Standard' 2008, p. 15, available online at www.cwdo.org/documents/Response-to-AODA-Transportation-Standard.doc (last accessed January 22, 2013).

47 'Feedback', ibid, p. 14.

48 For an account of the work of the Committee, see G. Quinn, 'A Short Guide to the United Nations Convention on the Rights of Persons with Disabilities' in G. Quinn and L. Waddington (eds) *European Yearbook of Disability Law, vol. 1*, Portland, OR: Intersentia, 2009, pp. 112–13.

49 See B. Sheldrick, *Perils and Possibilities: Social Activism and the Law*, Halifax: Fernwood, 2004.

50 Sheldrick, ibid, pp. 10–12. See M. Galanter, 'Why the Haves Come Out Ahead: Speculations on the Limits of Legal Change' *Law and Society Review*, 1974, vol. 9, pp. 95–160.

51 K. Klare, 'The Judicial Deradicalization of the *Wagner Act* and the Origins of Modern Legal Consciousness, 1937–1941' *Minnesota Law Review*, 1978, vol. 62, pp. 318–25 (noting how the NLRB approved permanent strike replacements and refused to sanction the sit-down strike). But see O. Lobel, 'The Paradox of Extra-Legal Activism: Critical Legal Consciousness and Transformative Politics' *Harvard Law Review*, 2007, vol. 120, pp. 937–88 (analyzing New Deal and civil rights reform movements to argue that extra-judicial social movements also risk co-optation).

52 For an early skeptical critique, see M. Mandel, *The Charter of Rights and the Legalization of Politics in Canada*, Toronto: Wall & Thompson, 1989. See also A.C. Hutchinson, *Waiting for Coraf: A Critique of Law and Rights*, Toronto: University of Toronto Press, 1995.

53 Armstrong, op. cit., n. 18.

54 See R. Malhotra 'The Politics of the Disability Rights Movements' *New Politics*, 2001, vol. 8, pp. 65–75.

55 See C. Kelly, 'Toward Renewed Descriptions of Canadian Disability Movements: Disability Activism outside of the Non-profit Sector' *Canadian Journal of Disability Studies*, 2013, vol. 2, pp. 1–27, available online at http://cjds.uwaterloo.ca/index.php/cjds/article/view/68/119 (last accessed January 18, 2013).

56 D.J. Connor *et al.*, 'Disability Studies and Inclusive Education—Implications for Theory, Research and Practice' *International Journal of Inclusive Education*, 2008, vol. 12, pp. 441–57 at p. 449.

57 See e.g. K.E. Nielsen, *A Disability History of the United States*, Boston, MA: Beacon Press, 2012.

58 See e.g. K.E. Nielsen, *The Radical Lives of Helen Keller*, New York, NY: New York University Press, 2004.

59 See H.G. Gallagher, *FDR's Splendid Deception: The Moving Story of Roosevelt's Massive Disability—and the Intense Efforts to Conceal It from the Public*, FDR Memorial Edition, St. Petersburg, Florida: Vandamere Press, 1999.

60 See R. Malhotra, 'Electioneering and Activism at the Turn of the Century and the Politics of Disablement: The Legacy of E. T. Kingsley (1856–1929)' *Review of Disability Studies*, 2011, vol. 7, pp. 34–42. One of us (Malhotra) is writing (with Benjamin Isitt) a biography of Kingsley under contract for University of British Columbia Press.

61 S. Taylor, 'The Right Not to Work: Power and Disability' *Monthly Review*, 2004, vol. 55, pp. 30–44.

62 J. Fudge and B. Cossman, 'Introduction: Privatization, Law and the Challenge to Feminism' in B. Cossman and J. Fudge (eds) *Privatization, Law and the Challenge to Feminism*, Toronto: University of Toronto Press, 2002, pp. 19–20; G. Albo, 'Neoliberalism, the State and the Left: A Canadian Perspective' *Monthly Review*, 2002, vol. 54, p. 46. See also D. Harvey, *A Brief History of Neoliberalism*, Oxford: Oxford University Press, 2005, pp. 76–77.

63 J. Visser, 'Union Membership Statistics in 24 Countries' *Monthly Labor Review*, 2006, p. 45 (showing significant decline in union density rates in the United States, Canada and Britain between 1970 and 2003). Interestingly, Canadian union density rates fell least of the three countries but this likely suggests the extreme weakness of the American and British labour movements in recent years, rather than any particular resilience for a Canadian labour movement still struggling to have its voice heard by policymakers.

64 See M.P. Thomas, *Regulating Flexibility: The Political Economy of Employment Standards*, Montreal and Kingston: McGill-Queen's University Press, 2009. For more sources, see Chapter 4.

65 Taylor, op. cit., n. 61.

66 Taylor, op. cit., n. 61.

67 Taylor, op. cit., n. 61.

68 S. Himmelweit and S. Mohun, 'Real Abstractions and Anomalous Assumptions' in I. Steedman *et al.*, *The Value Controversy*, London: Verso, 1981, p. 225; A. Callinicos, 'Assault on Marx's Theory of Value' *International Socialism*, 1976, No. 90, pp. 24–25. The labour theory of value is controversial among scholars and we cannot canvass the full debate here. For other views, see the papers collected in Steedman *et al.*, ibid; G.A. Cohen, 'The Labour Theory of Value and the Concept of Exploitation' *Philosophy and Public Affairs*, 1979, vol. 8, pp. 338–60; J. Schwartz, 'What's Wrong with Exploitation?' *Nous*, 1995, vol. 29, pp. 158–88. For a recent defense, see A. Freeman, A. Kliman and J. Wells (eds), *The New Value Controversy and the Foundations of Economics*, Northampton, MA: Edward Elgar, 2004.

69 Himmelweit and Mohun, ibid, p. 225; Callinicos, ibid, pp. 24–25; Steedman *et al.*, ibid, p. 225; Cohen, ibid, pp. 338–60; Schwartz, ibid, pp. 158–88; Freeman, Kliman and Wells, ibid.

70 See the classic text articulating a new post-capitalist society: C.L.R. James, G.C. Lee and C. Castoriadis, *Facing Reality*, Detroit, MI: Correspondence, 1958.

71 Kelly, op. cit., n. 55, p. 11.

72 F. Pelka, *What We Have Done: An Oral History of the Disability Rights Movement*, Amherst, MA: University of Massachusetts Press, 2012, p. 376; Taylor, op. cit., n. 61.

73 Pelka, ibid, p. 376; Taylor, op. cit., n. 61.

74 S. Thomas, 'I Was There . . .', ADAPT History Project, available online at http://www. adapt.org/freeourpeople/adapt25/narratives/12adapt.htm (last accessed February 4, 2013). Interestingly, Thomas was apparently among the few college educated members of ADAPT.

75 Thomas, ibid.

76 Thomas, op. cit., n. 74.

77 Pelka, op. cit., n. 72, p. 395.

78 *Federal Reporter, Second Series*, 1989, vol. 867, p. 1471 (3d Cir.).

79 D.Z. Fleischer and F. Zames, *The Disability Rights Movement: From Charity to Confrontation*, updated edn, Philadelphia, PA: Temple University Press, 2011, p. 269.

80 *Federal Reporter, Second Series*, 1989, vol. 881, p. 1184 (3d Cir.).

81 Ibid.

82 See Fleischer and Zames, op. cit., n. 79, p. 4.

83 C. Coleman, L. Nee, and L. Rubinowitz, 'Social Movements and Social-Change Litigation: Synergy in the Montgomery Bus Protest' *Law and Social Inquiry*, 2005, vol. 30, pp. 663–737.

84 M. Russell, *Beyond Ramps: Disability at the End of the Social Contract*, Monroe, ME: Common Courage Press, pp. 128–29.

85 The first book length treatment is M. Staudenmaier, *Truth and Revolution: A History of the Sojourner Truth Organization, 1969–1986*, Oakland, CA: AK Press, 2012.

86 R.M. Unger, *Urgent Tasks*, Summer 1981, No. 12. This issue featured some of the most prominent radicals of the time including Paul Buhle, E.P. Thompson, Manning Marable and Peter Linebaugh. One of us (Malhotra) co-organized a conference, with Professor Joanne St. Lewis, at the University of Ottawa Faculty of Law devoted to the political legacy of C.L.R. James in 2009.

87 M. Staudenmaier, 'Unorthodox Leninism: Workplace Organizing and Anti-Imperialist Solidarity in the Sojourner Truth Organization' in D. Berger (ed.) *The Hidden 1970s: Histories of Radicalism*, New Brunswick, NJ: Rutgers University Press, 2010, p. 163.

88 STO lawyers were able to provide advice on the legality of ostensibly wildcat strikes. See Staudenmaier, op. cit., n. 85, p. 38.

89 Staudenmaier, op. cit., n. 87, p. 155.

90 Staudenmaier, op. cit., n. 87, pp. 156–57. One of its key members, Noel Ignatiev, wrote a foundational text in this regard on the history of Irish Americans and racial identity. See N. Ignatiev, *How the Irish Became White*, Abingdon: Routledge, 1995. Thus, our reference to white skin privilege with respect to anti-capitalist organizing refers to dismantling structures of racial oppression and should not be confused with every dispute over diversity on university campuses.

91 See T.W. Allen, *The Invention of the White Race: Volume 1: Racial Oppression and Social Control*, 1st edn, London: Verso, 1994; J.B. Perry, *Hubert Harrison: The Voice of Harlem Radicalism, 1883–1918*, New York, NY: Columbia University Press, 2008. Perry's biography, the first of two volumes to appear, is arguably one of the most important contributions to African American history in years. For an account of Hubert Harrison's extraordinary legacy for critical race legal theory, see R. Malhotra, 'The Legal Politics of Hubert H. Harrison: Excavating A Lost Legacy' *Columbia Journal of Race and Law*, 2012, vol. 1, pp. 382–401.

92 Unfortunately, this is all too rare. The *News and Letters* newspaper, founded by the late Marxist theoretician, Raya Dunayevskaya, who closely collaborated with C.L.R. James for many years, is one exception. See e.g. S. Rose, 'Handicap This!' *News and Letters*, 2013, vol. 58, no. 1, p. 9.

93 For an attempt to incorporate anti-racism into disability studies scholarship, see Ferri, op. cit, n. 6.

94 See e.g. C. Teelucksingh, 'Environmental Racialization: Linking Racialization to the Environment in Canada' *Local Environment*, 2007, vol. 12, pp. 645–61 at p. 651 (discussing poor transit options in largely racialized communities such as Scarborough, a Toronto suburb).

95 See C. Thomas, *Female Forms: Experiencing and Understanding Disability*, Buckingham: Open University Press, 1999, pp. 42–44.

96 B.S. Turner, 'Disability and the Sociology of the Body' in G. Albrecht, K. Seelman and M. Bury (eds) *Handbook of Disability Studies*, Thousand Oaks, CA: Sage, 2001, pp. 252–66. We discuss this in more depth in Chapter 1.

97 M. Oliver and C. Barnes, *The New Politics of Disablement*, Basingstoke: Palgrave Macmillan, 2012, p. 22.

Bibliography

Abbas, J. 'A Legacy of Exploitation: Intellectual Disability, Unpaid Labor and Disability Services' *New Politics*, 2012, vol. 14, no. 1, pp. 22–26.

Abberley, P. 'The Concept of Oppression and the Development of a Social Theory of Disability' *Disability, Handicap & Society*, 1987, vol. 2, pp. 5–19.

Abrams, K. 'Hearing the Call of Stories' *California Law Review*, 1991, vol. 79, pp. 971–1052.

Aiken, A. and Buitenhuis, A. 'New Veteran Charter Shortchanges Our Disabled Soldiers' Toronto *Globe and Mail*, August 24, 2010, available online at http://www.theglobeandmail.com/commentary/new-veterans-charter-shortchanges-our-disabled-soldiers/article1213169/ (last accessed September 24, 2012).

Albo, G. 'Neoliberalism, the State and the Left: A Canadian Perspective' *Monthly Review*, 2002, vol. 54, pp. 46–55.

Albrecht, G.L., Seelman, K.D. and Bury, M. (eds) *Handbook of Disability Studies*, Thousand Oaks, CA: Sage, 2001.

Aleshire, J. 'Eye of the Beholder' in R. O'Brien (ed.) *Voices from the Edge: Narratives about the Americans with Disabilities Act*, Oxford: Oxford University Press, 2004.

Allen, T.W. *The Invention of the White Race: Volume 1: Racial Oppression and Social Control*, 1st edn, London: Verso, 1994.

— *The Invention of the White Race: Volume 1: Racial Oppression and Social Control*, 2nd edn, London: Verso, 2012.

Armstrong, S. 'Disability Advocacy in the Charter Era' *Journal of Law and Equality*, 2003, vol. 2, pp. 91–102.

Ashe, M. 'Zig-Zag Stitching and the Seamless Web: Thoughts on "Reproduction" and the Law' *Nova Law Review*, 1989, vol. 13, pp. 355–84.

Atkinson, R. 'The Life Narrative Interview' in J.F. Gubrium and J.A. Holstein (eds) *Handbook of Interview Research: Context & Method*, Thousand Oaks, , CA: Sage, 2002.

Bagenstos, S.R. 'Comparative Disability Employment Law from an American Perspective' *Comparative Labor Law and Policy Journal*, 2003, vol. 24, pp. 653–55.

— 'The Future of Disability Law' *Yale Law Journal*, 2004, vol. 114, pp. 14–18.

Baker, D. *Moving Backwards: Canada's State of Transportation Accessibility in an International Context*, Winnipeg: Council of Canadians with Disabilities, 2004.

Baker, D. and Godwin, S. 'ALL ABOARD!: The Supreme Court of Canada Confirms that Canadians with Disabilities Have Substantive Equality Rights' *Saskatchewan Law Review*, 2008, vol. 71, pp. 39–77.

Balandin, S. *et al.*, 'Older Disabled Workers' Perception of Volunteering' *Disability and Society*, 2006, vol. 21, p. 680.

Baldwin, T. 'The Humanism Debate' in B. Leiter and M. Rosen (eds) *The Oxford Handbook of Continental Philosophy*, Oxford: Oxford University Press, 2007.

Banks, K. 'The Impact of Globalization on Labour Standards: A Second Look at the Evidence' in J. Craig and S.M. Lynk (eds) *Globalization and the Future of Labour Law*, Cambridge: Cambridge University Press, 2006.

Barile, M. 'Globalization and ICF Eugenics: Historical Coincidence or Connection? The More Things Change the More They Stay the Same' *Disability Studies Quarterly*, 2003, vol. 23, pp. 208–23.

Barnartt, S.N. and Scotch, R.K. *Disability Protests: Contentious Politics 1970–1999*, Washington, DC: Gallaudet University Press, 2001.

Barry, K. 'Toward Universalism: What the *ADA Amendments Act of 2008* Can and Can't Do for Disability Rights' *Berkeley Journal of Employment and Labor Law*, 2010, vol. 31, pp. 217–21.

Barton, E.L. 'Disability Narratives of the Law: Narratives and Counter-Narratives' *Narrative*, 2007, vol. 15, pp. 95–112.

Barton, L. 'Inclusive Education: Romantic, Subversive or Realistic?' *International Journal of Inclusive Education*, 1997, vol. 1, pp. 231–42.

Basas, C.G. 'The New Boys: Women with Disabilities and the Legal Profession' *Berkeley Journal of Gender, Law & Justice*, 2010, vol. 25, pp. 32–124.

Bauman, R.W. *Ideology and Community in the First Wave of Critical Legal Studies*, Toronto: University of Toronto Press, 2002.

Bê, A. 'Feminism and Disability: A Cartography of Multiplicity' in N. Watson, A. Roulstone and C. Thomas (eds) *Routledge Handbook of Disability Studies*, London: Routledge, 2012.

Bell, D. *And We Are Not Saved: The Elusive Quest for Racial Justice*, New York, NY: Basic Books, 1987.

Berrey, E. and Nielsen, L.B. 'Integrating Identity at the Bottom of the Dispute Pyramid' book review of *Rights of Inclusion: Law and Identity in the Life Narratives of Americans with Disabilities* by D.M. Engel and F.W. Munger, *Law & Social Inquiry*, 2007, vol. 32, pp. 233–60.

Bickenbach, J.E. *Physical Disability and Social Policy*, Toronto: University of Toronto Press, 1993.

Bird, M. 'Where is VIA Going? A Case Study of Managing a Commercial Crown Corporation' in A.M. Maslove (ed.) *How Ottawa Spends, 2009–2010: Economic Upheaval and Political Dysfunction*, Montreal and Kingston: McGill-Queen's University Press, 2009.

Blumberg, L. 'Public Stripping' in B. Shaw (ed.) *The Ragged Edge: The Disability Experience from the Pages of the First Fifteen Years of the Disability Rag*, Louisville, KY: Advocado Press, 1994.

Boltanski, L. and Chiapello, E. *The New Spirit of Capitalism* trans. G. Elliott, London: Verso, 2005.

Booher, A.K. 'Docile Bodies, Supercrips, and the Play of Prosthetics' *International Journal of Feminist Approaches to Bioethics*, 2010, vol. 3, p. 71.

Borsay, A. 'Personal Trouble or Public Issue? Towards a Model of Policy for People with Physical and Mental Disabilities' in L. Barton (ed.) *Overcoming Disabled Barriers: 18 Years of Disability and Society*, Abingdon: Routledge, 2006.

Bourke, S. and Burgman, I. 'Coping with Bullying in Australian Schools: How

Children with Disabilities Experience Support from Friends, Parents and Teachers' *Disability & Society*, 2010, vol. 25, pp. 359–71.

Boyce, W. *et al.*, *A Seat at the Table: Persons with Disabilities and Policy Making*, Montreal and Kingston: McGill-Queen's University Press, 2002.

Braddock, D. and Parrish, C. 'An Institutional History of Disability' in G.L. Albrecht, K.D. Seelman and M. Bury (eds) *Handbook of Disability Studies*, Thousand Oaks, CA: Sage, 2001.

Bradshaw, T. *Canadian Forces Military Nursing Officers and Moral Distress: A Grounded Theory Approach*, MS thesis, University of Ottawa, Ottawa, 2010.

Broderick, A.A., Reid, D.K. and Valle, J.W. 'Disability Studies in Education and the Practical Concerns of Teachers' in S. Danforth and S.L. Gabel (eds) *Vital Questions Facing Disability Studies in Education*, New York, NY: Peter Lang, 2006.

Brodsky, G., Day, S. and Peters, Y. *Accommodation in the 21st Century*, Ottawa: Canadian Human Rights Commission, 2012, available online at http://www.chrc-ccdp.ca/pdf/accommodation_eng.pdf (accessed January 4, 2012).

Broverman, A. 'Toronto Wheelchair Taxi Cabs Price Gouge Patrons with Disabilities', *Wallet Pop*, October 31, 2010, available online at http://www.walletpop.ca/blog/2010/10/31/toronto-wheelchair-taxicabs-price-gouge-patrons-with-disabilitie/ (last accessed November 28, 2012).

Brown, L.M. *Girlfighting: Betrayal and Rejection among Girls*, New York, NY: New York University Press, 2003.

Brown, S.C. 'Methodological Paradigms That Shape Disability Research' in G. Albrecht, K. Seelman and M. Bury (eds) *Handbook of Disability Studies*, Thousand Oaks, CA: Sage, 2001.

Browne, S.E., Connors, D. and Sterne, N. (eds) *With the Power of Each Breath: A Disabled Women's Anthology*, Pittsburgh, PA: Cleis Press, 1985.

Bruner, J. *Actual Minds, Possible Worlds*, Cambridge, MA: Harvard University Press, 1986.

— *Acts of Meaning*, Cambridge, MA: Harvard University Press, 1990.

— 'The Narrative Construction of Reality' *Critical Inquiry*, 1991, vol. 18, pp. 1–21.

— 'Identity as Inclusion' *Buffalo Law Review*, 2005–2006, vol. 53, p. 347.

Bryant, J. and Lasky, B. 'A Researcher's Tale: Dealing with Epistemological Divergence' *Qualitative Research in Organizations and Management: An International Journal*, 2007, vol. 2, pp. 179–93.

Brydon-Miller, M. 'Breaking Down Barriers: Accessibility and Self-Advocacy in the Disabled Community' in P. Park *et al.* (eds) *Voices of Change: Participatory Research in the United States and Canada*, Westport, CT: Bergin & Garvey, 1993.

Burge, P. *et al.* 'A Quarter Century of Inclusive Education for Children with Intellectual Disabilities in Ontario: Public Perceptions' *Canadian Journal of Educational Administration and Policy*, 2008, vol. 87, pp. 1–18.

Butler, J. 'Performative Acts and Gender Constitution: An Essay in Phenomenology and Feminist Theory' in S. Case (ed.) *Performing Feminisms: Feminist Critical Theory and Theatre*, Baltimore, MD: Johns Hopkins University Press, 1990.

Callinicos, A. 'Assault on Marx's Theory of Value' *International Socialism*, 1976, No. 90, pp. 24–25.

Campbell, J., Gilmore, L. and Cuskelly, M. 'Changing Student Teachers' Attitudes towards Disability and Inclusion' *Journal of Intellectual & Developmental Disability*, 2003, vol. 28, pp. 369–79.

Canadian Labour Congress, *Toward Inclusion of People with Disabilities in the Workplace*, Ottawa: Canadian Labour Congress, 2008.

Canguilhem, G. *The Normal and the Pathological*, trans. by C.R. Fawcett and R.S. Cohen, New York, NY: Zone Books, 1991.

Carbado, D.W. and Gulati, M. 'Working Identity' *Cornell Law Review*, 1999–2000, vol. 85, pp. 1259–308.

— 'The Law and Economics of Critical Race Theory' *Yale Law Journal*, 2003, vol. 112, pp. 1784–85.

Carlson, L. 'Cognitive Ableism and Disability Studies: Feminist Reflections on the History of Mental Retardation' *Hypatia*, 2001, vol. 16, pp. 124–46.

Cellard, A. and Thifault, M. 'The Uses of Asylums: Resistance, Asylum Propaganda and Institutionalization Strategies in Turn-of-the Century Quebec' in J.E. Moran and D. Wright (eds) *Mental Health and Canadian Society: Historical Perspectives*, Montreal and Kingston: McGill-Queen's University Press, 2006.

Cepko, R. 'On Oxfords and Plaster Casts' in M. Saxton and F. Howe (eds) *With Wings: An Anthology of Literature by and about Women with Disabilities*, New York, NY: The Feminist Press, 1987.

Chadha, E. 'Running on Empty: The "Not So Special Status" of Paratransit Services in Ontario' *Windsor Review of Legal and Social Issues*, 2005, vol. 20, p. 1.

Charmaz, K. 'Grounded Theory: Objectivist and Constructivist Methods' in N. Denzin and Y. Lincoln (eds) *Handbook of Qualitative Research*, London: Sage, 2005.

— *Constructing Grounded Theory: A Practical Guide Through Qualitative Analysis*, London: Sage, 2006.

Charmaz, K. and Rosenfeld, D. 'Reflections on the Body, Images of Self: Visibility and Invisibility in Chronic Illness and Disability' in D. Waskul and P. Vannini (eds) *Body/Embodiment: Symbolic Interaction and the Sociology of the Body*, Burlington, VT: Ashgate Publishing Company, 2006.

Chesler, P. *Woman's Inhumanity to Woman*, New York, NY: Thunder's Mouth Press, 2001.

Chow, A. 'This is Not Going to Control My Life: Young and Living with Fibromyalgia' in D. Driedger and M. Owen (eds) *Dissonant Disabilities: Women with Chronic Illnesses Explore Their Lives*, Toronto: Canadian Scholar's Press/Women's Press, 2008.

Cohen, G.A. *History, Labour and Freedom: Themes from Marx*, New York, NY: Oxford University Press, 1988.

— 'The Labour Theory of Value and the Concept of Exploitation' *Philosophy and Public Affairs*, 1979, vol. 8, pp. 338–60.

Coleman, C., Nee, L. and Rubinowitz, L. 'Social Movements and Social-Change Litigation: Synergy in the Montgomery Bus Protest' *Law and Social Inquiry*, 2005, vol. 30, pp. 663–737.

Colker, R. 'Winning and Losing under the Americans with Disabilities Act' *Ohio State Law Journal*, 2001, vol. 62, pp. 241–42.

— 'The Disability Integration Presumption: Thirty Years Later' *University of Pennsylvania Law Review*, 2006, vol. 154, pp. 789–862.

Connor, D.J. *Urban Narratives—Portraits in Progress: Life at the Intersections of Learning Disability, Race & Social Class*, New York, NY: Peter Lang, 2008.

Connor, D.J. and Ferri, B.A. 'The Conflict Within: Resistance to Inclusion and Other Paradoxes in Special Education' *Disability & Society*, 2007, vol. 22, pp. 63–77.

Connor, D.J. *et al.*, 'Disability Studies and Inclusive Education—Implications for

Theory, Research and Practice' *International Journal of Inclusive Education*, 2008, vol. 12, pp. 441–57.

Couser, G.T. 'Undoing Hardship: Life Writing and Disability Law' *Narrative*, 2007, vol. 15, pp. 71–84.

— *Signifying Bodies: Disability in Contemporary Life Writing*, Ann Arbor, MI: University of Michigan Press, 2009.

Cover, R.M. 'The Supreme Court, 1982 Term – Foreword: Nomos and Narrative' *Harvard Law Review*, 1983–84, vol. 97, pp. 4–68.

Cox, J. 'Crossroads and Signposts: The ADA Amendments Act of 2008' *Indiana Law Journal*, 2010, vol. 85, pp. 201–2.

Craig, R. *Systemic Discrimination in Employment and the Promotion of Ethnic Equality*, Leiden: Martinus Nijhoff, 2007.

Crawford, C. *Scoping Inclusive Education for Canadian Students with Intellectual and Other Disabilities*, Toronto: The Roeher Institute, 2005.

Crenshaw, K. 'Demarginalizing the Intersection of Race and Sex: A Black Feminist Critique of Antidiscrimination Doctrine, Feminist Theory and Antiracist Policy' *University of Chicago Legal Forum*, 1989, pp. 139–67.

— 'Mapping the Margins: Intersectionality, Identity Politics, and Violence against Women of Color' *Stanford Law Review*, 1991, vol. 43, pp. 1241–99.

Crooks, D.L. 'The Importance of Symbolic Interactionism in Grounded Theory Research on Women's Health' *Health Care for Women International*, 2001, vol. 22, pp. 11–27.

D'Aubin, A. 'We Will Ride: A Showcase of CCD Advocacy Strategies in Support of Accessible Transportation' in D. Stienstra and A. Wight-Felske (eds) *Making Equality: History of Advocacy and Persons with Disabilities in Canada*, Toronto: Captus Press, 2003.

— 'Making Federally Regulated Transportation Systems Accessible to Persons with Disabilities' in M.A. McColl and L. Jongbloed (eds) *Disability and Social Policy in Canada*, 2nd edn, Concord, Ontario: Captus University Publications, 2006.

— 'Working for Barrier Removal in the ICT Area: Creating a More Accessible and Inclusive Canada' *The Information Society*, 2007, vol. 23, pp. 193–201.

Davis, K. 'Intersectionality as Buzzword: A Sociology of Science Perspective on What Makes a Feminist Theory Successful' *Feminist Theory*, vol. 9, 2008, pp. 67–85.

Davis, L.J. (ed.) *The Disability Studies Reader*, 3rd edn, New York, NY: Routledge, 2010.

Delgado, R. *The Rodrigo Chronicles: Conversations about America and Race*, New York, NY: New York University Press, 1995.

— 'Storytelling for Oppositionists and Others: A Plea for Narrative' in R. Delgado and J. Stefancic (eds) *Critical Race Theory: The Cutting Edge*, Philadelphia, PA: Temple University Press, 2000.

Dempsey, P.S. 'The Civil Rights of the Handicapped in Transportation: The Americans with Disabilities Act and Related Legislation' *Transportation Law Journal*, 1990–91, vol. 19, pp. 330–33.

Denzin, N.K. 'Grounded Theory and the Politics of Interpretation' in A. Bryant and K. Charmaz (eds) *The SAGE Handbook of Grounded Theory*, London: Sage, 2007.

Denzin, N. and Lincoln, Y. (eds) *The Landscape of Qualitative Research*, 2nd edn, London: Sage, 2003.

Department for Transport, *Railways for All: The Accessibility Strategy for Great Britain's Railways*, London: Department of Transport, 2006, p. 5, available online at http://

assets.dft.gov.uk/publications/railways-for-all-strategy/railways-for-all-strategy.
pdf (last accessed November 28, 2012).

Deputy Minister of Education, 'Policy/Program Memorandum No. 124a' available online at http://www.edu.gov.on.ca/extra/eng/ppm/124a.html (last accessed September 27, 2012).

Dinerstein, R.D. '"Every Picture Tells a Story, Don't It?": The Complex Role of Narratives in Disability Cases' *Narrative*, 2007, vol. 15, pp. 40–57.

Donovan, L.A. 'For a Paralyzed Woman Raped and Murdered While Alone in Her Own Apartment' in M. Saxton and F. Howe (eds) *With Wings: An Anthology of Literature by and about Women with Disabilities*, New York, NY: The Feminist Press, 1987.

Dossa, P. *Racialized Bodies, Disabling Worlds: Storied Lives of Immigrant Muslim Women*, Toronto: University of Toronto Press, 2009.

Dosse, F. *History of Structuralism, Volume 1: The Rising Sign, 1945–1966*, trans. by D. Glassman, Minneapolis, MN: University of Minnesota Press, 1997.

Driedger, D. *Living the Edges: A Disabled Women's Reader*, Toronto: Inanna Publications and Education, 2010.

Driedger, D. and Gray, S. (eds) *Imprinting Our Image: An International Anthology by Women with Disabilities*, Charlottetown: Gyenrgy Books, 1992.

Driedger, D. and Owen, M. (eds) *Dissonant Disabilities: Women with Chronic Illnesses Explore Their Lives*, Toronto: Canadian Scholar's Press/Women's Press, 2008.

Duckett, P.S. and Pratt, R. 'The Researched Opinions on Research: Visually Impaired People and Visual Impairment Research' *Disability & Society*, 2001, vol. 16, pp. 815–35.

Duclos, N. 'Disappearing Women: Racial Minority Women in Human Rights Cases' *Canadian Journal of Women and the Law*, 1993, vol. 6, pp. 25–51.

Duff, D.G. 'Disability and the Income Tax' *McGill Law Journal*, 2000, vol. 45, pp. 873–74.

Dunn, W. 'Best Practice Philosophy for Community Services for Children and Families' in W. Dunn (ed.) *Best Practice Occupational Therapy in Community Service for Children and Families*, Thorofare, NJ: SLACK, Inc., 2000.

Durflinger, S. *Veterans with a Vision: Canada's War Blinded in Peace and War*, Vancouver: University of British Columbia Press, 2010.

Edwards, E. and Timmons, S. 'A Qualitative Study of Stigma Among Women Suffering Postnatal Illness' *Journal of Mental Health*, 2005, vol. 14, pp. 471–81.

Edwards, S. and Gabbay, M. 'Living and Working with Sickness: A Qualitative Study' *Chronic Illness*, 2007, pp. 155–66.

Engel, D.M. and Munger, F.W. 'Rights, Remembrance, and the Reconciliation of Difference' *Law and Society Review*, 1996, vol. 30, pp. 7–54.

—— 'Civil Rights and Self-Concept: Life Stories of Law, Disability, and Employment' *Droit et Cultures*, 1998, vol. 35, pp. 43–73.

—— 'Re-Interpreting the Effect of Rights: Career Narratives and the Americans with Disabilities Act' *Ohio State Law Journal*, 2001, vol. 62, pp. 285–333.

—— *Rights of Inclusion: Law and Identity in the Life Stories of Americans with Disabilities*, Chicago, IL: University of Chicago Press, 2003.

—— 'Narrative, Disability and Identity' *Narrative*, 2007, vol. 15, pp. 85–94.

Erevelles, N. *Disability and Difference in Global Contexts: Enabling a Transformative Body Politic*, Basingstoke: Palgrave Macmillan, 2011.

Eskridge Jr, W.N. 'Gaylegal Narratives' *Stanford Law Review*, 1994, vol. 46, pp. 614–16.

Estrich, S. 'Rape' *Yale Law Journal*, 1986, vol. 95, pp. 1087–184.

Evans, P.B., Rueschemeyer, D. and Skocpol, T. (eds) *Bringing the State Back In*, Cambridge: Cambridge University Press, 1985.

Ewick, P. and Silbey, S.S. 'Conformity, Contestation, and Resistance: An Account of Legal Consciousness' *New England Law Review*, 1992, vol. 26, pp. 731–49.

— 'Subversive Stories and Hegemonic Tales: Toward a Sociology of Narrative' *Law and Society Review*, 1995, vol. 29, pp. 197–226.

— *The Common Place of Law: Stories from Everyday Life*, Chicago, IL: University of Chicago Press, 1998.

Farber, D.A. and Sherry, S. 'Telling Stories Out of School: An Essay on Legal Narratives' *Stanford Law Review*, 1992, vol. 45, pp. 835–38.

— *Beyond All Reason: The Radical Assault on Truth in American Law*, Oxford: Oxford University Press, 1997.

Farley, A.P. 'The Black Body as Fetish Object' *Oregon Law Review*, 1997, vol. 76, pp. 457–535.

Ferri, B.A. 'Changing the Script: Race and Disability' *Weights' International Journal of Inclusive Education*, 2008, vol. 12, pp. 497–509.

— 'Disability Life Writing and the Politics of Knowing' *Teachers College Record*, 2011, vol. 113, pp. 2267–82.

Field, S., Sarver, M.D. and Shaw, S.F. 'Self-Determination: A Key to Success in Postsecondary Education for Students with Learning Disabilities' *Remedial and Special Education*, 2003, vol. 24, pp. 339–49.

Fine, M. and Asch, A. 'Disabled Women: Sexism without the Pedestal' in M. Deegan and N.A. Brooks (eds) *Women and Disability: The Double Handicap*, New Brunswick: Transaction Books, 1985.

Finger, A. *Past Due: A Story of Disability, Pregnancy and Birth*, Berkeley, CA: Seal Press, 1990.

— *Elegy for a Disease: A Personal and Cultural History of Polio*, New York, NY: St. Martin's Press, 2006.

Finkelstein, V. *Attitudes and Disabled People*, New York, NY: World Rehabilitation Fund, 1980, available online at http://www.leeds.ac.uk/disability-studies/archiveuk/finkelstein/attitudes.pdf (accessed December 18, 2012).

Fleischer, D.Z. and Zames, F. *The Disability Rights Movement: From Charity to Confrontation*, updated edn, Philadelphia, PA: Temple University Press, 2011.

Floersch, J., Longhofer, J.L. and Kranke, D. 'Integrating Thematic, GT and Narrative Analysis: A Case Study of Adolescent Psychotropic Treatment' *Qualitative Social Work*, 2010, vol. 9, pp. 407–25.

Ford, C. 'Disability Politics in a Time of Capitalist Crisis' *New Politics*, 2012, vol. 14, no. 1, pp. 10–15.

Foucault, M. *Discipline and Punishment: The Birth of the Prison*, trans. by A. Sheridan, New York, NY: Vintage Books, 1995.

Frazee, C., Gilmour, J. and Mykituk, R. 'Now You See Her, Now You Don't: How Law Shapes Disabled Women's Experiences of Exposure, Surveillance, and Assessment in the Clinical Encounter' in D. Pothier and R. Devlin (eds) *Critical Disability Theory: Essays in Philosophy, Politics, Policy and Law*, Vancouver: University of British Columbia Press, 2006.

Freeman, A., Kliman, A. and Wells, J. (eds), *The New Value Controversy and the Foundations of Economics*, Northampton, MA: Edward Elgar, 2004.

Freedman, R. *Beauty Bound*, Lexington Books: Toronto, 1986.

Fries, K. *Body, Remember: A Memoir*, New York, NY: Dutton, 1997.

Fudge, J. 'The Gendered Dimension of Labour Law: Why Women Need Inclusive Unionism and Broader-Based Bargaining' in L. Briskin and P. McDermott (eds) *Women Challenging Unions*, Toronto: University of Toronto Press, 1993.

Fudge, J. and Cossman, B. 'Introduction: Privatization, Law and the Challenge to Feminism' in B. Cossman and J. Fudge (eds) *Privatization, Law and the Challenge to Feminism*, Toronto: University of Toronto Press, 2002.

Galanter, M. 'Why the Haves Come Out Ahead: Speculations on the Limits of Legal Change' *Law and Society Review*, 1974, vol. 9, pp. 95–160.

Galer, D. 'A Friend in Need or a Business Indeed? Disabled Bodies and Fraternalism in Victorian Ontario' *Labour/Le Travail*, 2010, vol. 66, pp. 27–30.

— 'Building an Accessible House of Labour: Work, Disability Rights and the Canadian Labour Movement' in R. Hanes and N. Hansen (eds) *Untold Stories: Disability History in Canada*, Winnipeg: University of Manitoba Press, forthcoming.

— 'Disabled Capitalists: Exploring the Intersections of Disability and Identity Formation in the World of Work' *Disability Studies Quarterly*, 2012, vol. 32, no. 3, available online at http://dsq-sds.org/article/view/3277/3122 (accessed January 12, 2013).

Gallagher, H.G. *FDR's Splendid Deception: The Moving Story of Roosevelt's Massive Disability—and the Intense Efforts to Conceal It from the Public*, FDR Memorial Edition, St. Petersburg, Florida: Vandamere Press, 1999.

Gardner, C.B. *Passing By: Gender and Public Harassment*, Berkeley, CA: University of California Press, 1995.

Garland-Thomson, R. *Staring: How We Look*, Oxford: Oxford University Press, 2000.

— 'Shape Structures Narrative: Fresh and Feisty Narratives of Disability' *Narrative*, 2007, vol. 15, pp. 113–23.

Gerschick, T.J. and Miller, A.S. 'Coming to Terms: Masculinity and Physical Disability' in M.B. Zinn, P. Hondagneu-Sotello and M.A. Messner (eds) *Through the Prism of Difference: Readings on Sex and Gender*, Needham Heights: Allyn & Bacon, 1997.

Gibson, B.E. *et al.*, 'Consumer-Directed Personal Assistance and "Care": Perspectives of Workers and Ventilator Users' *Disability and Society*, 2009, vol. 24, pp. 317–30.

Gibson, S. 'Beyond a "Culture of Silence": Inclusive Education and the Liberation of "Voice"' *Disability & Society*, 2006, vol. 21, pp. 316–17.

Gilbert, L. and Dikeç, M. 'Right to the City: Politics of Citizenship' in K. Goonewardena *et al.* (eds) *Space, Difference, Everyday Life: Reading Henri Lefebvre*, New York, NY: Routledge, 2008.

Gill, C.J. 'Divided Understandings: The Social Experience of Disability' in G.L. Albrecht, K.D. Seelman, and M. Bury (eds) *Handbook of Disability Studies*, Thousand Oaks, CA: Sage, 2001.

Glaser, B.G. *Theoretical Sensitivity: Advances in the Methodology of Grounded Theory*, Mill Valley, CA: Sociology Press, 1978.

— 'Doing Formal Theory' in A. Bryant and K. Charmaz (eds) *The SAGE Handbook of Grounded Theory*, London: Sage, 2007.

Glaser, B.G. and Strauss, A.L. *The Discovery of Grounded Theory: Strategies for Qualitative Research*, Chicago, IL: Aldine Publishing Company, 1967.

Glassner, V. and Keune, M. 'The Crisis and Social Policy: The Role of Collective Agreements' *International Labour Review*, 2012, vol. 151, pp. 354–58.

Gleeson, B. 'Disability Studies: A Historical Materialist View' *Disability & Society*, 1997, vol. 12, pp. 179–202.

— *Geographies of Disability*, London: Routledge, 1999.

— 'Disability and the Open City' *Urban Studies*, 2001, vol. 38, pp. 251–65.

Goffman, E. 'The Stigmatized Self' in C. Lemert and A. Branaman (eds) *The Goffman Reader*, Malden, MA: Blackwell Publishing, 1997.

Goode, J. '"Managing" Disability: Early Experiences of University Students with Disabilities' *Disability & Society*, 2007, vol. 22, pp. 40–41.

Goodwin, D.L. and Staples, K. 'The Meaning of Summer Camp Experiences to Youths with Disabilities' *Adapted Physical Activity Quarterly*, 2005, vol. 22, pp. 160–78.

Gorman, R. *Class Consciousness, Disability and Social Exclusion: A Relational/Reflexive Analysis of Disability Culture*, PhD Dissertation, Toronto: University of Toronto.

Green, J. and Thorogood, N. *Qualitative Methods for Health Research*, London: Sage, 2004.

Gutting, G. 'What Have We Been Missing? Science and Philosophy in Twentieth Century French Thought' in B. Leiter and M. Rosen (eds) *The Oxford Handbook of Continental Philosophy*, Oxford: Oxford University Press, 2007.

Hahn, H. 'Advertising the Acceptably Employable Image: Disability and Capitalism' in L.J. Davis (ed.) *The Disability Studies Reader*, New York, NY: Routledge, 1997.

Hall, J.P. 'Narrowing the Breach: Can Disability Culture and Full Educational Inclusion Be Reconciled?' *Journal of Disability Policy Studies*, 2002, vol. 13, pp. 144–52.

Hallberg, L.R-M. 'The "Core Category" of Grounded Theory: Making Constant Comparisons' *International Journal of Qualitative Studies on Health and Well-being*, 2006, vol. 1, pp. 141–48.

Hanna, W. and Rogovsky, B. 'Women with Disabilities: Two Handicaps Plus' in L. Barton (ed.) *Overcoming Disabled Barriers: 18 Years of Disability and Society*, Abingdon: Routledge, 2006.

Hansen, N. 'Spaces of Education: Finding a Place That Fits' *Review of Disability Studies*, 2005, vol. 1, pp. 22–36.

Hardesty, C. 'Pain' in M. Saxton and F. Howe (eds) *With Wings: An Anthology of Literature by and about Women with Disabilities*, New York, NY: The Feminist Press, 1987.

Harvey, D. *A Brief History of Neoliberalism*, Oxford: Oxford University Press, 2005.

Heyer, K. 'A Disability Lens on Sociolegal Research: Reading *Rights of Inclusion* from a Disability Studies Perspective' book review of *Rights of Inclusion: Law and Identity in the Life Narratives of Americans with Disabilities* by D.M. Engel and F.W. Munger, *Law and Social Inquiry*, 2007, vol. 32, pp. 277–88.

— 'From Special Needs to Equal Rights: Japanese Disability Law' *Asian-Pacific Law & Policy Journal*, 2000, vol. 1, pp. 7:1–7:21.

— 'The ADA on the Road: Disability Rights in Germany' *Law & Social Inquiry*, 2006, vol. 27, pp. 723–62.

Hibbs, T. and Pothier, D. 'Post-Secondary Education and Disabled Students: Mining a Level Playing Field or Playing in a Minefield?' in D. Pothier and R. Devlin (eds) *Critical Disability Theory: Essays in Philosophy, Politics, Policy and Law*, Vancouver: University of British Columbia Press, 2006.

Himmelweit, S. and Mohun, S. 'Real Abstractions and Anomalous Assumptions' in I. Steedman *et al.*, *The Value Controversy*, London: Verso, 1981.

Hine, J. and Mitchell, F. 'Better for Everyone? Travel Experiences and Transport Exclusion' *Urban Studies*, 2001, vol. 38, pp. 319–32.

Hockenberry, J. *Moving Violations: A Memoir: War Zones, Wheelchairs and Declarations of Independence*, New York, NY: Hyperion, 1995.

Holzbauer, J.J. and Conrad, C.F. 'A Typology of Disability Harassment in Secondary Schools' *Career Development for Exceptional Individuals*, 2010, vol. 33, pp. 143–54.

Hones, D.F. 'The Transformational Power of Narrative Inquiry' *Qualitative Inquiry*, 1998, vol. 4, pp. 225–48.

Howes, C. 'Upgrading California's Home Care Workforce: The Impact of Political Action and Unionization' *State of California Labor*, 2004, vol. 1, pp. 70–105.

Hubbard, R. and Paquet, G. 'Design Challenges for the Strategic State: Bricolage and Sabotage' in A.M. Maslove (ed.) *How Ottawa Spends, 2009–2010: Economic Upheaval and Political Dysfunction*, Montreal and Kingston: McGill-Queen's University Press, 2009.

Hughes, B. *et al.*, 'Love's Labours Lost? Feminism, the Disabled People's Movement, and an Ethics of Care' *Sociology*, 2005, vol. 39, pp. 263–64.

Hughes, B. and Paterson, K. 'The Social Model of Disability and the Disappearing Body: Towards a Sociology of Impairment' *Disability and Society*, 1997, vol. 12, pp. 325–40.

Hutchinson, A.C. *Waiting for Coraf: A Critique of Law and Rights*, Toronto: University of Toronto Press, 1995.

Ignagni, E. 'Disabled Young People, Support and the Dialogical Work of Accomplishing Citizenship', PhD Dissertation, Ryerson University, 2011.

Ignatiev, N. *How the Irish Became White*, Abingdon: Routledge, 1995.

Immen, W. 'Fewer Drivers Makes It Harder to Hire' Toronto *Globe and Mail*, December 10, 2012, available online at http://www.theglobeandmail.com/report-on-business/small-business/sb-managing/human-resources/fewer-drivers-makes-it-harder-to-hire/article6114058/(last accessed December 10, 2012).

Imrie, R. *Disability and the City: International Perspectives*, London: Paul Chapman, 1996.

— 'Universalism, Universal Design and Equitable Access to the Built Environment' *Disability & Rehabilitation*, 2012, vol. 34, pp. 873–82.

Information and Research Utilization Center in Physical Education and Recreation for the Handicapped, *Involving Impaired, Disabled and Handicapped Persons in Regular Camp Programs*, Washington, DC: American Alliance for Health, Physical Education, and Recreation, 1976.

Iwakuma, M. 'The Body as Embodiment: An Investigation of the Body by Merleau-Ponty' in M. Corker and T. Shakespeare (eds) *Disability/Postmodernity: Embodying Disability Theory*, London: Continuum, 2002.

Jakle, A. 'Surveyors, Reporters, and Detectives: A Typology of Qualitative Interviews' paper presented to the 2012 Law & Society Association Conference, June 2012, unpublished.

James, C.L.R., Lee, G.C. and Castoriadis, C. *Facing Reality*, Detroit, MI: Correspondence, 1958.

Jeon, Y. 'The Application of Grounded Theory and Symbolic Interactionism' *Scandinavian Journal of Caring Science*, 2004, vol. 18, pp. 249–56.

Jones, C. 'Drawing Boundaries: Exploring the Relationship Between Sexual

Harassment, Gender and Bullying' *Women's Studies International Forum*, 2006, vol. 29, pp. 147–58.

Kanter, A. 'The Globalization of Disability Rights Law' *Syracuse Journal of International Law & Commerce*, 2003, vol. 30, pp. 241–70.

Katsiyannis, A. *et al.* 'Postsecondary Education for Individuals with Disabilities: Legal and Practice Considerations' *Journal of Disability Policy Studies*, 2009, vol. 20, pp. 35–36.

Kelly, C. 'Making "Care" Accessible: Personal Assistance for Disabled People and the Politics of Language' *Critical Social Policy*, 2011, vol. 31, pp. 562–82.

— 'Toward Renewed Descriptions of Canadian Disability Movements: Disability Activism outside of the Non-profit Sector' *Canadian Journal of Disability Studies*, 2013, vol. 2, pp. 1–27, available online at http://cjds.uwaterloo.ca/index.php/cjds/article/view/68/119 (accessed January 18, 2013).

Kelly, M. 'Regulating the Reproduction and Mothering of Poor Women: The Controlling Image of the Welfare Mother in Television News Coverage of Welfare Reform' *Journal of Poverty*, 2010, vol. 14, pp. 76–96.

Kelman, M. *A Guide to Critical Legal Studies*, Cambridge, MA: Harvard University Press, 1987.

Klare, K. 'The Judicial Deradicalization of the *Wagner Act* and the Origins of Modern Legal Consciousness, 1937–1941' *Minnesota Law Review*, 1978, vol. 62, pp. 318–25.

— 'Workplace Democracy & Market Reconstruction: An Agenda for Legal Reform' *Catholic University Law Review*, 1988, vol. 38, pp. 1–68.

Kraus, K. 'McGuinty's Axing of the Special Diet Program is a Catastrophe to Poor and Sick Ontarians', Rabble.ca, May 7, 2010, available online at http://rabble.ca/news/2010/05/mcguintys (last accessed January 26, 2013).

Krause, C. (ed.) *Between Myself and Them: Stories of Disability and Difference*, Toronto: Second Story Press, 2005.

Ladson-Billings, G. 'Racialized Discourses and Ethnic Epistemologies' in N.K. Denzin and Y.S. Lincoln (eds) *Handbook of Qualitative Research*, 2nd edn, Thousand Oaks, CA: Sage, 2000.

Lang, R. *The Development and Critique of the Social Model of Disability*, London: Leonard Cheshire Disability and Inclusive Development Centre, 2007, available online at http://www.ucl.ac.uk/lc-ccr/centrepublications/workingpapers/WP03_Development_Critique.pdf (accessed December 27, 2012).

Law Commission of Canada, *Is Work Working? Work Laws that Do a Better Job*, Ottawa: Law Commission of Canada, available online at http://dalspace.library.dal.ca/bitstream/handle/10222/10307/Work%20Discussion%20Paper%20EN.pdf?sequence=1 (accessed February 1, 2013).

Lawand, N. and Kloosterman, R. 'The Canada Pension Plan Disability Program: Building a Solid Foundation' in M. McColl and L. Jongbloed (eds) *Disability and Social Policy in Canada*, 2nd edn, Concord, Ontario: Captus University Press, 2006.

Lawson, A. 'Disability and Employment in the Equality Act 2010: Opportunities Seized, Lost and Generated' *Industrial Law Journal*, 2011, vol. 40, pp. 359–83.

Lazar-Meyn, H. 'Paratransit Services Are Not "Special Programs"' *ARCH Alert*, June 13, 2006, available online at http://www.archdisabilitylaw.ca/sites/all/files/ARCH%20Alert%20-%20June%2013%2006%20-%20Text.txt (last accessed December 15, 2012).

Lempert, L.B. 'Asking Questions of the Data: Memo Writing in the Grounded

Theory Tradition' in A. Bryant and K. Charmaz (eds) *The SAGE Handbook of Grounded Theory*, London: Sage, 2007.

Lepofsky, M.D. 'The Long, Arduous Road to a Barrier-Free Ontario for People with Disabilities: The History of the *Ontarians with Disabilities Act*—The First Chapter' *National Journal of Constitutional Law*, 2004, vol. 15, pp. 125–333.

Lero, D., Pletsch, C. and Hilbrecht, M. 'ntroduction to the Special Issue on Disability and Work: Toward Re-conceptualizing the "Burden" of Disability' *Disability Studies Quarterly*, 2012, vol. 32, para. 3.

Lewiecki-Wilson, C. and Cellio, J. (eds) *Disability and Mothering: Liminal Spaces of Embodied Knowledge*, Syracuse, NY: Syracuse University Press, 2011.

Lewyn, M. '"Thou Shalt Not Put a Stumbling Block before the Blind": The Americans with Disabilities Act and Public Transit for the Disabled' *Hastings Law Journal*, 2001, vol. 52, pp. 1037–100.

Linton, S. *Claiming Disability: Knowledge and Identity*, New York, NY: New York University Press, 1998.

Lipman, F. 'Enabling Work for People with Disabilities: A Post-Integrationist Revision of Underutilized Tax Incentives' *American University Law Review*, 2003, vol. 53, pp. 395–97.

Lipsky, D. and Gartner, A. 'Inclusion, School Restructuring, and the Remaking of American Society' *Harvard Educational Review*, 1996, vol. 66, pp. 762–96.

Lobel, O. 'The Paradox of Extra-Legal Activism: Critical Legal Consciousness and Transformative Politics' *Harvard Law Review*, 2007, vol. 120, pp. 937–88.

Locke, R.M. 'The Political Embeddedness of Industrial Change: Corporate Restructuring and Local Politics in Contemporary Italy' in T.A. Kochan and M. Useem (eds) *Transforming Organizations*, Oxford: Oxford University Press, 1992.

Long, A. 'Introducing the New and Improved Americans with Disabilities Act: Assessing the ADA Amendments Act of 2008' *Northwestern University Law Review Colloquy*, 2008, vol. 103, pp. 220–21.

Longmore, P.K. 'Conspicuous Contribution and American Cultural Dilemmas: Telethon Rituals of Cleansing and Renewal' in D. Mitchell and S. Snyder (eds) *The Body and Physical Difference: Discourses of Disability*, Ann Arbor, MI: University of Michigan Press, 1997.

Lorber, J. and Moore, L. *Gender and the Social Construction of Illness*, Walnut Creek, CA: AltaMira Press, 2002.

Lord, J. and Hutchison, P. 'Individualized Funding in Ontario: Report of a Provincial Study' *Journal on Developmental Disabilities*, 2008, vol. 14, pp. 44–53.

Lord, J.E. and Stein, M.A. 'Social Rights and the Relational Value of the Rights to Participate in Sport, Recreation, and Play' *Boston University International Law Journal*, 2009, vol. 27, pp. 251–52.

Lubet, A. *Music, Disability and Society*, Philadelphia, PA: Temple University Press, 2010.

Lynk, M. 'Accommodating Disabilities in the Canadian Workplace' *Canadian Labour and Employment Law Journal*, 1999, vol. 7, p. 191.

— 'Labour Law and the New Inequality' *University of New Brunswick Law Journal*, 2009, vol. 59, pp. 14–41.

McCormack, K. 'Stratified Reproduction and Poor Women's Resistance' *Gender & Society*, 2005, vol. 19, pp. 660–79.

McGuire, J., Scott, S. and Shaw, S. 'Universal Design and Its Applications in Educational Environments' *Remedial and Special Education*, 2006, vol. 27, pp. 166–75.

MacKinnon, C. 'Feminism, Marxism, Method and the State: An Agenda for Theory' *Signs*, 1982, vol. 7, pp. 516–17.

McMahon, L., Murray, C. and Simpson, J. 'The Potential Benefits of Applying a Narrative Analytic Approach for Understanding the Experience of Fibromyalgia: A Review' *Disability and Rehabilitation*, 2012, vol. 34, pp. 1123–30.

Madriaga, M. 'Enduring Disablism: Students with Dyslexia and their Pathways into UK Higher Education and Beyond' *Disability and Society*, 2007, vol. 22, pp. 399–412.

Mahoney, M.R. 'Legal Images of Battered Women: Redefining the Issue of Separation' *Michigan Law Review*, 1991, vol. 90, pp. 1–94.

Mairs, N. *Waist-High in the World: A Life among the Non-Disabled*, Boston, MA: Beacon Press, 1996.

Malagon, M.C., Huber, L.P. and Velez, V.N. 'Our Experiences, Our Methods: Using Grounded Theory to Inform a Critical Race Methodology' *Seattle Journal of Social Justice*, 2009–2010, vol. 8, pp. 252–72.

Malhotra, R. 'The Politics of the Disability Rights Movements' *New Politics*, 2001, vol. 8, pp. 65–75.

— 'Empowering People with Disabilities' *New Politics*, 2006, vol. 11, no. 1, pp. 55–59.

— 'The Legal Genealogy of the Duty to Accommodate American and Canadian Workers with Disabilities: A Comparative Perspective' *Washington University Journal of Law and Policy*, 2007, vol. 23, pp. 1–32.

— 'The Implications of the Social Model of Disablement for the Legal Regulation of the Modern Workplace in Canada and the United States' *Manitoba Law Journal*, 2009, vol. 33, pp. 1–41.

— 'Electioneering and Activism at the Turn of the Century and the Politics of Disablement: The Legacy of E. T. Kingsley (1856–1929)' *Review of Disability Studies*, 2011, vol. 7, pp. 34–42.

— 'The Legal Politics of Hubert H. Harrison: Excavating A Lost Legacy' *Columbia Journal of Race and Law*, 2012, vol. 1, pp. 382–401.

Malhotra, R. and Hansen, R. 'The United Nations Convention on the Rights of Persons with Disabilities and its Implications for the Equality Rights of Canadians with Disabilities: The Case of Education' *Windsor Yearbook of Access to Justice*, 2011, vol. 29, pp. 73–106.

Mandel, M. *The Charter of Rights and the Legalization of Politics in Canada*, Toronto: Wall & Thompson, 1989.

Marleau, V. 'Globalization, Decentralization and the Role of Subsidiarity in the Labour Setting' in J.D.R. Craig and S.M. Lynk (eds) *Globalization and the Future of Labour Law*, Cambridge: Cambridge University Press, 2006.

Martin, B. 'British Rail Privatisation: What Went Wrong?' 2002, available online at http://www.publicworld.org/docs/britrail.pdf (accessed October 22, 2012).

Marx, K. *A Contribution to the Critique of Political Economy*, trans. by N.I. Stone, Chicago, IL: Charles H. Kerr & Co., 1904.

— *Capital, vol. 1*, London: Penguin, 1976.

Mason, M.G. *Working against Odds: Stories of Disabled Women's Work Lives*, Boston, MA: Northeastern University Press, 2004.

Matthews, B. 'The *Disability Discrimination Act* and Developments in Accessible Public Transit in the U.K.' *World Transport Policy and Practice*, 2002, vol. 8, pp. 42–49.

Meikle, J. 'Minister Calls for Change in Attitude as Wheelchair User Takes on Bus Companies' *The Guardian*, 11 July 2012, available online at http://www. guardian.co.uk/society/2012/jul/11/row-wheelchairs-buses-minister-attitude (last accessed November 29, 2012).

Menzies, H. and Falvey, M.A. 'Inclusion of Students with Disabilities in General Education' in T.C. Jiménez and V.L. Graf (eds) *Education for All: Critical Issues in the Education of Children and Youth with Disabilities*, San Francisco, CA: Jossey-Bass, 2008.

Merleau-Ponty, M. *Phenomenology of Perception*, trans. C. Smith, London: Routledge and Kegan Paul, 1962.

Meyer, E.J. *Gender, Bullying and Harassment: Strategies to End Sexism and Homophobia in Schools*, New York, NY: Teachers College Press, 2009.

Mitchell, D. and Snyder, S. (eds) *The Body and Physical Difference: Discourses of Disability*, Ann Arbor, MI: University of Michigan Press, 1997.

Morris, C. 'Fewer Young Canadians Are Getting Their Driver's License' *Shine On*, April 9, 2012, available online at http://ca.shine.yahoo.com/blogs/shine-on/fewer-young-canadians-getting-driver-licence-184210177.html (last accessed November 28, 2012).

Morris, J. *Pride against Prejudice: Transforming Attitudes to Disability*, London: The Women's Press, 1991.

— 'Personal and Political: A Feminist Perspective on Researching Physical Disabilities' *Disability, Handicap & Society*, 1992, vol. 7, pp. 157–66.

Mulvey, L. *Visual and Other Pleasures*, Indianapolis, IN: Indiana University Press, 1989.

Nakagawa, J. and Blanck, P. 'Future of Disability Law in Japan: Employment and Accommodation' *Loyola of Los Angeles International and Comparative Law Review*, 2010, vol. 33, pp. 173–221.

Nelson, B. and Stambrook, D. 'Economics of Accessible Transportation in Canada' paper delivered at the 12th International Conference on Mobility and Transport for Elderly and Disabled Persons (TRANSED 2010), 2010, available online at http://www.sortclearinghouse.info/cgi/viewcontent.cgi?article=1622&context=research (accessed November 22, 2012).

Nielsen, K.E. *The Radical Lives of Helen Keller*, New York, NY: New York University Press, 2004.

— *A Disability History of the United States*, Boston, MA: Beacon Press, 2012.

Norway, R. 'Ending Participatory Research?' *Journal of Intellectual Disabilities*, 2000, vol. 4, pp. 27–36.

O'Brien, R. (ed.) *Voices from the Edge: Narratives about the Americans with Disabilities Act*, Oxford: Oxford University Press, 2004.

— 'Defining Moments: (Dis)ability, Individuality and Normalcy' in R. O'Brien (ed.) *Voices from the Edge: Narratives about the Americans with Disabilities Act*, Oxford: Oxford University Press, 2004.

Office for Disability Issues, *Consultation on Improving Protection from Disability Discrimination*, London: Office for Disability Issues, 2008.

Olesen, V.L. 'Feminist Qualitative Research and Grounded Theory: Complexities, Criticism, and Opportunities' in A. Bryant and K. Charmaz (eds) *The SAGE Handbook of Grounded Theory*, London: Sage, 2007.

Oliver, M. *The Politics of Disablement*, London: Macmillan, 1990.

Oliver, M. and Barnes, C. *The New Politics of Disablement*, Basingstoke: Palgrave Macmillan, 2012.

Oliver, M. and Omansky, B. 'Unmet Promises of Disability Law and Policy' in M. Oliver (ed.) *Understanding Disability: From Theory to Practice*, 2nd edn, Basingstoke: Palgrave Macmillan, 2009.

Ontario Human Rights Commission, *Human Rights and Public Transit Services in Ontario: Consultation Report*, Toronto: Ontario Human Rights Commission, 2002.

— *Ontario Human Rights Commission Annual Report 2007–2008*, Toronto: Ontario Human Rights Commission, 2008.

— *Policy and Guidelines on Disability and the Duty to Accommodate*, Toronto: Ontario Human Rights Commission, 2009, available online at http://www.ohrc.on.ca/en/policy-and-guidelines-disability-and-duty-accommodate (last accessed September 6, 2012).

Ontario Ministry of Education, *Standards for School Boards' Special Education Plans*, Toronto: Queen's Printer for Ontario, 2000.

Organisation for Economic Co-operation and Development, *Ageing Populations: High Time for Action*, Paris: OECD, 2005.

— 'Disability Programmes in Need of Reform' in B. Marin, C. Prinz and M. Queisser (eds) *Transforming Disability Welfare Policies: Towards Work and Equal Opportunities*, Aldershot: Ashgate, 2004.

Panitch, M. *Disability, Mothers and Organization: Accidental Activists*, New York, NY: Routledge, 2008.

Parr, H. and Butler, R. 'New Geographies of Illness, Impairment and Disability' in R. Butler and H. Parr (eds) *Mind and Body Spaces: Geographies of Illness, Impairment and Disability*, London: Routledge, 1999.

Parsons, T. 'The School Class as a Social System: Some of Its Functions in American Society' *Harvard Educational Review*, 1959, vol. 29, pp. 297–318.

Paterson, K. and Hughes, B. 'Disability Studies and Phenomenology: The Carnal Politics of Everyday Life' *Disability and Society*, 1999, vol. 14, pp. 597–610.

Peck, J. *Workfare States*, New York, NY: The Guildford Press, 2001.

Pelka, F. *What We Have Done: An Oral History of the Disability Rights Movement*, Amherst, MA: University of Massachusetts Press, 2012.

Penney, J. 'A Constitution for the Disabled or a Disabled Constitution? Toward a New Approach to Disability for the Purposes of Section 15 (1)' *Journal of Law and Equality*, 2002, vol. 1, pp. 83–94.

Perry, J.B. *Hubert Harrison: The Voice of Harlem Radicalism, 1883–1918*, New York, NY: Columbia University Press, 2008.

Pfhal, L. and Powell, J.J.W. 'Legitimating School Segregation: The Special Education Profession and the Discourse of Learning Disability in Germany' *Disability & Society*, 2011, vol. 26, pp. 449–62.

Pina, D., Gannon, T. and Saunders, B. 'An Overview of the Literature on Sexual Harassment: Perpetrator, Theory, and Treatment Issues' *Aggression and Violent Behavior*, 2009, vol. 14, pp. 126–38.

Polanyi, K. *The Great Transformation: The Political and Economic Origins of Our Time*, Boston, MA: Beacon Press, 1944.

Polat, F. 'Inclusion in Education: A Step towards Social Justice' *International Journal of Educational Development*, 2011, vol. 31, pp. 50–58.

Polit, D.F. and Beck, C.T. *Nursing Research: Principles and Methods*, 8th edn, Philadelphia, PA: Lippincott, Williams & Wilkins, 2008.

Polletta, F. '"It Was Like A Fever . . ." Narrative and Identity in Social Protest' *Social Problems*, 1998, vol. 45, pp. 137–59.

— *It Was Like A Fever: Storytelling in Protest and Politics*, Chicago, IL: University of Chicago Press, 2006.

Porter, A. *Gendered States: Women, Unemployment Insurance, and the Political Economy of the Welfare State in Canada, 1945–1997*, Toronto: University of Toronto Press, 2003.

Posner, R. 'Skin Trade' *New Republic*, 1997, vol. 217, pp. 40–43.

Pothier, D. 'Book Review of *Rights of Inclusion: Law and Identity in the Life Narratives of Americans with Disabilities* by D.M. Engel and F.W. Munger' *Social and Legal Studies*, 2008, vol. 17, pp. 139–43.

— 'Legal Developments in the Supreme Court of Canada Regarding Disability' in D. Pothier and R. Devlin (eds) *Critical Disability Theory*, Vancouver: University of British Columbia Press, 2006.

Pottie, L. and Sossin, L. 'Demystifying the Boundaries of Public Law: Policy, Discretion and Social Welfare' *University of British Columbia Law Review*, 2005, vol. 38, pp. 147–87.

Potts, B. 'Disability and Employment: Considering the Importance of Social Capital' *Journal of Rehabilitation*, 2005, vol. 71, pp. 20–25.

Priestley, M. *Disability: A Life Course Approach*, Cambridge: Polity Press, 2003.

Puttee, A.H. (ed.) *Federalism, Democracy and Disability Policy in Canada*, Montreal and Kingston: McGill-Queen's University Press, 2002.

Quinn, G. 'A Short Guide to the United Nations Convention on the Rights of Persons with Disabilities' in G. Quinn and L. Waddington (eds) *European Yearbook of Disability Law, vol. 1*, Portland, OR: Intersentia, 2009.

Reaume, G. *Remembrance of Patients Past: Patient Life at the Toronto Hospital for the Insane, 1870–1940*, Toronto: University of Toronto Press, 2000.

— 'Patients at Work: Insane Asylum Inmate Labour in Ontario, 1841–1900' in J.E. Moran and D. Wright (eds) *Mental Health and Canadian Society: Historical Perspectives*, Montreal and Kingston: McGill-Queen's University Press, 2006.

— *Lyndhurst: Canada's First Rehabilitation Centre for People with Spinal Cord Injuries, 1945–1998*, Montreal and Kingston, McGill-Queen's University Press, 2007.

Reichetz, J. 'Abduction: The Logic of Discovery of Grounded Theory' in A. Bryant and K. Charmaz (eds) *The SAGE Handbook of Grounded Theory*, London: Sage, 2007.

Rice, C. *et al.*, 'Creating Community across Disability and Difference' in D. Driedger (ed.) *Living the Edges: A Disabled Women's Reader*, Toronto: Inanna Publications and Education Inc., 2010.

Riddell, S., Tinklin, T. and Wilson, A. 'New Labour, Social Justice and Disabled Students in Higher Education' *British Educational Research Journal*, 2005, vol. 31, pp. 623–43.

Riessman, C.K. *Narrative Analysis*, Newbury Park, CA: Sage, 1993.

Riley, R. 'Preservation, Modification or Transformation? The Current State of the Department of Veterans Affairs Disability Benefits Adjudication Process and Why Congress Should Modify, Rather than Maintain or Completely Redesign the Current System' *Federal Circuit Bar Journal*, 2009, vol. 18, pp. 8–9.

Rioux, M. and Valentine, F. 'Does Theory Matter? Exploring the Nexus between Disability, Human Rights and Public Policy' in D. Pothier and R. Devlin (eds) *Critical Disability Theory: Essays in Philosophy, Politics, Policy and Law*, Vancouver: University of British Columbia Press, 2006.

Rose, S. 'Handicap This!' *News and Letters*, 2013, vol. 58, no. 1, p. 9.

Rosenbaum, P. and Chadha, E. 'Reconstructing Disability: Integrating Disability Theory into Section 15' *Supreme Court Law Reports*, 2006, vol. 33, pp. 343–65.

Rosenwald, G.C. 'Conclusion: Reflections on Narrative Self-Understanding' in G.C. Rosenwald and R.L. Ochberg (eds) *Narratives Lives: The Cultural Politics of Self-Understanding*, New Haven, CT: Yale University Press, 1992.

Roulstone, A. 'Disabled People, Work and Employment: A Global Perspective' in N. Watson, A. Roulstone and C. Thomas (eds) *Routledge Handbook of Disability Studies*, London: Routledge, 2012.

Ruocco, J. 'Town to Cover Taxi Voucher Program Increase Until New Year' *Whitecourt Star*, October 3, 2012, available online at http://www.whitecourtstar. com/2012/10/03/town-to-cover-taxi-voucher-program-increase-until-new-year (last accessed November 28, 2012).

Russell, M. *Beyond Ramps: Disability at the End of the Social Contract*, Monroe, ME: Common Courage Press, 1998.

— 'Inequality, Neo-Liberalism and Disability' *Disability Studies Quarterly*, 1999, vol. 19, p. 372.

— 'Backlash, the Political Economy and Structural Exclusion' *Berkeley Journal of Employment and Labor Law*, 2000, vol. 21, pp. 335–66.

— 'What Disability Civil Rights Cannot Do: Employment and Political Economy' *Disability and Society*, 2002, vol. 17, pp. 117–35.

Russell, M. and Malhotra, R. 'Capitalism and Disability' *Socialist Register*, 2002, pp. 211–28.

Ruth, B. 'In My Disabled Women's Group' in M. Saxton and F. Howe (eds) *With Wings: An Anthology of Literature by and about Women with Disabilities*, New York, NY: The Feminist Press, 1987.

Sager, J. 'Just Stories' in S.E. Browne, D. Connors and N. Sterne (eds) *With the Power of Each Breath: A Disabled Women's Anthology*, Pittsburgh, PA: Cleis Press, 1985.

Samoy, E. 'Activation Through Sheltered Work? Not *If* But *How*' in B. Marin, C. Prinz and M. Queisser (eds) *Transforming Disability Welfare Policies: Towards Work and Equal Opportunities*, Aldershot: Ashgate, 2004.

Saxton, M. and Howe, F. (eds) *With Wings: An Anthology of Literature by and about Women with Disabilities*, New York, NY: The Feminist Press, 1987.

Scambler, S. 'Long-Term Disabling Conditions and Disability Theory' in N. Watson, A. Roulstone and C. Thomas (eds) *Routledge Handbook of Disability Studies*, London: Routledge, 2012.

Schmid, G. 'The Future of Employment Relations: Goodbye 'Flexicurity'—Welcome Back Transitional Labour Markets?' Working Paper 10-106, Amsterdam: University of Amsterdam, 2010, available online at http://www.uva-aias.net/ uploaded_files/publications/WP106-Schmid.pdf (accessed February 1, 2013).

Schultz, V. 'Life's Work' *Columbia Law Review*, 2000, vol. 100, pp. 1886–92.

Schwartz, J. 'What's Wrong with Exploitation?' *Nous*, 1995, vol. 29, pp. 158–88.

Scotch, R.K. and Shriner, K. 'Disability as Human Variation: Implications for Policy' *Annals of the American Academy of Political and Social Science*, 1997, vol. 549, pp. 148–59.

Scott, J. 'Stories of Hyperembodiment: An Analysis of Personal Narratives of and through Physically Disabled Bodies' *Text and Performance Quarterly*, 2012, vol. 32, pp. 100–20.

Sevenhuijsen, S. *Citizenship and the Ethics of Care: Feminist Considerations on Justice, Morality and Politics*, London: Routledge, 1998.

Shaffer, A. *et al.*, 'Changing the Food Environment: Community Engagement Strategies and Place-Based Policy Tools that Address the Influence of Marketing' *Loyola of Los Angeles Law Review*, 2006, vol. 39, pp. 675–76.

Shakespeare, T. 'Disability, Identity and Difference' in C. Barnes and G. Mercer (eds) *Exploring the Divide*, Leeds: The Disability Press, 1996.

— *Disability Rights and Wrongs*, Abingdon: Routledge, 2006.

Shakespeare, T., Gillespie-Sells, K. and Davies, D. *The Sexual Politics of Disabilities: Untold Desires*, New York, NY: Cassell, 1996.

Shapiro, J. *No Pity: Disabled People Forging a New Civil Rights Movement*, New York, NY: Times Books, 1993.

Shapiro, S. *et al.*, 'Identity and Meaning in the Experience of Cancer: Three Narrative Themes' *Journal of Healthy Psychology*, 1997, vol. 2, pp. 539–54.

Sharma, U. *et al.*, 'Impact of Training on Pre-Service Teachers' Attitudes and Concerns about Inclusive Education and Sentiments about Persons with Disabilities' *Disability & Society*, 2008, vol. 23, pp. 773–85.

Sheldrick, B. *Perils and Possibilities: Social Activism and the Law*, Halifax: Fernwood, 2004.

Siebers, T. *Disability Aesthetics*, Ann Arbor, MI: University of Michigan Press, 2010.

Silbey, S.S. 'After Legal Consciousness' *Annual Review of Law and Social Sciences*, 2006, vol. 1, pp. 326–27.

Siller, J. 'Commentary on Finkelstein's 'Changing Attitudes and Disabled People': Issues for Discussion' in V. Finkelstein, *Attitudes and Disabled People*, New York, NY: World Rehabilitation Fund, 1980.

Silver, P., Bourke A. and Strehorn, K.C. 'Universal Instructional Design in Higher Education: An Approach of Inclusion' *Equity & Excellence in Education*, 1998, vol. 31, pp. 47–51.

Silverman, K. *Male Subjectivity at the Margins*, London: Routledge, 1992.

Silvers, A. 'Reprising Women's Disability: Feminist Identity Strategy and Disability Rights' *Berkley's Women's Law Journal*, 1998, pp. 81–116.

Singer, J. 'Legal Realism Now' *California Law Review*, 1988, vol. 76, pp. 478–82.

Slee, R. *The Irregular School: Exclusion, Schooling and Inclusive Education*, London: Routledge, 2011.

Smith, A. 'Disability and Inclusion Policy Towards Physical Education and Youth Sport' in H. Fitzgerald (ed.) *Disability and Youth Sport*, London: Routledge, 2009.

Smith, A.M. 'Persons with Disabilities as a Social and Economic Underclass' *Kansas Journal of Law and Public Policy*, 2002–2003, vol. 12, p. 21.

Soffer, M., Rimmerman, A., Blanck, P. and Hill, E. 'Media and the Israeli Disability Rights Legislation: Progress or Mixed and Contradictory Images?' *Disability & Society*, 2010, vol. 25, pp. 687–99.

Soldatic, K. and Meekosha, H. 'Disability and Neoliberal State Formations' in N. Watson, A. Roulstone and C. Thomas (eds) *Routledge Handbook of Disability Studies*, London: Routledge, 2012.

Stack, R. 'Progress and Uncertainty: The Educational Rights of Special Needs Children in British Columbia' *Appeal*, 2001, vol. 7, p. 29.

Staudenmaier, M. 'Unorthodox Leninism: Workplace Organizing and Anti-Imperialist Solidarity in the Sojourner Truth Organization' in D. Berger (ed.) *The Hidden 1970s: Histories of Radicalism*, New Brunswick, NJ: Rutgers University Press, 2010.

— *Truth and Revolution: A History of the Sojourner Truth Organization, 1969–1986*, Oakland, CA: AK Press, 2012.

Stein, M.A. 'The Law and Economics of Disability Accommodations' *Duke Law Journal*, 2003, vol. 53, pp. 79–191.

— 'Labor Markets, Rationality and Workers with Disabilities' *Berkeley Journal of Employment and Labor Law*, 2000, vol. 21, pp. 314–34.

— 'Under the Empirical Radar: An Initial Expressive Law Analysis of the ADA' book review of *Rights of Inclusion: Law and Identity in the Life Narratives of Americans with Disabilities* by D.M. Engel and F.W. Munger, *Virginia Law Review*, 2004, vol. 90, p. 1167.

Stern, P.N. 'On Solid Ground: Essential Properties of Growing Grounded Theory' in A. Bryant and K. Charmaz (eds) *The SAGE Handbook of Grounded Theory*, London: Sage, 2007.

Stienstra, D. 'Race/Ethnicity and Disability Studies: Towards an Explicitly Intersectional Approach' in N. Watson, A. Roulstone and C. Thomas (eds) *Routledge Handbook of Disability Studies*, London: Routledge, 2012.

Stienstra, D. and Wight-Felske, A. (eds) *Making Equality: History of Advocacy and Persons with Disabilities in Canada*, Toronto: Captus Press, 2003.

Stone, D. *The Disabled State*, Philadelphia, PA: Temple University Press, 1984.

Stone, K.V. *From Widgets to Digits: Employment Regulation for the Changing Workplace*, New York, NY: Cambridge University Press, 2004.

— 'A Labor Law for the Digital Era: The Future of Labor and Employment Law in the United States' in K. Dau-Schmidt *et al.* (eds) *Labor and Employment Law and Economics*, vol. 2, *Encyclopedia of Law and Economics*, 2nd edn, Northampton, MA: Edward Elgar Publishing Ltd, 2009.

Strauss, A.L. and Corbin, J. *Basics of Qualitative Research: Grounded Theory Procedures and Techniques*, London: Sage, 1990.

— *Basics of Qualitative Research: Techniques and Procedures for Developing Grounded Theory*, 2nd edn, London: Sage, 1998.

— *Basics of Qualitative Research: Techniques and Procedures for Developing Grounded Theory*, 3rd edn, London: Sage, 2008.

Supiot, A. 'The Transformation of Work and the Future of Labour Law in Europe: A Multidisciplinary Perspective' *International Labour Review*, 1999, vol. 138, pp. 31–46.

— 'Introductory Remarks: Between Market and Regulation: New Social Regulations for Life Long Security?' in P. Auer and B. Gazier (eds) *The Future of Work, Employment and Social Protection: The Dynamics of Change and the Protection of Workers*, Geneva: International Labour Organization, 2002.

Supiot, A. *et al.*, *Beyond Employment: Changes in Work and the Future of Labour Law in Europe*, Oxford: Oxford University Press, 2001.

— 'Possible Europes' *New Left Review*, May–June 2009, No. 57, pp. 59–60.

Tavory, I. and Timmermans, S. 'Two Cases of Ethnography: GT and the Extended Case Method' *Ethnography*, 2009, vol. 10, pp. 243–44.

Taylor, S. 'The Right Not to Work: Power and Disability' *Monthly Review*, 2004, vol. 55, pp. 30–44.

Teelucksingh, C. 'Environmental Racialization: Linking Racialization to the Environment in Canada' *Local Environment*, 2007, vol. 12, pp. 645–61.

Thomas, C. *Female Forms: Experiencing and Understanding Disability*, Buckingham: Open University Press, 1999.

Thomas, M.P. *Regulating Flexibility: The Political Economy of Employment Standards*, Montreal and Kingston: McGill-Queen's University Press, 2009.

Thomas, S. 'I Was There . . .', ADAPT History Project, available online at http://www.adapt.org/freeourpeople/adapt25/narratives/12adapt.htm (accessed February 4, 2013).

Thomas, S.B. 'College Students and Disability Law' *The Journal of Special Education*, 2000, vol. 33, p. 248.

Tomasevski, K. *Human Rights Obligations in Education: The 4-A Scheme*, Netherlands: Wolf Legal Publisher, 2006.

Torjman, S. 'Canada's Federal Regime and Persons with Disabilities' in D. Cameron and F. Valentine (eds) *Disability and Federalism: Comparing Different Approaches to Full Participation*, Montreal and Kingston: McGill-Queen's University Press, 2001.

Tremblay, M., Campbell, A. and Hudson, G.L. 'When Elevators Were for Pianos: An Oral History Account of The Civilian Experience of Using Wheelchairs in Canadian Society. The First Twenty Five Years: 1945–1970' *Disability and Society*, 2005, vol. 20, pp. 103–16.

Turner, B.S. 'Disability and the Sociology of the Body' in G. Albrecht, K. Seelman and M. Bury (eds) *Handbook of Disability Studies*, Thousand Oaks, CA: Sage, 2001.

Turner, W. 'Preface: Abilities and Disabilities' in W. Turner and T. Pearman (eds) *The Treatment of Disabled Persons in Medieval Europe: Examining Disability in the Historical, Legal, Literary, Medical, and Religious Discourses of the Middle Ages*, Lewiston: The Edwin Mellen Press, 2010.

Unger, R.M. *False Necessity: Anti-Necessitarian Social Theory in the Service of Radical Democracy*, Cambridge: Cambridge University Press, 1987.

—— *What Should Legal Analysis Become?*, London: Verso, 1996.

—— *The Critical Legal Studies Movement*, Cambridge, MA: Harvard University Press, 1983.

—— *Urgent Tasks*, Summer 1981, No. 12.

Union of the Physically Impaired Against Segregation, *Policy Statement*, Leeds: Union of the Physically Impaired Against Segregation, 1974, p. 1, available online at http://www.leeds.ac.uk/disability-studies/archiveuk/UPIAS/UPIAS.pdf (last accessed November 28, 2012).

Vickerman, P. and Blundell, M. 'Hearing the Voices of Disabled Students in Higher Education' *Disability & Society*, 2010, vol. 25, p. 30.

Visser, J. 'Union Membership Statistics in 24 Countries' *Monthly Labor Review*, 2006.

von Benzon, N. 'Moving on from Ramps? The Utility of the Social Model of Disability for Facilitating Experiences of Nature for Disabled Children' *Disability & Society*, 2010, vol. 25, pp. 622–23.

Vosko, L. (ed.) *Precarious Employment: Understanding Labour Market Insecurity in Canada*, Montreal and Kingston: McGill-Queen's University Press, 2005.

Watson, N. *et al.* '(Inter)Dependence, Needs and Care: The Potential for Disability and Feminist Theorists to Develop an Emancipatory Model' *Sociology*, 2004, vol. 38, pp. 331–50.

Weber, M.C. 'Beyond the Americans with Disabilities Act: A National Employment Policy for People with Disabilities' *Buffalo Law Review*, 1998, vol. 46, pp. 127–74.

—— *Disability Harassment*, New York, NY: New York University Press, 2007.

—— 'A Nuanced Approach to the Disability Integration Presumption' *University of Pennsylvania Law Review Pennumbra*, 2007, vol. 156, pp. 174–87, available online at http://www.pennumbra.com/responses/10-2007/Weber.pdf (accessed January 22, 2013).

— *Understanding Disability Law*, 2nd edn, New Providence, NJ: LexisNexis, 2012.

Webley, L. and Duff, L. 'Women Solicitors as a Barometer for Problems within the Legal Profession—Time to Put Values before Profits?' *Journal of Law and Society*, 2007, vol. 34, pp. 382–83.

Weisbrod, C. 'Divorce Stories: Readings, Comments and Questions on Law and Narrative' *Brigham Young University Law Review*, 1991, pp. 143–96.

Wendell, S. *The Rejected Body: Feminist Philosophical Reflections on Disability*, New York, NY: Routledge, 1996.

Whitehead, S.M. *Men and Masculinities*, Cambridge: Polity Press, 2002.

Williams, F. 'In and Beyond New Labour: Towards a New Political Ethics of Care' *Critical Social Policy*, 2001, vol. 21, pp. 467–93.

Williams, P.J. *The Rooster's Egg: The Persistence of Prejudice*, Cambridge, MA: Harvard University Press, 1995.

Williams, V. *Disability and Discourse: Analysing Inclusive Conversation with People with Intellectual Disabilities*, Hoboken, NJ: John Wiley & Sons Ltd, 2011.

Wilson, L. 'An Overview of the Literature on Disability and Transport' Manchester: Disability Rights Commission, 2003.

Wilton, R. 'Working at the Margins: Disabled People and the Growth of Precarious Employment' in D. Pothier and R. Devlin (eds) *Critical Disability Theory: Essays in Philosophy, Politics, Policy and Law*, Vancouver: University of British Columbia Press, 2006.

Withers, A.J. *Disability Politics and Theory*, Halifax: Fernwood Publishing, 2012.

Wood, R. 'Care of Disabled People' in G. Dalley (ed.) *Disability and Social Policy*, London: Policy Studies Institute, 1991.

Young, I. *Inclusion and Democracy*, Oxford: Oxford University Press, 2000.

Young-Welke, B. *Recasting American Liberty: Gender, Race, Law and the Railroad Revolution, 1860–1920*, New York, NY: Cambridge University Press, 2001.

Zames, D.Z. and Zames, F. *The Disability Rights Movement: From Charity to Confrontation* updated edn, Philadelphia, PA: Temple University Press, 2011.

Zola, I.K. 'Bringing Our Bodies and Ourselves Back in: Reflections on a Past, Present and Future "Medical Sociology"' *Journal of Health and Social Behavior*, 1991, vol. 32, pp. 1–16.

Index